Deconstructing Nationality

Deconstructing Nationality

Edited by

Naoki Sakai, Brett de Bary,
and Iyotani Toshio

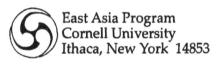 East Asia Program
Cornell University
Ithaca, New York 14853

The Cornell East Asia Series is published by the Cornell University East Asia Program (distinct from Cornell University Press). We publish affordably priced books on a variety of scholarly topics relating to East Asia as a service to the academic community and the general public. Standing orders, which provide for automatic notification and invoicing of each title in the series upon publication, are accepted.

If after review by internal and external readers a manuscript is accepted for publication, it is published on the basis of camera-ready copy provided by the volume author. Each author is thus responsible for any necessary copyediting and for manuscript formatting. Address submission inquiries to CEAS Editorial Board, East Asia Program, Cornell University, Ithaca, New York 14853-7601.

Cover illustration: "Sending a Soldier Off to War" (oil painting mounted on cloth, 1995), by Tomiyama Taeko, in the collection of Kyoto Seika University.

Number 124 in the Cornell East Asia Series
Copyright © 2005 by Naoki Sakai, Brett de Bary, and Iyotani Toshio. All rights reserved
ISSN 1050-2955
ISBN-13: 978-1-885445-34-6 hc / ISBN-10: 1-885445-34-2 hc
ISBN-13: 978-1-885445-24-7 pb / ISBN-10: 1-885445-24-5 pb
Library of Congress Control Number: 2005922990

23 22 21 20 19 18 17 16 15 14 13 12 11 10 09 08 05   9 8 7 6 5 4 3 2 1

Contents

Preface to the English Edition

Brett de Bary

The essays translated and collected in this book are the product of collaborative work done between 1992 and 1994 by Japanese and American scholars in a series of workshops and conferences held in Japan, Germany, and the United States, but primarily on the campuses of Tokyo University of Foreign Studies and Cornell University in Ithaca, New York. The collaboration resulted in the publication of a book *Nashionritei no datsukōchiku,* edited by Naoki Sakai, Brett de Bary, and Iyotani Toshio (Kashiwa Shobō, 1996). This English edition contains translations of eight of the original essays in the book, including a translation of the Japanese introductory essay by Naoki Sakai, and new essays by Brett de Bary and Hirata Yumi.

In undertaking, in the early 1990s, the project of *Deconstructing Nationality* specified in the title, our group sought to address both the academic discourses institutionalized as "Japanese Studies" in Japan, North America, and Europe, as well as to engage the theoretical debate on "nation-ness" and the nation-state that was gaining prominence at that time. Within the first context, that of the academic discourse of Japanese Studies, the writings featured here represent one of the first attempts to break new ground by historicizing and problematizing the self-evidence of that very "Japan" that provided the routine organizational unity and narrative telos for area-studies work in the postwar period. Such a deconstructive effort necessitated, on the one hand, a turn to topics and texts that had been relatively neglected in previous studies precisely because their subject matter was seen to exceed the geographical boundaries of the postwar Japanese state. At the same time, as our meetings progressed, we found we had embarked on a conceptual odyssey that involved experimentation with, and the articulation of, new modes of analysis once the assumed positivities of "Japan" and "Japanese culture" had been challenged. Collectively, then, these essays seek to envision and point the way toward a post-national era of intellectual discourse and exchange.

Within the second context, our book was envisioned as an extension of, but also as a critical rejoinder to, a growing volume of writing produced in the decade of the 1990s on the problem of the nation. While initially salutory in its defamiliarizing effect, analysis of the nation as an "imagined community" or cultural imaginary, we felt, had also often led to preoccupation with a realm of reified representations ("culture") taken as divorced from conflictual social relations and histories involved with nation-building, as well as from the exercise of power. If the nation and nationality has by now to a large extent eclipsed work on the state and capitalism as a focus of attention for critical intellectuals, there has nevertheless been a nagging tendency to reserve connotations of violence and repressiveness for the older term, "nationalism," still taken to be a historical aberration or an extreme form of the more quotidian "nationality." Our interpretive stance thus differs in degree from that of those who would define nationality nonnormatively as a "variable cultural artifact," albeit in an attempt to avoid the privileging of Eurocentric models.[1] Historically, the emergence of national communities in much of the globe was neither spontaneous nor benign, this book argues, but necessitated by the invasive presence of Western colonialism and imperialism, and productive, in its turn, of violence toward new groups of "others" deemed neither citizens nor civilized. Neither "false consciousness" nor pure "artifact," nationality, as our essays interpret it, is a series of practices and behaviors nonetheless violent and regulatory for being deeply embedded in daily life.

The question of how to articulate the relationship of the "cultural" to the "national," then, loomed large among our concerns in carrying out this project. What sorts of links might be traced between diverse practices deemed "cultural" without having recourse to the nation as a cohering frame, or without positing the nation as a unitary subject of history? Could we even speak of a coherent modern "Japanese" culture given the far-flung nature of the Japanese Empire's territorial expansion between 1895 and 1945? What methods were available, which were neither reductive nor deterministic, for conceptualizing the relationship between the cultural and the economic, or between culture and the state?

Essays in the introduction and Section One of this book, by Naoki Sakai, Tomiyama Ichirō, Oguma Eiji, Kawamura Minato, and Kang Sangjung, all explore ways of problematizing the imbrication of the "cultural" and the "national," and of understanding the role of the "cultural" in modern imperialisms. Perhaps the most significant departure of this first group of essays from current approaches in Japanese Studies, as argued in Naoki Sakai's essay, is the suggestion that the ideology of the "homogeneous Japanese" be understood as a *post*-World War II, rather than a prewar, historical product. (Indeed, as several authors point out, it was a form of the multiculturalism usually seen as a relatively recent phenomenon that constituted the official policy of the prewar Japanese Empire, as it sought to unify peoples with diverse languages, collective identities, and histories under its aegis: between 1895 and 1945, 30% of the population of the Japanese Empire was composed of peoples who belonged to non-Japanese ethnic groups.) While analyzing extensively how the demand to identify as "Japanese" is addressed to contemporary subjects in the course of their day-to-day experience of heterogeneous social relations, Sakai links the production in Japan of ideologies of "culturalism" and "cultural particularism" to the historical exigencies of the U.S. occupation and the ensuing global Cold War order. Because the image of the nation as an organic unity always relies on the co-figuration of that nation's cultural "other," notions of the homogeneity of Japanese culture (including the apparently exceptionalist arguments of *Nihonjinron*) and those of the "West" as a coherent entity have been, in fact, mutually reinforcing and interdependent. Similarly, because they both so often rely on unitary notions of ethnic and racial particularities, more recent advocates of liberal multiculturalism may be seen as paradoxically complicitous with their apparent opponents, the anti-multiculturalists who seek to preserve the distinctiveness of national cultural traditions.

It was precisely the resonance between these discursive anomalies provoked by the border-crossing movement of global capital in the late twentieth century and those of prewar imperialisms that behooved us to also reexamine earlier-twentieth-century Japanese notions of the "cultural." In terms of the topics taken up by these essays, this meant considering afresh the salience for the imperial, metropolitan "center" of cultural practices and productions previously designated "peripheral," as well as foregrounding ways in which prewar discourses on citizenship and ethnicity sought to suture the contradictions arising from the Japanese state's exercise of colonial violence.

Essays by Tomiyama Ichirō and Kawamura Minato subvert canonical narratives on the formation of modern Japanese culture by looking at the crucial role played by writings done in Japanese-occupied "peripheries" in the consolidation of knowledge in the "homelands." They thus participate in the movement to understand the emergence of modern societies in terms of what Amy Kaplan has called "decentered cosmopolitanism," one that rejects the notion of national frontiers as "primitive margins of civilization," and seeks to redefine the improvisatory cultural practices characterizing borderlands not so much as "foreign relations" but as constitutive of national identity.[2] As Tomiyama demonstrates, integral to the development in Japan of the modern academic disciplines of anthropology, medicine, labor sciences, and others were the "testing grounds" set up in Japanese territories in the South Seas by the Japan Society for the Promotion of Science, the South Seas Agency, and research hospitals. Critical studies of imperialism and science, he notes, had earlier relied on instrumentalist conceptions of knowledge that confined them, for example, to such topics as the use of human subjects for research on bacteriological warfare. But for Tomiyama it is not simply to "fanatical nationalism" that responsibility for colonial violence should be traced, but to routinely institutionalized academic discourses in the human and natural sciences. He vividly demonstrates how ethnographic and other writings produced in the South Seas exhaustively described an "islander" inseparable from a normative positing of the "Japanese," and how these writings themselves, as representational practices, entailed social relations inseparable from Japanese management of the islands.

Equally provocatively, Kawamura Minato unfolds a history according to which principles of composition developed for teaching the Japanese language to non-native subjects of the empire led to transformations in composition pedagogy on the mainland, both before the Pacific War and under the American occupation. The sources of the twentieth-century realist style, he even suggests, might be more meaningfully studied in relation to this primary and secondary school composition pedagogy than to the histories of Naturalist and Proletarian schools. Looking at the differing experiences of novelist Nakajima Atsushi, and the educators Ashida Einosuke and Ishimori Nobuo in Japanese-occupied territories, Kawamura traces how an emphasis on "free composition" and "writing from daily life" developed amid the severe contradictions involved in implementing colonial education policies. By calling attention to the disparity between the emphasis on "spontaneity" and "immediacy" of writing and what was, in practice, rigid censorship of language and subject matter, his essay suggests that it is not surprising that the pedagogical philosophy of "writing from daily life" flourished as vigorously during the period of imperialism as it did during more ostensibly liberal periods. While dedicated to spontaneity, daily composition practice produced an interiority more distinctive for its malleability to bureacratic supervision than its critical spirit.

Perspectives on culture and nationality offered in Section One are rounded out by analyses provided by Oguma Eiji and Kang Sangjung that focus more specifically on the historical conditions of emergence of modern non-Western discourses of nation. Taking up writings from the 1920s produced by well-known figures in modern Japanese intellectual history, who span the political spectrum from "Taisho democrat" (Uehara Etsujirō), to liberal (Ishibashi Tanzan), to right-wing populist (Nakano Seigō), Oguma seeks to foreground often-overlooked discrepancies that rendered coherent public articulation of the nature of Japanese national identity during this period, in fact, a logical impossibility. His method is to bring about an interface between writings on issues that have for long been considered as separate spheres: his subjects' inconsistent reactions of outrage toward racially discriminatory U.S. policies toward Japanese immigrants, on the one hand, and of opposition to movements of ethnic self-determination for colonized Koreans, on the other. Oguma discloses an unstable situation where the discourse of national identity, always a relativized and comparative rhetorical construction to begin with, was rendered all the more contradictory insofar as modern "Japan" was produced through hierarchized oppositions constructed vis-á-vis both the West and Asia. Homogenized and racialized as "Asians" in the gaze of the West, Japanese could nevertheless not overcome the sense of their "difference" from other Asians, an identity both produced and necessitated by modern processes of nation-building and imperial expansion.

Finally, Kang Sangjung's essay contributes a broad theoretical frame for all the considerations in this section. Citing as the historical condition for the emergence of non-Western nationalism the expansion of capital into a world system with the West as its privileged center, Kang observes that movements to resist this system economically and politically (whether defined as attempts at "demodernization" or at developing alternate forms of modernity) were often linked to modes of cultural resistance conceived of as "dewesternization." In countering Western culture's claims to universality, non-Western nations developed equally totalizing concepts of their own cultures and traditions, with the attendant phenomena of cultural essentialism and, in the case of Japan, "Occidentalism" or "Orientalism" vis-á-vis other Asians. In the mosaic-like distribution of races, ethnicities, and nations that characterizes the contemporary world, Kang finds evidence of both the historical transformation and a powerful legacy of this form of nineteenth-century imperialism. No longer an intentional radiation from an imperial center, the movement of global capital now appears random and "free," while a tendency to exercise power through the production and regulation of cultural categories has rendered the concept of "cultural resistance" less and less viable. Nevertheless, the legacy of the intertwined and mimetic relationship between imperial and colonized cultures may be detected in the persistence of ethnic and national self-determination movements that define culture in ever more rigid and fundamentalist ways. Contemporary critical intellectuals, Kang concludes, should avoid the historical trap of clinging to static notions of cultural boundaries.

Essays in Section Two present literary and textual analyses. Drawing on her research on the long-neglected topic of writing by and about women in the first three decades of the Meiji period, Hirata Yumi's essay analyzes discourses on geisha and female deviancy in the national imaginary shaped by the emergence of modern print capitalism at this time. Her essay meticulously reconstructs literary and journalistic narratives surrounding the sensationalized murder trial of the geisha Hanai Oume in 1888. She shows the contradictory ways in which women, not yet fully recognized citizens of the modern state, were simultaneously targets of educational reform associated with the emergence of *koshinbun* (illustrated newspapers written in simple syllabary) and objects of highly stereotyped representations in those same newspapers. Thus representations of Oume can be seen as a nodal point around which discourses on national morality, the education of women, prostitution, the role of the newspaper, and the emerging ideology of literary realism all converged. As voices repudiating the social institution of geisha as a blot on Japan's national honor swelled, the parameters of this narrative were reconfigured. Hirata demonstrates the way representations of gender and the nation impinge on each other.

Continuing to focus on literary history, Nakano Toshio examines debates surrounding the controversial relationship of Takamura Kōtarō's poetry to the Pacific War. He attempts to tease out assumptions about national identity and modernity that have, in fact, underlain and unified what have been taken to be differing strands in the interpretation of the life and work of the well-known poet and artist. Although Takamura's poetry eulogizing the Emperor and Japan's role in the Pacific War were at the center of debate over the "war responsibility of writers" in the early postwar period, through a certain process of "selective memory," such poems have been erased from the works of Takamura now prominently featured in high school text books. Nakano calls our attention to a surprising isomorphism that may be observed in modern criticism, according to which models of individual growth and maturation are invoked that closely parallel those employed to describe the growth and maturation of the Japanese nation-state (conceived, of course, as an active subject of history). Interpretive schema put forth, however contritely, by critics and the poet himself to explain his war cooperation in terms of a "break-down," brought on by external pressures and resulting in reversion to premodern (more "primitive") attitudes, are the same as those that have been used to explain the war itself in terms of historical aberration or the Japanese state's relapse into "semi-feudalism." As long as such isomorphism goes unremarked, investigation into continuities between the war order and the present will be forestalled. Moreover, the continuing appeal—for modern, supposedly "autonomous" individuals—of national identity as a form of collective identity, will be underestimated.

A similar trajectory is pursued in Kasai Hirotaka's discussion of the political philosopher Maruyama Masao. While the significance of Maruyama's influential writings on the nature of the modern Japanese political system and the ethical responsibilities of its subjects have been widely studied, Kasai argues, the way in which Maruyama's mode of argumentation itself may have reproduced a notion of the "cultural identity of Japan" has constituted a blind spot in Maruyama scholarship. In attempting to specify the historical singularity of Japanese modernity vis-á-vis a Western-derived "ideal-type," Maruyama defined Japan's transition from premodern to modern in terms of an emerging awareness of the relative, or "invented," rather than absolute, nature of social institutions and values. Yet for Maruyama, the internalized, subjective investment of the modern citizen in the state was the crucial factor differentiating the democratic nation from ultra-nationalism. By assuming a preexisting ethnos that was the volitional subject of the transition from premodern to modern (which Kasai understands as the transition from an emphasis on "nature" to an emphasis on "invention"), Maruyama both smuggles the characteristics of the "natural" back into the "invented" modern state, and perpetuates a discourse of Japanese homogeneity.

Iyotani Toshio's essay opens a final section of essays dealing with "Contemporary Nationality" by situating the academic preoccupation with the nation within the context of the intensified global division of labor and transnational flows of commodities and labor that have destabilized the contemporary nation-state. While the hierarchical center-periphery relationships that characterized the age of European, American, and Japanese imperial power appeared to have dissolved, for example, in the face of rising economic power of regions such as the East Asian "NIC"s, global exchange of commodities simultaneously produced greater uniformity among cultures in a "non-coercive" manner. Rejecting the plethora of arguments that explain East Asian growth in terms of cultural particularities, Iyotani finds in these societies a faithful reproduction of Western-style nationalism. But because the capitalism historically nurtured by the nation-state must also, in its global orientation, eventually exceed the nation-state's sovereign boundaries, he predicts that "the age of world orders based on a specific country" is coming to an end. Countries of the former center and the former peripheries are gradually losing the characteristics of earlier nationalisms.

Brett de Bary's essay on the writings of *Sākuru Mura* member Morisaki Kazue concludes this book by turning to the processes by which a discourse of Japanese cultural identity is reproduced in American Japan Studies. She points out that the expert's knowledge of Japan is often authorized by a claim to mastery of the national language and contact with "native speakers" that, in turn, posits an authentic self-knowledge of Japanese as members of a linguistic community. A Japanese colonial repatriated from Korea after the war, Morisaki produced essays that described her hybrid subjectivity as "two languages, two souls." de Bary analyses ways in which the writings of this former colonial resisted recuperation into a postwar "community of remorse," and sought to challenge notions of consensus and ease of communication often used to buttress arguments about Japanese homogeneity. Our volume thus ends on a note of critical reflection on the multifaceted processes of representing "Japan" with which all of us, as authors and scholars, have been engaged for quite some time.

As mentioned above, the results of this collaborative project were first published in Japanese in the book *Nashionaritei no datsukōchiku* (Tokyo: Kashiwa Shobō, 1996). Over the course of the long process of translating and editing this book for the English edition, two authors, Hirata Yumi and Brett de Bary, replaced their essays in the Japanese edition (*"Onna no monogatari to iu seido"* and *"Nihon basshingu no jidai ni okeru Nihon kenkyū,"* respectively) with the essays included here. We are grateful to *positions: east asia cultures critique* for letting us reprint Alan Christy's translation of Tomiyama Ichirō's essay, which was first published in that journal's *Special Issue on Marxist Scholarship,* Volume 3, Number 2, Fall, 1995. Finally, we wish to acknowledge support for our endeavours (especially for conferences, workshops, and translation) generously provided by a scientific research grant from the Japanese Ministry of Education, by the Rōdō Mondai Risāchi Sentā in Tokyo, by the Japan Foundation, and by Cornell University and its East Asia program. Two anonymous readers for the Cornell East Asia Series called our attention to many fine points that, it is hoped, have enhanced the quality and readability of this English edition. Thanks to Gail Blake for copyediting assistance. Finally, Rebecca Jennison assisted us in our negotiations with the artist, Tomiyama Taeko, who has graciously allowed us to reproduce her oil painting, "Sending Off a Soldier," on our cover. It is a visual deconstruction of nationality most appropriate to our theme.

Notes

1. Parker, Russo, Sommer, and Yaeger argued for this view of "nationalism" and "nationality" in their influential introduction to *Nationalisms and Sexualities*, an essay in which there is considerable slippage between the terms "nation," "nationality," and "nationalism." Implicitly affirming the progressive aspects of certain non-Western nationalisms, they emphasize Benedict Anderson's "redescription" of "nationalism as a variable cultural artifact that is neither reactionary nor progressive in itself," and recommended that it not be classified as a form of "ideology" or "false consciousness." See Andrew Parker, Mary Russo, Doris Sommer, and Patricia Yaeger, ed. *Nationalisms and Sexualities* (London and New York: Routledge, 1992), 5.

2. Amy Kaplan, "Left Alone with America," in *Cultures of United States Imperialism*, edited by Amy Kaplan and Donald E. Pease (Durham: Duke University Press, 1993), 17.

Contributors

Brett de BARY	Professor, Cornell University; modern Japanese literature and cultural theory
HIRATA Yumi	Professor, Osaka University of Foreign Studies; modern Japanese literature
IYOTANI Toshio	Professor, Hitotsubashi University; international economics and sociology
KANG Sangjung	Professor, Tokyo University; political thought, social theory
KASAI Hirotaka	Associate Professor, Tsuda College; political science
KAWAMURA Minato	Professor, Hosei University; literary criticism
NAKANO Toshio	Professor, Tokyo University of Foreign Studies; social theory, social thought
OGUMA Eiji	Associate Professor, Keio University; sociology, history
Naoki SAKAI	Professor, Cornell University; intellectual history, Japanese literature, cultural theory
TOMIYAMA Ichirō	Professor, Osaka University; historical sociology

INTRODUCTION
Nationality and the Politics
of the "Mother Tongue"

Naoki Sakai

INTRODUCTION

The myth of Japan's monoethnic society no longer goes unquestioned. It is becoming increasingly common to see Japan as neither constituted by a single ethnic group nor as making up a homogeneous society. What this means is that the view that once seemed so self-evident has been cast into doubt. Japan is no longer seen as a monoethnic nation, with a high degree of cultural conformity, which will not have to deal with problems related to racism and immigration, for example, that exist in multi-ethnic societies such as the United States and Australia.[1] Regardless of whether one lives in Japan or not, the image of a single ethnic society has long constrained the thinking of those who are interested in Japanese society.[2] And yet it seems we have somehow begun to free ourselves from the spell, cast upon us since the era of the Second World War, of this myth of Japan and the discourse on Japanese culture it has implied.

In which direction, however, are we being freed? Indeed, what does it mean to be freed from the myth of the monoethnic society? Above all, how do we understand the collapse of this myth?

If, as a result of the gradual internationalization that has made foreign workers a not uncommon sight in Japan, Japan has already ceased to be a monoethnic society, does this mean that, up until the 1970s, such a myth was to a certain extent correct? Or was it merely the case that Japanese were simple-minded enough, until quite recently, not to have noticed that there were within Japan, not only those referred to as "foreigners" or *gaijin*, but also resident Koreans, Ainu, and Okinawans? Alternatively, if we had possessed sufficient knowledge of Japanese society (gained through books

1

and other audiovisual media that informed us of the existence of minority peoples) to know that it was something of an exaggeration to refer to Japan as monoethnic, would this myth ever have cast a spell on our consciousness? A thoroughgoing problematization of the myth of the monoethnic society, however, can never rest with merely empirical attempts to illuminate its truth or falsity. The myth of the monoethnic society is not a matter, in other words, of people forgetting about the existence of different ethnic groups that reside in Japan. On the contrary, what constitutes this myth is the very assumption that, since the Japanese people are one ethnos, communication of ideas and sentiment among them is guaranteed from the start. What I am calling a myth refers to the very situation in which such an assumption makes it possible for people to attribute meaning and intentionality to their everyday actions. This myth entails, moreover, the preconception that one ethnos can be simply recognized as distinct from another. In other words, the myth of the monoethnic society is accompanied by the epistemological myth that ethnic identity can be directly and objectively experienced within everyday life. At the core of this myth of the monoethnic society, we can find the epistemological myth that ethnic identity is an experiential fact. From this is born the convenient conviction that, among Japanese, mutual understanding and natural compassion are possible. Conversely, from this myth is also born the belief that, "among foreigners" one is bound to experience discomfort and impediments to smooth communication.

We may agree that persons who have an intense conviction of their own "Japaneseness" often seem to be those who have visited foreign lands and have, themselves, been plagued by anthropophobic feelings toward foreigners. Yet, when we probe the source of the vaguely defined "foreigner" of these encounters that give rise to shyness and anthropophobia, we find that the encounter may have been with a North American male or some other person. On the basis of the narrator's extremely limited experience, such encounters will often be freely augmented so as to emotively sustain his or her sense of identity as "Japanese." In the case of Japan, neither Koreans, Thais, nor Indians are implied in this conception of "foreigner." Or perhaps, even if they are implied in the conception of "foreigner," this does not entail a palpable emotional content. I have the vague memory of a commonsensical understanding—however strange as a concept—widespread until about the year 1960 within the environs of Tokyo (I cannot be certain of areas outside this) according to which the terms "foreigner," "American," and "whites" were held to be equivalent to one another. This sense of "foreigner," which perhaps conversely determines that of "we Japanese," is entirely devoid of any conceptual coherence. Nevertheless, it is something that emotionally sustains the self-consciousness of individual "Japanese." While it is certainly the notion of "foreigner" that defines "Japanese," as its conceptual opposite, the sentimental persuasion that one is "Japanese," which we mistakenly think of as an actuality, is not a self-evident concept. Moreover, it is overwhelmingly the case that this emotional conviction itself is what provides the internal reality of being "Japanese." In other words, the sense of being Japanese cannot be analyzed according to a methodology of the history of ideas, which would seek the origins of the "Japanese" through chronologically pursuing the name or concept of "Japanese."

The myth of the monoethnic society functions perhaps through this emotional dimension. In other words, emotional convictions arising out of personal experiences that differ for each individual are, from time to time, constellated around the term "foreigner," in such a way that one becomes persuaded that the object, "foreigner," the antithesis of the conviction that one is "Japanese," actually exists. It is when various experiences of discomfort become the source of predicates (when, for instance, one is overwhelmed by the sense that "After all, foreigners are very different from us!") or when the discomforts and social obstacles that are organized around the schema of "Japanese" vs. "foreigner" become predicated of "the foreigner," that one's awareness of being "Japanese" comes into existence.

In this sense, examination of the myth of the monoethnic society would certainly not simply be a problem of postwar Japan. Rather, such an examination would lead us more broadly to an inquiry into the regime of fantasies and conceptual forces present when national identity is believed to be an actual sensation. In order to examine this regime, moreover, we must necessarily take up the problem of the representations of community within the nation-state, as well as the general problem of how sentimental feelings of solidarity are produced.

I would first like to suggest the following definition for the words "nationality" or "national polity" (*kokutai*): nationality is constituted through representations of community conveyed through a regime of fantasies and conceptual forces; it is the sentimental feeling of the "we" enabled by these regimes within modern national communities. I align "nationality" and "national polity" since the word *kokutai* was first introduced during the early part of the Meiji period as a translation of "nationality." Fukuzawa Yukichi, for example, asserted the necessity of a consciousness through which the national populace could be regulated and unified in his rebuttal of the arguments of *Kokugaku* (National Studies) scholars who insisted that Japan's superiority lay in its nature as a state in which politics and religion were fused, based on "a line of emperors for ages eternal." In addition to the "flawless" imperial line, Fukuzawa said, it was necessary to have, on the national level, "a structure in which things are collected together, made one, and distinguished from other entities." *Kokutai*, according to Fukuzawa, was "a race of people of similar feelings, the creation of a distinction between fellow countrymen and foreigners, the fostering of more cordial and stronger bonds with one's countrymen than with foreigners. . . . In Western countries it is called 'nationality.'" Fukuzawa's "nationality" was, moreover, to be expressed through certain emotions (*kokutai no nasake*):

"A sentiment of nationality may originate in similarity of physical characteristics, or religion, or language, or geography. Although the reason may differ from country to country, the most important factor is for a race of people to pass through a series of social forms and share a common past."[3] This represented a nearly exact rendering of John Stuart Mill's 1861 explanations of "nationality" and "the society of sympathy" displaced onto the situation in Japan.[4] The definition of "nationality" varied, as the sentiment of nationality was derived from the sameness of race, the permanence of the governmental body, language, or customs. As Oguma Eiji has described, it was on the basis of these different definitions that various and quite distinct discourses of nationality consequently developed in Japan. There were also instances in which "nationality" was translated by words like *kokusui* or "national essence."[5]

It cannot, of course, be concluded that Fukuzawa's interpretation has dominated views on "national body (*kokutai*)" in Japan since the Meiji period. It is necessary to refer to his views, however, in order to understand why "nationality" has played such an important role as a device by which to produce the sense and sympathy of being "Japanese." Fukuzawa realized, moreover, that it was impossible to construct the nation without a distinction between Japanese and non-Japanese. In this sense, we can say that he regarded the "division between self and other" as important. Although Fukuzawa rejected a type of Christian image of the Emperor denoting "impartial and universal brotherhood" (*isshi dōjin shikai kyōdai*),[6] it was later conceded that the sentiment of nationality should accompany the expansion of the Japanese empire and extend beyond merely the residents of the Japanese mainland. In this way, "impartial and universal brotherhood" came to be understood as implying a broad universalism that extended beyond the Japanese archipelago. In the history of the modern emperor system, up until the inauguration of the New Constitution in 1946, the first half of the phrase "impartial and universal brotherhood" (*isshi dōjin shikai kyōdai*), that is, "one gaze, equal love" (*isshi dōjin*), was irreparably associated with the figure of Emperor and symbolically represented the very relationship between the Emperor and the individual subject, between the state and individuated Japanese, as one between the one who provides love to his subjects individually and the one who demands such love. It is no accident that the figurative representation of the relationship between the Emperor and his subject (a parent and his or her baby) eerily resembled that of the shepherd and the lost sheep. It is precisely in this respect that the modern Japanese state has been an actualization of what Michel Foucault called "pastoral power."[7] Yet, as is well known, Japan's defeat in World War II and the loss of the Japanese empire meant that, once again, the "sentiment of nationality" came to based on the myth of the single ethnic society living within the discrete boundaries of the Japanese archipelago. The argument that consciousness of "we Japanese" has existed since ancient times, so often found in *Nihonjinron* and the imperial histories—an argument whereby Japanese seek the origins of their own communality within the past—was in fact anticipated in Fukuzawa's definition of "nationality." The absurd myth that consciousness of "we Japanese" existed since ancient times has been, in fact, the necessary condition upon which a "sentiment of nationality" has been brought about.

While keeping these historical circumstances in mind, I will now examine the regime of representations of community constituted through the apparatuses of fantasies and imagination within the modern national community. It will also be necessary to investigate the imagined sense of "us" enabled by these apparatuses, as well as the series of devices—such as national culture and national language—that have played such an important role in relation to the "sentiment of nationality."

NATIONAL CULTURE AND ETHNIC CULTURE

Let us, for the moment, set aside the vague notion of culture as an omnipresent medium existing within a national or ethnic community. Instead, let us begin by calling into question those views, which immediately link culture to a nation or an ethnicity. In their place, let us conceive of cultures as modes of behavior or regimes of practices. Swimming, for example, a regime of practices based on certain modes of bodily action, could be considered as a culture. Common experiences are produced among people who are able to swim, to the extent that one could say that a certain incommensurability of experience, based on cultural difference, separates them from those who cannot swim. Likewise, cultural differences may be said to exist between people who can drive a car and those who cannot. We all know how extremely common it is for things understood by people who are able to drive to not be grasped, no matter how exhaustively explained, by people who have never previously driven. Hence, swimming or automobile driving could be said to constitute "cultures." When culture is seen in this way, we realize that many "cultures" coexist, like patchwork, within our societies. Such examples also make it clear that, in our everyday lives, we constantly encounter "cultural differences" that might give rise to incommensurabilities among people. Moreover, we can easily assent to the fact that the "culture" of swimming cuts across differences of ethnicity, nation, and race. This should make it clear that, while nation-states can produce various "cultures" that are broadly shared among their citizens (standardized language is one example), no organic unity necessarily underlies the various cultures produced in this manner. Education in the national language facilitates the production of a language generally held in common by national citizens. But an annual school dance (held at the same educational facility) no doubt also plays a large role in fostering intergender relations as well as a culture of sociability. This does not mean there is an inherent relationship between national language and dance parties. (Schools that do not hold dance parties nevertheless offer instruction in the national language.) Thus, while it is possible to recognize the existence of "Japanese culture" as a random assemblage of various "cultures" within Japan, it does not follow that this assemblage is an organic unity that bears the essence of Japanese people. Here the differences become clear between our position and that of so-called culturalism, in which group and culture are seen as overlapping. Culturalism postulates cultural difference only between the interior and exterior of a certain national or ethnic community. It should also now be clear that it is only by means of a certain institutionalized discourse that culturalism comes to locate certain differences uniquely to the boundary between the inside and outside of national collectivities. It is culturalism, in fact, that has invented the notion that the sphere of the collective and that of culture overlap, in disregard of the infinite number of cultural incommensurabilities that already exist within a community.

This institutionalized discourse is necessarily sustained by several rules, which we may now explicate. We should begin by bearing in mind that, by definition, any incommensurablity is initially unintelligible to the person encountering it, and thus can be grasped neither in the form of a symmetrical binary opposition nor in the form of a particularity within a generality.[8] One comes across cultural difference as something initially impossible to understand: impossibility of understanding, in this case, means, above all, an inability to predicate the experience of cultural difference through the use of existing categories. Such incommensurablities are therefore neither given as "representations" nor as "phenomena." Neither are they apprehended as culturally specific difference, in the sense of being a difference between two particularities subsumed within the same generality. Such encounters do not present themselves to us as experiences of cultural difference or as problems of cognition, but rather as practical tasks. It is impossible, for example, to establish a "phenomenology of cultural difference." For an object of consciousness is regarded as a "phenomenon" only insofar as it is posited as something describable in terms of concepts; it is, so to say, placed in the field of conceptualization. Cultural difference is precisely what is *not* given in this manner, and thus does *not* rise to consciousness. From a culturalist viewpoint, however, cultural incommensurability is invariably seen as registered by consciousness. It is understood as that which can be posited as an object of the epistemological subject, and as a specific difference between two communities, which are presupposed in advance. Culturalism therefore attempts to ignore the practical relation to cultural difference by dissolving this latter within culturally specific difference.

Second, in classical logic, the concept of specific difference is based on the distinction between genus and species, and is used to differentiate between two particularities within a common generality. Within culturalism, however, these two particularities are invariably understood as properties of one community and another community outside it. For example, let us take the difference between a writing style that has developed honorific usage and one that has not, or the often-cited cultural difference observed in the distinction between a style of painting in which the center is left blank and one in which it is filled in. In each case, we could understand what we observe as differences existing within distinct generalities (of the grammatical function of the personal demonstrative, or of the spatial arrangement of painting, respectively). Within culturalism, however, all of these specific differences will be reduced to the distinction between Japanese culture and non-Japanese culture. The result is that all the particularities that can be indicated by these specific differences are taken to be predicates of the single propositional subject, "Japanese culture." If we were to think of this in terms of figures of speech, we could say that, in "culturalism," specific differences are seen synecdochically as marks of the whole that is Japanese culture. The totality of Japanese culture can thus be represented by reference to a particular example. Of course, a question mark needs to be attached to the very assumption that there is a totality of Japanese culture, as tacitly premised through the use of the synecdoche.

Let us now take up a more complex argument from the actual development of discourses on culture. In these discourses, such terms as "Japanese culture," "Japan," and "Japanese people," are treated as propositional subjects. Various particularities are then made the predicates of these propositional subjects through the citation of specific differences, which are their properties. This procedure is quite common. That is to say, because within culturalism the propositional subject, "Japanese culture," has been established in advance as the theme (or thetic subject), it becomes impossible to problematize the very assumption that "Japanese culture" exists in the first place. Similarly, because the propositional subject is singly posited, Japanese culture must logically be homogeneous. The apparent appropriateness of the statement, "Japanese culture is homogeneous," is an effect of the fact that the view that regards national culture as heterogeneous has been logically excluded in advance. For the same reason, heterogeneity can only be found where other ethnic cultures are located within Japanese society, and it is immediately ascribed to such minority cultures as Korean or Okinawan ones. From a culturalist position, cultural heterogeneity can only be understood as the coexistence of different ethnic cultures.

Culturalism constrains debates on so-called multiculturalism as well as on national cultures. The view of culture as organic unity is just as much assumed by those who affirm multiculturalism as a return to ethnic cultural authenticity, as by those who denounce it as something that divides the national community into fragmented ethnic communities. Thus we see that culturalism can survive as an inversion of itself, especially in the form of those apparently anticulturalist arguments that oppose multiculturalism. The reproach of multiculturalism for fragmenting national societies is based on the premise that the unity of culture equals the unity of ethnos. What critics of multiculturalism fail to understand is that all social formations, not just multicultural ones, are composed of multiple cultures, and that this multiplicity of cultures should not be conceived of as a numerical multiplicity of coexisting units.

While it is true that social formations invariably include incommensurabilities and discontinuities, this does not necessarily mean that societies must be divided into racial and ethnic units. The dominant critique of multiculturalism could not have emerged without a naïve acceptance of culturalist premises, and a conception of culture as something that overlaps with ethnic and racial groups. In fact, those who promote a particularistic multiculturalism adhering to the notion of ethnic and racial identities are complicit with their seemingly "universalist" critics who reject multiculturalism in favor of the unity of the nation in general. It is not only in the myth of the single ethnos, but in the form of nationalism that affirms the multi-ethnic nation, that culturalism exists.

The correlation between culturalism and racism, furthermore, is exceedingly clear. Since the myth of the mono-ethnic society is one of the logical conclusions of culturalism, it is better to think of this myth as produced through the perspectival device of culturalism rather than primarily as a proposition grounded in direct experience of Japanese culture.

But, above all, it is through narration that the Japanese culture is produced through culturalism as an object of knowledge; it is a means by which to organize the personal experiences of the narrator. Although the same can be said of any "sentiment of nationality," the lived and imagined reality of "us Japanese" cannot be dissected merely by indicating its logical inconsistencies. This is because belief in something called "Japanese culture" is interwoven with the very sense of "being Japanese." All attempts to grasp the institutionalized aspect of this sentiment will fail if they do not consider the manner by which such a narrative comes to be produced. This does not mean we should overlook the extreme violence, often revealed in racism and nationalism, that is potentially contained within culturalism as well as the "sentiment of nationality." But just as a "sentiment of nationality" produces the fantasy of a community of sympathy in which those compatriots who are injured are pitied and comforted in and by the community as a whole, so, too, does this sentiment invariably create a fantasized anxiety over, as well as pre-emptive discrimination against the intrusion of, "foreigners." It is this that needs to be taken into account when we analyze of the sense of "being Japanese." What is even more worrisome about this community of sympathy is the fact that fear of, and discrimination against, "foreigners" are frequently governed by a sentiment that "we" are the victims.

THE NARRATIVE OF NATIONAL CULTURE

Why do people wish to explain their own culture? And to whom do people wish to explain it? If "cultural difference" gives rise to difficulties in social interactions with foreigners and people of different ethnic groups, explanation of the practices and customs of one's own society would no doubt be an attempt to smooth these over. But we could say this is no different from the situation in which a new member of a baseball team is taught team rules and baseball techniques by his seniors. The player enters the group and is expected to learn its rules and customs. Similarly, the addressee of cultural explanations would be the foreigner or immigrant placed in the position of learner. Because the role of "student" is, at the very least, premised upon absorbing the explained practices and customs, their acquisition is presented as positive and desirable—much like the knowledge transmitted in school from teacher to pupil.

Explanations of culture, however, do not take place in such situations. Let us take the narrative of so-called *Nihonjinron* as a typical cultural discourse.[9] The scope of *Nihonjinron* is quite broad: it includes a branch of the comparative cultural discourse taught in university lectures as well as the genre of travel journal that thrives in tourist guidebooks and magazines. While it is difficult to discuss these collectively, it is possible to conceive of several distinguishing features when we consider the implicit patterns manifested in this genre.

First, let us consider the pattern of narrative address. For the most part, the scene of the narration of *Nihonjinron* is characterized by the *absence* of those foreigners and different ethnic groups that are its supposed listeners. Absence in this case does not simply mean that *Nihonjinron* is not narrated in a language directed at foreigners, nor that few foreigners live in those areas where it is produced. In fact, it is exceedingly obvious that *Nihonjinron* is not addressed to those newcomers to the collectivity called Japan, i.e., to foreigners. The addressees of this narrative are in fact Japanese: *Nihonjinron* takes the form of Japanese narrating to Japanese. Yet, even if "foreigners" are absent from the scene of narration, this does not mean that they are entirely removed from the narrator's consciousness. Foreigners, in the sense of all those people throughout the world who are not Japanese, are generally not present in this scene of narration. But the narration, in most cases, contrasts "Westerners" with Japanese and is premised on the fact that "Westerners" are the bearers of that culture that is being contrasted with Japanese culture. Thus, we have a form of narrative, apprising Japanese of the fact that they can never be anything but Japanese, premised upon the existence of the "Westerner" they are unable to become. Try as one might, one can never be more than a superficial imitation of a Westerner, because one's upbringing and cultural baggage are such that, in the end, a Japaneseness deep within one's very body calls one back despite oneself—such is the basic thrust of most *Nihonjinron* arguments that fellow Japanese address to one another.

In *Nihonjinron*, the narrator, while using personal experiences of the West as a reference point, returns to his or her "Japanese" origins by awakening to his or her essence as Japanese. While the culture referred to as a point of contrast may be that of France, the United States, or Germany, the differences among these entities are commonly obscured within a vague and all-encompassing notion of "the West." Let us note first that the cultures that constitute points of contrast here are national cultures, and that these European—and, moreover, "Western"—cultures are understood as an organic whole. The aspects of culture that cut across national communities (for example, certified public accountants, automobile driving, rock music, video games) are deliberately excluded from *Nihonjinron*'s view of culture. It goes without saying that this is because any position that conceives of Japanese culture as the equivalent of a unitary national community would be jeopardized if the Western culture it were contrasted with was seen as either diffusive or something that straddled different geographical areas. Previously, cultures that cut across national boundaries were lumped together under the notion of modern machine culture, which became a cultural index symbolizing the progress of the "West." (The industrial development of various countries of the so-called "non-West," of course, has now invalidated this conception of modern machine culture.) If we are looking at this trajectory, the "West" might be another name for capitalism. In this sense, any of those countries in which capitalism has made the most rapid advances, and that carry out the role of "center" in an imperialist division of labor, can be called the "West." As Iyotani Toshio puts it, the "West" is another name for anything that functions as a "center" within the configuration of power that is the modern world system. As such, there is no particular reason that it must designate such fixed areas as Europe and North America.[10] Interestingly, the belief that the "West" is advanced and is a model to be studied often comes to merge with *Nihonjinron*. I use the phrase "come to merge with" because most advocates of *Nihonjinron* present themselves as opponents of Eurocentrism. This is precisely the reason why they argue against the Eurocentric demand that everyone become like the "West." On the contrary, they assert that actual experience has taught them that "Western" culture is not everything, and that, however much one tries to accommodate it, what is different is simply different. As I have already noted, such a "West" is occasionally conflated with "foreigners," and even sustains the everyday sense of "being Japanese" that is posited by contrast to being "foreign."

However, the demand for recognizing one's own particularity while rejecting the universality of the West arises in fact only under the hegemony of Eurocentrism. Recent works by scholars from so-called "non-Western" societies, such as Partha Chatterjee's *The Nation and its Fragments*, quickly reveal that the problem is not one of *Nihonjinron* alone.[11] The demand to be recognized in one's particularity is in fact complicitous with Eurocentric universalism. It has been necessary for me to consider how *Nihonjinron*'s mode of address produces a sense of one's "Japanese essence" in order to clarify this point.

It is precisely the demand to "become like a Westerner!" or to "acquire the standards of the West," that makes one aware of those historical and cultural traces that have accumulated within the body that make it impossible, try as one might, to comply with this demand. Facing the command, "become like a Westerner!" the "non-Westerner" hears something like a cry of protest from his or her own body, which resists and defies this demand, forcefully bringing about an awareness of these traces. Such a reaction is comparable to those of people from the provinces who stammered when they were required to speak in standard Japanese. As Kawamura Minato's work has shown, people in colonies and annexed territories of the Japanese empire responded similarly when forced to learn the Japanese language.[12] Similarly, Tomiyama Ichiro has studied how Okinawans living in Osaka discovered their own "Okinawan-ness" upon receiving the command, "become Japanese!"[13] It is only when one faces the demand to internalize the standards of the dominant group as part of a process of modernization that the particularist argument acquires the force of an emotional impulse that protests against these standards. This is true of the relations between metropolis and provinces in the nation-state, but also in the hierarchized relations between classes and genders. That the cultures of Asia, Africa, or South America are only very rarely proposed by *Nihonjinron* as points of contrast with Japanese culture can be explained by the fact that, unlike the encounter of a provincial with someone from Tokyo, that of a Japanese with someone from these areas is not conducted under the command that one learn the customs and modes of acting of this other.

Can we not say, then, that the interest in Japanese culture, as well as the fervor with which Japanese essence is constantly narrated in *Nihonjinron*, derive from the fact that it is fundamentally a narrative of "excuse"? It is, moreover, within this narrative of "excuse" that the unity of that national culture known as "Japanese culture" has come to be articulated.

We can call this narrative one of "excuse" because the existence of various commands constitute the preconditions for confirming oneself as Japanese, and the particularity of Japanese culture is offered as an explanation for the impossibility of complying with these commands. Moreover, if we were to speak dialectically, the preconditions themselves are elided in *Nihonjinron*, and only the explanation is posited as an immediacy. Thus, we can see that the particularity of Japanese culture is not immediately given in experience but is evoked as a reaction, the refusal of a demand. Japanese culture is constituted only within dialectic mediation. Without the effort to execute these commands, there would be no self-consciousness of cultural essence itself. Nor would there be any consciousness of cultural origins in the sense of bodily nature as that which resists the execution of these commands. In order to become conscious of oneself as Japanese, therefore, one must execute these commands under threat from a non-Japanese "other." The explanation constantly repeated within *Nihonjinron* to the effect that, "I am Japanese"—which means that Japanese have such-and-such customs and cannot escape from such-and-such a disposition—is in fact prefaced by the following: "You demand of me that I act, feel and think like you, and yet it is impossible for me to satisfy your demand." This is uttered within the form of address of an "excuse," that is to say, a "demand for love," in which forgiveness is begged from the other person in the form of an apology for one's inability to satisfy the stipulated expectations. The "Westerner," who is generally this other, however, is absent from the scene of narration of *Nihonjinron*.

The preceding argument, however, should not be taken to constitute the command to "become civilized" as immediately "Western," while the disposition and habits of those who are unable to follow such a command are not immediately "non-Western" or "Japanese." There must first exist a certain apparatus of fantasy that posits as "Western" those whose demands cannot be accomplished, and considers as "Japanese" the inability to accomplish them. To take either the "West" or the "Japanese" resistance to it to be such immediately existing realities is to ignore the necessary existence of this mechanism. In other words, an apparatus of fantasy must take individual experiences of frustration within the modernizing process and "represent" them through the schema of binary opposition between the "West" and "Japan." Such a regime transforms these experiences into a narrative in which the desire to return to the national community "Japan" may be satisfied. This regime, which treats these experiences of frustration as equivalent to representations of binary oppositions between cultures seems to me to be analogous to the schema of "translation" through which the relationship between the *operation* of translation and the *representation* of that operation are reversed.[14] This regime of fantasy has long since been institutionalized. The culturalist discourse of *Nihonjinron* comes to seem natural only when efforts to articulate another regime by which to invalidate the schema of binary opposition of "West" versus "non-West" are lacking.

Discourses of national culture also assume that in the course of history people have experienced deep losses, and that it is impossible to grasp the origins of these historical losses without tracing them back either "genealogically" or "archaeologically." (It might be better to conceive the temporality of these historical injuries as inverted, much as trauma is understood within psychoanalysis. This tracing back, then, would not merely involve a retracing of chronological time.) If we want to go beyond simply reproaching culturalism and undertake a more fundamental critique, we must unearth the history that produced it. We must be attentive to the way *Nihonjinron* forecloses interrogation of appropriateness of the very command that "we" can never satisfy. *Nihonjinron* removes the possibility of historicizing this command, concealing the fact that the operation of providing cultural representations is always political.

But let us return again to the question of whether "Western" standards are really "Western."

Most men in the business district of today's Tokyo wear suits. While probably all of these men know that the design of such suits originates in Europe, to wear a suit today is in no way taken as an indication that one is dressing in particularly "Western" style and hence accepting the standards of the West. As has been remarked countless times, it is not at all the same thing that certain customs or articles of use originated in the West and that they are considered "Western" even now. This is also true of culture: while its origins can be found in some cases in the Japanese archipelago or in others in Western Europe, this does not at all mean that such approaches are an expression of ethnic or national identity. There are many Nintendo computer games produced in Japan, and yet most of the children throughout the world who enjoy these games do so without realizing that they are made in Japan. Of course this is one effect of transnational capitalism. But, even so, this situation is probably a result of the fact that computer games are not caught up within a discourse that emphasizes national culture. They are not, for example, like perfumes, which also spread across the world through the circuit of transnational capitalism, but are sold as a symbols of French national culture and national essence—and hence caught up within a discourse that does emphasize national culture. In both cases, however, the relation or non-relation to national culture is nothing more than a result of advertising and the image making of marketing. Anticipating, for a moment, the conclusion of this argument, let me propose that there is no reason whatsoever that culture must symbolize ethnos or nation in the absence of a discourse that attributes certain cultures to ethnic or national identity. Culture is, in the first instance, exactly like the suit or the computer game, in the sense that it is indifferent to its status as either "Western" or "Japanese." The investigation of cultural pedigrees is best left to the "connoisseurs" of the "culture state." The arbitrary linking of culture to ethnos or nation is a characteristic of discourses that are fixated on national culture and national character. Culture itself does not inherently bear the marks of either ethnos or nation.

We can proceed from this to ascertain that various entities lumped together as "Western" constitute an assemblage of elements from an array of different binomial oppositions—the "West" is in this sense overdetermined, since these elements cannot logically coexist with each other. It simply cannot be assumed that the "West" is an inherently unified substance. At times "the West" refers to the Judeo-Christian tradition, while at other times it refers to highly industrialized capitalist institutions. As mentioned earlier, the "West" may refer to "centers" within the configuration of power of the modern world system, or equally well to those parliamentarian forms of government that are grounded upon the concept of individual human rights. The "West" refers at times to liberal democracy, at times to the hereditary privilege of those who are "white" in the racial systems of classification. It is exceedingly contradictory for all of these definitions to determine what the "West" is, insofar as each produces an entirely different object. It must be said, then, that the notion of "West" is based on a collection of mutually contradictory definitions. Or rather, that the "West" is the conviction that these mutually contradictory definitions can all be subsumed within one totality, regardless of the fact that this is a patchwork, assembled quite arbitrarily, of entities that are sometimes called "Western" and sometimes not. In this sense, the "West" is a typical cultural imaginary.

What this cultural imaginary implies is a history in which it has been possible to force commands upon people in a threatening form. That we can only allude to this indirectly is because the multiple violences entailed in the separate histories through which such coercive hegemony was established remain with us in as yet unspecified forms. That the "West" is still seen as the source of commands to be obeyed is a legacy of histories of annihilation against those who could not internalize the demands of the system that established its coercive hegemony throughout the world—first peoples in the New World, and colonized Asian and African peoples. Although these regimes of domination were established neither simultaneously nor in one stroke, and involved entirely different historical processes and groups, the "West" has come to refer uniformly to the dominating force. This overlaps with the process through which the vague category of "the white race" is conceived as that which sustains the identity of the "West." The problem with this view of modernity as the era in which the "West" dominates the world, however, is that it leaves unanswered the question of whether there was a "West" prior to this as well. (Such a view is, of course, closely connected to the view that modernity established the "white man's superiority.") Such a manner of speaking is, however, mistaken. We should rather understand modernity as the process through which the unitary category of the "West" and the racial category of "white" were established. These categories of "West" and "the white race," moreover, not only concealed discrete histories of domination through violence, but appeared as their displacements. For, in addition to erasing the histories inscribed by overbearing force, the terms "West" and "white" perpetuate the lived sense of inferiority foisted upon peoples throughout the world through precisely that history. When the "West" is taken as uniform, therefore, the traces of complex struggles can no longer be seen. These include, for example, the history of colonial violence between the British and Irish and an infinite number of other discriminations and disputes between "whites," as well. In order to be recognized as "white," one identifies with one's "white-like" self at the expense of one's non-whiteness and excludes, in particular, other non-white groups. The historicity of the category "white" is suggested by the fact that, in recent history, those people possessing Japanese citizenship were treated in certain countries as "honorary whites." Of course, Japanese also were exposed to colonial violence in the process of constructing the modern nation. But in order to "Westernize," they simultaneously posited other people in Japan and Asia who had to be colonized and civilized, who then became objects of violence. The binary opposition "West" and "non-West" does not represent the essential identities of ruler and ruled. Instead, it conceals the instability inherent on the putative identity of the "West," as well as modernity's entangled history of conflicts.[15]

Many narrators of *Nihonjinron* repeatedly tell the miniaturized history of such a "West" within their personal experiences. They are keenly made to feel the threatening force of these commands. This premise is, however, erased from their culturalist narration, from which the diversity and over-determined aspect of "the West" is similarly expunged. Like the binary opposition between "West" and "non-West," *Nihonjinron* conceals the history that such a discourse has necessarily produced.

Thus, we may say that *Nihonjinron*, this culturalist discourse of Japan, is not produced simply to explain the cultural differences that exist between the "West" and "Japan." Cultural difference must be explained so that those Japanese who have attempted to imitate the West and failed may have a common narrative of "excuse," and on this basis may return to a shared culture. Such a cultural discourse must be produced because it is the shared belief in the existence of the absent "West" that allows the contrasting figure of "Japan" to come into being. Such a schema of co-figuration makes possible the representation (and "re-presentation") of "Japan" and the "West" as organic unities. One can say that forms of cultural particularism like *Nihonjinron* could not exist without Eurocentric universalism, insofar as they are a means of concealing the fact that Eurocentrism entails compliance with these threats and commands. This is one example of the complicity between particularism and universalism.

Indeed, disputes about the origins of national cultures can clarify the otherwise obscured premise of narratives of cultural particularism and can help us to once again problematize that "West" they posit in a very vague form. This would make it possible to no longer ascribe those commands that must be accepted to an amorphous "West," but to assess the appropriateness of each in turn. Those judged correct would be accepted whether "Western" or not, whereas those judged incorrect would be rejected. For this reason, it is absolutely necessary that we make the schematism of co-figuration an object of analysis.

Once *Nihonjinron* is apprehended in this light, however, it can be seen that it is by no means a phenomenon particular to Japan. When *Nihonjinron* speaks as if Japanese culture and society were exceptional, it is simply embodying the kind of exceptionalism that is commonplace in discourses of national culture. Moreover, although it is not identical to culturalism, American exceptionalism springs to mind as another example of how commonplace cultural exceptionalism is. In its most familiar form, American exceptionalism is expressed in that "sentiment of nationality" that is an obsession with how unusual and special "my country" is. And no matter how "contagious" nationalism has proven to be in other parts of the world, it is always through this kind of exceptionalism—or belief in the particularity of one's nation—that it has been transmitted. Analysis of *Nihonjinron* is, therefore, useful for us, because it provides an opportunity to consider the process through which national culture comes to be figured.

Actually, the narrative in which the narrator continuously expresses awareness of his or her own cultural particularism may be produced in various contexts. For example, Japan scholars from the United States and Europe must live under the professional demand that they learn the Japanese language. There are many cases in which these scholars are made conscious of their own cultural origins, finding themselves unable, despite their best efforts, to comply with the demand to speak fluent Japanese. Such frustration may lead to a paranoid sense of being a "Westerner" and of how one's Western origins are inscribed upon one's own body. On this basis, a certain argument can be constructed that acts as a complement to *Nihonjinron*. Of course, such scholars do not generally go on from here to develop an argument about Western particularity, but this is because they operate within the framework of the broader demand described above that makes the dominant West the center of the world. That system of commands that takes "Japan" as its locus ("You must learn Japanese!" and "You must act like a Japanese!") is applicable only within an extremely limited professional context. Moreover, the system of commands that makes the West its center, and extends over a much broader area, is a tacitly recognized presence in Japan, as well. Depending on fluctuations in economic and social conditions, however, the center from which demands are assumed to be issued actually shifts constantly.

Moreover, it cannot, perhaps, be forgotten that the identity "West" confers a certain pride upon "Westerners" who identify with the "West." Because identification with the West asserts one's superiority vis-à-vis "non-Westerners," the non-Westerners inevitably feel coerced or threatened by the Westerners who stress their own "Western" identity. In other words, because "Western" pride is perceived through a contrast with non-Westerners, the "non-West" becomes for "Westerners" a type of mirror on which the desire to be one's own self-image is elicited. In this respect, it is interesting to note that the self-representations of the "West" always involve relations of gender. This is why relations between "West" and "non-West," and especially between colonial ruler and ruled, are often metaphorically represented by the gender relations symbolized by the trope of "Madame Butterfly." As a discourse that thematizes the "non-West," *Nihonjinron* takes Japanese people to be its thetic subject, yet it remains in fact a narrative of "Western" desire. The obfuscation of the division between "West" and "non-West"—which is otherwise maintained through such binary oppositions as modern versus premodern, white versus nonwhite, and progress versus tradition—brings about a kind of crisis for those who have identified with the "West." This crisis is similar to that which occurs when women, who sustain male subjective coherency through the assumption of male desire, cease to play that role. Through woman's internalization of male desire, a relationship of mutual interdependence is established in which women receive recognition by men.[16] When a woman abandons this role, we find a collapse of male self-esteem as well as the loss of a position of masculine privilege. Women who have internalized male desire and act "woman-like" in relation to men provide, as it were, a type of fulcrum of identity by which men are able to know themselves as men. Recognition that countries in East Asia might attain the universality of the modern has more recently threatened to disrupt the binary opposition between "West" and "non-West"—producing a situation that could perhaps be described as the West's loss of self-esteem.

Changes in the relations between areas that have functioned as center and periphery of the world economy have destabilized the apparatus of "Western superiority" that sustained the system of commands we have analyzed. In areas like the United States and Western Europe that, heretofore, through either colonial or imperialist power structures, had been the source of commands to "others," we have suddenly witnessed the eruption of greatly expanded possibilities for the production of discourses like that of "the return to the West," or cultural essentialist theories about the "West" that are simply an inversion of *Nihonjinron*. As writings by Paul Gilroy and Etienne Balibar have shown, in anti-immigrant movements of the late twentieth century, we find cultural essentialist discourses on "the English" and "the French" that are subdivisions of this broader discourse on the "West."[16]

We cannot, however, overlook the way in which the belief in cultural homogeneity upon which culturalism depends is also related to national homogeneity in the sense of the "society of sympathy" Fukuzawa derived from Mill. In order for an event that occurs in one part of the national community to be felt as if it belonged to the whole community, a mechanism for diffusing sentimentality must exist here. Without such a device, it is extremely difficult to create the sense, for example, of "we Japanese."

The diffusion of sentimentality I refer to here is not, of course, a certain feeling that spreads among people. Rather, we might compare the sentiment of nationality to the emotion one has when attending the funeral of someone one does not know. Through conforming to such rules of etiquette as maintaining a "solemn bearing" and wearing a "sad expression," one comes imperceptibly to actually maintain a "solemn bearing" and "feel sad." Rather than feeling, it is sentimentality that is diffused here. *Sentimentality* is that state of affairs in which the appearance demanded by "etiquette" is unquestioningly accepted as "reality." "Sentimentality" is analogous to the types of emotion one experiences when, on the basis of formalities rooted in preconceived ideas, one forms a stereotype of another and then respects, scorns, or fears him or her. Diffusion of these emotions is rooted in a community's possession of a common etiquette or patterns of behavior. It is for this reason that sentimentality will not be diffused among children and others who are ignorant of such etiquette and bold enough to say, "The Emperor is naked." What device diffuses sentimentality in the case of national community?

The discourse of national culture is one such device. The device takes those who narrate or listen to it and forms them into national subjects. We might best speak of this device as a "subjective technology," through which a subject constructs itself or performs its *poiesis* as a subject. National history may be cited as another example of such "subjective technologies." In this sense, the roles of national history and of discourses of national culture overlap. They are devices for making us feel as if events that are distant in both social space and historical time are in fact "our events." Without such devices, it would be extremely difficult to constitute the "nation" as community of sympathy.

THE DEVICE OF SYMPATHY: THE POSITIVITY OF NATIONAL LANGUAGE

The most effective device for producing a palpable "sentiment of nationality," however, is to create the *positivity* of a "mother" tongue. Closely related to this is the idea of the "native speaker." If we are to criticize the constructs of national and ethnic culture, we must begin by analyzing unitary notions of the mother tongue, native language, or national language. This is because the figure of culture as an organic unity in most cases depends upon the figure of a linguistic unity as its original form. Moreover, the regime, by which cultural difference is figured out in terms of specific difference between two cultures posited as entities, relies on the same schema that is mobilized to represent failure in communication as taking place between two different languages. The critique of culture as a unity cannot be accomplished without asking how language can be represented as a unity. Unless the concept of language is submitted to critical examination, all critiques of national culture will invariably remain incomplete.

Let us first note that the thought of the mother tongue as determined by an immediate relation to language is simply a fantasy of communion. As Lacan well understood, the acquisition of language takes place through the thorough alienation from the kind of immediacy symbolized in the notion of a "mother tongue." The fact that humans are capable of acquiring language is premised upon their definitive alienation from anything like a symbiotic relationship with the mother, and in this sense represents the loss of a mother tongue. Humans are always foreigners vis-à-vis language, and in this sense languages can only be "foreign" languages. One's linguistic ability is constituted in that relationship of severance, or alienation, from the mother tongue. This, it would not be too far-fetched to say that it is possible for me to learn the Japanese language precisely because I am a foreigner, or, that it is only insofar as I am not Japanese that I am able to identify with the national community called "Japan." In Hegelian terms, my capacity to be Japanese must be premised on a negation of that capacity. The notion of the mother tongue as that medium that allows me to express absolutely immediately my own desires and emotions is itself a reactive function. It can only be understood as an imaginary response to moments of failure or difficulty in expression. In Nietzsche's words, the notion of the native tongue bears the character of a fundamental *ressentiment*, in that it posits a certain transcendent essence as preceding its own emergence. The thought of the mother tongue, that is, preserves the desire to return to a moment prior to injury, i.e., a hypothetical state in which injury as a reaction to certain historical scars is absent. This is similar to the status of the "excuse" within *Nihonjinron*: although the mother tongue was produced through scars, its imagined existence is determined by the wish to erase them.

Let me now explain why the mother tongue can only be in the register of the imaginary.

First, the notion of the mother tongue (as that which guarantees unmediated and direct relation between myself and my desires) conflicts with the basic condition in which the speaking subject cannot be identical to itself within the utterance, inasmuch as all utterances create a schism between the subject of the enunciation and the subject of the enunciated. The subject's schism within the utterance is similar to that schism that exists between the empirical ego and transcendental subject that, since the time of Kant, has come to be known as the aporia of the modern epistemological subject. While I can, of course, believe that my relation to my desires and emotions is unmediated, this relation can only be conceived of as an aspect of spontaneity of my own imagination. My relation to my mother tongue, as that which immediately expresses my own interiority, can therefore only be understood as imaginary. In other words, just as "representations/representations" of notions of national and ethnic culture are offered as "excuses" for the frustrations experienced within modernization and then taken by people to be "their own," so, too, through experiences of frustration and oppression do people discover their "mother tongue."

Intensely bound up with the notion of the mother tongue may be memories such as a mother's tone of voice, the feel of contact with her body, the repose brought about through symbiosis with her, nostalgia for her cooking, and the figure of the "family" constructed around her. In other words, the mother tongue is a notion, and, as a notion, it does not preserve actual memories, but gathers random memories, which include putative non-linguistic events, around it. It resembles the notion of a home: various memories swarm within this collection, including fabricated memories of things that never existed. It is a fundamentally nostalgic notion. I am directly related to this notion insofar as I think "this is *my* mother tongue." In other words, the immediacy of the mother tongue is something that is *imaginarily* related to the *notion* of the "mother tongue." Let us note, moreover, that these memories have no immediate relation to language. The taste of a mother's cooking and the feeling of contact with her body are not generally referred to as linguistic experiences. Furthermore, while "mother tongue" is a word, it does not refer to a tone of voice. This is because insofar as a language is a medium of expression, it does not bear the distinctive features of either individual morphemes or personal diction. Rather, it is necessarily constituted as a *unity* of linguistic rules within a certain regime.[18] Although the mother tongue as indicated through the figure of the mother is for the speaker the most primordial collective language, this community cannot be identified or represented outside of discourse. The unity of the mother tongue, like that of the "national mother tongue" or a national language, can be given only within discourse. It is a unity not to be discovered by those who live experientially in the "mother tongue" but rather by those who objectify it within a discourse on language, as in the discourse of philologists and linguists. Unless it has been first postulated as a unity through a discourse, we will never be able to discover the primordial and unmediated "mother tongue" upon which another language has supposedly been imposed.

We have established that the unmediated relation between myself and the mother tongue can only be understood as reactively imagined in relation to moments of failure or difficulty in expression. In other words, something like the mother tongue cannot be understood without the mediation of negativity. That which provides the identity of the mother tongue is the chance encounter with something negative to itself.

Nevertheless, the existence of historical scars or antagonisms within a collective does not necessarily enable us to return to the mother tongue or national mother tongue. In order for us to do this, there must be established in advance a discourse that represents historical scars in terms of the division between the mother tongue and that which is not the mother tongue. We may also come to understand the overwhelming importance of the perspective first referred to in the 1960s by Jacques Derrida as "phonocentrism"—in which speech and writing *are something that can be originally divided* into the opposition between the immediate and the mediated—with regard to the construction of the imaginary relation to the mother tongue. In order to ascertain the mother tongue, the immediate and mediate must both be posited as knowable. In other words, if we locate difficulties and failures of communication on the side of mediation, we can assume an authentic relation that is, for me, an intimacy devoid of such interruptions. The mother tongue becomes the figure of an intimate relation to language where difficulties and failures do not exist. Hence, for example, an immediate relation to language via the spoken words of someone who neither reads nor writes may be opposed to the elites' mediated relation to language of a ruler who has knowledge of the written word. This may then be figured as the opposition between a natural mother tongue acquired at birth and the artificial language of civilization that is only learned through training. Whatever we consciously recognize as the mother tongue will change according to the contrastive term with which it is paired. Thus, at times it will be the dialect contrasted to the standard language; at other times it will be the national language contrasted with an international language. Or, it may be the informal "spoken word" contrasted to the public "written word." The relation between myself and the figure of a unitary mother tongue is entirely controlled by ideology.

Needless to say, we should not view this process of figuration in an ahistorical manner. It is a process that first becomes possible through phonocentrism. In this sense, thought of the mother tongue prepares for the transition to the notion of a native language, or national mother tongue. It is only under such conditions that it is possible to consider the Japanese language as a lost mother tongue.[19] It is for this reason that the mother tongue must be conceived as constitutive of the ideological core of "the national body."

Once the notion of the Japanese language has been invented, it becomes possible to regard the unthinkable as that which always emanates from *outside* a determinable area (such as Japan). Those things that resist thought (or create difficulties or failures in expression and understanding) are established in advance as coming "from outside," and incapable of arising within the "interior" of that immediacy figured through phonocentrism. In short, the establishment of the mother tongue and the notion of a native language or national mother tongue does not merely produce the idea of a speaker of the mother tongue ("native speaker"); through homogeneity, it also creates the matrix of the "ethnos" or "nation" as a region of flawless communication. Investigation would reveal that, within such so-called multi-ethnic nations as the United States, Australia, and Canada, the demand for linguistic homogeneity that has emerged as part of the logic of national integration derives, in fact, from phonocentrism. Moreover, the invention of the Japanese language makes possible both consciousness of an ethnocentric "we" and the nationalistic sense that this "we" exists as an archetype. The invention of the Japanese language, as well as of national language in general, produces an imaginary relation of unmediated bonding between the subject of the enunciation and the mother tongue. The Japanese language comes into being as an institution when many people begin to experience their everyday lives in accordance with this relation.

This does not, however, mean that the Japanese language thus produced appears as transparent and absolutely immediate to those who are, literally, "Japanese people." This is because, as mentioned earlier, the very possibility of language acquisition means that it cannot be true that those people within a national language or mother tongue are nothing but native speakers. As I stated earlier, the relation between myself and an assumed mother tongue is, in an essential sense, "broken." Nobody can be at home within a mother tongue, a national mother tongue, or national language. If it were in fact possible to be so at home, we would have to abandon the basic human rules of sociality in the sense of being open to the Other.

That is to say that the unities of the mother tongue, national mother tongue, and national language are all established within discourse. The thought of the mother tongue must itself be historicized. These unities can be conceived only as discursive positivities. Because these unities are discursive *a prioris*, they emerge and disappear as discourse itself changes.

The unity of a language is, firstly, regulated through the formation of an idea that provides that unity, and, secondly, defined in terms of a specific difference with another language. Thus, such unities as ethnos, nation, race, and national/ethnic culture may be thought of as produced by nearly identical regimes.

A particular language, especially national language, while playing a role in regulating our experience, is not itself experienced. Neither ethnos nor national language is given within verifiable experience. Rather, the unity of a language is posited as an idea. This is not to deny that individual morphemes and rules are understood as belonging to specific languages. Nevertheless, when we investigate the regimes that judge such parts as belonging to the whole, we come face to face with language's mode of being as a regulative idea.

Let us, for example, adopt the position that the regulative idea of the "Japanese language" came into being at a certain period of time, and that, prior to this, it did not exist. A situation could then be imagined in which the various elements of language could be known, not as the special features of the Japanese language, but rather as the elements or styles of different social formations that need not be synthesized within a unity called the Japanese language. Without including various styles (e.g., the ancient Chinese classical style, noh chants, waka poetry, the epistolary style, everyday village conversation, or that village speech sometimes known as "dialect," formal aristocratic speech, and so forth) within the unity of the Japanese language, it would still be possible to identify different languages used in different social settings, on the basis of a pragmatics approach. So-called "Japanese writing" (*wabun*) would be a loose grouping of certain styles within such a discursive space. This could be distinguished from "Chinese writing" (*kanbun*), just as the style of contemporary novel writing is contrasted with the style of laws published by the government. If we followed such a manner of pragmatic classification, the languages presently subsumed within the category "Chinese language" could also be grasped in continuity with "Japanese writing," and seen as a particular style in which the differences between "Chinese writing" and other styles would not be privileged and exclusive boundaries created.

It is, moreover, necessary to consider the following problem. The relevance of pragmatics is not limited to those conditions that relate to the utterance and its hearing, such as movements of the speaker's body, facial expressions, and the present circumstances of speech. There are also conditions typically found in written texts that have to do with sight and movements of the pen. From the viewpoint of pragmatics, the boundaries between texts that are seen, read, felt, and heard are mutually interpenetrating. There is no reason to think of texts, in general, purely from a linguistic standpoint. The text of a book, for example, can be considered merely as *language* (as sentences constituted by a series of words) only if one disregards such things as the style of its letters, the social occasions where the book is presented, its design, and the feel of its paper. If written texts were classified on the basis of their letters, then the "stiff" style of calligraphy (*kaisho*) and the "grass" style (*sōsho*) would constitute two different genres. Likewise, if texts were classified on the basis of the frequency of usage of Chinese characters (*mana*) and Japanese syllabary (*kana*), two different genres would also appear. The opposition between these genres, however, would have nothing to do with the opposition between one language and another. When the text of a book is not recognized merely as a *language* text, then, it is possible to see it as belonging to many different, intersecting genres. Our consideration of texts would then not be limited by the principle of ascending rank, in which the highest rank, as represented by the order of family-species-genus, would be the category of the universal or general. Rather, a series of genres could be seen as linking up with another series rhizomatically. It would not, therefore, be unusual for two different grammars to coexist within the same text, just as "stiff" and cursive styles, or illustrations and written letters, are able to coexist within the same space of the utterance. Before the unity of a language is established—a unity established by expunging other languages from it—new rules of classification have to be established that make language an exclusionary category that takes precedence over other genres. The idea that a text is a purely linguistic entity requires that such reorganization of categories has already taken place.

Prior to such reorganization, it would have been impossible to conceive of a discursive formation in which (to use the current terms) the "Chinese language" and "Japanese language" coexisted not as different languages but as different genres. Of course, any reference to these genres as indicated by the names of nations such as "Chinese language" or "Japanese language" is, rigorously speaking, inappropriate. Conversely, the coming into being of national languages must, at the very least, accompany a substantial change in classifying regimes. Speaking in the most abstract and general terms, it can be said that *the establishment of the idea of a national mother tongue or national language (as would be the case, for example, when* wabun *or "Japanese writing" is taken as signifier of the national language) entails removing a genre from that level of species where it coexists with other species and placing it on the level of a "genus" that subsumes other genres understood as its "species."* In other words, genre is formed arborescently.[20] It is easy to conflate the word "genre" with "genus," inasmuch as the former derives originally from the latter. Yet, in the era when *wabun* and *kanbun* coexisted as two different genres, it was no more strange for a writer to shift from "Chinese writing" (*kanbun*) to an epistolary writing style (*sōrōbun*) than it was for a writer to shift between the style of private correspondence and one in which ordinances were written in government notices. Of course, it is another question entirely whether a certain individual could, at the same time, properly use both a legal and epistolary style. Although some people even today are incapable of writing in a legal style, such people are usually not thought of as foreigners. And yet those who are able to expertly write letters in the style of "Chinese writing" are regarded now as foreigners. Only seventy or eighty years ago, however, such people within the Japanese archipelago were regarded not as being of a different nationality but rather as being intellectuals who came from different social class and educational backgrounds. Such movements between genres were actually anticipated in systems of classification that existed prior to the formation of the positivity of the national mother tongue or national language (the question of people's actual capacity to write in different genres is one I will set aside for the moment). The assumption did not exist that people using "Chinese writing" could only be of a certain origin, or that "Japanese writing" determined one's personal authenticity. Such restrictions bearing on such practices were not related to ethnic, national, or racial authenticity, but rather to social ranking. Under the rules of this system of classification, "Chinese writing" was not defined as the "Chinese language" or as an ethnic language. It goes without saying that, when these writing practices were understood in terms of differences between genres, people considered it reasonable to shift from one genre to another in accordance with the necessities of pragmatic context. Let me state once again that, *in order for a certain "language" to be accepted as determining an individual's total and personal identity, almost as if it were a fate, it is necessary for a category once loosely classified as, for example, a "classical style" of writing to relinquish its status as one genre among many. And if what was once thought to be genre is now taken as logically extending over an entirety of social relations, it must be shifted to the logical category of the "genus" that, in turn, subsumes within itself many genres.*

Once this occurs, the shift from one "language" to another in accordance with pragmatic necessity can be perceived as if it were a betrayal of authenticity, an escape from fate, so to speak. Or perhaps this shift begins to be understood not as a transition from genre to genre but as a relation to people who speak a foreign language, by means of the regime of translation. At such a time, it becomes impossible to conceive of "Chinese writing" and classical "literary Japanese" (*gikobun*) as coexisting within the same enunciative situation. Rather one "language" and another "language" will be assumed to exist within an exclusionary relation to each other. The mother tongue (or national mother tongue) acquires its identity as a negation of the "other" language, in such a way that people are seen to possess their authentic "mother tongue" by virtue of their own ethnic or national origins. This is precisely the manner by which the native speaker is born— as one who bears the mother tongue or national mother tongue as the ground of personal authenticity.

This same argument is possible on the level of morphology as well. Let us take as an example the two Japanese nouns, "Western confectionery" (*yōgashi*) and "cake" (*kēki*). At first, perhaps, the word "*yōgashi*" might be understood as an approximate substitute for the English word "cake." But there are also times when "*kēki*" indicates an object distinct from "*yōgashi*," and a distinction is made between the two words. In this sense, the word "cake" may be seen as contained within the Japanese language. Nevertheless, "cake" (*kēki*) may also be understood to refer to the English word "cake." On the basis of pragmatic conditions, however, it is a matter of indifference whether "cake" is a Japanese or English word. Such ambiguity appears most clearly in the case of Chinese characters, which appear to straddle both Japanese and Chinese languages. The question of whether Chinese characters "belong" to either the Japanese or Chinese language, when raised without attention to the historicity of such unities as "Japanese language" and "Chinese language," is clearly foolish. When such inquiries are made, they reveal the historicity of the question itself. I hardly need to add that the distinction between Chinese characters and the Japanese syllabary needs to be historicized as well.

It can be said that the idea of national language is produced by erasing those multiplicities inherent in the act of enunciation, which should itself be understood as a form of sociality. On the Japanese archipelago in the premodern period, there existed *multilingual social formations, formed through multiplicity, which did not correspond to the coexistence of plural languages and cultures as individualized unities.* These multilingual social formations were gradually reorganized and replaced by that which took as its standard a single language. It may be possible to locate the birth of the Japanese language and people at the point of rupture between this unilingual social formation and the multilingual social formations that preceded it.

Yet it is perhaps important to distinguish between at least two levels of argument here. First, the thought of language cannot be determined unambiguously. The concept of language itself varies depending upon time, region, and social class. It is for this reason that our inquiry must not take as its guiding thread a concept of language popularized by modern linguistics.[21] To do so would be to ignore the political role played by linguistics and historical linguistics. It would entail not only disregarding the politicality of those requirements (homogeneity, grammaticality, normativity) in accordance with which linguistics posits its object, but also to ignore the connection between language and pragmatics. At the same time, I am not making a judgment about the empirical knowledge taken up by linguistics. My argument deals rather with the conditions of possibility of the historical emergence of this empirical knowledge.

There is also the difference between, on the one hand, the positivity of national or ethnic language as a regulative idea within those social formations that take as their standard a monolingual and monoethnic society, and, on the other, the various aspects of social formations that contradict this idea. As stated earlier, a single language is an idea, something that is not empirically observed within social reality. Unless this difference is taken into account, the contemporary Japan that is supposedly monolingual and monocultural is literally taken as such. And it is for this reason that those who try to attack the myth of a monolingual and monoethnic Japan by calling attention to the existence of foreigners and other ethnic groups end up, themselves, perpetuating and affirming the assumption of unitary languages and ethnic cultures. We must, for example, be extremely wary of propositions that assert that premodern Japan was a multilingual and multicultural society due to the great cultural divide that existed between the Kansai and Kantō regions during the medieval period. Multilingualism does not mean the coexistence of a plurality of ethnic languages: rather, the identity of language itself can only be represented through the suppression of multiplicity. The Japanese language is ceaselessly deconstructing itself. In other words, an institution that suppresses multilingualism must be in constant operation in order to sustain the conviction that the social formations of contemporary Japan are monolingual and monocultural. The unities of the Japanese language and people cannot be conceived as apart from the institution that suppresses the recognition of multilingualism.

"THE SAME" AND HOMOGENEITY

We have thus far seen that, in the absence of a culturalism that regards culture as an organic unity pervasive throughout the nation, it is impossible to stipulate the homogeneity of a national body that shares common customs and a common culture. We have also seen that the identity of community cannot be directly equated to the identity of language. How can one determine what constitutes the "same" language? Language is capable of countless divisions; it is a positivity whose content changes constantly throughout history. If this is the case, then the assumption that a given community is homogeneous and constituted by "the same" people must once again be submitted to rigorous revision. Dealing with this question requires us to confront the idea of assimilation, as that process that ultimately produces homogeneity.

The violence implicit in the notion of assimilation is largely unleashed in situations where discrimination and social conflict prevail. The most conventional response is that discrimination is what those people incapable of assimilation are fated to endure. Added to this is the notion that inability to assimilate is determined by ethnic origin, against which individual will can do nothing. This argument is similar to the argument that holds that the "mother tongue" is grounded in an ethnic or racial identity constitutive of the core of personality. Assimilation has, in fact, frequently been explained by recourse to the example of immigrants entering a certain society, or of native peoples subsumed within national territory through expansion of empire. Supposedly, it is a process in which such people gradually acquire the customs and ways of life of that society, becoming in time indistinguishable from the majority.

What is at stake here, however, is not simply a question of permitting differences in habits and customs. No matter how homogeneous the society, it is impossible for all adult members to share the same habits and customs. Within, for example, the United States, different clothing, manners, and performance of duties are required for men and women. Differences in habits and customs are made to represent the difference between men and women; the desire to maintain such basic institutions as education and the family, moreover, is controlled in accordance with these markings. These differences are skillfully organized to coincide with social status, so that homogeneity does not necessarily mean that everyone acts in the same way or has the same tastes and sense of duty. Homogenization is not, therefore, simply the process by which people become the same.

Would it be natural, then, to assume that ethnic groups are discriminated against because of differences in their habits and ways of life? Is it cultural difference that produces differences between immigrants, or ethnic minorities, and the national majority? Here we must once again emphasize the distinction between the notions of cultural difference and culturally specific difference.

The difference between red and blue is understood to be a particular difference within the generality or universality of color. Red and blue are "species" within the genus of color, and thus this difference can be seen as constituting a "specific difference." Red and blue are "continuous" with each other within the generality of color, and thus can be seen as "continuous particular differences." We could, in a similar manner, define cultural difference as a matter of cultural particularities within the continuity of culture, in which case they could be "species" ("specific differences") within the same genus. In those cases where another person cannot be understood or gotten along with, however, there is an encounter with incommensurability that cannot be grasped as particular difference within a "continuous" generality. Insofar as something is incommensurable, it indicates a situation of discontinuity. It goes without saying that such discontinuity in social relations is what I call "cultural difference," which is something we above all encounter practically. Culturally specific difference is a problem for epistemology. But our relationship to cultural difference is a practical one.[22]

As previously stated, members of a national community are involved in a countless number of cultures. Incommensurabilities of experience and behavior arise constantly between those who drive cars and those who do not. While these could be considered practical experiences of cultural difference, which have social effects such as disparities in job opportunities or mobility, they are nevertheless rarely recognized as the kind of differences that give rise to discrimination. Yet the different customs of an ethnic group, even when in a practical sense their social effects are negligible, are represented as differences belonging to one group rather than another, and to this extent, as differences between one particularity (or species) and another. This has the result of producing the other ethnic group as an externality. In a similar manner, for example, the observer of another ethnos (such as the cultural anthropologist) often represents as closed that gathering of people that constitutes his or her object of observation. Despite living among these people, the anthropologist "externalizes" himself or herself, representing the experience of various incommensurabilities as discordance between "insiders" and "outsiders," as if spatially outside the closed-off entity. Incommensurability is, in other words, understood spatially as a culturally specific difference.

Assimilation is not a monolithic becoming of the same. People produce their own desires in accordance with a regime of prearranged expectations: women act "woman-like" and students "student-like" in accordance with the relevant circumstances. Assimilation is nevertheless represented as an entering from the outside, as if something becomes steeped in the atmosphere of a self-enclosed area and dissolves within it. "Cultural difference" is that which is perceived when people are unable to meet such expectations. A person encounters cultural difference when, in a dialogic situation, that person finds it impossible to understand the actions of others, or when a person encounters obstacles in the execution of a collective task. When these obstacles and impossibilities to mutual understanding are represented as the difference between one particularity and another, cultural difference has been displaced onto culturally specific difference. As I stated earlier, since it is precisely the *inability to understand* that constitutes cultural difference, it is impossible to determine it (to predicate, of course, is already one mode of determination). Determination is the displacement of cultural difference onto culturally specific difference. Through actions in the face of cultural difference, one displaces cultural difference with culturally specific difference. Because specific difference is inscribed within a certain discursive formation, however, cultural difference itself can only be apprehended with these existing formations as incomprehensible. Cultural difference, in other words, indicates the exteriority of a discursive formation. The terms "ethnos" and "race" have already been assumed to fall within the category of "particularity," among many other kinds of positivities incorporated within these discursive formations. As a purely practical issue, cultural difference alone could never produce the notion of ethnic difference.

The positivity of ethnos is maintained only within discourse—which means that ethnos as a category that sustains specific difference has nothing to do with cultural difference. Conversely, we can say that discrimination against immigrants and ethnic minorities has no immediate relation to cultural differences between the majority and themselves. Assimilation does not, therefore, put an end to discrimination. Jews who were in their lifestyles completely Germanized were arrested by the Nazis solely on the basis of their race. Likewise, Korean residents in Japan who have become indistinguishable from Japanese in both language and customs still continue to suffer from discrimination. When their ethnic and racial identities are not known, they are safe. But they are turned into objects of discrimination as soon as their ethnic or racial origins are discovered. The knowledge that they belong to another "species" distinguishes "them." The most subtle differences are perceived after the fact as ethnic or racially specific difference in such a way that, when these are taken as indices of difference, these people become objects of discrimination. It is only when, through discourse, specific differences come to be seen that it becomes possible to mobilize the specific differences of ethnos and race for social discrimination. That is to say, people are not discriminated against on the basis of experienced difference. Rather, discrimination takes place when the positivities of ethnos and nation, which themselves can never be experienced, function as givens or preconceptions. In the absence of such preconceptions, all these varied differences would never be problematized. Indeed, immigrants and migrant workers are not, in the first place, discriminated against because of different customs or incomprehensible behavior. Discrimination against them arises from the stereotyped understanding of the difference between "them" and "us."

Robert Miles says the following about discrimination against migrant workers: "From the moment of their arrival, therefore, they have participated in commodity production and exchange and, through the taxation of their wages and the expenditure of their income, they have sustained the welfare (not to mention the 'law and order' and 'warfare') state. Moreover, migrant workers have reproduced their labor power and themselves: they required accommodation and food, they engaged in leisure practices, and they organized social relations within which to reproduce themselves. While many of these practices were accomplished in a culturally distinct manner, they were nevertheless an immediately present part of the social fabric of the social formation. The notion of integration therefore *exteriorises* in thought, and in politics, those populations that are already, indeed have always been, a constituent element of the social formation."[23]

Discrimination comes to be recognized as a problem insofar as cultural difference is represented. Discrimination is, in fact, rarely grounded on the incommensurabilities between people; rather, it is produced when the political process of articulating culturally specific difference attaches a fantasy to a certain subject position. And yet, identities based on culturally specific differences that are attributed to migrant workers and immigrants always contain within them the mechanism that produces the identity of one's own group. Discrimination against a different ethnos or race occurs when "we" and "they" are grasped as specific difference through a schema of cofiguration. Moreover, no matter how thoroughly appropriated within existing regimes of specific difference a person may be, not every social relation can be contained within existing classification systems. An excess will always remain. It is impossible to fully eliminate discontinuity, and it is because of this discontinuity that people do not fully lose their singularity. People are, in other words, "irreplaceable," because they always contain something that deviates from that possibility of equivalence upon which the continuity of specific difference is premised. This excess renders problematic the very justification of culturally specific difference. Social relations from which discontinuities are absent cannot be said to be realistic, but are rather fantasized. It is precisely this excess that disrupts the conviction (or dream of communion) that holds that social formations have a transhistorical basis, and that harmonious and self-realizing communities will someday become possible. This excess exposes the ungroundedness of social formations, always indicating the possibility of social change. Because of this excess, the possibility can never be entirely erased that someone, no matter how assimilated, may become feared and become the object of a violent exclusion. As Franz Fanon says of mimicry, the gesture of mimicry that is performed by the minority for the purpose of assimilation may always potentially be regarded as a threat by those who see themselves as the social mainstream. Assimilation of the minority reveals the ungroundedness of the position of those who seek confirmation of their own superiority through dependence upon the hierarchical structure of discrimination. The cause of discrimination, in many cases, does not lie with immigrants and ethnic minorities; rather discrimination becomes necessary in order to represent the discriminator's own ethnic or national identity. The nation constructs itself as culturally homogeneous by "externalizing" alien cultures. Hence the notion of assimilation always contains the danger of a constant "externalizing" of immigrants and migrant workers. Homogeneity within the nation can, moreover, only be posited as a negative reflection through accounts of other nations, races and ethnic groups. This "other" that constitutes the term of contrast is ceaselessly transformed and shifted. To speak of the unity of the nation as imaginary is to recognize that it is a reflection that takes place via the "other."

As we have seen, the sense of "being Japanese" cannot escape this basic principle of reflection, either. When this awareness is naturalized and taken to be derivative of a long and continuous history, it also naturalizes the contrast with another "species" and hence becomes dependent upon the category of the designated, contrasting ethnos or race. Whether supporting a belief in the "unbroken imperial line" or in cultural homogeneity, those arguments that attempt to ground themselves upon the national community are sustained by the conviction that the boundaries of this community are determinable on the basis of an index that is natural and impervious to human change. It is precisely because of this that nationalism seeks to ground itself in that category of "ethnos" considered more natural than nation itself, and an ethnos, in turn, attempts to seek its foundations in that category of "race" that is understood to be fully natural in origin. As such, neither nationalism nor ethnicism can escape that logic of "race" that is the most typical category of collective specific identity within modernity.[24]

We have already invalidated the notion that "ethnos" and "race" are more natural and historically constant than the nation. Since "ethnos" and the positivities of "mother tongue" and "national mother tongue" that sustain it have been historically generated, they cannot be conceived as naturally given in comparison with the nation.

And yet, it must not be thought that racism occurs only within those societies in which the myth of monoethnic society (in which race = ethnos = nation) is openly displayed. Racism should not be understood only within the narrow framework of that argument that posits an overlap between race and the sphere of national community. The equality between nation and ethnos was widely accepted in such places as postwar Japan, in which the myth of the single ethnic society was dominant. Naturalization of the nation through naturalization of the ethnos, i.e., national racialization, progressed largely without criticism. As has already been shown through analysis of *Nihonjinron*, the discourse on national culture and its various premises can be utilized exactly as is by the logic of national racialization. This, however, does not mean that we can act as if racism and ethnicism were less important within so-called multi-ethnic societies, in which the words "ethnos" and "race" have become taboo, or where there is an overemphasis on the contradiction between concepts of "ethnos" and "nation." Taken in by the *Nihonjinron* myth of the single ethnic society, for example, some American critics attempt to denounce Japan for being a single ethnic nation. But such criticism becomes merely nationalistic self-praise on the part of multi-ethnic America. Similarly, criticism of monoethnic discourse or of the discourse of ethnic minorities on their ethnic cultures functions at times to conceal the intimate link between multi-ethnic nationalism and racism in the United States. As is well known, racism is most visible within so-called multi-ethnic societies. This is not because people become more racist because of multi-ethnic societies, nor because monoracial societies are more harmonious. Generally speaking, people within those nation-states that flaunt their status as monoethnic societies are not aware of their own racism. Such people believe themselves to be in a position to denounce somebody else's racism because they rarely self-consciously confront their own racism.

In such so-called multi-ethnic societies as Australia after 1970 and the prewar Japanese Empire, anti-racist arguments were often vigorously set forth because people generally had to deal with racial problems constantly. It cannot, however, be concluded that societies in which the antiracist claim is strong are necessarily ones in which racism is not often practiced. In such societies, where anti-racist arguments were vigorously set forth, it was also true that a colonial social ranking was frequently based on a hierarchy of races, relations between the colonial ruler and ruled were maintained as racial relations, and racism was considered indestructible insofar as the structure of such social stratification was taken as unchanging.

As we can see, in "white Americanism" and "white Australianism," the ranking, on the basis of degrees of assimilation, between more and less legitimate citizens within multi-ethnic nation-states often takes the form of a hierarchy of races. Because a greater degree of assimilation to the image of the western European bourgeoisie is often taken to be the equivalent of becoming a more "legitimate" citizen, advancement in rank through assimilation must be preserved in order to maintain the command to assimilate. (There is, at the same time, a strong tendency among American citizens to distinguish themselves from Europe. The worship of and the hatred of Europe inherent within American nationalism are in a relationship of ambivalence.) Here, as well, assimilation "externalizes" minorities, and it is through this "externalizing" that the conviction of the unity of national community is maintained.[25]

Many of the anti-multiculturalist arguments that have recently flourished in the U.S. hold that American national culture is of European (i.e., white) descent. They therefore insist that minorities should assimilate themselves to this legitimate culture, arguing that multiculturalism diminishes the desire to assimilate, and hence dissolves national culture and fragments the national community. As we have just seen, these anti-multiculturalist arguments are in fact of the same type as essentialist multiculturalism, in that they also regard culture as an organic unity. They are no different from the discourse of national culture (nor from that of ethnic culture). Anti-multiculturalist discourse is complicitous with an essentialist discourse of culture. Anti-multiculturalists, obsessed with the supremacy of the West, constantly remind those who are unable to assimilate of their own "non-Western" origins, and stir up their nostalgia for their own ethnic culture. Anti-multiculturalism constantly produces an essentialistic culturalism, while an essentialistic culturalism will continue to evoke a reaction of anti-multiculturalism. If, moreover, the collective culture of minorities ever became dominant, people of European descent would then have to assimilate to minority culture. In other words, inasmuch as cultural difference is reduced in advance to specific difference from the point of view of assimilation, exchange between different groups can only be conceived in terms of pure power relations according to which one side becomes subordinate to another and accepts its culture. In sum, assimilation and essentialist culturalism may be understood as invariably producing both insecurities between majority and minority populations and a mutual intensification of adherence to their respective ethnic identities. The majority quickly becomes the minority when its political and economic superiority collapses, in which case adherence to its own cultural origins becomes natural. A "return to the West" carries with it many fantasized insecurities evoked by such a logic of culturally specific difference. And yet, this does not mean that ethnic struggles and discrimination would immediately disappear in the absence of culturalism. Social relations are invariably antagonistic, just as it is also true that culturalism is a reactive response against such antagonisms.

An essentialist multiculturalism and the anti-multiculturalism that protests it are two poles of the debate surrounding "nationality." Both sides
begin their arguments by regarding as an entity the "we" of ethnic minority
groups as well as, for example, the "we Americans" sentimentally produced
by a "sentiment of nationality." In other words, both arguments are, In this
sense, homologous to *Nihonjinron*. When its roots in the discourse of "nationality" are overlooked and its own premises and historical conditions
concealed, essentialist multiculturalism lends support to anti-
multiculturalism, which attempts to assert the supremacy of the "West."

It is for this reason that the "deconstruction of nationality" is necessary.
As a method of confronting racism, the "deconstruction of nationality" must
by all means be undertaken, whether in Japan, the United States, or elsewhere. This deconstruction would force us, moreover, to problematize the
very idea of a distinction between monoethnic and multiethnic societies.

I am not, of course, suggesting that we must deny the identities of ethnos and nation simply because they are dependent upon the regimes of
imagination. As imaginary constructs, race, ethnos and nation are unques-
tionably social realities. That the deconstruction of "nationality" is not
equivalent to its dissolution strictly confirms the nature of such regimes.
Yet we might say that, regardless of the fact that nationality exists as a social reality, by rigorously coming to terms with its modes of existence we
are already engaging in social relations that are not governed by a sentiment
of nationality. In doing so, we are, moreover, living emotional lives that
depart from the society of sympathy. This shows that "nationality" is always in fact being betrayed. Although a "sentiment of nationality" incites
us to distinguish ourselves from "foreigners" and perceive them as "strang-
ers," for example, there are countless cases in which relations with an individual identified as "foreigner" can be closer and more dependable than
those with "compatriots." And there are countless cases of social relations
that are not governed by the categories of "race," "ethnos," and "nation."
"Nationality" is continually deconstructing itself. This is why what we must
really be concerned about is that histories exist of people who could not
find a way to live without the categories of "race," "ethnos," and "nation."
Rather than denying or forgetting such "histories," our task is to discover
them at the very heart of these social formations governed by the regime of
"nationality," and hence to find a path by which we may answer to such
histories without appeal to "nationality."

An attack on nationalism that simply discredits ideas of ethnicity and
race can easily become complicitous with the logic of imperial nationalism,
which produces a more inclusive sense of the solidarity of the nation. In
order to maintain an awareness of the distinction between ethnic nationalism, with its essentialized ideas of race and nation, and the equally dangerous logic of imperial nationalism, it is absolutely necessary that we turn our
attention to the "deconstruction of nationality."

Translated by Richard Calichman and Brett de Bary

Notes

1. In his critique of the discourse on Japanese homogeneity and closure, which may be understood as the corollary of the myth of the monoethic society, Iyotani Toshio has stated the following: "Many writers have even positively appraised the 'homogeneity' and 'harmony' of Japanese society as the foundation of its international competitiveness. They regard the loosening of restrictions on the influx of foreigners with caution, asserting the social foundation does not exist by which to accept their heterogeneous existence.

Those arguments that seize upon the particularity of Japanese society as compared with the various countries of Europe and the United States are above all grounded in this kind of exclusionism and homogeneity. The extreme intensity by which Japanese society refuses to tolerate heterogeneous existences is a fact that does not, of course, need restating. There are various obstacles within the daily lives of foreigners understood in the sense of "others," not only (as is predictable) among Asians, but as well among European and American whites.

And yet, given differences in mode of expression, socio-cultural discrimination and exclusion against foreigners may be seen in all countries. The modern nation has been constituted as an entity within which only a specific group has been demarcated as citizens. The creation of "minority" groups within this territory has been accompanied by the exclusion of foreigners vis-à-vis its outside. But contempt for Asians and adulation of Europeans and Americans is not restricted to Japan alone. In Europe and the U.S., as well as in those countries engulfed by these latter within the world economy, the dichotomous conception of "civilized" and "barbarian" has been the common worldview of capitalism. Emphasis on the notion of "escape from Asia" (*datsua shisō*) that emerged in Japan in the Meiji period placed excessive emphasis on the particularity of Japanese society and caused us to lose sight of the structure of discrimination against the foreign *within* Japan. While there exists within Japan discrimination against foreigners and ostracism, as well as heterogeneity, these features are rather common in modern nation states." "*Sakerarenai kadai: sengo nihon ni okeru gaikokujin rōdōsha*," in Kajita Takemichi and Iyotani Toshio, *Gaikokujin rōdōsharon* (Tokyo: Kōbundō, 1992), 126.

2. The myth of the single ethnic society is not to be found only within postwar Japan. We should not overlook the fact that many "Japan experts" within the United States also hold a view of Japan that is governed by this myth. The existence of this myth, moreover, should not be seen as a problem of Japan alone. It need hardly be said that the image of the U.S. played a major role in reproducing Japanese national identity following World War II. The role that the image of Japan played in reproducing American national identity, however, has been underestimated. The myth of the single ethnos would appear to be an irreplaceable aspect of the regime of mutual reproduction of the two nations. The various obstacles created in the reproduction of American and Japanese

national identities have been frequently displaced onto the image of the other nation. This myth about Japanese society has become the framework through which various insecurities arising in the mutual relations between Japan and the U.S. are displaced. Examples of texts published within the U.S. that have attempted to displace these insecurities through the wholesale acceptance of the myth of monoethnic are David Pollack, *The Fracture of Meaning* (Princeton: Princeton University Press, 1986), and *Japan 2000*, Andrew Dougherty, ed., (Rochester: Rochester Institute of Technology, 1991).

3. Fukuzawa Yukichi, *Bunmeiron no gairyaku* (Tokyo: Iwanami Shoten, 1931), 37. [English translation by David A. Dilworth and G. Cameron Hurst, *Fukuzawa Yukichi's 'An Outline of a Theory of Civilization'* (Tokyo: Sophia University, 1973), 23. Translation has been slightly modified.]

4. Concerning such central notions of nineteenth-century liberal representative government as "national sentiment," "national character," and "the society of sympathy," cf. John Stuart Mill, "Considerations of Representative Government," in *John Stuart Mill*, H. B. Acton, ed. (London: Everyman's Library, 1972), 187–428.

5. Oguma Eiji, *Tanitsu minzoku shinwa no kigen* (Tokyo: Shinyōsha, 1995).

6. Fukuzawa Yukichi, op. cit., 237. [English translation, p. 177.]

7. Michel Foucault, "«*Omnes et singularis*»: *vers une critique de la raison politique*," in *Dits et Écrits 1954–1988, vol. IV* (Paris: Éditions Gallimard, 1994), 134–161.

8. To avoid misunderstanding, let me offer here a brief explanation of the terms "particularity" and "generality" ("universality"). As set forth in classical logic, particularity is the generality (universality) of the rank of species that is opposed to the generality (universality) of the rank of genus. Inasmuch as neither particularity nor generality constitute singularity, both belong equally to the realm of generality/universality.

9. *Nihonjinron* refers to the pervasive discourse, in postwar Japanese scholarship as well as the mass media, that sought to define unique characteristics of Japanese culture.

10. See Iyotani Toshio's essay in this volume.

11. Partha Chatterjee, *The Nation and its Fragments* (Princeton: Princeton University Press, 1993).

12. Kawamura Minato, *Umi o watatta nihongo* (Tokyo: Seidosha, 1994).

13. Tomiyama Ichirō writes the following concerning the self-consciousness of "Okinawans": "From the moment they tried, through diligence, to become outstanding workers, workers from Okinawa became objects of surveillance under the mark of being "Okinawan." This is because the actions of their everyday lives, which made up their being as "Okinawans," became objects of a surveillance that sought to ascertain if they could continue to perform as excellent workers. "Okinawan" no longer referred simply to their efficiency, but referred to their very physical existence. This kind of surveillance of the body, and the threat it implied, constituted a function of power that

disciplined those from Okinawa. As a result, these Okinawans came to aspire to a change in markings, i.e., to be seen as 'Japanese.' . . . To the extent that human beings are fated to be marked in one way or another, however, aspiring to change one's mark causes an increase in fantasy. Those who attempt to change their fated mark become lost in the process of pursuing the invisible fantasy of their goals. Becoming 'Japanese,' then, meant nothing more than having one's body and everyday actions drawn into a mystified world produced by one's fantasy of being Japanese on the one hand, and one's fated identity as Okinawan, on the other." *Kindai Nihon shakai to "okinawajin"-"nihonjin" ni naru to iu koto* (Tokyo: Nihon Keizai Hyōronsha, 1990), 242–243.

14. See Naoki Sakai, *Translation and Subjectivity* (Minneapolis: University of Minnesota Press, 1998.)

15. We may recall on this point the classic words of Antonio Gramsci: "To understand exactly what might be meant by the problem of the reality of the external world it might be worth taking up the example of the notions of 'East' and 'West,' which do not cease to be 'objectively real' even though analysis shows them to be no more than a conventional, that is, 'historico-cultural,' construction. (The terms 'artificial' and 'conventional' often indicate 'historical' facts that are products of the development of civilisation and not just rationalistically arbitrary or individually contrived constructions.) . . . What would North-South or East-West mean without man? They are real relationships and yet they would not exist without man and without the development of civilisation. Obviously East and West are arbitrary and conventional, that is historical, constructions, since outside of real history every point on the earth is East and West at the same time. This can be seen more clearly from the fact that these terms have crystallised not from the point of view of a hypothetical melancholic man in general but from the point of view of the European cultured classes who, as a result of their world-wide hegemony, have caused them to be accepted everywhere. Japan is the Far East not only for Europe but also perhaps for the American from California and even for the Japanese himself, who, through English political culture, may then call Egypt the Near East." *Selections from the Prison Notebooks*, Quintin Hoare and Geoffrey Nowell Smith, trans. (New York: International Publishers, 1971), 447.

16. The problem of the coherency of male subjectivity and the support of such by women in film is addressed vis-à-vis film in Kaja Silverman, *Male Subjectivity at the Margins* (New York and London: Routledge, 1992).

17. Paul Gilroy, *"There Ain't No Black in the Union Jack": The Cultural Politics of Race and Nation* (Chicago: University of Chicago Press, 1987); Robert Miles, *Racism after 'Race Relations'* (London: Routledge, 1993); Etienne Balibar, with Immanuel Wallerstein, *Race, Nation, Class* (London: Verso, 1991).

18. While the unity of a national language can be grasped as a regime, this in no way implies that the unity of language constitutes a closed system that conforms to a finite number of individual rules. The unity of language is given as an "idea" in the Kantian sense.

19. While Derrida tends to directly link phonocentrism with Western metaphysics, in this argument, phonocentrism is strictly conceived as a historically identifiable formation. This is in no way to conceive of an empirically existing outside to Western metaphysics, but any historically specific phonocentrism will contain its own exteriority.

20. Concerning the notions of "arborescent formation" and "rhizome," cf. Gilles Deleuze and Felix Guattari, *Mille Plateaux* (Paris: Les Éditions de Minuit, 1980).

21. It is well known that 30 years ago Michel Foucault incorporated in his terminology the widely used everyday word *discours*, or discourse, hence introducing a new concept to historical analysis. Foucault's *discours* prepared a new viewpoint from which it was possible to review and historicize various positivities within our institutionalized knowledge.

As such, one of the categories that requires historicization is that of language. *Discours* does not objectify language within the purview of linguistics or literary study. Rather, it enables us to grasp it as a positivity that emerged at the same time as a complex of institutional conditions concerning the production of repetition, circulation, change, succession, and knowledge. It is related to the attempt to historicize not only individual languages but language in general. In the final analysis, language can be historicized because it is *within discours*; not within language. The description of discursive formations, therefore, opens the possibility for history to be written without placing language within descriptive categories. This possibility is, however, immediately lost when *discours* is conflated with such things as conversation, argument, historical documents, as well as, for example, the complete works of individual authors, schools of learning, contemporary intellectual climate, national culture, and intellectual traditions. It is, of course, possible to employ *discours* without adhering to Foucault. And yet, what I find to be especially valuable in his use of *discours* is that discursive analysis does not consider historical data as documents (in the sense that they accurately convey acts of meaning, intention, and historical reality alone, i.e., historical materials regarded merely as linguistic texts) but rather allows them to be seen as archaeological monuments. When historical data are viewed as documents, such aspects as the sight, feel, and corporeal linkage of those texts that came into being prior to national language can no longer be examined. When one thinks, for example, of the genre of song (*uta*), not in the narrow sense of *waka* poetry, but of songs in general, it will immediately be understood why the texts that belong to this genre must be read as monuments as opposed to documents. This is because a reading of the text of a song that concerns itself solely with its acts of meaning would not constitute a reading of its texts. A song is usually neither an expression of the singer's intentions nor a portrayal of reality as seen by the song's author. The text of a song can be an event in terms of such nonlinguistic aspects as musicality, its power to evoke collective emotion, the correlation between bodily movement and rhythm, as well as its rituality. A text can be described within *discours* when read so as to include the relation to its various pragmatic aspects. Conversely, language as positivity that emerges within *discours* can then be analyzed. When, moreover, there is no dimension by which to relativize language, people are forced to read past documents through projecting national or ethnic languages into the past. Concerning these notions of "documents," "monuments," "enunciative," and "discursive formation," see Michel Foucault, *L'Archéologie du savoir* (Paris: Éditions Gallimard, 1969) and *The Archaeology of Knowledge and the Discourse on Language*, A. M. Sheridan, trans. (New York: Pantheon Books, 1972).

Still, the use of *discours* as that dimension by which to relativize language is not necessarily consistent in Foucault. Foucault insisted that historical accounts be without any hypothesis of totality whatsoever, and yet it is from this point that the concept of *discours* must be critically examined. It must also be rigorously investigated whether discursive analysis is able to sufficiently target sensible things. Cf. Beverly Brown and Mark Cousins, "The Linguistic Fault: the Case of Foucault's Archaeology," in *Towards a Critique of Foucault*, Mike Gane, ed. (London and New York: Routledge and Kegan Paul, 1986), 33–60.

22. See Tanabe Hajime, *"Shakai sonzai no ronri," Tanabe Hajime zenshū* (Tokyo: Chikuma Shobō, 1963), 51–168; and Nishida Kitarō, *"Sekai no jikodōitsu to renzoku," Nishida Kitarō zenshū* (Tokyo: Iwanami Shoten, 1965), 7–107. Tanabe's book was originally published in 1934 and Nishida's in 1935.

23. Robert Miles, op. cit., 175.

24. Let me offer some broad observations about the difference between the basic principles of the modern national community and those of the premodern community. In the modern national community, specific identity is taken to be equal to direct and unmediated relationship with the totality. Premodern social formations, by contrast, are based upon relational identity. Within relational identity, group belonging occurs via such status relations as father/son and master/retainer. Status relations are not necessarily fixed. In other words, individual identity is determined by a social network and kinship. Within specific identity, however, relations of belonging that do not occur via status relations are dominant, such as individual/race, individual/ethnos, and individual/nation. Here, for the first time a notion of social relations of institutionalized equality becomes possible. "Equality" refers to those relations that are sustained by an immediate link to the totality. Here, the immanence of the totality within the individual becomes possible. As such, the individual becomes autonomous. The independence of the nation becomes the independence of the individual.

Still, determinations such as "modern" and "premodern" are period divisions that are proposed strictly to understand the historical materials of the past. It is impossible to predict the future. Although we could predict that the twenty-first century will follow the twentieth century, we cannot as easily posit the "aftermath" of modernity.

25. Robert Miles, 79 and 148.

I. Nationalism and Colonialism

Colonialism and the Sciences of the Tropical Zone: The Academic Analysis of Difference in the "Island Peoples"

Tomiyama Ichirō

"THE SOUTHERN ISLANDS" AND THE SCIENCES OF THE TROPICAL ZONE

The Sciences of the Tropical Zone and the Memory of the Empire

Many independent nations were born after World War II as a result of the long struggle for freedom from colonialism. The demise of colonialism was also a process of subsuming people everywhere within nation-states as a reversal of a widely trumpeted internationalism. However, as we can see in the rise of multinational corporations and world-class cities, capitalist accumulation has now become global. On the other hand, Benedict Anderson's "long-distance nationalism" suggests the chaotic and violent dissolution of the nation-state, in the movement of immigrants and refugees on a worldwide scale across national borders.[1]

In particular, this process is related to the revival of memories of the empire among those nations that had the experience of governing colonies. The postcolonial condition in those countries that had been at the center of their empires is a situation in which the notion that the empire disappeared after the war is gradually exposed by the destabilization of recently developed nation-states. This is probably also a process in which the postwar national consciousness, which had been formed as the memories of empire were forgotten, ceaselessly reawakens those memories.

Masao Miyoshi questions the ability of academic discourse to inscribe this situation from his understanding of the postwar world order as a new continuation of colonialism.[2] While this is a problem for the popular variety of studies related to cultural difference, it first and foremost calls for another critical examination of the relationship between colonialism and academic discourse. My attempt to deal with academic discourse in the Southern Islands (*Nan' yō guntō*) controlled by Japan over the 30 years from their military occupation in 1914 to their "shattering jewel" demises (*gyokusai*) in World War II, is based on this problematic.

We need to be careful that this kind of examination does not end as a mere inquiry into whether scientific research was used in the control of the colonies. This understanding of academics as a tool has the effect of reducing the area of politics related to colonialism while also unconditionally establishing academics as objective and unrelated to colonialism. One may even go so far as to say that it is precisely in such a discursive space, seen as objective and neutral, that the memory of empire is preserved. What needs to be questioned is the academic discourse that analyzes cultural differences included within the empire.

As is well known, the history of modern Japan is the history of an expanding empire from the Ainu/Moshiri, to the Ryūkyūs, Taiwan, Korea, Micronesia (the Southern Islands), "Manshū" (Manchukuo), and finally the "Greater East Asia Co-Prosperity Sphere." Corresponding to this imperial history, the human sciences in Japan, particularly anthropology, ethnography, geography, and medicine, took the subsumed peoples in these areas, one after the other, as their objects of inquiry. The relationship between these disciplines and colonialism has rarely been examined up to the present, apart from such limited themes as the human experiments carried out by Unit 731.[3] In the background of this problematic relationship, we find not only the problem described above of understanding of academics as a tool, but also the particular national consciousness of postwar Japan in which the historical process of the liberation of the colonies and the breakup of the empire—a history that should have been experienced—is already seen as someone else's affair through the reduction of the end of the Japanese empire to the single event of the loss of the war. Similarly, the notion that it was a fanatical nationalism that established the Japanese empire is also related to the failure to critique science in the empire. The beginning of the postwar era and the closure and erasure of the empire are two sides of the same coin.

As part of its participation in World War I, Japan occupied the German Territories in the islands of the Marianas, Palau, the Caroline Islands, and the Marshall Islands in October of 1914. Those islands, which are called Micronesia today and were called the South Sea Islands at the time, came under the Japanese mandate through the Treaty of Versailles. In 1922, the South Seas Agency was established on the island of Koror in the Palau islands. This was the first acquisition of territory in the tropics for Japan, which had advanced through Ainu/Moshiri territory, the Ryūkyūs, Taiwan, and Korea. The significance of the South Sea Islands for Japanese imperialism was in their position as a base for military invasion of the Philippines, Indonesia, and New Guinea, more than in the economic benefit or burden of the islands themselves. After Japan's departure from the League of Nations in 1933, the area came to be called "the Inner Southern Seas" (*uchi nan 'yō*), further emphasizing its military importance. This shift clearly reveals an expansionist policy from inner to outer territories.

However, the significance of the South Sea Islands in the Southern Advance does not end with its military possibilities. For example, in a call for papers in the monthly magazine, *The South Sea Islands* (*Nan' yō guntō*), published in the islands at the time, the ad reads, "Life in the South Sea Islands is the training ground for the southern development of the Japanese race. The experience of daily life is valuable material."[4] The South Sea Islands, as the first tropical territory acquired by Japanese imperialism, were "an integrated testing ground in preparation for a southern advance."[5] And the various disciplines anthropology, ethnography, archaeology, medicine, labor sciences, agricultural sciences, and biology were all developed on the stage of this "testing ground" as sciences of the tropical zone. As institutions supporting these sciences, the Society for the Promotion of Science established the Palau Tropical Biology Research Center in 1934, and the South Seas Agency established Tropical Industry Research Centers (on Palau in 1922, on Ponape in 1926, and on Saipan in 1930). In addition, there were hospitals established in every part of the South Sea Islands, and the Pacific Association, established in 1938, organized investigations and research in the area.

How were the academic discourses of the sciences of the tropical zone that were formed in the South Sea Islands related to the colonial conditions there? In order to pursue this problem, this paper will look at how the differences between the residents of the islands—called "islanders," "natives," "*kanaka*," or "*chamoro*"—and "Japanese" were inscribed and analyzed through these disciplines.

Discourse and Practice

In discussing the difference between "islanders" and "Japanese," we naturally come across points at issue related to the "Orientalism" described by Edward Said.[6] Namely, the very process of representing the "islanders" as Other is precisely an operation to ascertain the self-identity of "Japanese." Consequently, I would like to try to show how "Japanese" were presented within colonial conditions in the South Sea Islands. But when dealing with academic discourse on the "islanders" in colonial conditions, I must consider the problem of the enunciative position of observation that forms the discursive space called academics, before I can bring out this relatively formalized framework.[7] What kind of process is the description and constitution, through observation, of the "islanders" in a discursive space within academics? Who is the observing subject that drives this process forward?

What the human sciences share in their formation of representations of people in academic discourse is that, like clinical medicine, which produces the "diseased" by reading the signs of a disease from the various symptoms of the patient, the symptoms that signify the disease before one's eyes are always in excess.[8] The human sciences are brought into being, and the observer is established as a subject, in the very process of suppressing this excess and confirming the signs through a system and its rules. In other words, the observing subject applies the filter of a system that only s/he has grasped to the observed object and then reads the symptoms as signs. This system that attributes meaning is the monopoly of the observer, so that the meaning of the signs is established as unrelated to the consciousness of the observed object. Consequently, the patient is told the meaning of the symptoms after the fact and the task of an enlightenment that cautions is thus established. As a result, the narrative of the observer who represents human beings within academic discourse is a powerful discourse that constrains the superfluity of symptoms within the sign and thereby opens a path for the task of enlightenment.

However, what I am trying to conceive of here is not a generalized theory of the human sciences, but the observing subject in colonial conditions. What needs to be problematized is the question of what is suppressed and denied when a researcher describes and constitutes the "islanders" within colonial conditions. While making a distinction between epistemological subjectivity (*shukan*) and the subject in practical relations (*shutai*), Naoki Sakai points out that, in the process of observing and describing cultural differences within academic discourse, the practical relations that bind the observer to the object s/he observes, as well as the temporality that courses through that relation, are both denied. It is the Other that is depicted according to this practical denial that guarantees cultural identity and produces "our time."[9] Furthermore, Sakai sees this expression of the observing subject that produces cultural identity as an "articulation"— described by Ernesto Laclau and Chantal Mouffe as the practice that organizes social relations[10]—and therein he locates the terrain of politics. "The articulation of cultural difference can only be expressed as a practical, in other words political, mediation of the strained contradiction between the practical subject and epistemological subjectivity."[11]

Frantz Fanon's dissension against and transformations to academic discourse brilliantly reveal this political terrain. For example, Fanon criticizes O. Mannoni's location of the primary cause of French colonial control in a psychoanalytical analysis of the inferiority complex of colonized peoples. Fanon notes, "After having sealed the Malagasy into his own customs, after having evolved a unilateral analysis of his view of the world, after having described the Malagasy within a closed circle," the analysis presents the inferiority complex as preceding colonial control, so that after the beginning of colonial control, "the Malagasy has ceased to exist."[12] Fanon attempts to reestablish the Other, which had been described by academic discourse, within the practical relations in colonial conditions that were denied in the enunciation of the observing subject.

But that was a problem in Fanon himself. Homi Bhaba notes, "As Fanon's texts unfold, the scientific fact comes to be aggressed by the experience of the street; sociological observations are intercut with literary artifacts, and the poetry of liberation is brought up short against the leaden, deadening prose of the colonized world."[13] Bhaba tries to find the possibility of a new articulation in Fanon's heterogeneous narrative that develops in the widening gap between the signs that are confirmed "scientifically" and the symptoms of the street that consume the signs. But, as Fanon attempts to reestablish practical relations within academic discourse, he gradually stops making statements as an observing subject. For Fanon, the practical relations under colonial conditions were not simply an opportunity for finding the possibility of new enunciations, but the real site of necessary struggle.[14] Fanon's development in this direction may be a retreat from the attempt at a new articulation. At the same time, not only is the enunciated academic discourse revealed as denying practical relations, it is also revealed as aggressively affirming colonial practice. For example, in Fanon's attack on the relation between medical examination and police interrogation, we can read how academic discourse and violence are a series of technologies that together support colonial control.[15]

When Fanon ceased observation, took back a denied practice, and turned to face a recognized practice, he changed from being a psychoanalyst to being a revolutionary. What I would like to investigate in the South Sea Islands is the academic discourse under colonial conditions that Fanon moved away from. In that case, it is precisely the political space that Sakai indicated in relation to the enunciation of the observing subject that needs to be emphasized. And again, as we know from Fanon's critique of academic discourse, there is also the issue of the observing subject, who, denying the practical relations under colonial conditions, also reveals other practices where the observed Other is redefined in a narrative revealing a practice. It is the purposive narrative that asks not "What are they?" but "What do we do to them?" that defines the epistemological object.

THE CLASSIFIED "ISLAND PEOPLES"

Ethnography

In 1929, seven years after the publication of Bronislaw Malinowski's *Argonauts of the Western Pacific*, Hijikata Hisakatsu began his 15 years of activity in the South Sea Islands, lasting until his collapse from disease in 1944. His anthropological texts, beginning with his investigations of the island of Satawan, off the island of Yap in the Palau archipelago, are still central to anthropology and ethnography even today and are seen as the results of detailed fieldwork. How do his texts describe those he met and lived with in the islands?

In the first portion of his ethnography *Driftwood* (*Ryūboku*), written on the basis of his seven-year stay on the island of Satawan, Hijikata records the following:

> How the lives of the uncivilized peoples are controlled by the smallest, most difficult regulations, almost as if they were struggling in a net of their own making! However, in this net—their blindly customary emotions that deserted their reason, their mysticism filled with contradictions unconcerned with logic—they have really quite magnificently lived their lives for several thousand years; there are morals and ethics—their whole lives are harmonized within this net.[16]

As in other ethnographies, Hijikata constitutes their morals, their harmony—one might even say the Other—as different from the society he is positioned in through the local narratives he collects with his masterful linguistic powers. I would like to take up these texts by Hijikata in relation to the problem of the fixation of the observing subject and its practical relations in ethnographic writing. The local narratives gathered in field work are formed in the practical relations between the storyteller and the anthropologist who goes to the storyteller. Moreover, it is impossible for this practice in the field to be established without any relation to the control, subjugation, and resistance in colonial conditions. To put it somewhat roughly, the background to the local narrative is not the harmony of the storyteller's people, but a practice that is never unrelated to the conditions of colonialism. Consequently, the ethnographic operation that observes the local narratives as the sign of the Other—and thus constructs the Other—always returns practical relations, which are never unrelated to colonial conditions, to the epistemological world. This is accompanied by a process that fixes the Other as observed object and the Self as observing subject.

Now, what needs to be scrutinized in Hijikata's writing is not how he organizes and reconstructs, according to academic themes, the broad matters of social relations, language, and religion heard from the Satawal, but how he records this along with his own activities. That is, *Driftwood* is both an ethnography that depicts an Other and a diary that records the activities of Hijikata himself. At the beginning of the text, Hijikata warns the reader, "This text is a record of my stay, but it is not a diary of my private life. It is not a romantic tale about me. It is a diary of the island and of the village; it is the reality of the island." We should note the discomfort of an expanding narrative of an ethnography that is supposed to depict the people of Satawal but that also ends up describing the ethnographer, so that the Self cannot be fixed as the observing subject.[17] There is also the possibility that the practical relations in colonial conditions that cannot be completely recovered to the epistemological world may come back to the surface.

But in Hijikata, this possibility is avoided through a different method than ethnography. Hijikata's activities in the South Sea Islands were not restricted to anthropological field work. Also a sculptor, Hijikata left works through a variety of forms of expression, in paintings, sculpture, poetry, and prose. How are the people he met and lived with in the islands depicted in these works?

In his works apart from ethnography, the words "young women," "children," and "nature" frequently appear in addition to the discourses on "pre-civilization" and "primitivity." For example, in Hijikata's prose poem "A Dream of Blue Lizards," submitted to the magazine *South Sea Islands* under the name Hisaki Isao, Hijikata regularly uses metaphors like "nature's queen" and "children" for the "archetypal native daughter" of the poem, Geruru.[18] That is, the prose poem represents originary, unchanging "islanders" through discourses on "primitivity," "young women," and "Nature." The division between Self and Other that could not be achieved in the ethnography is completed here. In addition, the Self is confirmed as "civilization," "man," and "adult."

The prose poem is concluded thus: "When we are alone / there will be nothing more we can say with words / when our hearts speak together silently / under the unbearable weight of an immense happiness / we might softly take each other's hands and weep."[19] The destined meeting of these two who, after all, need no words, is anticipated in the essential and unchanging division of the Self and the Other. The practical relations that could not be recovered in Hijikata's ethnography are represented in another discursive space as a fortunate meeting with destiny. In other words, the instability of the observing subject in field work and the romantic and destined division, then unification, of the Self and the Other in the poem exist for Hijikata in mutual support.

This kind of design/complicit relation is tied to the denial of practical relations in colonial conditions. Later, Hijikata himself records the following from a meeting with some young men who criticized the suppression of a religious movement in Palau that proclaimed itself anti-Japanese: "I didn't think I could talk about difficult things with these garrulous young Palauans. If I did, I would spend some several thousand words on them, and I would probably only tell them whatever was convenient."[20] He astutely acknowledges an area that has been denied, and also recognizes that, the moment he enters that area, his Self, as an observing subject, will be destroyed and will be unable to write any further. It is as an extension of the denial of this kind of practice that Hijikata redefines their world as an object of the practice of "enlightenment." Despite the instability of the diary as writing, the practice of "enlightenment" appears rather suddenly. "If we don't untie the knots of the net that have been tied so tightly over many years, then they cannot be civilized quickly. Now is the time when it has become the responsibility of the Japanese to untie those knots."[21] The Other depicted in the ethnography is redefined as an Other who must be "civilized," in the affirmation of practical relations that appear suddenly. At the same time, the "Japanese" appear, not as someone to observe, nor as someone to enact a romantic meeting, but as someone to guide and instruct the "islanders."

However, to repeat, Hijikata's ethnography itself develops as an unstable narrative in which the Self and the Other cannot be completely distinguished. This denial and affirmation of practice does not proceed directly from the writing of his ethnography, but is found throughout his unconsolidated, multi-layered narrative. Again, this multi-layeredness is a problem of the observing subject that cannot completely return practical relations to the epistemological world. I would now like to consider the fixation of the observing subject as academia in the process of integrating the denial and affirmation of a multi-layered and ubiquitous practice in Hijikata.

Observation and Classification

The anthropologist Sugiura Ken'ichi shared with Hijikata the attempt to depict the world of the people who lived in the South Sea Islands as a closed, anticipatedly harmonious world, different from the society in which he himself was located. Sugiura, who had been an assistant in the Anthropology section of the Department of Science at Tokyo University, was commissioned by the South Seas Agency to undertake an "investigation of old customs among the islanders" throughout the South Sea Islands area from 1938 to 1941. "The unique culture of the islanders," in Sugiura's investigation, was composed of such signs as the land system, social organization, religion, fishing tools, fishing methods, hand crafts, and so on, unlike Hijikata's unbounded inscription.[22]

For example, after investigating the social system in villages on Palau, Sugiura attributed significance to the system in the context of political function. Then, to further reinforce this significance, he invoked "their own consciousness."[23] In the end, the significance attributed to the narratives observed on location came not from the narratives, but from a function discovered by the observer Sugiura, and their narrative was used as reinforcement for the significance attributed by Sugiura. In this way, as long as the final right of determining significance is held solely by the observer, the local narratives that arise out of practical relations can be recorded as signs, and the Other can be constituted. The symptoms can be completely read as signs constituting the Other. We must note how Sugiura, unlike Hijikata, fixed the observing subject that can return to an affirmation of practical relations.

Again, Sugiura, a pioneer in functionalist cultural anthropology in Japan, rejected "self-serving prejudice" that viewed the culture of other races as inferior, and instead argued that "the unique cultures of the islanders" must be investigated.[24] Sugiura's posture of a cultural relativism that would not attribute a hierarchy to cultures simultaneously saw the "unique culture of the islanders" as a culture of an Other, revealing Hijikata's romantic division of the Self and the Other as unnecessary. The stable determination of the observing subject is closely tied to cultural relativism.

This monopoly on the right to determine significance is even more striking in the field of natural anthropology called anthropometry. Hasebe Kotondo, an anthropologist and anatomist who occasionally visited the South Sea Islands from 1927, classified the "islanders" by race according to measurements of skulls, faces, and bodies.[25] Apart from Hasebe, there were many others, particularly the doctors at the South Seas Agency Hospitals, who classified races by measuring the blood type, skin color, sweat glands, and fingerprints of the "islanders."[26] In this kind of study, the signs to be measured are determined in advance and the meaning of the signs is attributed unilaterally, utterly unrelated to local narrative. It is no longer an issue whether the signs measured in racial categorization are cultural or physiological. What is important is that, through the complete acquisition of the right to attribute meaning, the observing subject that constitutes the "islanders" is established in a place completely separated from practical relations.

Now then, how are the "islanders" classified by this observing subject? In many cases, the "islanders" are classified as existing closer to "Japanese" than to "whites." The relative racial resemblance between the "islanders" and "Japanese" clearly resonates well with the following kind of claim about the Japanese advance into the South Seas. Takano Rokurō, a doctor, and Chief of the Prevention Agency in the Ministry of Health and Welfare described the southern advance of Japanese in 1942 thus:

> The Japanese race is actually well suited for life in the South Seas as the Europeans clearly are not. Our skin already exhibits a South Sea color, and the content of that color is not so different from the South Sea races of today. A certain biologist has studied Japanese sweat glands and reported that our sweat glands are close to those of the South Sea peoples. In addition, the South Sea sunlight is not too bright for the Japanese eyes, nor do our noses stick out like those of the Northern peoples. . . .There would be no sense in saying that the Japanese race, which is far more inclined toward and appropriate to the south than the Europeans, cannot be active in the South Sea paradise. Physically and temperamentally, we are a South Sea people.[27]

The resemblance of "Japanese" and the "islander peoples" is reread as a statement representing "Japanese" as "South Seas people" advancing into the South Seas. Takano was not the only one to reread things in this way; it also comes up frequently in discussions of the "Greater East Asia Co-Prosperity Sphere."[28] Of particular note is how this resemblance is frequently claimed to be a resemblance of ancient "ancestors." Thus, the advance of the Japanese into the South Seas is, unlike the control of South Sea peoples by "whites," "a return to the land of our distant ancestors."[29] At that point, the "islanders" are constructed as existing like archaeological remains that have not changed through the ages. They are not seen as having an existence that can produce the same kind of history.[30] The practical relations in colonial conditions are recuperated as a relationship between the observer in an archaeological museum and the items on display. Furthermore, the huge remains, such as the Namantaal remains and the Rero castle ruins, discovered in the South Sea Islands by anthropologists and archaeologists, exist as archaeological displays. Strangely enough, these huge remains were discussed as if they were totally unrelated to the people currently living in the South Sea Islands and as if their successors were "the Japanese."[31]

What we need to note here is that this discussion of the relations between the racial classification of the "islanders" and colonial control is not to tie colonial control to a racism that views races as superior or inferior. It is not a matter of a value judgment between superior and inferior. The distance measured in the classification of the relative resemblance between "the Japanese" and "the islanders" depicts the colonial advance of Japan as something that was destined. We might even say that at the moment in which a sign is observed and classified, colonialism has already begun. The establishment of an observing subject in academic discourse that denies the relationship with the people before one's eyes should be taken as a problem of colonialism.

"ISLANDERS" AS PATIENTS

Sex and Labor

From 1920 to 1937, the population of Yap in the Palau archipelago decreased by 30 percent. The Standing Committee on the League of Nations Mandate protested to the Japanese government twice, in 1930 and 1933, on the suspicion that this decrease was related to problems in the management of local labor in the government-operated phosphorous mines. The Palau Agency had mines on Pelelieu, Rota, Fais, and Tokobai, but the mine on Angaur was continued throughout the period of the mandate. Most of the workers in that mine were workers brought forcibly from the island of Yap and working conditions in the mines were extremely poor. During the period of 1930 to 1935, 337 workers were employed on average per year, of which 31 suffered severe injuries each year, while 1343 were injured over all.[32] The doctors at the South Seas Agency Hospital, headed by Fujii Tamotsu, formed the core of a group that undertook an investigation of this population decrease among the Yap islanders. How were the "islanders" constituted in the medical discourse related to this population decrease?

Their research reports recorded measurements of birth rates, death rates, and illness rates and sought the causes for low birth rates and high death and disease rates in connection with the population decrease, in customs and practices related to hygiene and sex.[33] In the case of hygiene, the group investigated diet, funerary customs, and the living environment and found that the "islanders' unclean and unsanitary" lifestyle was the cause of the high disease rate. In the case of customs and practices related to sex, the group investigated in great detail birth rituals, the management of menstruation, the frequency and methods of sexual intercourse, methods of masturbation and so on, and concluded that "perversity" in sexual life was tied to the low level of the birth rate. The gaze of the observer here focused in particular on women.

This kind of medical discourse was also an anthropological discourse that constructed the "islanders" from a variety of signs. From the signs of an "abnormal" sexuality or an "unclean" diet, the "islanders" were constituted as diseased and the "island customs" were produced as a source of infection. Again, in the same manner as anthropology, the observing subject who formulates the "islanders" from a place utterly untouched by practical relations exists by his acquisition of the right to determine meaning. The romantic "native woman" of Hijikata Hisakatsu no longer appears at this point. All that is left is a thoroughly scrutinized sexual practice seen as "perversity," viewed by a pathological gaze that attempts to discover the source of infection in the population decrease. The "native daughter" is exposed as a body under the bright sunlight of medical discourse.

Apart from the problem of the population decrease, this pathological gaze could also be found in discourses related to labor proficiency, discussed in the terms of colonial administration studies and labor sciences. In these sciences, the native view of work was observed and theorized as the source of the low labor capacity of the people of the South Sea Islands. The peoples' activities, put under observation, were constituted as an "indolent" native culture. For example, Yanaihara Tadao, a professor at Tokyo University and a scholar of colonial administration, pointed to the "island peoples'" unique view of labor in such activities as long-distance sea travel and dance, and concluded that the "island peoples" were not suited for "temporal, duty-regulated, continuous labor."[34] It is in this kind of statement by Yanaihara that we must find the establishment of an observing subject who observes signs and unilaterally constitutes the source of infection as the "indolence" of the "islanders."

What we must also take note of is not only how the "island peoples" were constituted as objects for observation, but also how they were produced as objects to be reformed, or, in other words, as objects of practice. Japanese colonialism constructed a school system in the South Sea Islands centered on medical treatment, hygiene systems, and employment education.[35] While the academic discourses of medicine, labor sciences, and colonial administration studies constructed the "islanders" as objects of these systems and apparatuses, these discourses were also technologies that revealed practical methods for medical treatment, hygiene, and education. At that point, the epistemological narrative of "what are they?" and the practical narrative of "what do we do to them?" adhered together, much as they do in the doctor who both observes the source of infection and also considers ways to heal the patient. From here on, let us call the "island peoples" who were constituted by practical narratives the "patient-'islanders'" and the practical methods revealed in the academic discourses of medicine, labor sciences, and colonial administration studies the "therapy." As a result of the union of the classified "island peoples" and the "patient-'islanders,'" the observing subject moves ever closer to the supervising subject who monitors the "therapy" in medicine, hygiene, and education.

This union is found not only in medicine and the labor sciences. For example, after the anthropologist Sugiura Ken'ichi constituted "the unique culture of the islanders" from his observation of various signs, he stated that "development is impossible if efforts are made only to preserve" this culture.[36] Instead, "we ought to guide them to reform through a knowledge of their past, and in accordance with their old customs."[37] Observing their "unique culture" was also an act of constituting the source of infection that should be treated. Moreover, Sugiura argued for the importance of employment education, in relation to the problem of "indolence," stating that "what is first necessary is that we sufficiently manage the natives' labor power."[38] The classified "unique culture of the islanders" is made the source of infection and further redefined as the object of "therapy" through medicine, hygiene, and education.

The union of epistemology and practice in this kind of academic discourse means that the denial of practical relations under colonial conditions in the establishment of the observing subject is continually reaffirmed in the practice of medicine, hygiene, and education. For example, the forced labor on Angaur Island should be noted as the primary factor in the population decrease on Yap Island. Therefore, the moment the medical observers attempt to find the source of population decrease within the observed "islanders" themselves, the practical relations under colonial conditions—that is, the fact of forced labor—are denied. Further, the denial of forced labor is continually upheld in the practice of "treating" the customs and manners related to sex and hygiene.

Also important in the issue of forced labor are the issues related to the problem of "lazy islanders," discussed as separate from the problem of population decrease. As I noted above, these "lazy islanders" existed in colonial administration studies and labor sciences as objects to be treated with employment education. However, Yanaihara argued the following about these unproductive "islanders":

> The islanders of the South Seas, like the Moro of the Philippines, the Papua of New Guinea, and the uncivilized tribes of inner Borneo, have not yet developed to the level where they would be useful as laborers in the modern sense. In principle, using these uncivilized tribes as laborers for modern industries requires a certain amount of coercion.[39]

Yanaihara was not the only one to argue for the necessity of forced labor with regard to their "indolence," which, when defined as untreatable, was placed at the limits of remedy.[40] Just as in the case of Mannoni, who sought the primary causes of French colonial control in the culture of the natives, we must note the affirmation, not the denial, of practice in this kind of statement. Not only did the medical discourse on the problem of population decrease not recognize the forced labor on Angaur, but the coercion of labor was also inevitably represented as unavoidable violence in the separate discussions of untreatable "indolence" at the limits of remedy.

What was this "indolence" existing at the bounds of treatment? In the Palau islands, there was a religious movement called the Modekngei[41] that raised the anti-Japanese standard a number of times, resulting in roundups by the Japanese—at the end of 1938, 26 people were arrested *en masse*. The South Seas Agency reported this as "a major incident, unprecedented in the history of the South Seas Agency."[42] The Modekngei was treated as a "heresy" in the South Seas Agency report, and Sugiura Ken'ichi argued that it came about due to changes in the "islanders' unique" religion under the influence of outside religions, and further, that it was politically manipulated.[43] In other words, this religious movement was understood as a deviation from the "islanders'" original native culture.

According to *The Monthly Report on Thought* (*Shisō gappō*), the Modekngei made the following appeals: "Do not rely on the medical treatment of outsiders. . . . We aboriginals receive the grace of the heavenly gods so that we might live and play naked. Why should we live painful, unfree lives, doing hard work and wearing Western clothes? . . . What good are society and government offices for us primitives?" That is, the anti-Japan stance of the Modekngei was a rejection of Japanese medical treatment and labor for Japan.

We may surmise from the Modekngei movement that "indolence" was a form of conscious resistance. It was precisely this resistance that the observing subject denied and for which that subject affirmed the inevitable use of violence in colonial control. Resistance was observed as a source of the infection of "laziness," subjected to treatment and finally crushed with violence.

The Invading Other— "Japan Kanaka"

Japanese imperialism, compared to German, aggressively developed colonial management in the South Sea Islands. Much of the necessary labor power for colonial management, apart from that for phosphorous mining operations, was brought in from Okinawa. The number of Okinawans in the territory especially ballooned during the 1930s, from 10,176 to 45,701. In these circumstances, a debate arose in medicine, labor sciences, and colonial administration studies that problematized the nature of "Japanese" in the South Sea Islands. In many cases, the problem was attributed to the low quality of the character of "Japanese" in the islands. How did this problem of character construct "Japanese" and "islanders"?

Kiyono Kenji, a doctor and anthropologist who was commissioned by the Pacific Association to conduct an investigation of the South Sea Islands, referred to this low character in such terms as "bodily strength," "birth rate," "work efficiency," "brain power," and "spirit of leadership."[44] It is easy to find a gaze similar to the pathological gaze that questions labor capacity and birth rates in this approach. In addition, Kiyono also prescribed treating the disposition of "Japanese of poor character" through medical, hygienic, educational, and lifestyle reforms. In other words, he constructed the "Japanese" as patient.

In the discourse of labor sciences concerning this "patient-Japanese," the classification of "Japanese" and "islanders" becomes confused. For example, as we can see in Kiyono's argument that "Japanese of poor character" have "psychological conditions similar to those of the islanders."[45] Here, the "Japanese" patient is discussed as a problem of "Japanese" and "islanders" becoming the same in the tropical environment.[46] In short, when a character (represented by low labor capacity and birth rate, etc.) that needs therapy is represented as a sign of common ground with the "islanders," the "islanders" classified as Other are discovered within the "Japanese" themselves. In addition, this is accompanied by an untreatable "indolence" and is threatened with an inevitable violence.

After discussing the "laziness" of the "islanders" in the discourse of the labor sciences, Suzuki Shun'ichi, a Labor Director, stated the following:

> It is difficult for the normal person, a person living in a society organized on the logic of superior and inferior, to understand this psychological condition. Some time ago, I was commissioned by the city of Tokyo to study a mental condition that one might call lethargy among the lumpen proletariat living in Tokyo. One might understand the psychological condition among the natives as being somewhat the same psychology.[47]

The invasion of the "islanders" did not stop with the "Japanese" in the South Seas. Suzuki views the "islanders" and the people in the slums of Tokyo as the same. What does this confusion of categories in the labor sciences and the invasion of the Other signify?

As I stated earlier, the "island peoples," observed and classified as Other, were, at the same time, the therapeutically treated "islanders." The unity of the epistemological and practical narratives in this kind of academic discourse shows that the self identity of those classified as "Japanese" was affirmed through therapeutic practices in medicine, hygiene, and education. This affirmation of self-identity through treatment promoted the redefinition of the Self and Other, which had been divided by the observing subject. That is, to establish an epistemological Other as an object of a purposive therapy is simultaneously to envelop the object of treatment in an otherness. As a result, the object of medical, hygienic, and educational treatment is represented as ever more closely adhering to the classified "island peoples," while the "poor" character that must be treated in "Japanese" appears as an existence wrapped in otherness that has seeped into the interior of the Self. Moreover, the self-identity of "the Japanese" is affirmed through the practice of a self-referential therapy against the Other that has invaded the interior of the Self.

The confusion of categories in the labor sciences is the instability of the observing subject that cannot completely recover in knowledge the self-identity of "Japanese" affirmed in practice. Further, this instability reveals the possibility of manifesting the various existences of those who are both "Japanese" and "islander," as well as those who cannot be classified as either.

Fifty to 60 percent of the "Japanese" in the South Sea Islands were from Okinawa. Okinawa was the first of the territories to be subsumed in the expansion of the modern Japanese empire. That is, the Ryūkyūan kingdom, which had already been invaded by the Satsuma domain at the beginning of the Edo period, was annexed to Japan by the Meiji government's military invasion from 1872 to 1879; this was an invasion that came to be known as the Ryūkyūan Management (*Ryūkyū shobun*). Okinawan history could be recalled in two forms, with regard to the movement of people from Okinawa to the South Sea Islands. One is that the destiny of the "Japanese" southern advance, in which the classification of "islanders" played a role, was told as a tale of Okinawan tradition. Another is that a unique history constituted an otherness in the self-identity known as the "Japanese." A representative of the former narrative is Asato Noboru's *The History of the Development of Japan's South* (Sanseido, 1941). This book, which had earlier been published as *The History of Okinawan Sea-faring Development*, deals with the history of the Ryūkyūan kingdom's trade with Southeast Asia as a tradition of "Japanese" southern development. Okinawan tradition is produced as the tradition of Japan's southern development.

For the latter narrative related to otherness, we must look to the derisive term for people of Okinawan birth living in the South Sea Islands: "Japan Kanaka."[48] For example, Yanaihara Tadao reacted to the appellation of people of Okinawan birth as "Japan Kanaka" as follows:

> Okinawans do not win the respect of the islanders because their lifestyle is so shabby. Consequently, the reform of Okinawan education and lifestyles is an urgent matter for the reform of Japanese colonial society in the south. I realized from my observations in the South Sea Islands how "the problem of Japanese overseas emigration is the problem of Okinawa."[49]

For Yanaihara, the problem of the character of "Japanese" in the South Sea Islands was a problem of "Okinawans" as "Japan Kanaka." The otherness of the "islanders" that had invaded the interior of "Japanese"—the source of an infection that should be treated—was here divided and removed from "Japanese" once again as "Japan Kanaka Okinawans," and reclassified as the Other. The derisive "Japan Kanaka" reveals the struggle to reclassify and redivide an otherness that required therapy intruding upon the interior of "Japanese" as an epistemological Other. Furthermore, this struggle over the Other is precisely the process of the "differend" (Lyotard) in the self-identity of "Japanese."

In Conclusion: the Tropical Sciences and the Dream of Greater East Asia

As I mentioned earlier, it was generally believed in postwar Japan that the Greater Japanese Empire was established on the basis of fanatic nationalism. This was linked to the argument, which reappeared in postwar Japan, affirming invasion by highlighting the so-called "cooperativist" aspects of the intellectual system of the "Greater East Asia Co-Prosperity Sphere." This argument held that war is bad, but that the "cooperativist" ideals in the "Greater East Asia Co-Prosperity Sphere" can be affirmed. In conclusion, then, I would like to examine historical epistemology in relation to this "cooperative spirit" on the basis of previous debates.

Hirano Yoshitarō, a prewar Kōza school Marxist and member of the Pacific Association (established in 1938 to organize surveys and research in the South Sea Islands), was a central theorist for "cooperativism." He writes, with regard to "cooperativism" in the "Greater East Asia Co-Prosperity Sphere":[50]

> Because ethnic policies, autonomism and cooperativism under "Co-Prosperism" respect the traditions of the social lifestyle of aboriginal peoples, recognize the fact of their historical existence, and attempt to bring about their development in accordance with their unique direction, these policies, being individualistic and particularistic, oppose the uniformity of assimilation policies.[51]

We can discern here both a relativistic epistemology of unique "traditions" and a shared universalistic practice of "development" in a "unique direction." This kind of "cooperativism" perfectly matches the cultural relativistic understanding of the "islanders' unique culture" demonstrated by the anthropologist Sugiura Ken'ichi, as discussed in this essay. To reiterate, after Sugiura constructed the "islanders' unique culture" from the various signs he observed, he claimed "development" based on this culture's "uniqueness."

As has been pointed out, "cooperativism" is nothing other than the "Greater East Asia Co-Prosperity Sphere" ideology, which attempts to justify Japanese invasion in contrast to "white" colonial rule. As Peter Duus has pointed out, the "Greater East Asia Co-Prosperity Sphere" was a response to the dilemma faced by "imperialism without colonies" of how to maintain colonialism when colonialism lost its validity during the war.[52] However, the resonance between the discourses of Hirano and Sugiura make it possible to understand the meaning of the "cooperativism" in Japanese colonialism in a context slightly different from its intellectual historical significance. The meaning of the "cooperativism" in the "Greater East Asia Co-Prosperity Sphere" lies in the fact that scientific discourse itself, which discerned and represented the Other, appeared as a major player in colonialism in place of outright racism.

The classification and treatment of the Other in the tropical sciences dealt with in this essay can be said to have been established precisely under the name of a "cooperativism" that respected unique cultures and asserted the inevitability of "development." And, conversely, the colonialism found in "cooperativism" was simply the denial and affirmation of a practice born in the midst of classifying and reforming the Other, not a naked racism or nationalism. In other words, colonialist practice was not narrated as an opposition of races and cultures; rather, this "cooperativism" reveals the existence of the "Greater East Asia Co-Prosperity Sphere" as a discourse connected with such social reforms as medicine, hygiene, and education.

The scientific observing subject, who reads signs from symptoms in a unidirectional fashion and constructs the Other, is secured in the denial and affirmation of this practice. When examining this observing subject, it is important to think once more about the academic genealogy of today's multicultural narratives, which have appeared in the midst of the unsettling of national polities. "Cooperativism" is by no means a problem of the past. The academic discourse constituted by the tropical sciences, which classify, discover, and treat sources of infection, has survived together with "cooperativism" up to the present day. What we need now is to find a site of resistance within "cooperativism" and multiculturalism where we can create ways of being that confuse categories or that are unclassifiable. This is also a task of searching for new articulations.

Notes

1. Benedict Anderson, "The New World Disorder," *New Left Review* 193 (1992).

2. Masao Miyoshi, "A Borderless World? From Colonialism to Transnationalism and the Decline of the Nation-State," *Critical Inquiry* 19 (summer 1993).

3. For studies of the relationship between Japanese colonialism and science, see the essays in the special issue on "Japanese Imperialism and the Sci-

ences," in *Kagakushi kagaku tetsugaku* 11 (1993), and Tomiyama Ichirō, *"Kokumin no tanjō to 'nihonjinshu',"* in *Shisō* 845 (1994). Unit 731 was the notorious biological warfare research unit that carried out experiments on prisoners of war in Manchuria.

4. *Nan'yō guntō* (Nan'yō guntō Bunka Kyōkai (1937), 3–8.

5. Hirano Yoshitarō and Kiyono Kenji, *Taiheiyō no minzoku seijigaku*, (Tokyo: Nippon Hyōronsha, 1942), 258–259.

6. Edward W. Said, *Orientalism*, (New York, Pantheon Books, 1978).

7. See Sakai Naoki, *"Bunkateki sai no bunsekiron to nihon to iu naibusei,"* in *Jōkyō* (December 1992).

8. On the relation of the symptom to the sign, I have in mind Michel Foucault's study of the medical gaze. See Michel Foucault, *Naissance de la Clinique* (P.U.F., 1963).

9. For discussions of this dual time, see the essay noted above by Sakai and also Homi K. Bhaba, "DissemiNation," in *Nation and Narration*, ed. Homi K. Bhaba (London: Routledge, 1990).

10. Ernesto Laclau and Chantal Mouffe, *Hegemony and Socialist Strategy* (New York: Verso, 1985).

11. Sakai, op. cit., 90.

12. Frantz Fanon, *Black Skin, White Masks* (New York: Grove Weidenfeld, 1968), 94.

13. Homi K. Bhaba, *The Location of Culture* (London: Routledge, 1994), 41.

14. There is a difference here between Fanon and Bhaba. In particular, it is the difference between their respective attitudes toward psychoanalysis. For more on this point, see R. Young's critique of Bhaba. Robert Young, *White Mythologies* (London: Routledge, 1990), 210.

15. Frantz Fanon, *A Dying Colonialism* (Grove Press, 1965), 133–139.

16. Hijikata Hisakatsu, *Ryūboku* (Tokyo: Oyama Shoten, 1943), included in *Chosakushū* 7 (San'ichi Shobō, 1992), 2.

17. One may call *Driftwood* a magnificent ethnography because of its unstable narrative. See Sudō Ken'ichi, "Minzokushika Hijikata Hisakatsu and *Ryūboku*," in *Chosakushū* 7.

18. *Nan'yō guntō* 7, no. 7 (Nan'yō guntō Bunka Kyōkai, 1941).

19. Hijikata Hisakatsu, in *Chosakushū* 6.

20. Ibid., 25.

21. Hijikata, *Chosakushū* 7, 3.

22. Sugiura's texts include the following: *"Parao tōmin no shūkyō,"* in *Minzokugaku nenpō* 1 (1938); *"Paraotō ni okeru shūraku no nibun sōshiki ni tsuite,"* in *Jinruigaku zasshi* 53, no. 3 (1938); *"Parao ni okeru iwayuru totemizumu ni tsuite,"* in *Jinruigaku zasshi* 55, no. 4 (1940); *"Minzokugaku to Nan'yō guntō tōji,"* in *Tainan'yō*, Taiheiyō Kyōkai, ed. (Kawade Shobō, 1941); *"Mikuroneshia no yashiba-sei amikago,"* in *Jinruigaku zasshi* 57, no. 10 (1942); *"Mashāru guntō ni okeru kon'in kankei,"* in *Jinruigaku zasshi* 58, no. 8 (1943); *"Mikuroneshia no tochi seido,"* in *Minzoku kenkyūjo kiyō* 1 (1944).

23. Sugiura, *"Paraotō ni okeru shūraku no nibun sōshiki ni tsuite,"* ibid.

24. Sugiura, *"Minzokugaku toNan'yō guntō tōji,"* op. cit., 178.

25. Hasebe Kotondo, *"Nihonjin to Nan'yōjin,"* in *Nihon Minzoku,* Tokyo Jinruigakkai, ed. (Tokyo: Iwanami Shoten, 1935); *"Nan'yō guntōjin,"* in *Jinruigaku, Senshigaku kōza ikkan* 1 (Tokyo: Oyamakaku, 1938).

26. Matsunaga Teruta and Hyōdō Shōichi, *"Waga Nan'yō guntō ni okeru 'kanaka'zoku no kesshokuso gan'yūryō narabini ketsuatsu, myakuhaku, dosū, taion, oyobi akuryoku nado ni kansuru chōsa"* and Takasaki Satarō, *"Dōshu kekkyū gyōshū hannō yori mitaru waga Nan'yō guntō domin no seibutsu kagakuteki jinshu keisū to jinshukata to ni oite,"* both in *Nan'yō guntō chihō byōchōsa: igaku ronbunshū* 2 (Nan'yōchō keimuka, 1933); Okatani Noboru, *"Waga nan'yō guntō saipantō ni okeru chamurozoku no ketsuatsu ni tsuite,"* *Minzoku eisei* 4 (1934); Kameshima Muneo, *"Māsharu guntō genjūmin (mikuroneshiazoku) no shimon kenkyū,"* *Minzoku eisei* 6 (1937); Sonoda Kazunari, *"Ketsuekigata oyobi tōbu tsumuji no sonzai bui yori mitaru nan'yō ponape tōmin danji (mikuroneshiajin) no kishitsu oyobi hatsuiku ni tsuite,"* *Nan'yō guntō chihō byōchōsa: igaku ronbunshū* 4 (Nan'yō keimuka, 1937); Furuhata Tanemoto, Haneda Yata, and Yoshie Tsuneko, *"Parao tōmin no ketsuekigara narabini shimon chōsa,"* *Minzoku eisei* 11 (1943).

27. Takano Rokurō, *"Nanpō hatten to jinkō mondai,"* in *Jinkō mondai* 4, no. 4 (1942): 22.

28. See, for example, Kiyono Kenji, *"Nihon no nanshin to nihonjin no takushoku nōryoku,"* in *Taiheiyō minzoku seijigaku,* Hirano Yoshitarō and Kiyono Kenji, eds. (Tokyo: Nihon Hyōronsha, 1942). Also, Noma Kaizō, *"Jinkō mondai kara mita nanshinron,"* in *Jinkō mondai* 4, no. 4, (1942).

29. Nakayama Eishi, *"Nettai ni okeru rōdō nōritsu,"* in *Shakai seisaku jihō* 260, (1942): 669.

30. J. Fabian calls this control of the time of the other through this kind of anthropological discourse a denial of "coevalness." J. Fabian, *Time and the Other* (New York: Columbia University Press, 1983).

31. Benedict Anderson makes the same point about the gap between the builders of reconstructions of archaeological remains and the residents of the area. Benedict Anderson, *Imagined Communities* (New York: Verso, 1991, revised edition), 181.

32. Details on the above figures are available in Suzuki Shun'ichi, *Nanpō rōdōryoku no kenkyū,* (Tokyo: Tōyō Shokan, 1942).

33. From 1933 to 1937, the South Seas Agency's Police Section published four volumes of *Nan'yō guntō chihō byōchōsa: igaku ronbunshū.* Volume three, *"Yapputō jinkō genshō mondai no igakuteki kenkyū,"* deals with population decrease.

34. Yanaihara Tadao, *Nan'yō guntō no kenkyū* (Tokyo: Iwanami Shoten, 1935), 107.

35. Mark R. Peattie, *Nanyō: The Rise and Fall of the Japanese in Micronesia, 1885–1945* (Honolulu: University of Hawaii Press, 1988), 86–96.

36. Sugiura Ken'ichi, *"Minzokugaku to Nan'yō guntō tōji,"* op. cit., 45.

37. Ibid., 38.

38. Sugiura, *Minzokugaku to Nan'yō*, 37.

39. Yanaihara Tadao, "*Nanpō rōdō seisaku no kichō*," in *Shakai seisaku jihō* 260 (1942): 151. Although Yanaihara argued for the necessity of forced labor, he was fundamentally pessimistic about the use of the "islanders'" labor power.

40. See for example, Kiyono Kenji, "*Nanpō minzoku no shishitsu to shūsei—nihonjin no nettai junka nōryoku*," in *Shakai seisaku jihō* 260 (1942): 105. Also, Suzuki, op. cit.

41. On the issue of the Modekngei, A. Vidich evaluates it as an anti-Japanese movement, while Aoyagi Machiko examines the question of class within Palau. A. Vidich, "Political Factionalism in Palau," *Coordinated Investigation of Micronesian Anthropology* 23 (1949); Aoyagi Machiko, *Modekugei* (Tokyo: Shinsensha, 1985).

42. *Shisô gappô* 62, (1939): 357.

43. Sugiura Ken'ichi, *Minzokugaku to nan'yō*, 217–218.

44. Kiyono Kenji, op. cit. Also, Nakayama Eishi, a doctor who was also commissioned by the Pacific Association to investigate the South Sea Islands, saw the low-natured "inferior people" as "people with poor mental capacity, lacking in education, character, being low in quality and lacking a racial consciousness (concept of the State)." Nakayama, "Nettai ni okeru rōdō nōritsu, 677.

45. Ibid.

46. The low labor capacity of "Japanese" in the South Sea Islands was occasionally expressed in the phrase "[one's] head becomes a papaya." This expresses the fear of becoming like the "islanders" in the tropical environment.

47. Suzuki, *Nanpō rōdōryoku*, 29.

48. The "Kanaka" are one of the "tribes" among the "islanders." There were other derogatory names for people of Okinawan birth in other places than the South Sea Islands, such as "home island savages" (Taiwan). "Home islands" refers to Japanese and "savages" refers to the minority ethnicities living in the mountain regions of Taiwan.

49. Yanaihara Tadao, "*Nanpō rōdō seisaku no kichō*," 156–157.

50. On the genealogy of "cooperativism" in Japanese colonialism, see Oguma Eiji, "*Sabetsu soku byōdō*," in *Rekishigaku kenkyū* 662 (1994).

51. Hirano and Kiyono, *Taiheiyō minzoku seijigaku*, 234.

52. Peter Duus, "Imperialism without Colonies" trans. as "Shokuminchi naki teikokushugi" in *Shisō* 814 (1992).

The Green of the Willow, the Flower's Scarlet: Debate on Japanese Emigrants and Korea under the Japanese Empire

Oguma Eiji

The Japanese Empire was a multi-ethnic empire. This is a fact that is liable to be forgotten at times. However, with the cession of Taiwan in 1895 and the annexation of Korea in 1910, and until their loss in 1945, the non-Japanese ethnic groups that comprised roughly 30 percent of this empire's total population were incorporated as Japanese subjects. For Japanese intellectuals at the time, then, the question of how to regulate ethnic relations within that multicultural empire was a subject of debate.

The work of Milton Gordon is well known as a classic typology of the principles of integration in the multi-ethnic nation of the United States of America. Here, Gordon elaborated three patterns according to which the process of integration of United States society could be envisioned. The first was "Anglo-conformity," which advocated a one-way assimilation into Anglo-Saxon culture. Second was the model of the "melting pot," where a new United States homogeneity is born through the mixture of various ethnicities. Third was "cultural pluralism," a mode within which various ethnic groups could integrated, with each preserving its own distinct culture. Horace Kallen, Randolph Bourne, and others held up by Gordon as forerunners of multiculturalist thought have later come to be highly regarded for the models of integration they proposed.[1]

In the Japanese Empire, as well, debate was not limited to those who conceived a multi-ethnic state including Korea and Taiwan to be a one-way assimilation into Japanese culture. One also found people embracing principles close to multiculturalism. But their thought was never able to forge a link with real events. It was not just a matter of the Japanese Empire lacking the objective conditions that would have made multiculturalism a possibility. There were fundamental problems arising from the geopolitical position in which Japan found itself at the time.

First and foremost, unlike immigrants to the United States who came of their own will, the peoples of Korea and Taiwan were forcibly incorporated during the period of Japanese Empire. (Of course, in the United States, Native American peoples, African-Americans, and the Hispanic peoples of California and Texas had not been incorporated by their own will.) Hence, advocating the integration of the Japanese Empire as a multi-ethnic nation, however broad-minded the concept, necessarily came into conflict with movements for independence simultaneously being waged by these peoples.

There was one more perplexing problem. At the time, Japan actually faced two different kinds of ethnic problem. One was the disposition of the Koreans, Taiwanese, and Ainu people internal to the Japanese Empire, while the other was the exclusion movement directed against Japanese immigrants in the United States. Deprived of the ability to acquire rights as citizens on the basis of their race as "non-naturalizable foreigners," and constantly threatened with the passage of new exclusionary laws, Japanese immigrants in the United States symbolized for the Japan of that time the prejudice of "white people." In the prejudice brought to bear within the empire against Korea and Taiwan, and the prejudice faced from the United States in international relations, then, Japanese intellectuals came face to face with the two-layered problem of "discriminating while being discriminated against." Clearly, this compound problem was generated from Japan's unique position: that of a non-white country sending immigrants abroad that was at the same time an empire holding colonial territories.

It goes without saying that there was no shortage of people who responded to this compound problem by embracing a double standard: condemning the racial prejudice of the United States while advocating oppressive policies toward Korea. But even among those who understood both problems as prejudice, the solutions they arrived at do not necessarily appear appropriate from today's perspective. This is because they ultimately chose solutions of a different order in resolving these two types of discrimination, advocating the acquisition of equality within the United States in the case of Japanese immigrants, and separation and independence from Japan in the case of Korea and Taiwan. That they did so was the result of an underlying structure that would have made it, in effect, a mistake to advocate a similar solution to both problems—either to have recommended the acquisition of equal rights internal to the affiliated country in both cases or, conversely, advocating separation in both cases.

Whether coincidence or not, both problems were entering critical phases around 1920. In 1910, Japan annexed Korea and began pursuing a policy of assimilation. Several years later, faced with the flood of immigrants from southern and eastern Europe into the country during and after World War I, the United States also found itself engaged in a program of semi-forced Americanization, including English language education and the urging of naturalization. In the United States, the exclusion movement against Japanese immigrants included the passage of laws restricting the rights of aliens to own land in California in 1913 and 1920, and a complete halt to the entry of Japanese immigrants with the Immigration Act of 1924.[2] During the Versailles Peace Conference following World War I, from February to April 1919, Japan proposed incorporating into the League of Nations Charter a clause prohibiting racial discrimination, with the immigration problem in mind. This proposal was blocked by the western powers. At precisely the same time, however, the March First Movement for independence broke out in Korea, and was bloodily suppressed by the Japanese military government.[3] As the Beijing Daily News, the Sydney Morning Herald, and others pointed out at the time, a Japan engaged in discrimination against Korea was in no position to be proposing a clause on racial equality.[4]

A number of contemporary Japanese intellectuals were engaging these two ethnic problems simultaneously, gradually bringing their own peculiar position to the level of self-consciousness. When they themselves were being excluded by the United States from immigration and were proposing a clause on racial equality, is it really defensible, they wondered, to discriminate against the Koreans?

This paper will use Gordon's social scientific approach as a point of reference in taking up the problem of how Japanese intellectuals discussed these issues. Gordon analyzed the arguments of Israel Zangwill, John Dewey, and many others, in terms of how their thinking corresponded to his own typology. Were he a historian, he might have asked about the extent to which the circulation of their books exerted an influence on United States immigration policy. Were he an intellectual historian, he might well have taken up the question of the place cultural pluralism occupied in Dewey's philosophical thought. As a social scientist, however, Gordon made it his goal to produce an abstract classification of ways of thinking about social integration, and the investigation of how different models functioned within society. Rather than analyzing a specific age or a specific thinker, such an approach aims to tease out a model that can be applied to multiple perspectives.

This paper will make use of Gordon's approach in examining how three men, Uehara Etsujirō, Nakano Seigō, and Ishibashi Tanzan, discussed the issues of Japanese immigrants and Korea in the 1920s. Each of these men has found a place in Japanese history: Uehara as a Taishō democrat and politician, Nakano as a right-wing populist, and Ishibashi as a liberal. They were selected as the object of this study because each sought to eschew a double standard and apply a consistent logic to these two problems; yet each of their solutions, however internally consistent it may have appeared, was quite different. Furthermore, while they did not, themselves, necessarily argue that the two problems were interrelated, one can extract from each thinker a common logic applied to both Japanese emigration and

Korea. In trying to identify this common logic in the three cases, I would propose that a typology in terms of "democratic assimilation" in the case of Uehara, a kind of "multiculturalism" for Nakano, and "peaceful separation" for Ishibashi, allows us to see how the different recommendations of the three men functioned in relation to the two issues of ethnicity they sought to deal with.

These three thinkers, in the context of the 1920s, constitute an ideal site for working out such a model. While there are a number of studies of the problem of Japanese emigrants and the reaction of the Japanese homeland to the expulsion movement in the United States in social history and the history of foreign policy, there have been relatively few studies that take this issue up in the context of the debates of Japanese intellectuals, and I am not aware of any studies that link it to debates about Korea.[5] This paper may be understood as an interdisciplinary attempt to bring Japanese intellectual history into an encounter with the kind of sociological concerns introduced above.

UEHARA ETSUJIRŌ

Uehara Etsujirō, who journeyed to the United States in 1899 at the age of 22 and spent eight years working his way from a Seattle middle school to Washington State University in jobs that included publishing a weekly magazine for Japanese emigrants, was representative of the pro-American wing of the Japanese intelligentsia of his day. Uehara did post-graduate study at the College of London and, upon his return to Japan, became a professor at Meiji University. In 1917, he was elected to the House of Representatives. The years centering on 1920 were his most prolific period for public debate, and he wrote many treatises on Korea and the problem of Japanese immigrants.

According to Uehara, "racial prejudice is not the chief cause of the anti-Japanese sentiment in California."[6] As he argued in the 1920 article, "The True Face of Anti-Japanese Sentiments and a Program for their Resolution" (*Hainichi no shinsō to sono kaiketsusaku*) "Even in the case of Japanese emigrants, if one acquires the same language as the Americans and establishes an assimilated lifestyle in order to attain mutual understanding, so-called racial discrimination disappears of itself. . . . American people in general do not have a great deal racial prejudice."[7] This argument was based on the premise that immigrants were indeed assimilating into a homogeneous United States culture.

> In America, neither the Jewish, the Irish, the Italians, nor the Spanish are the objects of much discrimination. . . . All these people assembled from various countries all over the world and now they are national citizens with a common language, customs, and habits. Hence, the American people in general are not possessed of a strong racial preju-

dice. If racial prejudice lies at the bottom of the anti-Japanese problem, the fault lies with the Japanese people in California, who are for the most part making no effort to become intimate with American culture and society.[8]

According to Uehara, support for the expulsion movement in California was coming mainly from the new immigrant laborers from southeastern Europe, "Latin peoples" who were "prone to extremes" and had yet to assimilate to the democratic United States.[9] Working from this understanding of the problem, Uehara was led to assert that exclusion movements were an unavoidable occurrence in the contemporary United States with its large numbers of new immigrants.

America's population has recently reached the 100 million mark. However, of those 100 million, 13 million are foreign-born residents in America, the great majority of whom cannot yet be called American citizens. . . . The 10 million blacks and 13 million unassimilated foreign immigrants are without a doubt an obstruction to the unification of the American state. From this perspective, the expulsion of Japanese by Americans cannot but be affirmed as a necessary outgrowth of American national policy.[10]

Uehara's thesis, which locates the cause of the exclusionary movement not in majority discrimination but in minority responsibility, and argues for consolidation of the United States through assimilation into a homogeneity, would appear to repeat verbatim the views of the American majority. However the assertion that one only has to go through the process of assimilation in language, manners and customs, and education to be received on a level of parity by American society is rooted in his own personal experience as a "model minority," who, as a result of arduous study, was able to make his way through an American college. Moreover, the aim of his polemic was actually not the justification of United States exclusionary policies, but criticism of the reclusive nationalism of Japanese immigrants.

Uehara charged that "Japanese residents have no contact with Americans . . . making Japanese villages completely separate from the society of white people," and that they enter into human relationships only within these boundaries. As a result, although "the majority have been resident in America 10 years or more . . . one would be surprised at the number who cannot converse freely in English." Most "cannot even take care of daily affairs in English." The reclusive character of Japanese immigrants is something that was deeply ingrained during "life under the (Tokugawa) isolation policy" of Japan's "feudal age" so that "even when they are in America, Japanese people organize themselves into societies of this-or-that province, making a kind of isolation policy at the group level." Uehara makes this the basis for the conclusion that "on the whole, Japanese have considerably stronger racial prejudice than Americans."[11]

Uehara's description of Japanese immigrants continues, "their only reading materials consist of newspapers published among the Japanese and the odd newspaper or magazine that arrives from the old country." These newspapers "frequently run articles that engender over-confidence in people ignorant of the actual level of strength of their mother country," and "because of this, though they reside in America, their way of thinking is narrower than when they lived in Japan ten or more years ago."[12] Uehara, himself involved in publishing a Japanese-language magazine, can be expected to have had some knowledge of the actual situation of the ethnic newspapers.

Moreover, the Japanese immigrants had "no conception of 'working hours,'" according to Uehara.[13] "In Japanese families, even the wife and children work in the fields, and working hours have no limit . . . and as a result white farmers in most cases simply can't compete with Japanese farmers. This is a very persuasive reason for white people to despise the Japanese."[14]

What lay behind this situation, according to Uehara, was that Japanese immigrants had come to the United States as "guest workers," with no intention of establishing permanent residence or becoming citizens. They remained in the United States on a long-term basis only when "they were not able to make a lot of money and repatriate" as they had planned. "From the day they emigrated to America they had no long-term intentions to stay, and applied themselves intensely so that they might make money and repatriate even one day sooner. Since they have no intention to learn the language and assimilate into American culture and no intention to build the foundation for permanent residence, there is no reason to expect them to be assimilated."[15]

That this type of immigrant would become the object of an exclusion movement, maintained Uehara, was little cause for surprise. Indeed, he argued that Japanese were mistaken in considering assimilation to be "mainly a question of language, manners and customs. The failure of Japanese to be assimilated is at root a matter of their way of thinking."[16] Uehara argued that, while the United States based its national policy on democracy, Japan was a "militarist state." He described Japanese immigrants in the United States building their own ethnic schools, and sending children there to undergo a "pure Japanese-style education," with "Japanese Ministry of Education-censored textbooks." It was an education that "preached the traditional moral precepts of our country, illustrating loyalty and devotion with references to Kusunoki Masashige, and inculcating a narrow-minded Japanese-style patriotism in Japanese children born in America."[17]

Moreover, under the laws governing citizenship in the Japanese Empire, renouncing one's nationality was difficult, and the duty to serve in the Japanese military remained even for second-generation emigrants born overseas. For this reason, too, Uehara concluded, the charge that Japanese immigrants constituted a reserve army for Japanese militarists was a persuasive reason for anti-Japanese sentiment. For Uehara, the charge made by expulsion advocates that "the militarism of the Japanese people makes them unassimilable" was quite reasonable.[18]

In conclusion, Uehara asserted that there were "a variety of reasons for anti-Japanese sentiment," but that "the root cause is the construction of Japanese villages" by immigrants.[19] His proposal for resolving the problem was simple: the Japanese immigrants should immediately dissolve their ethnic collectives and assimilate into democratic United States society. As he put it, "a foreign race that insists on maintaining the difference of its own language, manners, feelings, and customs no matter where it goes, separating off from the host society and living in its own little corner, is not desirable for that society's healthy development."[20]

We can perceive a similar pattern in the logic of tracts on the administration of Korea that Uehara was writing at the same time. However, unlike most participants in the debate (who affirmed Japan exactly as it was and argued for assimilation), he argued for the reconstruction of the Japanese Empire based on principles of parliamentary democracy, and asserted that Korea should be assimilated into a democratized Japan.

In the book, *Democracy and the Reconstruction of Japan* (*Demokurashii to Nihon no kaizō*, 1919), published eight months after the March First Movement in Korea, one finds democratic reform argued from a variety of perspectives including extension of voting rights, opposition to military cliques, advocacy of local self-government, raising of the status of women, freedom of speech, etc. The problem of Korea and Taiwan is taken up there under the question of "reform of the administration of the New Territories."[21]

According to Uehara, "the Korean people are the brothers of the people of our country,"[22] and it is of utmost importance "to make the peoples of the New Territories feel themselves to be members of our nation."[23] This is not, however, to be through the force-fed patriotism of the education system he was criticizing in the case of Japanese immigrants in the United States, but through a shift from the "political despotism" of subjecting Korea and Taiwan to military government toward administration under an Imperial Assembly and incorporation with the mainland under a "unified policy," which would wipe out any trace of discrimination.

> The peoples of the New Territories will be able to place their demands immediately before the Imperial Assembly. Moreover, through this they will begin to feel a sense of responsibility as subjects of the empire. . . . Once the peoples of the New Territories awake to a true feeling as imperial subjects, then they and their representatives must be granted at once full authority in line with the Imperial Assembly. In this way, discrimination between the peoples of the New Territories

and those of the homeland will be completely abolished, and each will take their place as subjects of the empire.[24]

Uehara stresses unification and the abolition of discrimination through the establishment of a deliberative assembly, but does not advocate the transplanting of Japanese manners and customs. The reason is that assimilation is, for him, less a question of "language and manners and customs," than of "ways of thinking." It is, in other words, a unification through democratization. Whether it be Japan or Korea, his interest in the indigenous cultures of Asia is small compared to his passion for the universal principles of democracy.

Uehara did not neglect to criticize Japan. He commented negatively on the discriminatory consciousness of the Japanese by maintaining that the administration of Korea by a military governor who relied on "military force or police authority" was "out of step with world posture." Further, he asserted that "the attitude of the Japanese people toward the Koreans must change from the bottom up. In general, Japanese have been unable to escape the vestiges of the feudal system . . . and this attitude has seriously wounded the feelings of the Korean people." Uehara, however, assumed that, "if Koreans were able to step into a position of political equality with the people of Japan, I would venture to say that, despite their Korean identity, the kind of independence movement we see occurring today would cease." He was unable to comprehend that people might remain attached to the concept of their own ethnic identity even after having been granted equality in political terms.[25]

We also cannot overlook the fact that, to Uehara, Korea represented a land lagging behind Japan in modernization and democratization. "Koreans lag behind us in development, although they are not inferior," he stated, envisioning, of course, that under the direction of Japan "a policy must be promoted according to which the culture of the Koreans advances in step with that of the people of our nation." The existence within a nation of an alien people that remains shut up within its own "narrow-minded" ethnic consciousness and fails to assimilate with the more-modern society, as with the Japanese immigrants in the United States, poses the danger of producing phenomena "less than desirable for that society's healthy development."[26]

In the end, Uehara advocated that the administration of Korea should consist in eliminating all discrimination between the home islands of Japan and Korea, building an environment where "national borders of the past will no longer be tolerated," and "all distinction between the two will be eliminated."[27] For Uehara, a firm believer in democratic assimilation, ethnic consciousness (whether in Japanese immigrants in America or in Koreans) was nothing but an irrational emotion provoked by the experiences of mutual exclusivity and discrimination.

NAKANO SEIGŌ

In 1920, Nakano Seigō was directing the magazine *The Eastern Times* (*Tōhō Jiron*) after serving as reporter for the *Asahi Shinbun*. He was elected to the lower house of the Diet in that same year.

Nakano had been harshly critical of the colonial administration since the 1910s when he had been dispatched to Korea as a reporter for the *Asahi Shinbun*. In a 1915 article, he compared the discrimination against Koreans to that against African-Americans, wondering aloud if "we will not soon see characters like Uncle Tom emerging from their midst." The alternatives Nakano proposed at that time, however—such as "appointing Koreans to official positions in the Korean administration," "accepting into both the upper and lower houses minority representatives to plead the interests of the people of the New Territories," or "extending greetings to Korea from the royal family"—were partial measures at best. [28]

Later, Nakano left the *Asahi Shinbun* company, and, as a special correspondent for *The Eastern Times*, attended the Paris Peace Conference, accompanying the Japanese delegation. After returning to Japan, he recorded his observations in the book *Witnessing the Peace Conference* (*Kōwa kaigi wo mokugeki shite*).[29] At the Peace Conference, Nakano was made painfully aware of Japan's impotence in the negotiations for the postwar order between the Allied powers of England, France, and the United States. What came as a particular shock in this respect was the blocking of the racial equality clause proposed by Japan, a development that Nakano saw as "betraying the humanitarian theses of Mr. Wilson, as well as his Fourteen Points." Though the racial equality clause had received the support of a solid majority, the American president, Wilson, chair of the conference at the time, declared the measure "shelved," claiming that it required a consensus of the entire conference.

In *Witnessing the Peace Conference*, Nakano bitterly criticized Wilson and the United States' position. How, he asked, could Americans preach righteousness and humanity while ignoring all manner of discrimination within their own borders? He described a New York spinning factory where it was "Jews, the Italians, and the newly arrived immigrants who get sucked into its giant mouth, and a pathetic 83% are women. Once thrown into the lion's den, they are sure to be worked to death." He observed that, "the treatment of black people is even more cruel, utterly beyond the ability of man to record in words."[30] On his way to the Peace Conference, Nakano found himself "on the same boat with American Federation of Labor President Samuel Gompers," but recorded that unfortunately "newly arrived immigrants appear to have no way to get into the unions . . . and most of the labor unions have passed special by-laws excluding the colored races. Chinese, Japanese, Indians, Negroes, all are lumped together in these so-called colored races. What kind of humanitarianism is this?"[31] Nakano described the United States as a hypocritical country, as it welcomed the victorious, ethnically mixed U.S. Army home from World War I with fanfare, "proclaiming that the different races are not discriminated against, and whipping up enthusiasm for American unity. And yet the U.S. continues as before to restrict Japanese immigration, and they are threatening to take away the right of immigrants to own property."[32]

Still seething from the events of the Peace Conference, Nakano learned of the outbreak of the March First Movement in Korea in March of 1919 from a newspaper he obtained in Singapore on his return trip home, and had this to say:

> Who among us can observe the developments in Korea without concern? Those who would be indifferent to the Koreans differ in no way from the politicians of certain Allied Powers, who under the cover of talk about justice and humanity would secretly oppress and control the world.[33]

Upon returning to Japan, Nakano lectured on the circumstances of the Peace Conference, and rode the crest of this passionate rhetoric to a seat in the lower house of the Diet. He then promptly left on a fact-finding tour of Korea and Manchuria in the fall of 1920. Based on his tour, he wrote the book *Reflections in the Mirror: Manchuria and Korea*.[34]

Beginning with the words "In Manchuria and Korea are reflected the shadow of an exhausted Yamato race," this book repeatedly indicts the ugliness of Japanese discrimination against the Koreans and Chinese. Nakano criticizes most sharply "the contemptible way of thinking of Japanese people" who "in the face of the strong, stick to a policy of accommodation, but who trample the weak underfoot." Nakano traces to this attitude "the present state of our nation, which, while prostrating itself in the face of American anti-Japanese measures, takes pride in acts of arson against schools in the territories as if they were military exploits." For him, an argument like Uehara's "which would find reason in anti-Japanese sentiment, and characterize Japanese in California as the party at fault" is based on the same "inferior logic of persecuting the weak and catering to the strong" that characterizes "the thugs who beat up Koreans." In response to a position like that of Uehara's, Nakano retorted that he was "not as willing as my colleagues to acknowledge the righteousness and humanity of the Allied powers."[35] Nakano was also well aware that the United States had stolen California from Mexico.

Unlike Uehara, who could see nothing but irrationality in a minority ethnic consciousness that would work against the unity of the nation-state, Nakano praised such a stance highly. He spoke of his on-the-scene conversations with Korean youths, "Is it not now the case that, in the name of independence, the so-called 'glib' Korean youth are arming themselves and hurling bombs in their anger? People scoff at this as fanaticism, but isn't social transformation the product of such fanaticism?"[36] Nakano also added that "while traveling through Korea, I discovered, not the 'deterioration' of the Korean people but their self-consciousness, and this made me very happy."[37]

Nakano was aware that "the arguments of Korean radicals firmly demand Korean independence." But he maintained that "however much we may sympathize with this in spirit, it is an impossibility today." To justify this position, Nakano not only cited Korea's importance as a foothold for Japan's advance into the Asian continent—he also claimed that if Korea, as a resource-poor nation, were to gain independence, the only road open to it would be industrialization. "In such a case, Korea would be destined to encounter the same hardships Japan continues to face." For Nakano, such difficulties included America's exclusion of Japanese immigrants, and impediments to both the import of raw materials and the export of manufactured items constituted by American shipping laws, Australia's discriminatory tariffs, and South Africa's rejection of people of color. Powerful, white nations, he felt, were not about to permit nations of people of color to emerge as players in the world economy, and would use any means at their disposal to suppress them. For this reason, "if the people of Korea intend to throw out Japan and take that step toward independence, they are certain to be plagued by the same kind of oppression. We can be certain that America's 'justice and humanity' will not soften the economic pressure brought to bear. The Korean people would experience a rude awakening from their delusions."[38]

Moreover, Nakano knew that the Korean government in exile in Shanghai that supported the Korean independence movement was "not entirely a Korean product. It is, to put it bluntly, made in America. President Syngman Rhee resides, in fact, in America."[39]

He argued that even the March First Movement had absorbed the influence of Wilson's doctrine of ethnic self-determination. During his visit to Korea, he recounted, he received a chorus of approval when he exhorted his audience to escape from European and American influence with the question, "Gentlemen, is not the word 'independence' (*dokuritsu*) written with the characters 'to stand alone?' Yet the independence movement of my esteemed listeners seeks to sever ties with Japan while throwing Korea's lot in with America's, does it not?"[40] According to Nakano "an America that lynches Negroes cannot be expected to have any true sympathy with the colored races. Of late, Americans they have taken to the sport of harassing Japan. They spend their leisure time plotting against us, and in the name of noble and gallant values."[41] For Nakano, the positive interest shown in the Korean independence movement by the United States aimed at breaking the solidarity of peoples of color, and was nothing less than a conspiracy to install a puppet government in Korea favorable to United States interests.

Nakano cites tyranny and discrimination by Japan as the cause of Korean calls for independence, and stresses that for Japan the proper course of action in regard to Korea is "not the violent suppression of riots . . . nor is it the torching of schools and meeting halls."[42] He urged Japan to grant voting rights to Korea and a status of equality within the Japanese Empire. In addition, he called for respect for independent ethnic cultures.

> Given that Japan is already an empire, what is needed now is the generosity to forge these several peoples into a whole.
> When we talk about having an assimilation policy, this must not be conceived of as identical to the shallow-minded, arrogant, assimilation policy of the Americans. They repress the individuality of Japanese living in California, and yet harp on how difficult it is for Japanese to assimilate, citing skin color—a feature that no one can change. Is it not rather that the green of willows, and the scarlet of flowers, both have their appeal?[43] An empire constituted by a single island country of Japan would lack the complexity of an empire. We must develop the culture of Korea and the individuality of the Korean people, regarding them as a treasured part of the Great Empire. . . . What we call an assimilation policy must not be the artificial Japanization of Korean culture, but the creation of a thoroughly consistent political and economic system in both societies.[44]

Although Nakano uses the phrase "assimilation policy," it is evident from the above that he held principles that are, in substance, close to a kind of multiculturalism. He was critical of the situation in which a Korean in the Japanese empire "could not hope to become a bureau chief or high government official, let alone a minister. A Korean person with a higher level of education than a Japanese person won't receive even half the salary. We must remove any impediment to the attainment, by Koreans, of even such posts as prime minister, army general, university president, banker, or Diet member." He pointed out that "Lloyd George, the Prime Minister of the United Kingdom, is actually a Welshman. The people of Wales are a Celtic people and are not Englishmen. They have a different language and their manners and customs differ. One may say that they are Koreans to the English." He asserted that Japan, too, "needs to have Koreans participating in international conferences (as Japanese delegates), and needs to draw on their strength to petition the world for fairness and equality."[45] It goes without saying that behind Nakano's argument lay the fear that, if matters in Korea were left to take their course, Korea might become "like Ireland, where the right to participate in central government, and the right of local government, were denied from the outset. Koreans, like the Irish, will soon enough come to demand nothing less than independence."[46] Still, one cannot deny that, in a certain respect, Nakano advocated the rebuilding of Japan as a pluralistic, multi-ethnic nation-state.

Nakano held up, however, as the mission of this new Japanese empire born of the union of the Japanese and Korean peoples, the strengthening of military preparedness in order to resist the threat of the white peoples. The

United States "used the Indians as hunting dogs. The cotton fields of the South are fertilized with the blood of the black slaves. The plains of the Pacific coast are watered with the sweat of the Chinese and Japanese. These hunting dogs and slaves and laborers now stand in their way, so they are stricken with anxiety about their continued propagation, and pray for their extinction . . . These are the same Americans who have such sympathy today for Chinese and Koreans. If, on another day, they end up successful in their bid to suppress the Japanese in the Far East, how do you think they would regard colored peoples then?"[47] From this perspective, "Japan's military preparedness is not simply the military preparedness of little Japan."[48] For Nakano, "of all the colored peoples, only Japan has attained power and authority on an international level, and that just barely. If Japan is pushed out of the ring, the future of people of color will be far less hopeful."[49]

In this way, Nakano's argument developed into a pan-Asianism or Monroe Doctrine of the Far East that sought to bring races of color into a coalition, centered in Japan, to resist white peoples. While we can discern, in both his argument about Japanese immigrants in Japan and about the Japanese in Korea, a common logic criticizing prejudice and affirming the autonomy and culture of minority groups, his conclusion is that military preparation must be stepped up in the struggle against the white race, and that Korea cannot be granted independence. As Nakano puts it: "While continuing to bolster its real power, Japan must seize this historic opportunity and charge ahead. We must bear this burden even if it breaks our backs. We can only pray that the Chinese and Koreans, whose fate is one with ours, will sympathize with our dilemma."[50]

ISHIBASHI TANZAN

In 1919, Ishibashi Tanzan was Acting Associate Editor for *The Oriental Economist* (*Tōyō Keizai Shinpō*), a magazine known for its liberal stance.[51] He, too, left us essays from this period on Korea and the problem of Japanese immigrants in the United States.

Ishibashi was an anti-emigration polemicist from the start. In 1913, for example, at the time the law was passed in California forbidding aliens from owning land, he had written an editorial entitled "Who Needs Emigration?" (*Ware ni imin no yōnashi*). In Japan at the time, the prevailing tone of debate was that emigration and territorial expansion were indispensable means of coping with the population surplus. Ishibashi, however, argued that, rather than having its labor power drained off to other countries through emigration, Japan should use its labor power to promote industrial development and carry out foreign trade. This would provide the basis for adequately caring for the population, and would benefit Japan over the long term, whereas "adhering to imperialist doctrine" or "forcing immigrants on an America that despises them" went against the national interest.[52] This view would hold consistently through his later arguments on emigration.

In the case of the clause on racial equality proposed at the Paris Peace Conference, for example, Ishibashi recognized the prejudice of the Allied Powers against people of color, but directed his main objections toward "the prejudicial treatment shown by our own country to insiders and outsiders alike." He pointed out that Japan had posted a ban on the entry of Chinese laborers, and had, through its restricted election system—in which the right to participate in government was granted only to those above a certain taxable income—"denied political equality even to our fellow countrymen." Beyond this, "Japan engages in prejudicial treatment of the Taiwanese and Koreans under its dominion." A proposal for racial equality launched from a position like this, argued Ishibashi, "would not be likely to carry much authority."[53]

As is clear from these examples, Ishibashi, too, was conscious of the parallels between the discrimination carried out by the Japanese against the Taiwanese and the Koreans and discrimination against the Japanese, beginning with that experienced by Japanese immigrants in the United States. His response, however, differed from that of both Uehara and Nakano.

Though Ishibashi understood from the first that the problem with Japanese immigrants was rooted in racial prejudice, in 1916 he praised highly a statement by Japanese immigrants in Hawaii declaring that "as American citizens, not Japanese subjects," they would not refuse to serve in the United States army in case of war, even a war against Japan. Ishibashi felt that if all the immigrants came to this kind of resolution it would go a long way to solving the immigrant problem.[54] His approach to the problem on this point can be said to be close to Uehara's. However, by 1920, against the backdrop of the rise of the movement to expel Japanese immigrants from the United States, Ishibashi (unlike Uehara, who had claimed that there was no racial discrimination in the United States) had come to express the belief that the source of the problem was "from first to last racial prejudice."[55] Unlike Nakano, however, Ishibashi did not go on to condemn racial prejudice:

> Now, when we come to ask what is the cause of the present state of affairs, it is, as I have said previously, the intractable difficulty in assimilating the yellow and white races. Further, this failure to assimilate is, as the American president Harding has said, neither the fault of the yellow man nor of the white man. Perhaps it is nature, or perhaps the long separation of our histories has created this situation, but in any case there is no reason for anyone to feel indignant. The only thing we can do is simply accept this as a fact for a while, and arrange all our actions accordingly. . . . And if it is clear that the root of the problem lies here, then the question of whether the Americans are arrogant or evil becomes a matter of secondary importance.[56]

Ishibashi asked almost rhetorically "if it is really possible to eradicate prejudice from Americans? It seems a bit difficult to me."[57] He asserted the existence of racial prejudice in the Japanese as well:

Let my reader imagine a situation in which eighty or ninety thousand American workers came and settled in a corner of Hokkaido, Taiwan, or Korea, cultivated and took possession of the land, and reproduced themselves copiously. If you can imagine that, I would venture to say that you will be able to contemplate the problem in California with a bit more equanimity.[58]

Elsewhere, he wrote:

There is no denying that America has voiced a number of grievances about Japanese immigrants, but, from the point of view of American citizens, this is not completely without basis. If laborers from another country, with a different language, manners, and customs (moreover, lacking education) built a large number of villages and settled within Japan's borders, this would not doubt cause considerable discomfiture.[59]

For Ishibashi, exclusion of immigrants was "common to every country. When thinking about this matter, the Japanese cannot simply censure America. To do so is to ignore human nature."[60] From this standpoint, he offered the following proposal for solving the problem of Japanese immigrants:

The best solution, from the point of view of cordial relations between Japan and America, will be to negotiate with the American government, to have them buy up the assets amassed by the Japanese in California, and to have the immigrants return to Japan.[61]

Ishibashi's proposal to return immigrants to their country of origin—however motivated by concern for "cordial relations" with the United States—effectively recognized the position of American expulsion advocates. His proposal was also shaped by his peculiar understanding of the United States. Although Ishibashi took up the question of Japanese immigrants any number of times, he never touched on the existence of newly arrived European immigrants or of African-Americans in his arguments. This was in contrast to the view of Uehara, who took it as a premise that the United States was composed of a complex ethnic mixture, and who asserted that any foreign people who made an effort to assimilate could coexist with others within it. Nakano, on the other hand, had emphasized the prejudice to which American blacks, immigrants, and Native Americans were subjected, and that could be overcome only through their allying against whites. Ishibashi's writings on the problem of Japanese immigrants in America, however, describes the United States as a mono-ethnic, Anglo-American society, into which only Japanese immigrants have intruded and become a problem.

How, we might ask, did Ishibashi envision the actual realization of cordial relations between Japan and the West, in an agenda that was admittedly complicitous with the views of exclusionists? It is in this context that his views on foreign trade come to the fore.

> It is difficult to imagine a more unwise proposition than for one country to send farm workers to carry out agriculture in another, in order to develop an economically advantageous relationship with that country. . . . Let us take the same fifty thousand people, and instead make them merchants and financiers. Who knows what marvelous activity we might see then? Beyond that, having Japanese citizens circulate throughout the entire territory of America to conduct trade would not make the same kind of vivid impression on American eyes that Japanese building Japanese villages in the single location of California do, and consequently the immigration problem would not arise. If we negotiated with the American government, so that Japanese immigrants received compensation for the assets they held in California, there would be nothing to regret. I would like to see Japan take an even broader perspective on this issue, so that we can develop our economic relations with America to much greater advantage.[62]

The logic of eschewing smaller, short-term gains in order to pursue larger ones based on a broad view of international relations runs consistently through Ishibashi's writings on diplomacy. In such a logic, however, the attachment immigrants might form to the land they opened and cultivated and to the status they attained in the society they were actually living in is subsumed within profit-loss calculations on the level of the nation-state. This same logic is visible in an argument from 1924:

> It must have been before the Sino-Japanese War—sometime after the twentieth year of Meiji (1887), but I remember from my childhood that quite a few merchants from China had made their way into Japan. We used to call them "Mr. Nanking" at the time, and on the streets they became an object of contempt. It seems to me that this phenomenon could easily produce scorn . . . toward the Chinese in general. To take the most vulgar of classes from among a national citizenry and send them abroad is ultimately to cause the citizenry as a whole to be despised. To judge from our experience with Chinese students, sending students abroad to study is not such a good idea either. The cause of the Japanese being excluded in America is not necessarily a simple matter, but one thing is beyond doubt, that for the Americans the word "Japanese"

is essentially defined by farm laborers, and that this has been disas-
trous. . . . Englishmen are well respected among Japanese in general,
but if the destitute of East London started going abroad in large numbers, that view would likely undergo a remarkable change.[63]

Is Ishibashi really claiming that the "vulgar classes" are unqualified to
participate in international relations? He continues:

That the only fundamentally effective method of eliminating the anti-
Japanese problem is to make the Japanese into a people respected by
foreigners is beyond doubt. However, becoming a citizenry worthy of
respect requires first that we raise the quality of Japanese citizens in
general, and, second, that we carefully investigate the quality of the
citizens who do go abroad. Now many will no doubt quibble with this
logic. "Ridiculous!" they will say. "Every country has people who lack
education or have poor morals. It is those who deride them when they
occasionally go abroad in large numbers who are at fault—and even
more so the modern, bourgeois sensibility that views such people as
low or inferior." Objections like these are the equivalent of saying,
"Ridiculous! Every house has a toilet. What is the problem with in-
stalling it in the parlor?"[64]

For Ishibashi, whether assimilation was preferable or not was not the
question. He regarded assimilation as impossible and saw the best solution
to discrimination to be separatism, with different ethnicities residing in their
own countries. Cordial relations between such countries could be maintained by a select group of people involved in trade. Forced repatriation of
settled immigrants would, in the broad view, be to the mutual economic
benefit of all. If one were to summarize Ishibashi's outlook on international
relations as it appears in the context of the problem of Japanese emigrants,
this would be its basic theme.

Let us turn now to Ishibashi's views on the relations between Japan and
Korea. With regard to the Koreans, Ishibashi was persuaded that "no matter
how excellent an administration we shower on them, there is no reason to
think they will be content. Consequently, until they obtain autonomous self-
government, there is absolutely no question of bringing an end to their resistance."[65] As can be seen from his use of Ireland as an example, Ishibashi
was aware of a rising trend around the world toward ethnic self-
determination, but his views on Korea were not inconsistent with the views
on international relations described above. This is because both arguments
share the assumption that discrimination will not cease, and that, therefore,
assimilation is impossible, and that the best solution to these problems is
separation and existence in separate countries. Whereas Uehara and Nakano
could at least envision the accommodation of Koreans within a multi-ethnic

Japanese nation, based on the granting of equality to all citizens or on an official multiculturalism, Ishibashi recognized no such possibility.

To bring emigrants home and substitute, for their presence abroad, trade-based international relations that would result in economic gains more broadly defined, was the basis of Ishibashi's diplomatic philosophy: a view he defined as "Little Japan-ism" (shōnihonshugi).[66] In his 1921 article, "The Chimera of 'Great Japan-ism'" (Dainihonshugi no gensō), he argued that maintaining Korea and Taiwan as territories not only carried a high economic cost, but was interfering with trade with the countries of Europe and Asia. Again invoking "the broad view of things," Ishibashi argued that Japanese should simply write off its losses and be "resigned to letting Korea and Taiwan go." In this article, Ishibashi combined a moral emphasis on maintaining harmonious international relations with a utilitarianism that calculated economic profit and loss. For him, the way to gain the trust and confidence of the countries of Asia was not through a military confrontation with the white race, but rather through the ethical action of "liberating Korea and Taiwan at once in some form or another, and pursuing a pacifist policy with regard to China and Russia."[67] At the same time, Ishibashi felt that sending workers and colonists in large numbers to other countries was folly. "As for laborers, we should be using those of the other country and bringing in only capital, technology, and industrial know-how. . . . To put it crudely, to bring one's own capital, technology, and industrial know-how and exploit the other country's labor" was a wise course in Ishibashi's eyes. "Even in India, the numbers of English are few," Ishibashi suggested.[68] These different views were not in contradiction for him, however. As a liberal who had studied Adam Smith and Herbert Spencer, Ishibashi was consistently critical of military incursion and the transfer of peoples through immigration and colonization, but he firmly believed that trade relations were peaceful, and mutually beneficial. Though it takes us somewhat beyond the period we are considering here, we may note that Ishibashi had this to say in celebrating Japan's surrender of Korea and Taiwan in October 1945, following World War II:

> There are some in this world who mistakenly believe that countries with colonies overseas can extract things from them free of charge. People with such views criticize England for exploiting India. There are Koreans who direct the same reproach toward Japan. They claim that, when Japan imports Korean rice, the Korean people are being robbed of their sustenance. Long ago, when the East India Company was establishing itself in India, they no doubt engaged in activities that would best be termed plunder. However today in India, and still more so in Korea, how does one obtain goods except through commercial transactions? One obtains a commodity by paying an equivalent price for it. A glance at the trade tables will make that clear.[69]

Peaceful separation of races and friendly international relations through commerce: this was Ishibashi's principle from first to last. Ishibashi's idea that one only has to bring about separation for race problems to be solved, however, assumed that after such separation trade relations would not be marred by friction or exploitation.

CONCLUSION

The problems taken up in the present study bear on four different nationalisms. They are the nationalism of the United States in excluding immigrants, the nationalism of Japanese immigrants, the nationalism of the Japanese home islands, and the nationalism of the Koreans seeking independence. What is problematic here is the middle ground occupied by the nationalism of Japanese immigrants. The argument about the latter turns on whether one regards the nationalism of Japanese immigrants as a kind of "long-distance nationalism" or in terms of a concept of "ethnic solidarity."

For Uehara, the nationalism of Japanese immigrants was "long-distance nationalism." He thought of the unification of a multi-ethnic nation-state as something that transcended individual nationalisms, and consistently prayed for the dissolution of "narrow-minded" nationalism through democracy. Following precisely this logic, he was able to argue simultaneously for the assimilation of Japanese immigrants into United States society, the reform of Japan through democracy, and the integration of Korea into a democratized Japan. The "democratic assimilation" that anchors Uehara's argument was incisive in the context of criticizing the closed nature of Japanese immigrant society. Ultimately, however, this led him to affirm without qualification the concept of the integration of all citizens into a multi-ethnic nation-state, and to reject the political and cultural independence of the minority.

Nakano regarded the issue of Japanese immigrants as a racist assault on an "ethnic collective." For him, whether in the case of Japanese immigrants or of Koreans, minority nationalism was to be affirmed at least as an emotion. Had Nakano been a minority intellectual in the United States, he would probably have been held in high esteem by later generations for his fierce criticism of racial prejudice and his advocacy of multiculturalism and coalition of peoples of color. However, in the context of Japan at the time, his thinking led instead to the denial of Korean independence, and the advocacy of pan-Asianism and militarization. Nakano's argument, in denouncing Europe and the United States while, at the same time, justifying the actions of his own country, also embodies an unfortunate side of third-world nationalism. We can also find hinted at here the possibility that even multiculturalism, insofar as it upholds the ideal of the state as a unity, can function as an oppressive force in the face of an independence movement.

For Ishibashi, the Japanese immigrants were another example of Japan's foolish incursions abroad, no different from Japanese colonists on the

Asian continent, Taiwan, or Korea. For him, nationalism exists whether one likes it or not, and is a given in international relations. His proposal for solving ethnic problems was for the complete severance of contact and mixing among different peoples—who should be confined within their respective ethnic nation-states. Following this logic, Ishibashi was able to call for Korean independence and the establishment of a Korean nation-state, as well as for the containment of Japan's aggressive actions. But his advocacy of the forced repatriation of immigrants to their countries of origin will be of little help in thinking about contemporary immigration problems. Thorough criticism of the "peaceful separation" that symbolizes his argument has to acknowledge that it functions to simply avoid the problem of imagining coexistence in a multi-ethnic state. Furthermore, it did not envision the possibility of exploitation in post-separation commercial relations.

After the period in question, these three men proceeded along their respective paths. Uehara and Ishibashi each opposed the war against the United States, and, after the war, became leading politicians in the conservative parties that would eventually form the Liberal Democratic Party. Ishibashi, in fact, became prime minister for a short period. Nakano leaned more and more strongly to pan-Asianism, celebrated the establishment of the puppet state in Manchuria, and advocated a "holy war for the liberation of Greater East Asia." He was, however, subjected to repression for opposing General Tōjō, and committed suicide midway through the Pacific War.

The two problems of Japanese immigrants' experiences of discrimination in the United States, and of the oppression of Koreans under Japanese colonial rule, eventually found wholly different resolutions. But insofar as the responses to the issue of ethnicity proposed by the men we have considered may be seen as representing their ideals, the comparison has enabled us to see the strengths and weaknesses of those ideals. The embryonic multiculturalism that arose under the Japanese Empire was cut off undeveloped, leaving only the tainted legacy of its opposition to Korean independence. Postwar Japan surrendered Korea and Taiwan, demilitarized, and rebuilt a mercantile country based on manufacture and trade, thus proceeding according to Ishibashi's general conception. In an age, however, when trade friction arose between Japan and the United States, and the economic penetration of third-world countries became criticized as exploitation, the limitations of this framework were exposed. In the present day, as immigrant laborers continue to flow into Japan, we find ourselves still without a logic by which we can live together.

Translated by Joseph Murphy

Notes

1. Milton M. Gordon, *Assimilation in American Life* (New York: Oxford University Press, 1964).

2. The Alien Land Act passed in California in 1913 prohibited aliens from owning land or leasing land for more than three years. In 1920, this limited right to lease land was denied completely to Japanese. Following a 1922 ruling by the Supreme Court of the United States that Japanese were ineligible for citizenship, the 1924 legislation was clearly directed at excluding Japanese immigrants. See Hane Mikiso, *Modern Japan: A Historical Survey* (Boulder: Westview Press, 1986), 200–201.

3. On March 1, 1919, a peaceful demonstration for independence was carried out nationwide in Korea. Its ruthless suppression resulted in 1,962 Korean casualties (according to Japanese officials) and nearly 20,000 arrests.

4. Wakatsuki Yasuo, *Hainichi no rekishi*, (Tokyo: Chuōkōron, 1972), 146.

5. Asada Sadao's *Nichibeikankei to iminmondai*, in *Demokurashii to nichibeikankei*, ed. Saitō Makoto (Tokyo, Nanundō, 1973), Hasegawa Yūichi's *1920 Nendai: Nihon no iminron*, in *Gaikō jihō*, 1265, 1272, 1279, published in 1990 and 1991, and others, are extant. However, they do not examine the three thinkers who are the object of this paper.

6. Uehara Etsujirō, "*Hainichi no shinsō to sono kaiketsusaku*," in *Taiyō* (November 1920):33. The quotations on the Japanese immigrant problem that follow are taken from two articles from the journal *Taiyō*: "*Beikoku kinji no hainichi mondai*" (September, 1920), hereafter abbreviated as "*Beikoku*" and "*Hainichi no shinsō to sono kaiketsusaku*" (November, 1920), hereafter abbreviated as "*Hainichi*." Further, in "*Beikoku kinji no tainichi taido*" (*Taiyō*, September, 1919), Uehara takes up the problem of Japanese immigrants, not as a racial matter, but as an economic one, and defends Wilson's opposition to the clause on racial equality. He argues that without an improvement in relations with China, Japan was in no position to be proposing a clause on racial equality. Studies of Uehara from the perspective of his discussion of Taisho democracy are available from Matsuo Takayoshi, Suzuki Masasetsu, Miyamoto Seitarō, and others, while Wakabayashi Masatake's "*Taishō demokurashii to Taiwan gikaisetchi seigan undō*," in Haruyama Akihiro and Wakabayashi, *Nihon shokuminchishugi no seijiteki tenkai* (Asia Seikeigakkai, 1980), sees his discussion of the problem of Korea as an example of the position advocating extending the laws and system of the homeland as a way of incorporating the colonial territories (*naichi enchōshugi*). I am not aware of any studies that take up Uehara's discussion of the Japanese immigrant problem.

7. Uehara, "*Hainichi*," 3–4.

8. Ibid., 4.

9. Uehara, "*Beikoku*," 57.

10. Ibid., 62–63.

11. Uehara, "*Hainichi*," 4.

12. Ibid.

13. Uehara, "*Hainichi*," 68.

14. Uehara, "*Beikoku*," 6.

15. Ibid., 5

16. Uehara, "*Beikoku*," 68.

17. Uehara, *"Hainichi,"* 12. In the confusion following the fall of the Kamakura shogunate in 1333, Kusunoki staunchly supported one of the imperial lines, and was defeated by the Ashikaga clan in 1336. He was held up as a model of unswerving loyalty in primary school ethics education at the time.
18. Ibid., 5. Also, *"Beikoku,"* 69.
19. Uehara, *"Hainichi,"* 20.
20. Uehara, *"Beikoku,"* 17.
21. The discussion of Uehara's writing on Korea that follows is taken from his *Demokurashii to Nihon no kaizō* (Tokyo: Yūhikaku, 1919), and the article *"Chōsen tōchisaku,"* published in *Nihon oyobi Nihonjin,* July 1, 1919.
22. Uehara, *"Chōsen tōchisaku,"* 24.
23. Uehara, *Demokurashii to Nihon no kaizō,* 189.
24. Uehara, *"Chōsen tōchisaku,"* 190–191.
25. Uehara, *"Chōsen tōchisaku,"* 23–24.
26. Ibid., 24.
27. Ibid., 23–25.
28. Nakano's best-known discussion of Korea from this period was his *"Sōtoku seijiron"* in *Tokyo Asahi Shinbun* (April 16–May 1, 1914), but the quotations in the present paper are from *"Dōka seisakuron* (Part 2)" published in *Nihon oyobi nihonjin,* April 15, 1915. Recent work on Nakano includes Nakano Yasuo, *Seijika Nakano Seigō* (Tokyo: Shinkōkaku Shoten, 1971); and, by the same author, *Ajiashugisha Nakano Seigō* (Tokyo: Aki shobō, 1988); Inomata Keitarō, *Nakano Seigō* (Tokyo: Yoshikawakō Bunkan, 1988); Kisaka Junichirō *"Nakano Seigōron"* (*Ryūkoku hōgaku,* 3, no. 1, 1973, and 6, no. 2, 1976). In English, see Tetsuo Najita, "Nakano Seigō and the Spirit of the Meiji Restoration in Twentieth Century Japan" in James W. Morley, ed. *Dilemmas of Growth in Prewar Japan,* (Princeton, New Jersey: Princeton University Press, 1971); Leslie R. Oates, *Populist Nationalism in Prewar Japan: A Biography of Nakano Seigō,* (Sydney, Allen & Unwin, 1985). Takasaki Sōji, *Nihonjin no Chōsentōchi hihanron,* in the journal *Kikan Sanzenri* 34, 1983, and Wakabayashi's study mentioned in note 6 also examine Nakano's discussion of Korea. All of these studies valorize Nakano's debate on Korea with reservations because, while affirming equality and sympathy, he did not recognize the Korean independence movement. None calls attention to his argument as an affirmation of a kind of multiculturalism.
29. Nakano Seigō, *Kōwa kaigi wo mokugeki shite* (Tokyo: Tōhōjironsha, 1919), 21.
30. Nakano, *"Kōwa kaigi wo mokugeki shite,"* 140, 148.
31. Nakano, *"Kōwa kaigi,"* 143.
32. Nakano, *"Kōwa kaigi,"* 191.
33. Nakano, *"Kōwa kaigi,"* 172.
34. The quotations that follow are from *Mansen no kagami ni utsushite* (Tokyo: Tōhōjironsha, 1921).
35. Nakano, *"Mansen no kagami,"* 1–13.
36. Nakano, *"Mansen no kagami,"* 76.

37. Nakano, "*Mansen no kagami*," 24.
38. Nakano, "*Mansen no kagami*," 90–91.
39. Nakano, "*Mansen no kagami*," 72.
40. Nakano, "*Mansen no kagami*," 107.
41. Nakano, "*Mansen no kagami*," 74.
42. Nakano, "*Mansen no kagami*," 1.
43. A stock phrase describing the beauty of contrasting colors in a landscape. Nakano used the phrase in a similar context in a speech to the Diet on January 30, 1921, in which he criticized the handling of the Taiwanese and Korean territories.
44. Nakano, "*Mansen no kagami*," 138–139.
45. Nakano, "*Mansen no kagami*," 128–133.
46. Nakano, "*Mansen no kagami*," 64.
47. Nakano, "*Mansen no kagami*," 105–106.
48. Nakano, "*Mansen no kagami*," 97.
49. Nakano, "*Mansen no kagami*," 91.
50. Nakano, "*Mansen no kagami*," 101.
51. Important recent work on Ishibashi Tanzan begins with Masuda Hiroshi, *Ishibashi Tanzan Kenkyū* (Tokyo: Tōyō Keizai Shinpōsha, 1990) and Jiang Ke-shi, *Ishibashi Tanzan no shisōshiteki kenkyū* (Tokyo: Waseda Daigaku Shuppankyoku, 1992), and by the same authors, *Ishibashi Tanzan* (Tokyo: Maruzen, 1994). The numerous studies on his advocacy of "Little Japanism" (*shōnihonshugiron*) include work by Chō Yukio, Matsuo Takayoshi, Asagawa Tamotsu, Andō Minoru, Ueda Hiroshi, Okamoto Shunpei, Kano Masanao, Kikuchi Masanori, Hanzawa Hiroshi, Matsumoto Toshirō, Tsutsui Kiyotada, Kojima Naoki, and others, while works examining his theses on the Korean problem include Onuma Hisao's "*Ishibashi Tanzan no Chōsen dokuritsuron*" in *Kikan Sanzenri* 32, 1982, and the Takasaki essay mentioned in note 9. With regard to his advocacy of "Little Japanism," interpretations "seem to divide into those who assess it as an 'anti-imperialism' and those who assess it as 'economic imperialism'" (Jiang Ke-shi, "*Sengoshoki no Ishibashi Tanzan shisō*," *Rekishigaku kenkyū* 652, 1993). Ishibashi's argument advocating "independent self-government" for Korea is highly regarded as rare for its time, but has also been criticized by Takasaki for showing "little sympathy for Korean nationalism." There is not much research on the question of Japanese emigrants, but chapter one of Masada's above-mentioned work makes a positive assessment of his argument for repatriating immigrants (as anti-expansionist) and argues that there was a linkage between the thesis of "Little Japanism" and the argument for surrendering the colonial territories. The present study, while sharing the perspective that sees a linkage between Ishibashi's argument on the Japanese emigrant problem and the advocacy of "Little Japanism," argues that, in certain respects, it effectively ratified the expulsion movement.
52. The quotations that follow are from the *Ishibashi Tanzan zenshū* (Tokyo: Tōyō Keizai Shinpōsha, 1971), hereafter abbreviated *ITZ*. Page 357 (the

source of the two phrases in this sentence) of *Zenshū* volume 1, for example, becomes *ITZ* 1, 357.

53. *ITZ* 3, 69–70.
54. *ITZ* 2, 415.
55. *ITZ* 3, 506.
56. *ITZ* 3, 521.
57. *ITZ* 3, 506.
58. *ITZ* 3, 521.
59. *ITZ* 4, 27.
60. *ITZ* 3, 507.
61. Ibid.
62. *ITZ* 3, 522.
63. *ITZ* 5, 510.
64. *ITZ* 5, 510–511.
65. *ITZ* 3, 78–79.
66. *Shōnihonshugi* qualifies the concept of *Dainihon teikoku as* "little-Englandism" might the idea of "Great Britain."
67. *ITZ* 4, 24.
68. *ITZ* 4, 21.
69. *ITZ* 13, 48.

The "Composition" of Empire: One Aspect of Cultural Imperialism in Modern Japan

Kawamura Minato

THE COMMAND OF LETTERS

In the fiction of Nakajima Atsushi, a novelist who lived as a child in Korea, Manchuria, and Micronesia during the Pacific War, the theme of a contrast between "cultures of writing" and "unlettered cultures" is often developed allegorically.[1] In a story called *"The Curse of Letters"* (*Mojika*), set in the reign of the Great King Ashurbanipal in ancient Assyria, the narrative opens as the Great King inquires of one of his sages whether such a thing as a soul of written letters exists, and if so what the nature of this spirit would be.[2] The scholar, representing the historical figure Nabuahe Eriba, ponders the question. But the more intensely he reflects on the nature of letters, the more understanding slips his grasp. If he focuses intently, the letters become reduced to a mere set of lines, and finally to a senseless jumble of scratches on a clay tablet. (Since Assyrians did not possess papyrus, clay tablets were used for writing.) Eriba can only conclude that meaning does not reside in an arbitrary collection of dots and lines inscribed in clay. If a spirit of letters exists to be found, surely it would reside in whatever regulates these random marks and produces "meaning" out of them.

I have previously analyzed this allegorical tale by Nakajima Atsushi in terms of an opposition between the "culture of lettered societies" and the "culture of unlettered societies."[3] There, I argued that the world of Nakajima Atsushi's writings was one characterized by a fissure between "lettered" and "unlettered" cultures, and filled with a spirit of conflict. Nakajima seems to suggest that, with the adoption of writing, human beings become enthralled by concepts and reflections of material objects—that they lose sight of the clarity of the very world they inhabit. This theme runs through *The Curse of Letters* and several other stories by Nakajima Atsushi. In stories like *The South Sea Island Tales* (*Nantōtan*), by contrast, Nakajima seems to want to evoke the happiness and peace of societies without written culture.[4]

In 1941, Nakajima Atsushi proceeded to a new appointment as Secretary for Japanese Language Textbook Compilation at the South Seas Agency, at Imperial Japan's southernmost rim.[5] The South Sea Islands (Micronesia) was a trust territory mandated to Japan by the League of Nations in the Treaty of Versailles, and were formally incorporated into the Japanese Empire after Japan withdrew from the League in 1933. Nakajima had been teaching Japanese at a women's school in Yokohama, but had requested a transfer to points south in hope that a change of climate might alleviate his chronic asthma. He was recommended for the position at the South Seas Agency of the Japanese colonial government by Tsurimoto Hisaharu, then an official in the textbook department at the Ministry of Education and friend from Nakajima's days at the No. 1 Higher School and Tokyo University. Nakajima boarded the *Saipan Maru* bound for the South Sea Islands, leaving behind the manuscripts for *Light and Wind and Dreams,* and *Ancient Tales* that he had penned under the tutelage of the novelist Fukada Kyūya.[6]

The South Seas Agency was the hinterlands of the bureaucratic structure of the Japanese Empire. And his was a title not likely to be taken seriously, to boot. While Nakajima's position was truly that of a lowly bureaucrat, he was a bona fide "official of empire," nonetheless. Despite the lowliness of his status, Nakajima's job of compiling textbooks to teach Japanese—the language of empire that was taught, as "the national language" (*kokugo*), to indigenous populations like the children of the South Sea Islands "natives"—was, by its very nature, the work of faithfully making manifest the prestige of empire, and its hallowed authority, here at its margins, at its farthest reach. Nakajima Atsushi, dispatched from the metropolitan center of empire in Tokyo, functioned here as a bodily manifestation of the spirit of imperial authority.

That is not to say that Nakajima himself was particularly conscious of the role. He had never shown much evidence of being possessed of a bureaucratic disposition, and had been known, during his days as a teacher, as a kind of guardian of the flowers and fields, beloved by his women students and languid, remote from worldly affairs. This Nakajima was charged with compiling Japanese language textbooks for the "native" children of the South Seas. For someone of his nature, the teaching of language and "letters" must have seemed an opportunity for playfulness on the same level as swimming in the warm coral waters and climbing the trees to pick coconuts. Nakajima's dreamy, storybook expectations, however, were dashed by his first look at the actual situation in the South Sea Island public schools (schools set up by the Japanese administration for indigenous peoples). In his diary, for example, he records witnessing this scene at a public school in Saipan.

> I was surprised at the severity with which the principal/drill leader handled the students. Several students who couldn't quite master the pronunciation for "*Ōkuni-nushi-no-mikoto*" were made to stand and repeat the word for an interminable period. One of the little ones holding a short whip and wearing a peach-colored shirt (apparently the class monitor) kept scolding them with an impertinent look on his face. The class monitor appeared to have been instructed to spend his time, even during lessons, walking around the classroom and smacking lackadaisical students with the whip. He seemed particularly taken by the idea of having the students remove their caps in unison, with a one-two cadence.[7]

In his diary, Nakajima refers to the instructors and officials of the public schools as the "petty dictators" of the island. What he witnessed was of course a naked expression at the perimeter of the power constituting the Japanese Empire. As the representatives of the Showa Emperor, the instructors transmitted authority to the South Sea Island populations, who were second-class citizens but apprentices to the role of imperial subject. Laws and institutions, social order and customs, language and education were truly what constituted the prestige and authority of "empire," and it was the task of these officials to make that authority tangible.

These Japanese living at the margins of the empire were charged with the task of teaching both "letters" and "history." The intoned phrase, "Ōkuni-nushi-no-mikoto," was a guarantee of continuity since the age of the gods of an imperial line unbroken for ten thousand generations. The name of the Sun Goddess, "Amaterasu Ōmikami," was incorporated into the textbooks side by side with that of the Meiji Emperor, constituting an essential point of instruction. There is nothing to suggest that Nakajima Atsushi had, up till that time, harbored any particular doubts toward this colonial instruction and nationalist myth. As a graduate of Tokyo Imperial University, he had been comfortably ensconced in the interior of empire, and in the language, laws, institutions, and education of the center. Yet, witnessing firsthand the way the spirit of empire manifested itself in these southern hinterlands planted a seed of doubt in his mind.

Nakajima used one of his favorite words "disorientation"—to describe his state of mind. What began as a seed of doubt expanded, and came to dominate his thoughts. In a letter to his wife he wrote:

> I've come to a clear understanding of the meaninglessness of this business of compiling textbooks for the native people (*dojin*). If we want to benefit the native people, there are scores of more important things to be done. Compiling textbooks is just the tip of the iceberg; it's a minis-

cule matter. There is, by the way, really no way of promoting the welfare of the native people at this point in time. Under the present conditions in the South Pacific, it's becoming increasingly difficult to provide sufficient food and shelter for the people here. At a time like this, what is the point in trying to slightly improve the quality of textbooks? Administering an ill-considered education policy will probably just make people more unhappy. I've lost all enthusiasm for my editing work. It's not out of contempt for the native people. It's because I love them.[8]

Surely there must be higher priorities, Nakajima suggests, than teaching the "native" children Japanese as the language of the empire. By this, of course, he meant raising the standard of living for the island people and improving the degraded living environment in the South Sea Islands. The South Seas Agency oriented itself not to the aboriginal peoples but to the offices of the central government in Tokyo. Noguchi Masaaki, who wrote a novel called *Outland* (*Gaichi*, 1942) based on a three-year tour of duty in the South Seas Agency, had one of his characters describe the situation this way:

I don't recommend it, entertaining hope, that is. South Seas Agency officials aren't in any position to be employing the kind of aggressive leadership you're talking about. Take a look at our section chiefs. At the high end, they're university graduates, who passed the high level civil service exam and until yesterday had been shuffling paper somewhere in the Colonial Ministry (*Takumushō*). Then they're pulled out of that job and suddenly find themselves in positions like that of section chief at the South Seas Agency. They're able people, but they have no practical knowledge or experience in administering colonies.

Then there are the ones who've been here forever. They've managed to achieve the position of secretary, and get promoted to section chief on the basis of seniority. Admittedly, they have a certain proficiency in office matters, that is to say, in shuffling paper, but the tradeoff is, their heads are now like papayas. They've languished down here in the heat so long. They don't read, they don't study, and if something new comes up, they can neither recognize nor comprehend it.[9]

The leadership of Japan's colonial administration was, in fact, just the kind of combination of bureaucrats, descending through the clouds from the central government, with a lackluster stratum of local officials, that Noguchi's novel described. Careerism (getting back to the capital) and a don't-rock-the-boat mentality were common (one wonders how different the situation is for provincial administration and officials stationed overseas today). Moreover, if no coherent policy for administering the mainland Japanese transferred to the colonies was discernible, it goes without saying that time was not devoted to serious consideration of how to improve the standard of living of the native peoples. In one episode, we are shown water in the colonial governor's residence flowing copiously from a tap, while the officials' quarters suffer drought conditions. *Outland* is concerned with detailing this kind of situation, one in which the administrative machinery of the colonies never extends to the native people, and treats it as an obvious fact of colonial life.

Insofar as Nakajima Atsushi translated into action the loss of enthusiasm that emanates from his diary and letters, he was open to charges of laziness and dereliction of his duty. But one can also see here his mistrust of the linguistic policies and education system of the Japanese Empire, that is to say, a resistance to the Japanese Empire's "spirit of letters." Not that Nakajima Atsushi could have articulated this clearly, but he seemed to have an unconscious understanding that the authority and power of empire dwelled precisely in this spirit of the written character. The work of the officials of the South Seas Agency consisted in "shuffling papers," after all a kind of service to the spirit of the written word, which consisted of lackadaisically imposing the will of the metropole on the island people.

That is why it was here, in that bald expression of imperial power that was the South Sea Islands, that Nakajima Atsushi gained such an intimate grasp of the contradictions and injustice of the *kokugo* policies of the Japanese Empire: a policy that consisted of molding the minds of the island children to fit an authoritarian order, and training them in rote memorization of phrases like "*Tennō Heika Banzai.*" Nakajima Atsushi was derelict in his textbook compilation in a way that ran counter to the will of "empire," eventually setting out with a fellow deviant from the imperial order, Tsuchikata Hisao, on a tour of the South Sea Islands. He finally retreated to Tokyo, having left behind no accomplishments to speak of as an official of the South Seas Agency. His was an all too passive resistance to "empire," but with this empire on the verge of collapse, there was little room for more.

THE KOKUGO READER AND ETHNIC CONSCIOUSNESS

As a study in contrast, we might next consider Nakajima Atsushi's predecessor in the South Sea Islands, Ashida Enosuke.[10] Already an influential figure in *kokugo* instruction and composition, Ashida set sail from Kobe on the *Tsukugo Maru* for a tour of the South Sea Islands some 17 years before Nakajima Atsushi, in 1924. His objective, like Nakajima's, was the compilation of *kokugo* (that is, Japanese) readers for the children of the "natives" at the request of the South Seas Agency, and he had set out on an observation tour of local conditions. Two years prior, Ashida had completed a six-volume set of normal school *kokugo* readers at the request of the Governor General of Korea, and the request for his services by the South Seas Agency was a follow-up to this work. At this point, Ashida had become known as an expert in the compilation of *kokugo* textbooks for the colonies, well on the way to becoming the leader in the field. It was he who set in place the basic format for teaching Japanese as *kokugo* to children for whom Japanese was not the mother tongue. The task Nakajima Atsushi had undertaken in 1941 was basically one in a series of revisions of a textbook Ashida Enosuke had compiled long before. In *Blessed by Rain (Keiu jiden,* 1972), Ashida wrote of his experience compiling writing primers for the South Sea Islands:

> A sense of wonder in the face of nature is something shared by all humans. This was brought home to me upon viewing the *urakasu* bird at night along with a sight-seeing group. We are, of course, always surrounded on all sides with an abundance of objects that call forth wonder, but through familiarity we no longer pay them any mind. The point here is that attending to the banalities of daily life can give rise to deep meaning. This awakening to the profound significance of one's surroundings is a crucial part of education, and so I set about gathering material in this vein for the South Seas readers.
>
> Whether it is in mainland Japan or the South Sea Islands, I don't think there is any great difference in the way language is produced or the circumstances of its use. However, since there is no way to administer a policy that does not respond to some inner need, I strove to gather for my materials the beautiful aspects of the local people's way of life, and to make those the starting point in fashioning my textbooks. On this basis, I contrived to develop a set of issues that flow necessarily from daily life—these ranged from ethics, hygiene, economics, and work, all the way to questions of order and law.[1]

Fukuda Sumiko has done considerable research into the circumstances surrounding the *kokugo* textbooks produced by Ashida Enosuke in Korea and the South Sea Islands. According to Fukuda, the *kokugo* readers Ashida compiled for general use in the schools administered by the Japanese colonial government in Korea

> out of a kind of solicitousness toward the fact that the students were being deprived of use of their own national language, tried to keep the face of "Japan, the invader" from being too visible. In the South Seas, by contrast, readers were compiled with the lightheartedness of one who comes bearing comfort and assistance. That the editors were conscious of the fact that readers were being compiled in order to further an assimilation policy is clear from the editor's statement of purpose, which declares, "As a key foothold in the southward advance of the Japanese race, the South Sea Islands are a place of profound significance. As a matter of national policy, it is important that we develop methods of education according to which the island people can learn to

understand the national language, and achieve the same level of culture as the Japanese people."[12]

In the foregoing, Ashida Enosuke seems free of doubt or misgivings about Japan's colonial rule (in his postwar work, *Blessed by Rain*, one finds passages that reveal such doubts). The difference between Ashida, who was successfully able to discharge his bureaucratic duty (really no more than a commission) of compiling textbooks that would be used to instill the language and ideology of empire into the children of the colonies, and Nakajima Atsushi, who was derelict, may perhaps be traced to a differing receptivity toward colonial rule in the Japanese Empire. Of course, this is not to reduce Ashida Enosuke to a simple embodiment of state power. On the contrary, when he agreed to take on the task of compiling a *kokugo* reader for the island children, he advised the South Seas Agency at the start that, as far as text and illustrations were concerned, he would tolerate no interference from amateurs offering their views.

Though editing authority nominally lay with the Governor General's Office of Korea and the South Seas Agency, *kokugo* textbooks in both territories bear the unmistakable stamp of Ashida Enosuke's personal philosophy and educational principles. In *Blessed by Rain*, he recalls:

> I sat down and applied myself to the question of what kind of national language textbooks needed to be made in Korea. Of course, I wanted to produce a text with *kokugo* drills that would be easy to use with Korean children. However, in the case of content, I wanted something that would raise national consciousness and lead to the students' future well-being. The merit of these Korean readers, to my mind, depended on the degree to which their form and content met these standards. . . . Let me make clear what I was aiming for in these Korean readers. To be perfectly frank, I wanted to fashion, through these readers, a people that yearned for peace. . . . Koreans had a strong sense of their own cultural superiority vis-á-vis the Japanese. Without injuring their pride, I wanted to educate them about the unceasing nature of change in this world, and the fact that there is no point clinging vainly to old ideas.[13]

Granted that this was written by Ashida after the war, we need not necessarily discount its sincerity. Ashida's goal of "raising national consciousness" might have seemed problematic to the Governor General at the time, but even this idea is fully elaborated in the lines that follow. That is to say, for Ashida the "national consciousness" of the Korean people was the consciousness of a people "that yearn for peace," which in the face of the "unceasing change" of contemporary reality, meant acquiescing to Japanese rule and not "clinging vainly" to old ideas, such as independence or national self-determination.

The general themes, which we see here, of Ashida Enosuke's *kokugo* education do not reproduce in any immediate way the "politics of the Governor General," infamous for depriving the Korean people of their national consciousness, of their names, and of traditional culture. Regardless of whether or not Ashida Enosuke's *kokugo* textbooks actually did raise national consciousness, one can say that materials derived from Korean sources are relatively well represented in his texts, and they appear somewhat estranged from the imperialist project of forcibly eradicating ethnic Korean culture. However, if one were to invoke Aesop's fabled analogy of the "north wind and the sun," one is led to say that Ashida—by contrast to the Governor-General's "north wind"—merely adopts the "softer" role of the "sun," ultimately affirming the legitimacy of control of Korea by Japan, and playing a supporting role in bringing it to fruition.

In *Blessed by Rain*, Ashida also writes:

> Whenever Koreans gather to talk, one hears the phrase, "we are without a country." But are they really without a country? To be sure, the name "Korea" (*Kankoku*) exists no more. But have they not secured all the rights enjoyed by citizens under the mantle of Japan? Though this is as plain as daylight, a veil seems to lie over the eyes of Koreans, which keeps them from reflecting on the obvious. They bring misery on themselves by clinging to some kind of obsession.[14]

Though called on to pay taxes, the "peninsula people" had neither voting rights nor the right to become candidates in elections. Also, though sea passage from Japan to Korea was virtually unrestricted, passage in the other direction required identification papers showing official permission (required of Koreans only). Koreans were made to memorize an "Oath of Loyalty as an Imperial Subject" unheard of on the mainland, and, while Korean soldiers were conscripted for "volunteer service" near the end of the war, privileges and rights commensurate with that duty were not forthcoming. Thus, we can discern in Ashida's claim that the Koreans had "secured all the rights enjoyed by citizens" the rationalization of one who had shut his eyes to systematic prejudice in occupied Korea. Ashida Enosuke probably knew of this discrimination. Perhaps he rationalized these measures as reflecting Japan's role as teacher for "late-developing Koreans," who were not fully mature (the right to vote, for example, cannot be exercised by children.). Since administration of the colonies under imperialism was done under the facade of "education" (which could be seen as consonant with the imperial ideology of "compassion for all under one gaze" or *isshi dōjin*), it could also lead to adoption of blatantly discriminatory practices and systems under the guise of an elder brother's tutelage of younger siblings, or a father's guidance of his son. Within this framework, such practices could be merely seen as pedagogical measures, completely unrelated to ethnic prejudice.

Ashida Enosuke became swept up in this fraudulent "pedagogical" logic. Just as in the Meiji era it had seemed natural to restrict suffrage on the basis of tax payments, or to legitimize gender discrimination through the allocation of political rights, the inclusion of "mainland Japanese" and "peninsular people" under the title of "citizen" made the structure of discrimination in occupied Korea invisible to people like Ashida. Still, if Korean students were members of the same imperial realm, why could they have not simply used the state-approved readers used on the mainland? It was Ashida who seemed to be unaware of the way in which his own work was being carried along by the tide of such discriminatory pedagogy—discrimination carried out through education. In occupied Korea, Ashida sought to persuade Koreans lamenting the loss of their homeland of the greatness of Japan, and to lead them into compliance with Japanese demands.

WRITING PEDAGOGY: FREE COMPOSITION

Ashida Enosuke's legacy in the world of *kokugo* education has been chiefly defined by the unique method of "composition pedagogy" (*tsuzuri-kata kyōiku*) he developed.[15] It was said to be Ashida's theory and pedagogical practice, known as "free composition," that effected the transition, in Japanese schools, to a modern composition class from old-style, practically oriented, rhetorical training in which students learned by copying famous essays, or model compositions using the classical styles, *sōrōbun*, and other epistolary styles.[16] Under methods in favor until Ashida's time, the instructor would propose a "theme" and have students compose something in accordance with it. By contrast, Ashida's method called for students to freely choose a theme and write about it in whatever manner they deemed suitable. In his book, *An Easy Method for Teaching Japanese* (*Kokugo Kyōiku Igyōdō*, 1935) he describes his method to his readers:

> I think the notion of free composition I have developed has its core in what I learned from my teachers Okada Torajirō and the venerable Takeo Raishō of Sōjiji temple. Children are at ease in this world, and I have to bow my head in admiration when I look at their spontaneous, artless productions. I don't need to offer examples—each of you has abundant evidence close at hand. As children get older and continue to be trained in schools, their writing gains a certain refinement, but that sparkle fades.
>   When I realized this, I began to think that there is nothing more precious than the daily life in which one is immersed. In one's own daily life, all is direct and immediate. At happy things, one rejoices; at painful things, one grieves. This rejoicing and grieving are not another's, rather for each, they are his or her own. They require no explanation and brook no interference from another.[17]

If the best writing is produced by children who "are at ease in this world," writing spontaneously and artlessly, the meaning of an education that only causes this quality to deteriorate might seem to be in question. But Ashida's theory of composition was concentrated around such notions of naturalness and lack of artifice. With his belief that "there is nothing as inspiring as one's own life," Ashida, indeed, can be regarded as the forerunner of the postwar concept of "writing from life" (*seikatsu tsuzurikata*). He advocated making the joys and sorrows of this life the basis of composition. The very phrase "*seikatsu tsuzurikata*" occurs in his works, and the fundamental tenets of the extraordinary revival, within postwar education, of the "writing from daily life movement" were drawn from his theories.

In Ashida's view, all human beings have the innate capacity to "compose." The young minds who learn to read and write *kokugo* in the course of regular, primary education are already equipped with this talent. Ashida appears to assume that, if one is a speaker of Japanese, one has only to learn to write in order to be able to produce compositions. Thus, he also states: "I believe that composition is a precious mode of self-cultivation. I may not be able to write in an elegant style. But I lack for nothing when it comes to writing down whatever floats through my mind. That this ability has been granted to me, as to every other human being, is something for which I am truly grateful. To be deprived of this would be to be condemned to existence as a mere lump of flesh."[18]

The capacity to compose, to "set down the things that come to mind"— that is to say, the capacity for self-expression through the national language—is, for Ashida, one of the natural rights of man. His belief approaches the religious. In *Exercises in Self-Cultivation for Instructors of Composition*, he argued that, in teaching composition, it is important to cultivate the self.[19] It goes without saying that this idea of "self-cultivation" resembles the kind of modern popular devotional practices that have roots in the quasi-religious tradition of Edo Shingaku. Underlying Ashida's pedagogical zeal was the unique notion of composition as a kind of religious discipline, entailing both self-cultivation and meditational practice. Such religious zeal must have been almost infectious in its ability to appeal to those teaching language for Imperial Japan, which would explain the remarkable popularity of Ashida's language-teaching and composition pedagogies.

As anyone who has experienced primary-school education will recall, however, there is no assignment in composition more difficult than to be told to set down freely whatever comes to one's mind. This is because nothing comes freely to mind when one is sitting down facing a blank piece of paper. One may be told to choose material from daily life, but the trifling joys and sorrows of daily existence hardly seem worthy of being set down in writing. During such composition periods, students sit perplexed, chewing the stubs of their pencils.

Write of "your daily life." Write "whatever comes to mind." Facilitating this operation requires that the fundamental principle of composition pedagogy be the freedom to write about whatever one chooses. Ashida Enosuke seized on this principle with such fervor it might be better to speak of "free composition" as an ideology. The meaning of terms like "self" (*jibun*), "life" (*seikatsu*), and "mind" (*kokoro*) are not self-evident. Rather, to see such things as self-evident, natural, and inherent in all beings is modern ideology par excellence. It is under the influence of such an ideology, taken to be self-evident, that composition students have had to labor to construct "their own lives," and what is in "their own hearts."

We can see this ideology at work in the writings of one of Ashida's followers, Suzuki Miekichi, who left his mark in the field of Japanese children's literature and the pedagogy and practice of children's composition as the editor and publisher of the journal *Red Bird* (*Akai tori*), published between 1918 and 1929, and then again from 1931 to 1936.[20] Suzuki encouraged children to use everyday language to set experiences down just exactly as they occurred. These views were, of course, resonant with Ashida's principles of composition. In both cases, the child was first recognized as a writing subject, in whom is apprehended the ability to write, and the study of composition is defined as a process of drawing out that latent capacity. In this sense, what one finds in Ashida's and Suzuki's notion of "free composition" expresses the essentials of the ideology governing modern writing in Japan as it had developed from *genbun itchi* to *shaseibun*.[21]

Suzuki Miekichi sought to popularize the methods of *tsuzurikata* education that Ashida Enosuke had propagated in the public schools. He called on readers to submit their compositions to *Red Bird*, ranked them according to categories such as "masterpiece" or "editor's choice," and published them in a volume entitled *A Composition Reader* (*Tsuzurikata dokuhon*).[22] In Part One of this reader, Suzuki featured children's compositions, while, in Part Two, he developed his own theories on composition and pedagogy. A number of works found in Part One are by Toyota Masako, the "girl genius of composition" discovered by *Red Bird*. Later, a volume called *Composition Classroom* (*Tsuzurikata kyôshitsu*) was published, devoted solely to writings by Toyota.[23] Suzuki gave considerable space to criticism of the children's essays featured in Part One of the *Reader*. He discussed strong points and particularly fine passages in meticulous detail and was sympathetic and thorough in the best tradition of practical composition pedagogy. We get a vivid sense in these writings of Suzuki Miekichi as educator. In Part Two, entitled "Composition as a Means of Educating the Human Being," he criticizes without remorse the deficiencies of the older tradition of composition education. He also develops his own views on composition, with emphasis on the idea of description or "sketching from life" (*seikatsu no shajitsu*)." In Part Two, we find the following:

Material for children's composition should, in general, be sought in the events of everyday life. This means that what we are looking for is none other than a record of ordinary, day-to-day life. The artistic value in this comes from the immediacy with which it is recorded. It is the value of description in its true sense. This is the ultimate standard for judging what may be achieved through composition.

One shouldn't view this kind of activity patronizingly, finding in it only the value of recording life as it is. To be human is to have an instinctive need to reproduce what one has experienced—whether by talking to others, or by drawing, sculpting, or writing about social and natural phenomena.

In composition based on "sketching from life," one experiences the true pleasure of art as a means of reproducing life. The reader, too, finds artistic meaning in this writing, and can discover the pleasures of writing about life in the truest sense, laughing at the sheer humor of everyday events, and the like.

As I will discuss in the sections to follow, there is a tempering of the spirit that takes place when a child gradually learns to "sketch from life," and, through the process, a child's emotions, sensibilities, and critical skills are deepened and sharpened. Insofar as composition augments and deepens a child's humanity, an important educational significance can be gleaned from it.[24]

For Suzuki Miekichi, the pleasure of reproducing experience and the capacity to do description (*shajitsu*) are predicated on an ability to express one's thoughts, feelings, and experiences just as they are. Like Ashida Enosuke, Suzuki stresses the child's experience of life, and conceives of composition as a mode of description that can be taken directly from life. It would be no exaggeration to say that the sources of realism as a literary style in Japan should be sought, not so much in Naturalist literature or Proletarian literature as in the methods of "composition from daily life" taught to children beginning in the Taisho period. It is, at any rate, true that, insofar as Toyota Masako's prewar *Composition Classroom* or other postwar collections of school children's writings such as *Echo School (Yamabiko gakkō,* 1951), *The Yamaimo Anthology (Shishū yamaimo,* 1951), *Nyan-chan (Nyan-chan,* 1956), and *Tsuzurikata Brothers and Sisters (Tsuzurikata kyōdai,* 1958) won a wide readership and were acclaimed as literary works of surpassing "realism," they gained currency and circulated more broadly among the general public than the work of professional writers.[25]

When Suzuki Miekichi speaks of "a recording of daily life," or of "reproduction," and "description," and when he speaks of "augmenting and deepening humanity," his ideas overlap with the principles of humanism and asceticism Ashida Enosuke urged upon instructors of *tsuzurikata* composition. While the journal *Red Bird* is often associated with a humanistic vision, this was not the humanistic thought of European modernity. Rather, the journal advocates a kind of philosophy of life based on self-cultivation, one that places the highest priority on human life and humanism. In answer to the question, "What is human life?" it urges readers to gaze into their "own hearts," to gaze at whatever floats up spontaneously from within. Though at first glance it may appear to be a kind of humanism, this philosophy of "self-cultivation" is different. The "humanism" (*jindōshugi*) of Mushanokōji Saneatsu and other members of the Shirakaba-ha, for example, was unable to take any kind of a critical stance toward the war of aggression waged by the Japanese Empire, or toward currents in the *bundan* such as the Japanese Literature Patriotic Society (*Nihon Bungaku Hōkokukai*).[26] Mushanokōji's brand of "humanism" found no contradiction between the pursuit of self-realization and exhaustive self-knowledge, and conducting oneself in accordance with the will of an imperialist nation-state.

Suzuki Miekichi's "humanism" cannot be exempted from this kind of criticism either. A "realism" unaccompanied by a critical spirit finds itself powerless to push beyond a sketch-like chronicling of life as it is. In the children's essays selected by Suzuki for compilation, we find many that take as their theme extreme poverty, social contradictions, and so forth. But these, of course, go no further than "description" through a child's eye. Since the goal of these individual compositions is a "re-presentation" of things, impoverished living conditions appear just as they are, social contradictions are accepted for what they are, and matters cannot be taken even a step further. What Suzuki Miekichi sought to exclude was abstraction, or whatever had to do with ideals (*kannen*)—that is, any material that was conceptual or detached from the sphere of children's daily life. The following essay was singled out in *A Composition Reader* for particularly negative treatment:

> In each of the world's sixty-odd countries is a set of colors with the country's insignia, which we call the national flag. The flag of our Japanese Empire is the rising sun flag.
>
> The figure cut by the rising sun flag glittering proudly in the dawn light perfectly embodies the plentiful energy of our Japan. When the Japanese people celebrate auspicious days like holidays and days of big festivals, we display the flag. We also fly the rising sun flag from the merchant ships, military vessels, and airplanes of our Japanese Empire. The national colors are also known as the "sacred pennant of the sun." Our country is located to the east of China and India, and so it is said that it is called "*nihon*" ("source of the sun"). This is why our flag is called "*hi no maru*" ("orb of the sun") and takes the shape of the heavenly sphere.
>
> My father told me the story of last year's Olympics, where the athlete Nanbe stood in for Oda in the triple jump because of Oda's leg injury. When he described how Nambe took first place, even though it

wasn't his specialty, and the rising sun flag was raised to the highest place on the mast, I was so happy I jumped for joy.

I am going to apply myself with all my strength to the task of learning and become a fine citizen, and devote myself to seeing our national flag raised in the farthest corners of the earth.[27]

Suzuki Miekichi commented sarcastically that the only impression he received from this work by a fourth-grade boy was of "the harshness involved in assigning a child this difficult topic, and extracting from him this stilted prose." But from the perspective of teaching composition in imperial Japan, this might seem to be an example of truly ideal "*sakubun*" in practice, and one might question whether Suzuki's impression that it was completely divorced from daily life was not itself a kind of prejudice. The saga of the athletes Oda and Nanbe at the Olympics circulated widely in Japanese society at the time, and it was quite plausible to imagine Japanese citizens and other imperial subjects (whether self-consciously or not) strongly moved by the sight of the rising sun flag flying on the main flagpole. There is no reason, in fact, to assume that even "jumping for joy" was anything but "natural" and described in this essay "just as it happened." While it may be difficult to imagine that a child's immediate feelings could be embodied in a phrase like "our Japanese Empire," this kind of formulaic expession was universally disseminated at the site of primary education at the time. One cannot simply erase these conditions, rejecting as too "idea-oriented" (*kannenteki*) the compositions submitted by patriotic little soldiers like this one.

In the so-called *Flag, Octopus, Top* (*Hata, Tako, Koma*) edition of the Ministry of Education approved second-generation textbooks (1910–1917), the rising sun flag occupies a full page illustration. As a symbol of the Japanese Empire, the image of the flag was a part of the indoctrination of new students in public primary education from its inception, and the notion that "the figure cut by the rising sun flag glittering proudly in the dawn light perfectly embodies the plentiful energy of our Japan" was indeed drilled into the heads of children and students in daily teaching . In 1891, the Ministry of Education had issued orders to each school to "take the portraits of His Majesty the Emperor and her majesty the Empress that had been distributed to each school and integrate them into the education process. Take the official copy of the Rescript on Education and assign it a fixed spot, so that it becomes the most hallowed place on the school grounds," thereby making reverence to the esteemed visage a duty. The rituals of imperialism, such as the obeisance to the shrine in each schoolyard housing the imperial visage and the copy of the Rescript (*hōanden*), and the custom of bowing in the direction of the imperial palace (*kyūjō yōhai*) were carried out on school grounds continuously from the Meiji period into the 1940s. Suzuki's rejection of essays whose content was too idea-oriented, at a time when school children from their earliest years of education were repeatedly spoken to about "beautiful and stalwart" symbols of empire, can only be deemed an ideological preoccupation with a different kinds of ideas. Suzuki indeed celebrated as "realistic" documentation of everyday life essays that did not depart from children's immediate experience of everyday life—"Fishing," "Fire," "Death of a Close Relative," "The New Bride," and "Festivals"— and did not select as "editor's choice" or "masterpiece" anything that deviated from such themes.

One can see here the contradictions of *tsuzurikata* education, as they were encapsulated in Ashida Enosuke's pithy comment that the higher one's educational level the more the content of composition suffered. For Suzuki, the immediate description of daily life in the school, the family, or the village community counted as material for "composition from daily life," while the content of what was taught, and the ceremonial life of school did not, and could not, become objects of "realistic description." This is analogous to the contradictions of imperialism we find in Ashida Enosuke's words cited above, in which he expressed the desire to raise the national consciousness of the Korean people at the same time that he exhorted them to become Japanese. Both Suzuki and Ashida instructed children to set down "just as it is" the things that come from within, "freely" and "of their own accord." Effectively, one might go so far as to say that under the name of education, this composition instruction brought the child's interior, or personal ways of thinking and feeling, under the bureaucratic observation and control of empire.

IMPERIALIST CONSCIOUSNESS IN "COMPOSITION" (*SAKUBUN*)

The following is a poem called "The Hundred-Day Pilgrimage" written by a Japanese woman student:

Hyakunichi kigan

ieie wa makkuro de	Dark houses line the way
hito wa mada neteiru noni	the rest of the world is still asleep
watashitachi wa Dairen Jinja *e aruiteiru*	but we are marching to Dairen Jinja
jidōsha wa donatte tōtte mo	Automobiles go screaming by
ashioto niwa kawari ga nai	but we don't lose a step
hyakunichikigan no ashioto *wa nigoranai*	the footsteps of the hundred-day pilgrimage are never sullied
daichi no hochō wa midarenai	in step with the great earth we cannot be scattered
ashioto yo	You, footsteps!
tsuki yo	You, moonlight!
kaze yo	You, breeze!

otōto yo   Little brother!
Nihon yo   Japan!
minna Nihon yo!   All is Japan![28]

This poem describes the practice of getting up before dawn for a hundred days to perform devotions at a shrine, but it is hard to tell what is being prayed for. From the fact that it was included in a volume called *Round Robin: A Collection of Poems by Schoolgirls* (*Joseigakushishū: Junsōkyū*, 1939), published after the so-called "China Incident" in 1937, one might guess that these "supplications" had something to do with the progress of the war between China and Japan. From the final lines ("Little brother! / Japan! / All is Japan!"), one might surmise that this hundred-day pilgrimage was to pray for Japan's victory in battle.

According to the flowery preface by the editor Nishihara Shigeru, this volume was drawn from work done by the students of the Dalian Yayoi Girl's Higher School. Nishihara wrote, "Japan is in the process now of conducting the greatest military advance since the founding of the nation. Both generosity of spirit and resources of time and money went into the publication of this book: that we are at this point in time blessed with both is due to the beneficence of this glorious imperial reign. It is with pure hearts, humbly offered, that we enter on the path of the *kotodama*, and I, along with our young women, express our most fervent gratitude on this occasion."[29]

The significance of this collection of women students' verse being published, not on the Japanese mainland, but in the city of Dalian in Kwantō (Liaoning) Province is evident from the editor's words. (This is said to have been the first publication in Japan of a poetry collection by women students.) That these young "daughters of Yamato" (*Yamato nadeshiko*) chanted "All is Japan!" for one hundred days at the Dalian shrine in the heart of Japan's colony of Manchukuo illustrates the degree to which the imperial will had come to penetrate the East Asia Co-Prosperity Sphere.

As a matter of fact, in Dalian at that time a great deal of energy was being poured into instructing the children of Japanese residents in composition and poetry. The verse collection *Round Robin* was part of a phenomenon whereby Dalian was becoming a Mecca of sorts for composition in Japanese. One of the specialists in *kokugo* pedagogy in Dalian was named Ishimori Nobuo, a promoter of instruction in composition, and well-known writer of children's literature.[30] Ishimori held the chair in the *kokugo* section at Dalian Yayoi Girl's Higher School at the same time Nishihara Shigeru was a *kokugo* instructor there. Nishihara contributed an essay to the encomium *In Memory of Ishimori Sensei* (*Ishimori Sensei no omoide*), noting that it was Ishimori who first told him about the writer Miyazawa Kenji.[31] This essay suggests that Nishihara looked up to Ishimori Nobuo in a personal way that went beyond the usual relation of junior and senior in the workplace. Over the course of his 10-year residence in Manchukuo, Ishimori authored a research volume on composition pedagogy called *The Path to Good Composition* (*Tsuzurikata e no michi*), in addition to managing and publishing a journal called *Sail* (*Ho*).[32] Ishimori's, then, was a theory and practice of composition developed not in the Japanese "homeland" but in the "outlying" territories (*gaichi*).

Ishimori Nobuo's position as an educator, researcher, and writer of children's stories was actually more prominent in the postwar period than during the war. His works *Whistling in Kotan* (*Kotan no kuchibue*) and *Mount Sengen* (*Sengendake*) are both well-known as classics of children's literature. His contributions to, and influence on, *kokugo* education as an editor of the first postwar *kokugo* textbooks is therefore not to be underestimated. Under the banner of a postwar democracy supposedly freed from the yokes of imperialism and militarism, the *kokugo* textbooks were compiled with an eye to developing reading and writing as the free and independent activity of students. Reading and writing were means to fostering such qualities as rational thought, the spirit of scientific inquiry, social conscience, and an active and critical disposition. In place of the militarism, imperialism, or so-called "remnants of feudalism" that characterized the coercive patriarchal morality that prevailed earlier, we see in the textbooks of this period a groping for an American-style system of "democratic education." Postwar *kokugo* textbooks were infused with this spirit.

There is no question that the production of essays in composition class played an important role in postwar *kokugo* education, with its concern for actively cultivating students who could formulate and articulate their own thinking. It is said that the *kokugo* textbooks published in 1947 in tandem with the launching of the new six-year–three-year system of primary and secondary education were heavily colored by the thinking of Ishimori, who was head of the editorial group. In the sense that these textbooks laid stress on the student's personal self-expression, they were called *hyōgen dokuhon* ("primers in expression").[33] One might say that in emphasizing the student's self-expression, the active, assertive behavior of learning about things through writing about them or thinking about them was rather over-emphasized. In other words, the passive matters of "reading" and "understanding" were neglected in order to stress the active matter of "writing." In all of this, it is possible to see the influence of Ishimori Nobuo, who had been specializing in composition pedagogy since before the war, and his personal outlook, theory of composition, and distinctive view of *kokugo* textbooks.

It is easy, in turn, to discern affinities between Ishimori Nobuo and Ashida Enosuke. Both left outstanding accomplishments in the theory and practice of *kokugo* and composition. But more importantly, in both cases, these achievements in the field of *kokugo* were generated in Japan's "peripheries"—the colonial territories. Ashida Enosuke produced his *kokugo* readers for the children of Korea and the South Sea Islands. Ishimori Nobuo's energy was poured into composition instruction for the Japanese children in Manchukuo, for whom he produced the *Supplemental Reader for the Manchukuo Territories*. But the affinity does not stop there. It would appear that there was a fundamental similarity in principles undergirding their outlook on composition.

In 1949, Ishimori wrote:

> As I have said in the past, composition should not be force-fitted into forms and genres. Students should write whatever they want to write. It doesn't matter what it is, if something is captured in characters and written down, that constitutes composition practice. Help children cultivate the space that is their innermost heart, and modes of expression heretofore undreamed of will blossom.[34]

The thinking embodied here is clearly similar to Ashida's notion of "free composition." Ashida's admonition for students to "write down whatever comes to mind" and Ishimori's admonition that students would do best to "write whatever they want to write" are ultimately headed in the same direction. The difference is that whereas the "humanist" bent of Ashida's ideas on education had the potential to be regarded as dangerous thought in the context of Japanese society under imperialism, Ishimori's advice to students to "write whatever you want to write" was rooted securely in a democratic postwar contrition over the tendency of prewar composition to rob students of independence and initiative by its formalism and fastidiousness about genre. Ishimori, no less than Ashida, departed not one iota from trends of the times. Less a question of what to write and how to write than an attempt to cultivate the independent creative impulse from which that springs, his method stressed individualism and the power to make statements. In seeing that an important task of education lies in drawing these capacities out of students, Ishimori's methods were also quite in line with the latest in progressive educational thought in the United States.

We must stress, however, that the outline of Ishimori Nobuo's principles and methodology of composition were in fact already in place while he was in Dalian in the colonial territory of Manchukuo. The arguments on composition that appear in the postwar are little more than a repackaging of ideas already given shape in the prewar *Path to Good Composition*. In his postwar volume he writes: "To put it another way, one shouldn't conceive of composition as a lesson that begins after pen or pencil is taken up. An important lesson is taking place before the student or child ever takes pen or pencil in hand, in fostering in his or her mind something that merits writing down. Before a child ever sits down before a blank sheet of paper, there must be enfolded within the child's consciousness a content so fresh and stimulating that it can barely be contained. When one has been able to stimulate a child's creative urge so that it reaches this level of intensity, it is no exaggeration to say that the task of composition instruction is 99% complete."[35]

There remains the prior question of how one discovers "something worth writing about" or "what one wants to write about." One senses a circularity in such phrases. Ishimori's notion that it is best for students to "write whatever they want to write" naturally leads to the question of how to draw out what the child or student "wants to write," which is not far from the question of whether something is to be "sown" for later harvesting. Recalling the girl student's poem that began this section, clearly, the theme of the "hundred-day pilgrimage" was spontaneous for the girl, and actively generated the verses "Little brother! / Japan! / All is Japan!" This hundred-day pilgrimage to pray for victory in battle suggested itself to her mind as a poetic theme, and she "wanted to write" these verses that came so vividly to her mind while on the road to Dalian Jinja. In this light, it is clear that the composition principle of letting the children write whatever they want to write about is in no sense a posture of resistance to topics that have to do with imperialism, but rather makes possible an unreserved affirmation of the logic of the composition of empire. This is less a forcible imposition on children of imperialism or a colonialist consciousness, than an effective strategy for implanting such a consciousness that would then well up from within a child's innermost feelings.

We find this passage in the above-mentioned *Path to Good Composition*:

> The facile view that, insofar as the act of composition is the transposition of words into written characters, mere glibness suffices to guarantee good composition, is a serious misconception. Furthermore, it is risky to assume that, because the act of stringing together characters is instinctive, if simply left alone, the ability to produce compositions will arise of itself. It is true of written characters just as of spoken words— if there is not some necessity to do so, one will not learn to use them.
>
> On the outskirts of Harbin, there is a monument to the legendary stalwarts Yokogawa and Oki. Each time I think of that story, I am taught anew that words are not something that can be forced into speech from outside. Disguised as Mongols, these two Japanese soldiers were taken prisoner by the Russian Army and interrogated, "You two are Japanese, aren't you . . . " But they wouldn't utter a word. This is the meaning of keeping one's silence. But when the time comes to speak, there is no holding back the words. . . . Words are the final refuge, and when the urge comes to speak, the words bubble forth. Even prayers are nothing less than spontaneous words to the gods.
>
> Words, like the fountain that gushes forth spontaneously with a rainbow in its spray, are a mysterious life form that cannot be revived by outside force once they have died away. *Kotodama* (the spirit of words) has existed from before the *Manyōshū*, and even now is hidden in every phrase and utterance.[36]

Here, the site at which language is produced is cloaked in a kind of mysticism. The question of why humans utter words is answered with a tautology: "When the urge comes to speak, out the words bubble forth." Ishimori uses the archaic term *kotodama* as another way of defining "something worth writing," "whatever one wants to write about," and "creative urge." Rather than being a substantive explanation, this word creates an even more mystical sense of language, which can only be described with references to a "spirit" of writing or of culture. Following this line of reasoning, children's composition, too, can only be grasped as a mysterious effect of *kotodama*.

Children are well aware that being told to "write whatever you want to write" is not the same as being told that they don't need to write if they don't want to. To be told to "write whatever you want" is, rather, a command to come up with the desire to write about something willy-nilly—the so-called "urge to create" is nothing other than this. In such a situation, themes that would truly emerge freely and spontaneously would be a function a number of interrelated factors such as the historical and social context of the time, the abilities of the composition instructor, and the creative capacity of the students. In the examples we have just seen, a fourth-year student in the 1930s chose the national flag and a female student in Manchuria selected the hundred-day pilgrimage, while the postwar students whose work was anthologized in *School In the Mountains* chose their own experiences of poverty in everyday life. This continuity between prewar and postwar composition education is aptly symbolized by the resonances in thinking between the representative prewar and postwar leaders in the field, Ashida Enosuke and Ishimori Nobuo. Ishimori's respect for, and acknowledgement of, Ashida as his mentor or may be glimpsed throughout the essay he wrote commemorating Ashida's death.[37] In this essay, Ishimori also describes soliciting an essay from Ashida while he was compiling his postwar *kokugo* textbooks, although the essay, " The Cosmos as Writing" (*Banbutsu wa moji nari*) ran into difficulties with Occupation censors and was ultimately dropped. Their relation was deep in many other ways, too, and there can be no question of the spiritual affinity underlying their approaches to composition pedagogy.

It seems fair to say that, in the end, Ishimori Nobuo, like Ashida Enosuke, harbored virtually no doubts about policies toward language, writing, and the imposition of *kokugo* under the Japanese Empire. In one of his children's stories called "Coming to Japan" (*Nihon ni kite*, 1941) we find a character uttering these lines:

You see what I mean, don't you? People speaking German must be German, and people speaking Russian are Russian. But most important, if a little fellow like you is speaking to me in Japanese, why, it's because we're both Japanese, isn't it?[38]

When one reads these words, it is not readily apparent that their author was a man with long experience in Manchukuo at a time when its official slogan had been "Five Tribes, One Republic" (*gozoku kyōwa*). In Manchukuo, in fact, there were at least three different languages spoken (Japanese, Manchurian or "Chinese", and Mongol), and its governors sought to bring about a situation where the Manchurian (Han Chinese), Korean, and Mongol peoples could all use "Japanese" as their national language. And as a matter of fact, the majority of "non-Japanese" in the territory—from Koreans to the people of Taiwan and Manchuria—were able to attain a functional fluency in the Japanese language. But even in this historical context, it was clearly not justifiable to assume that a person using the Japanese language was "Japanese." It is only the myth of a homogeneous ethnic unity, wherein the frames of national language, national citizenship and race coincide, that makes the speech above plausible. From such a standpoint, however, the kind of multi-ethnicity and linguistic pluralism implied in the motto "five tribes, one republic" can only be seen as a travesty.

> Skies so beautiful, Manchuria!
> We, we are the children of Manchuria!

These lines in Japanese, written by Ishimori Nobuo himself, which grace the very first page of the *Supplemental Reader for the Manchukuo Territories*, indeed amount to a fairly straightforward claim over Manchurian territories in the name of the children of these Japanese-speaking Japanese people. In another short story by Ishimori that takes "five tribes, one republic" as its theme, we find expressed this frankly imperialist view of race:

> Well, things will all work out. Weren't we just talking about this a little while ago? The best thing for the mental outlook of Japanese living on the continent is to be able to speak Japanese beautifully and correctly. And there's one more thing. When we use the Japanese language, we have to be absolutely sure to treat foreigners with whom we may be speaking with respect and love. The reason the Chinese have become such a misguided race is that they have been so downtrodden by various foreign powers. It's warped them somehow.[39]

What is clearly revealed in this speech from the tale of "A Youth Brigade Reaching Its Peak" (*Sakidasu shōnengun*) is a sense of linguistic hegemony, a belief in the superiority of the language called "Japanese" as a medium of expression for the youth of empire. And certainly, if we can see in these words a kind of "unconscious imperialist consciousness," we would have to say that such attitudes were fostered in Dalian under Japanese colonial occupation by the composition pedagogy that was one part of *kokugo* instruction. Of course, this is not to imply that Ishimori alone was responsible for the propagation of such attitudes. One can find similar views expressed, for example, in a book by Ishimori's contemporary, Miyatake Shirokichi, who published his report *Observations on the Present State of Reading Instruction in Manchuria* (*Manshū ni okeru gendai yomikata kyōiku no ichikōsatsu*) in 1936. "Manchukuo should be the headquarters of national expansion based on language. Those of us who work as cultural facilitators here on the frontlines have been blessed with the opportunity—which is also our destiny—of carrying out pioneering activities under the banner of our *kokugo* policy." As for "children of the Japan proper," he writes, "because they are as yet few in this land, we must quickly provide them with that efficacious weapon of *kokugo*." Miyatake urges that "the people of Manchuria must be made to understand that if they do not use Japanese it will work to their disadvantage, while those employing Japanese will find it redounds to their benefit."[40]

In any case, by looking at such documents we can hardly escape the conclusion that proliferation in Manchuria of research on Japanese language pedagogy and composition pedagogy (as well as their practical application) was rooted in the unfolding of a "consciousness of empire." The "outlying region" of Manchuria, in fact, might be seen as a kind of experimental classroom where methods that became the basis for postwar education policies in these two areas were tested. This could not have occurred had there not been an inextricable relationship between the institutionalization of *kokugo* pedagogy, including the teaching of composition in *kokugo*, and Japanese imperialism, which extended to the consciousness of empire of each of its members. We can see such a consciousness expressed in the following examples, culled from collections of student compositions compiled by Japanese-language instructors working for the colonial governments of Korea and Taiwan.[41]

Our school just got a new national flag. Every Monday we have a colors ceremony. This happened one morning when we were all at colors.

We lined up in the playground and, facing east, we paid our deepest respect to the Emperor, then faced our teachers and gave the morning bow. When that was done our teacher gave the order, "Right, face! Half right, face! All face the flag." We all concentrated on the flag. As we watched the colors rising to the strains of *Kimi ga yo*, which echoed softly from the phonograph, our heads bowed spontaneously and our minds were at attention. The teacher shouted the command, "*Saikeirei!*"[42] With gratitude in our hearts, we all made our deepest obeisance to the Emperor.

—Korean primary school student

When I was in public school, we had a lot of trouble distinguishing between "da" and "ra" and "do" and " ro." We would say "ra" in place of "da," and "da" in place of "ra," and just couldn't make them sound different. One day, during reading hour, the teacher wrote on the board, *"dorodoro shita doromichi ni, yoidore ga koronde dorodarake ni narimashita."* The teacher started at one end of the room and made us say it one by one, but there wasn't a single student who got it right from beginning to end.

When the bell rang and class was over, the teacher scolded us by saying, "Born Japanese and can't speak Japanese correctly! Why don't you leave and go to some other country?" . . . To be told I wasn't Japanese in this way made me burst into tears.

—Taiwanese girl student

My mother can't read, and can't speak the national language (*kokugo*). She isn't the kind of person who cooks from a book; she just tries making things she liked to eat as a child. Knowing this, we eat whatever she makes without complaining and, sure enough, what we eat with a smile, we grow to like. We talk about the day's events as we eat her delicious meals. We usually begin speaking in Taiwanese, but before you know it, we've shifted into *kokugo* and there is no stopping it. The four or five of us will chat as if it were the most natural thing in the world, but my mother, who can't speak the national language, just sits there listening. Occasionally, I'd glance at my mother with a start, drop my head, and speak in Taiwanese.

—Taiwanese girl student

In my school, the teachers thought anyone in the family could learn the national language, so we started getting sheets with one Japanese word a day to take home. I carried the first sheet straight home and put it up on the wall beside my desk. When my mother asked "What's that?" I said, "Well, it's the one-word-a-day plan!" From that time on my mother learned one word every day for me. She was very happy and tried so hard for me . . .

Now she speaks so nicely, she can say *nashi, ringo, kuchi, mimi,* "*Konbanwa,*" and "*Gohan wo agarinasai.*" Just the other day she said, "Teach me the Oath of Loyalty of the Imperial Subject," so I'm teaching her that.

—Korean grade school student

These essays are the fruits of *kokugo* education and composition instruction in the colonies. Taking material from their own daily lives, using the unadorned words they use everyday, these students are realistically describing, "just as they are," the actual conditions of their lives. The compositions record things that came to their minds spontaneously, without artifice or sham. It does not seem possible to read them as "flowery phrases," produced in a desperate attempt to conform to their teachers' desires. At the same time, what we see here are model essays produced by the "New Japanese" (*Shin Nihonjin*) students in the colonies. They are stunning products of the colonial education policies of Ashida and Ishimori, achieving just what these policies were designed to attain. They represent the ultimate triumph of their teaching methods. Here we see children in the colonies thinking in Japanese, composing in Japanese, and eventually reaching the point where they think of themselves as "Japanese." They are consummate models of "Japaneseness," who more than correspond to the subject meant to be nurtured and formed by *kokugo* education, and training in composition, in modern Japan. And here the hypothesis of my essay reaches one conclusion, that "composition instruction" in modern Japan was a way of organizing an inner consciousness of empire in the children who constituted a reserve army, awaiting recruitment as loyal subjects of the Emperor.

Translated by Joseph Murphy

Notes

1. Nakajima Atsushi (1909–1942). Novelist. The son of a scholar of Chinese Studies, Nakajima lived in Korea and Manchuria as a child. In 1941, while he was teaching English and *kokugo* at a Yokohama girl's school, Nakajima accepted a position compiling public school textbooks for the South Seas Agency, partly for health reasons. Nakajima's principal works include *Light, Wind, and Dreams* (*Hikari to Kaze to Yume*, 1941) and *Moon Over the Mountains* (*Sangetsuki*, 1942). In the postwar period, the inclusion of *Sangetsuki* in middle- and high-school textbooks has made Nakajima better known as a writer than during his lifetime.

2. The last great king of Assyria, Ashurbanipal (r. 668–627 BC) assembled at Nineveh (present-day Mosul, Iraq) the first systematically organized library in the ancient Middle East. The scholar Nabuahe Eriba was Ashurbanipal's tutor and advisor.

3. Kawamura Minato, "*Ryūhyō to yashi no mi—Shōwa bungaku no 'kita' to 'minami'*," in Kawamura, *Nanyō, Karafuto no Nihon bungaku* (Tokyo: Chikuma Shobō, 1995), 159–166.

4. Nakajima Atsushi, *Nantōtan*, (Tokyo: Konnichinomondaisha, 1942). In this essay, I have consulted the text found in *Nakajima Atsushi zenshū*, Vol. 2 (Tokyo: Chikuma Shobō, 1993).

5. I have used the term "Japanese Language" to translate *kokugo* in this instance. During this period, *kokugo* (literally "national language") was used to refer only to the Japanese language, and not to other languages, such as Korean or Chinese. However, use of the term *kokugo* became increasingly ambiguous from 1910 to 1945, as Japanese colonial governments increasingly administered Japanese language instruction outside the "*kokudo*" (national territory). The ambiguity of the term is illustrated most clearly in the quotations from colonial student essays in the final section of this essay. *Kokugo* will be rendered in this

translation alternately as "national language" or the romanized "*kokugo*," as seems appropriate. A related set of terms that Kawamura uses in this essay is "*naichi/gaichi*," or "inner territory/outer territory," which was common usage during this period to distinguish Japan from the colonies. "*Naichi/gaichi*" will, in general, be rendered "mainland/outlying territories," though with the inevitable loss of symmetry. For a discussion of the pressure colonialism brought to bear on the term *kokugo*, see Kawamura's "*Nihongo no jidai*" in *Hihyō Kūkan* 11 (1993): 125–139. (Translator's Note)

6. Entitled *Tsushitara no shi* in manuscript, *Hikari to kaze to yume* (1941) details the life of Robert Louis Stevenson. The book *Kotan* (1940) is a collection of short stories.

7. Nakajima Atsushi, *Nakajima Atsushi zenshū*, Vol. 3 (Tokyo: Bunjidō Shoten, 1959), 379.

8. Ibid., Vol. 2, 457.

9. Noguchi Masaaki, *Gaichi*, (Tokyo: Kaiyō Bunkasha, 1942), 219–220.

10. Ashida Enosuke (1873–1951). Educator. Through such works as *Tsuzurikata Kyōju* (1913) and *Yomikata Kyōju* (1916), Ashida exercised great influence in *kokugo* education circles. He edited *kokugo* readers in the occupied territories of Korea and the South Sea Islands. A devotee of Okada Torajirō's *keiu* method of seated meditation, he incorporated this into his pedagogical practice, and made it the touchstone of his autobiography *Keiu jiden* (see following note).

11. Ashida Enosuke, "*Nanyō guntō kokugo dokuhon no henshū*," in *Keiu jiden*, vol. 1(Tokyo: Jissensha, 1972). The term *keiu*, containing the characters for "to be blessed" and "rain," is the name of a style of seated meditation advanced by Okada Torajirō and practiced by Ashida throughout his life.

12. See Fukuda Sumiko, "*Ashida Enosuke no Chōsen kokugo kyōkasho*" in *Kokugakuin Daigaku kyōiku kenkyûshitsu kiyō* 22 (March, 1987), and "*Ashida Enosuke no Nanyō guntō kokugo tokuhon*," in *Seijō bungei* 126 (March, 1989).

13. Ashida, "*Chōsen Sōtokufu henshūkan haimei*,"op. cit., 243–244.

14. Ashida, op. cit., 253.

15. From this point on, Kawamura uses the Japanese terms *tsuzurikata* and *sakubun* as synonyms for "composition" or essay-writing as taught in Japanese schools. Both terms actually designate the same subject. Composition in Japanese schools was known as *sakubun* in the Meiji period. However, in 1900, the Elementary School Law Enforcement Regulations changed the name to *tsuzurikata*. This was changed again in 1947, from *tsuzurikata* to *sakubun*, accompanied by considerable public debate. Because Kawamura's argument will ultimately posit a continuity between prewar *tsuzurikata* and postwar *sakubun*, both will be rendered "composition" and the reader may assume that prewar references are to *tsuzurikata* and postwar to *sakubun*. (Translator's Note)

16. Ashida used the term *zui-i sendai* (choosing one's subject in a free and spontaneous manner). (Translator's Note)

17. Ashida Enosuke, *Kokugo kyōiku igyōdō* (Tokyo: Dōshidōkōsha, 1935), 249.

18. Ibid.

19. Ashida Enosuke, *Tsuzurikata jugyō ni kansuru kyōshi no shūyō* (Tokyo: Ikuei Shoin, 1915).

20. Suzuki Miekichi (1882–1936). Inspired by Natsume Sōseki, Suzuki first emerged as a novelist, but ultimately devoted himself to the writing of children's literature. As the editor of the children's journal *Akai tori,* he secured contributions by Akutagawa Ryūnosuke, Kitahara Hakushū and other leading writers of the day. *Akai tori* also published essays written by children, and Suzuki's meticulous corrections and subsequent organization of these essays into published volumes gave him status as one of the founders of modern composition education in Japan.

21. *Genbun itchi* and *shaseibun,* respectively "unity of spoken and written languages" and "sketching from life," name movements around which a standardized style of Japanese literature emerged out of the diversity of classical, Chinese, and colloquial styles that circulated in the Edo period.

22. Suzuki Miekichi, *Tsuzurikata dokuhon* (Tokyo: Chūōkōronsha, 1935).

23. Ōki Kenichirō and Shimizu Kōji, eds. *Tsuzurikata kyōshitsu* (Tokyo: Chūōkōronsha, 1937).

24. Suzuki, *Tsuzurikata dokuhon,* 517.

25. *Yamabiko gakkō* was edited by Muchaku Seikyō (Tokyo: Seidōsha, 1951). The poetry collection formally entitled *Ōzeki Matsusaburōshishū: Yamaimo* was edited by Sagawa Michio (Tokyo: Yuri Shuppan, 1951). *Nyanchan* was edited by Yasuo Sueko (Tokyo: Kōbunsha, 1956). *Tsuzurikata* was edited by Nogami Tanji, Yōko, and Fusao (Tokyo: Rironsha, 1958).

26. The *Nihon Bungaku Hōkokukai* was established by the Japanese government in 1942 and given authority to approve the quantity and type of text produced by publishing facilities throughout the country.

27. Suzuki, *Tsuzurikata dokuhon,* 504–505.

28. Excerpted from Nishihara Shigeru, ed., *Jogakuseishishū: Junsōkyū* (Tokyo: Daiichi Shobō, 1939).

29. Ibid.

30. Ishimori Nobuo (1896–1987). *Kokugo* educator and writer of children's literature. In Manchuria, Ishimori compiled a supplementary *kokugo* reader and edited a journal on composition. A major influence on postwar composition pedagogy, he is best known for *Kotan no kuchibue,* a story about Ainu children.

31. Nishihara Shigeru, "*Hoshuburi,*" in *Ishimori-sensei no omoide,* published in 1967 by *Ishimori Nobuo Sensei Kyōiku Bungakuhi Kensetsu Sanjōkai*), 120.

32. Ishimori Nobuo, *Tsuzurikata e no michi* (Tokyo: Keibunsha, 1935).

33. See Ōuchi Zenichi, *Sengo sakubun kyōikushi kenkyū,* (Tokyo: Kyōiku Shuppan Sentaa, 1984), 35.

34. Ishimori Nobuo, *Kokugo kyōiku shotō* (Tokyo: Chūōsha, 1949), 262–263.

35. Ibid., 228.

36. Ishimori, *Tsuzurikata e no michi*, 23–25.

37. Ishimori, et al., *Kaisō no Ashida Enosuke* (Tokyo: Jissensha, 1957), 89–90.

38. Ishimori Nobuo, *Nihon ni kite* (Tokyo: Shinchōsha, 1941), 9.

39. Ishimori Nobuo, *Sakidasu shōnengun* (Tokyo: Shinchōsha, 1939), 254–255.

40. Miyatake Shirokichi, *Manshū ni okeru gendai yomikata kyōiku no ichikōsatsu* (A report presented to the *Kokugo* Department of Chiyoda Elementary School, Fengtian, China, 1936), 6–7.

41. The composition excerpts that follow have been taken from the following sources: *Shina zairyū Nihonjin shōgakusei: Tsuzurikata genchihōkoku*, Nii Itaru, ed. (Tokyo: Daiichi Shobō, 1939), 54–55; *Gaichi, Tairiku, Nanpō: Nihongo jugyō jissen*, edited and published by the Kokugo Bunka Gakkai, 1943; and *Nyūmon: Chōsen no rekishi*, edited by the Kokugo Bunka Kenkyūjō and the Chōsenshi Kenkyūkai (Tokyo: Sanseidō, 1986).

42. *Saikeirei* is the highest formal expression of respect, usually reserved for the emperor.

In Range of the Critique of Orientalism

Kang Sangjung

PHILOSOPHIES OF "DE-MODERNIZATION" AND "DE-WESTERNIZATION"

If we regard attempts to think a way out of modernity (*datsukindai no shisō*) as roughly coeval with attempts to articulate a philosophy of "escape from the west" (*datsuseiyō no shisō*), it is interesting to note that such attempts are by no means the monopoly of the non-west.[1] In fact, several daring attempts at de-westernization of thought have been undertaken in the heart of Europe itself.

One might consider the ideas of Max Weber, who, on the outbreak of the first Russian Revolution, attempted to discern in the future of the new Russia one last opportunity for the construction of the "free culture" that was disappearing before global capitalism's "virtually limitless" expansion.[2] Of course, Weber had the acumen to foresee that eventually a "mighty influx of western ideas" would mercilessly destroy the communism that rose out of old Russia's agrarian communities, and force Russia up capitalism's Hill of Golgotha.[3] But, in spite of this, or perhaps I should say, because of it, he had high hopes for a strong revival of "de-westernization thought" in western Europe's outer frontier, the half-European, half-Asian hybrid that was Russia.

It is important to note that Weber's hope for "de-westernization" was not paired with a hope for "de-modernization." On the contrary, modernity for Weber meant something akin to what it means in Hegelian historical philosophy: "the end of history." This is not to deny that Hegel's vision of world history as the self-actualization of the idea of freedom was laughable to Weber. Perhaps it is more accurate to say that Weber conceived of the limits of modernity in the Nietzschean sense, as the end of a long process of decline. This being the case, what was it about the new Russia's struggle to be born that aroused Weber's sympathy? It must have been something other than the mere advent of a nonsynchronicity with the modern west. I would argue that, within the global simultaneity of advanced capitalism (*hochkapitalismus*), Weber glimpsed an exuberance in the new Russia that was not to be found in Europe, whose people in Weber's eyes were "the last to discover happiness." Russia had not so much escaped modernity as manifested an alternative modernity.

Nevertheless, the subsequent Russian revolution dashed Weber's short-lived hopes. Venting the indignation and despair that he felt toward the Bolshevik revolution, Weber's "Russia's Transition to Pseudo-democracy" ("Rußlands Übergang zur Scheindemokratie," 1917) depicts the event not as a socialist revolution that "overcame" modernity, nor as an actualization of "de-modernization," but rather as a senseless revolution that confined Russia to a new cage of slavery.[4] Judging from the upheavals in modern history since then, it seems safe to say that Weber's predictions have, unfortunately, come true. Attempts in the non-western world to glean inspiration from the Russian revolution and accomplish "de-modernization" as a form of "de-westernization" have largely followed in the tragic footsteps of the Soviet Union.

Have we reached a point, then, when attempts to link de-westernization thought with de-modernization thought, or with an "overcoming" of modernity, have all been suspended? The answer is no. For we still witness attempts to resuscitate an eastern "spirit" or "culture" in opposition to the west. Representative of such attempts is that of Takeuchi Yoshimi. Takeuchi sensed that, even if, west and east being opposite concepts, to understand and actualize "the East" was a quintessentially European act, by Europe, nevertheless this "East" could not simply be an insubstantial western invention. In the logic of Hegel's master-slave dialectic, he argued that this was because it was only by resisting this same "east" that Europe had ever found the historical opportunity to *become* Europe. It is well known that this sensibility was extolled as an "overcoming" of modernity, and that it escalated during the war into a commitment to "perpetual war" and "war without mercy." This now-infamous school of thought captivated a great number of intellectuals, declaring a return to the Asian principle (*tōyō*) born of the aporia of modern Japan. Even if we acknowledge that it was narrated from within an intellectual drunkenness, there is still no mistaking that this "overcoming" of modernity, which made Asia or "the East" its fundamental principle, was fantasized as a resistance to and a rehabilitation from the west/modernity, and from the state of psychosis to which modern Japan had succumbed as a result of contamination by the west. In reality, however, Asia so conceived was little more than an "imagined community" produced by the schizophrenia of a modern Japan capable of validating its own identity only by equating modernity with the west.

Initially, of course, the corresponding image, a "West" that stood as the unification of the civilized world, was the nineteenth-century product of Hegelian historical philosophy. But was western Europe, as Hegel had made it out to be from within his ideal world, a unique topos housing world-historical universality? Or was it merely a small promontory on one end of the Eurasian continent? Allowing the viability of these extremes, certainly the former "West" was the creation of German nationalism in a Germany that was more or less lagging behind as a world power. In this respect, it is not at all surprising that modern Japan, having been christened by a German nationalism that aimed to pursue and overcome the world powers England and France, should have rallied behind an Asian Principle, touting it as the breakthrough that would completely bypass the sort of aporia of modernity experienced by Germany. In the same way that Pan-Germanism viewed World War I as the struggle of German culture against western civilization, Japanese nationalism or "Japanism" (*nihonshugi*) existed as an attempt to use this Asian Principle to accomplish an "overcoming" of the modern west. If this topos, "the West," purported to be the locus of world historical universality, could be said to have reached its saturation point—to have begun seeping out into what had until then been nothing more than regional areas—then what could be posited as the unique topos where world historical universality should be housed anew was none other than Asia—specifically, a certain island nation in Asia.

Clearly this sort of "de-modernization" thought actually operated completely within modernity, just as Hegel's had when it disguised German nationalism as western Europe's "world-historical mission." In this sense, we may say that the "overcoming" of modernity was a contorted but still recognizable version of Europeanized modernity in all its confusion and doubt.

Today, postwar Japan has completely jettisoned "de-westernization thought" and "de-modernization thought," together with any commitment to addressing the aporia of defeat, by means of a facile gesture that simply equates Japan with America and Europe. Outraged by such a total collapse of intellectual integrity, Takeuchi Yoshimi had leveled the following critique:

The problem is not that in today's Japan "mythologies" hold sway; rather, the problem is that the same pseudo-intellectualism that already proved itself incapable of overcoming "mythologies" is now, despite its obvious failures, simply being reinstated. Have the "modernizationists" (*kindaishugisha*) and the "traditionalists" (*nihonshugisha*) not become one and the same, predicting peace and an unprecedented level of civilization as they clap their hands joyfully and proclaim, as Fukuzawa Yukichi's *Autobiography* did, that "today's Japan is truly a Japan of civilization and enlightenment" and that "we have achieved a 'state of grace and auspiciousness'?"[5]

CULTURAL HEGEMONY AND THE ONE-DIMENSIONAL SYSTEM

In the postwar period, as well, Takeuchi nevertheless sought to promote the themes of "overcoming" modernity, and "Asia as method." For him, the Chinese Revolution was something to be conceived of—indeed, longed for—as the "denial, or the overcoming of European modernity." Despite China's modernization and the activity of its "liberation policy," however, the Chinese revolution is now widely held to have forcibly perpetuated many traits inherited from the old China, and is even viewed as an impediment to modernization. At this moment, contemporary China has been transformed to the point where it pursues comprehensive marketization policies in the name of the "general model of a de-ideologized nation state." Thus, the oppositional schema of de-westernization thought—the very gesture of opposing the "West" as a privileged topos, and seeking to reinstate non-western regions, is in need of fundamental reconfiguration. Indeed, that reconfiguration has become inevitable.

What I mean when I speak of a reconfiguration is that today, in the midst of a monolithic new order where the world is dominated by the self-regulating market principles that economic anthropologist Karl Polanyi once compared to a "satanic mill," we must continue to be skeptical about the possibility of de-modernization thought and de-westernization thought.[6] We must, that is, question the very meaning of attempts to deconstruct Eurocentrism by bringing the positions of non-western geocultures in line with the position of the west, and privileging them as new and different locations for civilization. As an example of this sort of attempt, I could cite the enormous body of scholarly work on Japan that is devoted to questions of "comparative civilization" and "comparative culture." These texts seem committed to transmitting the message that "we Japanese can *also* practice 'civilization'," or, in an Orientalist inflection of the same message directed not to the "West" but to other Asian nations, "we Japanese are actually *better* at 'civilization'" (to use Carol Gluck's characterization of this position). There is also something like a photographic negative of the foregoing views, according to which some scholars incline towards an "Occidentalism" that insists it was the west that made the originality of the "concentric" structure of Japanese geoculture visible. Nevertheless, as the one-dimensional market system continues to engulf everything that lies in its path, and since within that system power continues to be wielded and articulated in the form of cultural dominance, it seems safe to say that these sorts of projects are already demonstrating their bankruptcy. Instead, we have no choice now but to identify ways out of modernity from within the resistances to that system itself. Indeed, by the end of the World War II, Polanyi already had a premonition of what the one-dimensional postwar system would be like (especially during the Cold War), writing:

For a century the dynamics of modern society was governed by a double movement: the market expanded continuously but this movement was met by a countermovement checking the expansion in definite directions. Vital though such a countermovement was for the protection of society, in the last analysis it was incompatible with the self-regulation of the market, and thus with the market system itself. That system developed in leaps and bounds; it engulfed space and time, and by creating bank money it produced a dynamic hitherto unknown. By the time it reached its maximum extent, around 1914, every part of the globe, all its inhabitants and yet unborn generations, physical persons as well as huge fictitious bodies called corporations, comprised it. A new way of life spread over the planet with a claim to universality unparalleled since the age when Christianity started out on its career, only this time the movement was on a purely material level.

Yet simultaneously a countermovement was afoot. This was more than the usual defensive behavior of a society faced with change; it was a reaction against a dislocation that attacked the fabric of society, and that would have destroyed the very organization of production that the market had called into being.[7]

Wherever we look in the post-Cold-War era we see precisely this spectacle: the "utopia" of a dreary self-regulating market system working globally as a "satanic mill" that grinds down the old social structure and attempts an unsuccessful "new integration of man and nature."[8] Just as Polanyi suggested, however, this colorless scheme was born of a nineteenth-century civilization whose simultaneous legacy has also been the contrastingly vivid movements of resistance that attempt to defend society from the social pulverization wrought by its giant machinery.

Resistance movements and efforts at self defense undertaken by societies that find themselves increasingly buried in the debris produced by the "satanic mill" have been called "antisystemic movements" by Immanuel Wallerstein.[9] If we posit socialism and nationalism as the classic "antisystemic movements" that shaped the nineteenth century, it becomes possible to view both the case of Russia, which I touched upon earlier, and modern Japan's return to the "East" (the "Asian principle," infused with nationalism), as manifestations of this sort of movement. Because the modern world system had been constituted with the west at its center, these movements designated some form of "de-westernization" as their rallying point.[10] But because the power to initiate and change was always maintained by the system, these "anti-systemic movements" were bound to fail. Accordingly, even revolutionary China, which Takeuchi idealized as "Asia as method," is now rushing to embrace the one-dimensionalization of the world system, despite the acrobatic contortions denoted by the term "socialist market economy." Paradoxically, these developments in China have not resulted from the coercive imposition of culture for which the old imperialism was so well known. Rather, China is being caught up in the awesome vortex of globalization in what appears to be a voluntary process.

Can we agree with John Tomlinson's hypothesis, that globalization today represents a "different configuration of global power" that bears no relation to the coercion of nineteenth-century imperialism?[11] Is what we are witnessing not a cultural hegemony radiating intentionally and coherently from the nucleus of power, but rather the beginning of a dismantling of culture—a playfulness amid scattered indeterminacy? It does indeed seem that the concept of globalization designates a situation in which, with the increase of intercommunication and interdependence among all the regions of the globe, there proceeds a structural reconfiguration, both qualitative and quantitative, of "TimeSpace" as we have known it.[12] In this sense, Tomlinson's argument that, compared with imperialism, globalization takes place with far less intent or design, is to the point. But the systematic aspects of cultural hegemony—its anonymity and elasticity—do not mean that it is not a form of cultural domination. If anything, quite the opposite is true: cultural control has deepened and expanded. That the world system, understood as the self-regulating market system, has succeeded in its one-dimensional expansion is the direct result of its having simultaneously accomplished the globalization of a cultural system. But this is not to say that its culture is faceless and neutral, free of the stamp of geoculture. On the contrary, the features of the west (Europe/America), until now a privileged topos, are etched clearly into it. But since the culture of this world system is also an amalgam of many regional cultures (including linguistic, religious, and ideological elements) it gives continuous expression, as well, to the various "anti-systemic movements" to which its mosaic distribution corresponds. If this were not the case, it would be unthinkable that paradigms of the present global order like that advanced by Samuel Huntington—who, taking stock of the vertigo of our split century, reduces the crises of the post-Cold-War era to confrontations of identity, as epitomized by the "Clash of Civilizations"—would meet with the sort of enthusiastic receptions that they do.[13]

Just as was once the case with "cultural imperialism," an arrogant trinity of western (European/American) civilization, modernization, and "universalism," lives tenaciously on, all the while positing the existence of an alien "other" that is irreducible to its three principles, and is therefore "premodern" (and anti-western), or "anti-modern," or "particularist." The huge proliferation of discourses in the wake of the Gulf War demonstrating the links between culture, civilization, and the world order suggests the extent to which whatever is regarded as alien has been relegated to the status of an opaque other who must be tamed by means of the one-dimensionalized order (the world market and the "interstate system," as well as by globalized imperialist culture).[14]

Latent in this post-Cold-War paradigm of the world order—in the deep structures of its discourse and its practices, its representations and systems—is a strong sense of cultures (organized around signifiers of cultural identity and of civilization) as self-same entities, a strategy some scholars have called "differentialist racism." "Differentialist racism" is an ideology whereby older, racist notions of immutable racial difference have been reconfigured in the form of advocacy of the "insurmountability of cultural differences."[15] It constructs a grid according to which cultures and collectivities other than one's own are forced into categories of irreducible cultural difference. At the same time, however, at both the margins of the world system and among oppressed minorities in the "center," we witness in response to this systematized racism an epidemic of ethno-national consciousness, manifested in phenomena that tend to be labeled "religious retaliation" or "racial retribution."

Amid processes that journalists tend to identify as "atavism" and cultural "regression," the identities of self and other are becoming essentialized, and "cultures"—in relation to individuals—are willy-nilly taking on the role of a kind of intransigent super-ego. The discrepancies between cultural identities have been forced into dramatic opposition even in such areas as personal experience and behavioral norms, state policy and individual beliefs, customs and traditions. What is more, these fissures are positioned in such a way that, for the most part, they overlap with the new configurations of power in the one-dimensionalized system. It is this picture of the world's geocultural division and domination—this very Manichean binary opposition—that is narrated as a split century within Huntington's *Clash of Civilizations*. No doubt this situation continues to provide fertile ground for nationalism and neo-conservatism.

Within actual cultural experience, however, we should recognize that, despite the desire for supremacy and hegemony in nationally established cultures, these cultures exhibit an almost uncanny hybrid character. This reveals the way in which the "imperial narratives" of the west (particularly of England and France), which exercised geopolitical dominance and intellectual authority in the nineteenth century, have actually existed by overlapping and becoming intertwined with the "oppositional narratives" that resisted them. That the phenomenon of cultural hybridity continues to intensify today, in spite of the ongoing dramatization of discrepancies in cultural identity and of essentialist conceptions of difference, represents nothing less than the legacy of nineteenth-century imperialism and colonialism. As the post-Cold-War incorporation of the world into a one-dimensional system progresses, however, these legacies and memories are aroused anew, igniting opposition and violent resistance. As Edward Said writes:

> There is no question, for example, that in the past decade the extraordinarily intense reversion to tribal and religious sentiments all over the world has accompanied and deepened many of the discrepancies among polities that have continued since—if they were not actually created by—the period of high European imperialism. Moreover, the

various struggles for dominance among states, nationalisms, ethnic groups, regions, and cultural entities have conducted and amplified a manipulation of opinion and discourse, a production and consumption of ideological media representations, a simplification and reduction of vast complexities into easy currency, the easier to deploy and exploit them in the interest of state policies. In all of this intellectuals have played an important role, nowhere in my opinion more crucial and more compromised than in the overlapping region of experience and culture that is colonialism's legacy, where the politics of secular interpretation is carried on for very high stakes. Naturally the preponderance of power has been on the side of the self-constituted "Western" societies and the public intellectuals who serve as their apologists and idealists.[16]

As this passage from Said makes clear, the relationships between the contemporary "West" and its others (the "Orient," Africa, Latin America) are in no way symmetrical. They are ruled by an obviously hierarchical system of cultural hegemony. The existence of such interstate disparities, however, does not mean that national intelligentsia in post-colonial societies are any less complicit with state power than they are in western countries.

As the world becomes increasingly bound together in a single system, self-definition (an activity practiced in every culture) has taken on much more than merely formal significance. Indeed, today, the process of defining a culture's identity can mobilize passion in the same way cultural atavism does, making it seem almost as if we were reverting to the age of imperialism. At the same time, however, things are just as overlapping and intertwined as ever; in no sense can they be said to constitute relations of binary opposition. This being the case, it is precisely the dismantling of these mythical oppositions that comprises radical intellectual practice in its most fundamental sense. It is in this gesture that Said, through the critique of Orientalism, locates a horizon of possibility. "If it eliminates the 'Orient' and 'Occident' altogether," he says, "then we shall have advanced a little in the process of what Raymond Williams has called the 'unlearning' of 'the inherent dominative mode.'"[17]

I would argue that the only way we can conceive of the possibility of de-westernization thought and de-modernization thought is to follow this course.

ORIENTALISM AND THE DECONSTRUCTION OF ITS "ORGANIZING PRINCPLES"[18]

Orientalism, as one form in which cultural power is exercised, gave rise to an expansive discursive system that divided the west from those worlds existing outside it, particularly "the Orient." The system is supported by a general awareness of the fact that a vast portion of the globe has been brought under western rule, while it simultaneously works to strengthen the same awareness. In this sense, it is inextricably linked with colonialism and imperialism. But Orientalism is not simply a kind of ideology supplemental to the pursuit of real political projects. It adheres in the inner recesses of government and power, realizing its own effectiveness through their operation, as a far more cunning and tenacious form of control. If anything, Orientalism precedes the actual construction of empire and the subjection of the colonies; it is a cultural device, a discursive system, that confines worlds remaining outside the west to a rigid framework of domination. The "Orient" was constructed by means of this system. It was represented arbitrarily by the transcendental subject that was the "West," which dealt with it "by making statements about it, authorizing views of it, describing it, teaching it, settling it, [and] ruling over it" in "scholarly discovery, philological reconstruction, psychological analysis, landscape and sociological description."[19] A group of affiliated concepts whose efficacy had been proven by a host of scholarly methods but that nevertheless had no relation to any actual "Orient" not only gave rise to the "narrative" of the "Orient," but proceeded to reproduce it again and again.

If we take "nation," as a product of modernity, to be none other than "narration," then the power to narrate one's own narrative and intercept the proliferation of opposing narratives becomes crucial for culture and imperialism, shaping the important relationship between them. Orientalism produces exactly this sort of cultural control; it works to guarantee for the west the unique position of narrating subject, while at the same time both excluding and concealing the possibility of other narratives. As a result of this powerful and permeating hegemony, Orientalism has had a surprisingly lasting influence, operating as a kind of coercion and constraint within thought itself, whether in Asia or the "West."

Even more surprising is the way in which various expressions of humanism achieved such harmonious coexistence with imperialism in Europe during what Polanyi calls the "hundred years' peace" (1814–1914) presided over by nineteenth-century civilization.[20] Until resistance to imperialism began to emerge in the imperial territories of Africa, Asia, and Latin America, these sorts of large-scale movements of opposition and containment were almost never seen in the main colonial countries. Drawn to this problem by his "awareness of being an 'Oriental' as a child growing up in two British colonies," Edward Said asks after exactly this phenomenon.[21]

When Said described Orientalism as its own specific history, reading it as the process by which humanism, inextricably bound up with Eurocentrism, continued to gain ascendancy throughout the nineteenth century, he became one of the first to get at the core of modern systems of knowledge and power. To claim this, however, is not to advocate that what Said analyzed as Orientalism be replaced by a kind of Occidentalism. Rather, what Said advocates is the discovery of new cultural narratives, amid the over-

lapping and intertwined social spaces that have become the common property, through imperialism, of both the Empire and its subjects, the "West"
and the "Orient":

> What does need to be remembered is that narratives of emancipation
> and enlightenment in their strongest form were also narratives of inte-
> gration, not separation, the stories of people who had been excluded
> from the main group but who were now fighting for a place in it. And if
> the old and habitual ideas of the main group were not flexible or gener-
> ous enough to admit new groups, then these ideas needed changing, a
> far better thing to do than reject the emerging groups.[22]

Said's argument resonates with a declaration once made by Franz
Fanon, himself in constant search of a new philosophy and a new emergence. Fanon wrote, "[t]his Europe, which never ceased talking about Man,
never ceased proclaiming that she was concerned only about Man, we know
today with what sufferings humanity has paid for each of the victories of its
spirit. . . . Remember, comrades, the European game is finished forever; we
must find something else."[23] As Immanuel Wallerstein has observed of
Fanon's *The Wretched of the Earth*, Fanon is not calling for a rejection of
the discourse that equates modernity with the west, nor is he advocating
flight into some hypothetical freedom that would exist at the margins of that
discourse. On the contrary, Fanon is aware of the depth of his own implication in the world system. For the sake of the "wretched of the Earth," he
looks not to the past or the present but to the future, proclaiming, "we must
invent, we must discover . . . we must grow a new skin, develop new concepts, try to create a new man."[24]

Extending Fanon's intuitions, Wallerstein sees the humanist mythology
created by "Europe, which never ceased talking about Man" as a reflection
of the modern world system, calling it an "organizing principle." At the
core of this principle, he says, lie both humanistic "universalism" and its
opposite, racism. While the two appear to maintain a relationship of mutual
cancellation, they actually operate in a mutually sustaining way, as the
functioning ideology of the world system.

Within the world system as a social system (the "capitalist world-
economy"), "universalism" functions as an integrating force, while on the
other hand racism works to articulate differences within the system, struc-
turing them hierarchically. The two share between them the responsibilities
for absorption into, and exclusion from, the system. Accordingly, racism
and underdevelopment become the inevitable products of the process
whereby the capitalistic world-economy is organized as a historical system.
At the same time, they sustain the process by supporting it systematically.
Fanon's "wretched of the Earth" are none other than people in the vast majority of former colonial states, who are oppressed by racism and underdevelopment. Orientalism, broadly understood as a form of cultural hegem-

ony, provides the index according to which such populations assess their identities in the world and come to internalize the world system's hierarchies of difference. This "organizing principle" attained its completed form in the nineteenth century. Taking the nation state as its basic unit for organizing social space, it makes the stages of development (*entwicklung*) of that state into a temporal axis around which a ladder or hierarchy among nations is constituted. Then, by linking concepts of race with concepts of culture as an interiorized order of meaning, it either facilitates or obstructs advancement up the ladder so as to legitimize economic and social disparities between different regions of the world. Certain societies and their social sciences played a role in the intellectual mediation of the world system by producing various permutations of this "organizing principle," and it became the paradigm for an entire age. Michel Foucault, whose project was to ask after the "*episteme* of Western culture" by means of an archaeology of knowledge, designates the beginning of the nineteenth century as point of rupture, a point of major discontinuity. I would suggest he is clearly calling attention to the era when the "organizing principle" of the world system emerged as a regime of knowledge, and when Orientalist discourse was decisively reinstated.

> [A]s things become increasingly reflexive, seeking the principle of their intelligibility only in their own development, and abandoning the space of representation, man enters his turn, and for the first time, the field of Western knowledge. Strangely enough, man . . . is probably no more than a kind of rift in the order of things, or, in any case, a configuration whose outlines are determined by the new position he has so recently taken up in the field of knowledge. Whence all the chimeras of the new humanisms, all the facile solutions of an "anthropology" understood as a universal reflection on man, half-empirical, half-philosophical.[25]

Like Fanon, who calls for new discoveries and inventions, and Said, who seeks an abandonment of "the inherent dominative mode," Foucault says, "[h]ow consoling, however, and a source of profound relief, to think that man is only a recent invention, a figure not yet two centuries old, a new wrinkle in our knowledge, and that he will disappear again as soon as that knowledge has discovered a new form."[26]

Of course, as Said points out, Foucault had relatively little direct experience of imperialism. Nevertheless, there is no mistaking the intensity of the gaze his "archaeology of knowledge" trained on the west, producer of Orientalism as a hegemonic discourse, a mode of discipline, and a mode of intellectual power.

Concerned as he is with the west's "outside," Said builds on Foucault's work to train the intensity of his own gaze on "the Orient" itself. "Part of

the impulse behind what I tried to do in my book *Orientalism*," he has written, "was to show the dependence of what appeared to be detached and apo-
litical cultural disciplines upon a quite sordid history of imperialist ideology
and colonialist practice."[27] Said's book in no way endorses the real asym-
metrical relations between the "West" and the "Orient." On the contrary, it
seeks to unravel the relationship of mutual dependence between cultural
topographies whose competing narratives and geographies, histories and
designs, reveal a constant mutual hostility even amidst the overlapping experience of "Westerner" and "Oriental," the coexistence of colonizer and
colonized.

His first step in this direction is to expose the definitive role played by
culture in colonial and imperial expansion. According to Said, after the beginning of Europe's Modern Age, imperialism differed from overseas
dominance in prior ages precisely because between Europe and its territories, a completely different form of power was maintained over a surprisingly long period of time, so that the extensive system of rules organized by
power extended its influence not only to everyday life's larger framework,
but even to its finest details. This is the extent to which Orientalism operated not merely negatively and restrictively, but productively as well. By
"productive," here I am speaking of a promotional role that served to insure
that what Foucault calls discipline and instructive power would correspond
to the production of the "subject," or in other words to subjectification. As a
force bent on penetrating the innermost reaches of human experience, this
power allowed no land or people to escape it unharmed. This enormously
obstinate, comprehensive, and cunning system of knowledge/power sought
to reform the non-Western periphery, observing it, and cruelly systematiz-
ing its classification.

> [T]he power even in casual conversation to represent what is beyond
> metropolitan borders derives from the power of an imperial society,
> and that power takes the discursive form of a reshaping or reordering of
> "raw" or primitive data into the local conventions of European narra-
> tive and formal utterance, or, in the case of France, "the systematics of
> disciplinary order." And these were under no obligation to please or
> persuade a "native" African, Indian, or Islamic audience: indeed they
> were in most influential instances premised on the silence of the native.
> When it came to what lay beyond metropolitan Europe, the arts and the
> disciplines of representation—on the one hand fiction, history and
> travel writing, painting; on the other, sociology, administrative or bu-
> reaucratic writing, philology, racial theory—depended on the powers of
> Europe to bring the non-European world into representations, the better
> to be able to see it, to master it, and, above all, to hold it.[28]

This passage suggests vividly why Orientalism can be seen as a form of
geographical violence. It is the attempt to establish, epistemologically and

existentially, a geographical boundary between here and there, "us" and "them"—to fix the latter within a rigid discursive order apart from the privileged topos of the former. Separating the two sides is a very definite fault line—an "internal boundary" that establishes imperialism's "imaginative geography."

When this imperialistic "imaginative geography" is backed by actual power, and when, accordingly, the "Orient" (or the non-European world) loses to outsiders the very soil on which its self-identity is founded, then the history of the servitude of the colonized begins. It is at this point also that ethnocentrism takes the stage, in search of an identity rooted in a specific geography, plotting its recovery from the total absence of identity.

Rejecting the positionality created artificially through imperialism's systematic articulation and hierarchization of geographical space, ethnocentrism labors both to discover and to construct its own original "essence." What it seeks is a created tradition—a directed "naturalness" attempted by means of an overthrow of the deprivations of the present. Thus, because the identity of decolonization is contingent upon ethnocentrism, we witness religious revivalism, movements to reclaim the "mother tongue," and efforts to excavate new ethnic narratives, all of them repeated with an obstinacy that seems to draw its support from some magical revelation or false alchemy. In them, as in Orientalism, totalizing discourses are at work.

> [I]mages of European authority were buttressed and shaped during the nineteenth century, and where but in the manufacturing of rituals, ceremonies, and traditions could this be done? This is the argument put forward by Hobsbawm, Ranger, and the other contributors to *The Invention of Tradition.* At a time when the older filaments and organizations that bound pre-modern societies internally were beginning to fray, and when the social pressures of administering numerous overseas territories and large new domestic constituencies mounted, the ruling elites of Europe felt the clear need to project their power backward in time, giving it a history and legitimacy that only tradition and longevity could impart. . . . Similar constructions have been made on the opposite side, that is, by insurgent "natives" about their pre-colonial past, as in the case of Algeria during the War of Independence (1954–1962), when decolonization encouraged Algerians and Muslims to create images of what they supposed themselves to have been prior to French colonization. This strategy is at work in what many national poets or men of letters say and write during independence or liberation struggles elsewhere in the colonial world.[29]

Clearly, this sort of strategy has proved extremely effective for the formation of nation-states in former colonies. As a result, the very same imperialistic mores that supported the acquisition of the colony remained unchanged, regardless of its independence. As long as these mores persist, the hegemonic mode that works to conceal and exclude the diversity of human experience in former colonial states remains firmly entrenched.

POSTCOLONIAL IDENTITY

As long as anti-colonialist movements subscribe to the same totalizing discourses of cultural identity that colonialism produced, imperialist values will stubbornly persevere despite the efforts of anti-colonialist "counternarratives." It is only by breaking from such discourses and values, and groping towards new conceptions of identity, that a fundamental dismantling of Orientalism and the modes of cultural hegemony it has sustained can be achieved. This will, no doubt, also entail the pursuit of the death of a hegemonic and overpowering system of knowledge. And it will be commensurate with the crucial resolution of the perplexing gap between knowledge and experience, two realms that arise as autonomous when subordinated groups enact oppositional movements against hegemony.

Said's image of a new identity is highly allegorical. In his own case, he adopts the identity of an "exile" in the United States, but his image of exile entails no sadness or deprivation. Instead, Said emphasizes that, by virtue of his membership on both sides of the Arab/American imperialist divide, he can understand each that much better. This is not a singular, binary, reductive identity but a compound, contrapuntal, and occasionally nomadic one. It is, indeed, an identity capable of reacting to historical experience with a rich sensibility. Said asserts this boldly.

But the kind of identity I describe in Said is not the sole possession of single, heroic individuals who occupy the position of intellectuals in exile. In reality, the modern world's political maps produce countless numbers of refugees and immigrants, emigres and exiles. Their plight results from conflicts between imperialist nations and their former colonies, and, ironically, it is often born of the "resolution" of such struggles. As independence movements fighting for ethnic self-determination produce new states and new borders, they also produce displaced persons, exiles and nomads. These are people who remain unassimilated into whatever new structures of institutionalized power are emerging, but who have nevertheless been expelled from the existing order for their refusal to compromise with it. Their position is nevertheless critical: "[I]nsofar as these people exist between the old and the new, between the old empire and the new state, their condition articulates the tensions, irresolutions, and contradictions in the overlapping territories shown on the cultural map of imperialism."[30]

Here is where the energy for hybrid resistance, and the prospect of liberationist struggles come into view. The focus of emancipatory movements is beginning to shift away from cultural efforts already domesticated by institutionalization or excessive stabilization. Instead, new emancipatory movements are characterized by a kind of unstable, entropic, and nomadic energy. The consciousness that generates these characteristics belongs precisely to artists and intellectuals who occupy the position of exile; it is a consciousness common only to refugees who occupy the spaces between regions, social formations, homelands, and languages. The responsibility of such intellectuals at the current historical moment is clear. It must be, first and foremost, to illuminate the states of wretchedness that blight modernity—population shifts and forced immigration, and the imprisonment and deportation of huge numbers of "foreigners" by nation-states.

Theodor Adorno's *Reflexionen aus dem beschadigten leben (Reflections from a wounded life)* draws a sharp distinction between the consciousness of the emigre and the stereotyped thinking produced by what he calls the "consciousness industry" in a "managed world." Said's project clearly takes Adorno as a point of departure.

Still, the liberationist struggles of which Said speaks are more aggressive than the ones Adorno cites. This is because they share a great deal, as I have mentioned, with what Immanuel Wallerstein calls "antisystemic movements":

> From another perspective, the exiled, the marginal, subjective, migratory energies of modern life, which the liberationist struggles have deployed when these energies are too toughly resilient to disappear, have also emerged in what Immanuel Wallerstein calls "antisystemic movements." Remember that the main feature of imperialist expansion historically was accumulation, a process that accelerated during the twentieth century. Wallerstein's argument is that at bottom capital accumulation is irrational. . . . Thus, Wallerstein's argument says, "the very superstructure [of state power and the national cultures that support the idea of state power] that was put in place to maximize the free flow of the factors of production in the world-economy is the nursery of national movements that mobilize against the inequalities inherent in the world-system." Those people compelled by the system to play subordinate or imprisoning roles within it emerge as conscious antagonists, disrupting it, proposing claims, advancing arguments that dispute the totalitarian compulsions of the world market.[31]

It is easy to imagine why Said's provocative language has given rise to a great deal of misunderstanding, meeting vehement rejection from both Arab and American audiences. At the same time, the passage reveals Said's characteristic hope for the "antisystemic movements" that are unfolding alongside contemporary liberationist movements and that exhibit many of the same characteristics. As Said emphasizes, quoting Fanon, "a rapid step [must be] taken away from national consciousness to political and social consciousness"; "needs based on identitarian (i.e., nationalist) consciousness must be overridden."[32] Whether we should understand these words as expressing a modern vision in a different form, or as an attempt to articulate a philosophy of de-modernization, is something that will require further debate. At the very least, what emerges here is a fierce determination to dismantle the "inherent dominative mode" that operates within the one-dimensionalized world 'system.

This will, capable of catalyzing the energy of a hybrid resistance, exists as a moment of renewed awareness that today it is impossible for any one person to have one identity. "Indian," "woman," "Muslim," "American": these are nothing more than points of departure. The belief that a person can have a single pure identity is, if anything, the product of a brilliant fusion between imperialism and culture, a product of the mode of cultural hegemony I have been calling Orientalism. It results from the way identity and culture were combined and fixed as imperialism attained a global scale, allowing individuals to think that they were exclusively white or black, western or eastern. Of course, just as people create their own histories, so too they create their own identities. We cannot deny the longevity and continuity of traditions and customs, languages and cultural geography. But this is markedly and crucially different from requiring a stubborn attachment to notions of separateness or conspicuous difference. The problem is how best to go about establishing relationships among and between these indices of difference. It is also a problem of understanding and preventing the gesture by which, in the name of defending freedom, one makes the other a victim of oppression and erasure. If we are to go on narrating the ideal and the possibility of de-westernization, and even more so of de-modernization from within a one-dimensional system, then we must begin to address this problem.

Translated by Margherita Long

Notes

1. This translation will use "de-westernization thought" for *datsuseiyō no shisō* and "de-modernization thought" for *datsukindai no shisō*.

2. Max Weber, *The Russian Revolutions*, trans. Gordon C. Wells and Peter Baehr (Cambridge, England: Polity Press, 1995), 110–111.

3. Ibid., 110.

4. See "Russia's Transition to Pseudo-democracy" in Ibid., 241–255.

5. Takeuchi Yoshimi, "*Kindai no chōkoku*" (1959) in *Takeuchi Yoshimi zenshū* 8 (Tokyo: Chikuma Shobo, 1980), 66.

6. See chapters three through ten, which fall under the heading "The Satanic Mill" in Karl Polanyi, *The Great Transformation: the Political and Economic Origins of Our Time* (Boston: Beacon Press, 1985), 33–129.

7. Ibid., 130.

8. Ibid., 33.

9. On "antisystemic movements" see Part II "Antisystemic Movements" in Immanuel Wallerstein, *The Politics of the World-Economy: the States, the Movements and the Civilizations* (New York: Cambridge University Press,

1988), 97–145. Also relevant is chapter two, "Crises: the World-Economy, the Movements, and the Ideologies" in *Unthinking Social Science: The Limits of Nineteenth-Century Paradigms* (Cambridge, England: Polity Press, 1991), 23–38.

10. "World-system" is Wallerstein's term. See *The Modern World-System*, 3 vols. (San Diego: Academic Press, 1989).

11. John Tomlinson, *Cultural Imperialism: A Critical Introduction* (Baltimore: Johns Hopkins University Press, 1991), 175.

12. "TimeSpace" is Wallerstein's concept. See "Why Unthink" in *Unthinking Social Science*, 1–4.

13. See Samuel Huntington, *The Clash of Civilizations and the Remaking of World Order* (New York: Touchstone, 1997).

14. On "interstate systems" see Part I "The States and the Interstate System" in Wallerstein, *The Politics of the World-Economy*, 27–96.

15. Etienne Balibar, "Is There a Neo-Racism?" in Balibar and Wallerstein, ed., *Race, Nation, Class* (London and New York: Verso, 1991), 21.

16. Edward Said, *Culture and Imperialism* (New York: Knopf, 1993), 35–36.

17. Edward Said, *Orientalism* (New York: Vintage, 1979), 28.

18. "Organizing Myth" is a term from Wallerstein. See "World-Systems Analysis: The Second Phase" in *Unthinking*, 268.

19. Ibid., 3, 12.

20. See Chapter one "The Hundred Years' Peace" in *The Great Transformation*, 3–19.

21. Said, *Orientalism*, 25. Said grew up in Palestine and Egypt.

22. Said, *Culture and Imperialism*, xxvi.

23. Frantz Fanon, quoted in Immanuel Wallerstein, "Fanon and the Revolutionary Class" in *The Politics of the World-Economy*, 261.

24. Ibid., 262.

25. Michel Foucault, *The Order of Things: An Archaeology of the Human Sciences*, trans. Alan Sheridan (New York: Vintage, 1973), xxiii.

26. Ibid.

27. Said, *Culture and Imperialism*, 41.

28. Ibid., 99

29. Ibid., 16.

30. Ibid., 332.

31. Ibid., 334–335.

32. Ibid., 273.

II. Nationality and Representation

Fragmented Woman, Fragmented Narrative

Hirata Yumi

On November 21, 1888, the Tokyo High Court handed down its verdict in a murder trial and sentenced the defendant, Hanai Ume, to life imprisonment. "Oume," as the woman, a former geisha, was popularly known, was thought to have been the model for the protagonist of the *The Life of a Meiji Woman* (*Meiji ichidai onna*), written by Kawaguchi Matsutarō and published in 1936.[1] Kawaguchi's tale, however, featured two main female characters, and a determination of which of these characters was actually modeled after Oume depends on our understanding of what kind of woman Oume was. For, in this novel, the historical Hanai Oume appears to have been split into two different characters: one, Kanoya Oume, is an introspective, industrious woman who supports her mother and younger brother by reluctantly assuming the role of geisha; the other, a character called Hideyoshi, is a spiteful older geisha who is Oume's rival for the attentions of a *kabuki* actor. Only insofar as we think of the historical Oume as the perpetrator of the murder of her attendant, Minekichi, can we see her as the model for Kanoya Oume in *The Life of a Meiji Woman*—a character who stabs the young man, Minekichi, to death as he advances on her with a dagger, denouncing her for her failure to part with the actor Senshi. In the novel's plot, Oume had been lent money by Minekichi, also her admirer, in exchange for her promise to sever her ties with Senshi. She had planned to use this money to pay for promotional materials for Senshi.

Extant trial records, however, tell us that the murder with which Hanai Oume was charged was listed in neither the category of "justifiable self-defense" nor "excessive self-defense." Not only that, but by contrast to the novelistic Kanoya Oume, who perishes at her own hand in the dressing room behind a stage upon which her lover is succeeding to the title "Sennosuke III," the historical Hanai Oume was released from prison 17 years later, after having her sentence reduced several times. The image of the historical Oume that emerges from these documents, then, differs substantially from that of the fictional Oume. They reveal that behind the sensational tale of Minekichi's murder another tale was hidden: that of the conflict between a daughter, who strove to attain independence within a patriarchal system, and the father who opposed her. Needless to say, the discourse surrounding Hanai Oume in her time was neither produced nor read from such a perspective. Rather, as the tale of a Meiji era murderess, the story of Oume has been typically paired with the scandalous story of Takahashi Oden and classified as a *dokufumono* or "poison woman tale."[2]

A gap, however, separates the narratives about Hanai Oume and Takahashi Oden, which can neither be explained by reference to the differing individual circumstances surrounding their crimes, nor to differences between their social backgrounds, life histories, and the consequences that followed from their convictions. As we examine the details, a contrast in the conditions of production of the two narratives emerges in relief— something we might see as one of the nodal points differentiating early modern (*kinsei*) from modern (*kindai*) literature. The following essay will look at the way this point of differentiation is manifested in the discourse surrounding woman as it evolved between the second and third decades of Meiji.

A TALE NO ONE READ

According to an indictment issued on November 8, 1888, Oume was 24 years and two months old on that date. The indictment records the place of her birth as Shimousa, her status as that of commoner.[3] However, Asai Masamitsu's *The Confessions of Hanai Oume (Hanai Oume zangebanashi)* suggests otherwise. A reporter for the *Kokueki shinbun* who succeeded in interviewing Oume when she was released from prison in 1904 is cited as saying that she declared, "At least, I never forgot my samurai heritage . . . although I was raised in free-wheeling Edo, thanks to that heritage, I always stayed away from shady dealings."[4] Oume also remarked repeatedly that her conflict with her father was rooted in their unyielding natures. Her father, she said, had "been born into a samurai family that had fallen on hard times, but was proud . . . and he had never forgotten his ancestry."[5] We can surmise that Oume's father, Sennosuke, was a samurai from the Sakura domain.

When Oume was four years old, in 1867, the whole family moved to Tokyo. At the time of the move, it is reported, her father was doing a business in dried seaweed. It is unclear how he made a living later, but around November, 1873, when Oume was just nine years old, she was sent as an adopted daughter to the home of one Okada Tsunezō. A trial lawyer of Oume's, Ōka Ikuzō, described Okada as a poorly educated man, who did not give the child a proper upbringing but simply apprenticed her to a geisha, calculating that she might be a future source of income. This kind of adoption agreement, entered into by Sennosuke and Okada, was a thinly disguised form of slave trade, as we can see from the wording of a Dajōkan proclamation issued on October 2, 1872. The proclamation stated that "anyone who, on the pretext of taking an adopted daughter as a monetary transaction, forces such child to become a prostitute or a geisha, is in fact engaging in slave trade and from now on shall be severely punished." Of course, it is well-known that this series of measures issued by the Meiji government prohibiting slave trade and the professions of geisha and prostitute, including the Ministry of Justice's famous Proclamation Freeing Beasts of Burden (*gyūba tokihodokirei*), had little real efficacy. Even when a girl was returned to her own family, it was common for the local headman to simply send a request to the Tokyo authorities, saying something to the effect that "the family was making it difficult to make ends meet, as an additional member added to its burdens." The typical document would state that since "the person in question wishes to help her family, please investigate the situation and give your seal of approval to a new contract that recognizes that she is now a free agent."[6] The new contracts, that is, were supposedly entered into voluntarily.

However, in Sennosuke's case, the handing over of his daughter to Okada seems not to have held the significance it commonly had in the society of the time. This is suggested by the following information, which for some reason was featured in the *zappō* ("general news") section of an 1879 issue of *Yomiuri shinbun*.

> News concerning the application of Oume, 14 years old, adopted daughter of Okada Tsunejirō of Kita-Shinagawa, for a license to work as a geisha. . . . Since Oume's father is Hanai Sennosuke of Azabutani-chō, the authorities made inquiries at this ward office. According to the real father, the application is out of the question, since when he sent Oume into her adoptive family there had been an agreement that she would under no circumstances work as a geisha or prostitute. Hanai said he would not agree to the plan. Tsunejirō, however, claims that Oume herself decided to become a geisha. Since he has agreed to it, he has asked the police office to try to persuade Sennosuke.[7]

Ultimately, it appears that Sennosuke's "agreement" with Okada was not binding, and in the same year the 15-year-old Oume received her license and began to commute from her home in Ryōgoku to work as a geisha. Despite the difficulties that had surrounded her debut, we can surmise that her career proceeded normally, since three years later she had established herself as a full-fledged geisha in Yanagibashi. Within just two more years, she was able to terminate her adoptive status and have her name restored to her natural family's registry. We have evidence that, "on the basis of good business" she was able, by the end of 1886, to move her residence from Yanagibashi to Shinbashi, and to change her geisha name from "Kohide" to the more impressive "Hideyoshi." The sum of money she earned from the sale of the Yanagibashi house was "about 1500 yen," suggesting that she was doing a thriving business as a geisha.

The "spirit of the Edokko," nurtured in Oume since the days of her early training as a geisha, and pride in her samurai heritage—these characteristics are cited in Oume's reminiscences as the qualities that led to her crime, but we can surmise that they also contributed to the verve that made her a best-selling geisha. Such independent geisha (known as *jimae geisha*) lived at the pinnacle of a hierarchically ordered world. On the lowest rung were young women called *kakaegeisha*, who lived in geisha houses under the care of a mistress who collected even their tips in repayment for debts they had previously incurred. Next were the *tatakiwake* geisha, who had older geisha take them in and provide rooms for them, but who had to split their earnings, always giving half to the older woman. By contrast, an independent geisha was neither constrained nor supervised by others. In the book, *Geisha of Tokyo* (*Tokyo gijō*), Tajima Ninten described the highest class of geisha as follows:

> She has neither husband nor parents. She is the mistress of her own house. Such a woman belongs to the highest class of geisha. Why is this? It is because she is bound to noone and noone can complain about her actions. Whatever she earns is completely hers. Her expenses are low. Moreover, if she encounters a customer she doesn't like, she politely refuses him, and no one will criticize her for doing so. But, supposing she takes a fancy to some fellow and decides to run off and spend a few days with him? All she needs to do is take down the sign at her establishment. She can close her business for weeks at a time. She can do exactly as she pleases. There is nothing to prevent her from living her life as she wants.[8]

Although she had her name reentered in the family register, Oume did not actually live with her family but in her own home, with one female and one male attendant. Her tie with her parents did not, we can imagine, prevent her from living a free and unencumbered life. One story, of dubious veracity, has it that during a dramatic lovers' quarrel with the *kabuki* actor Sawamura Gennosuke IV, Oume took out a razor. But even this kind of behavior was probably overlooked by the public as a manifestation of the independent geisha's tendency to become infatuated with *kabuki* stars, and would have occasioned little censure. Oume's tragedy, it would seem, stemmed neither from her lifestyle nor her indomitable will, but from the fact that, in the end, she could not make this spirit prevail.

Less than two years after she moved to Shinbashi, Oume filed for the closing of her independent business. The date was May 13, 1888. She returned her geisha's license and on the following day opened the kind of teahouse, commonly called *machi-ai jaya* in the Tokyo area, where geisha entertained customers. Problems soon arose in the management of this teahouse, which had been given the name Drunken Moon Teahouse or Suigetsurō, but they seem to have been related not so much to Oume, who had developed considerable business expertise over the years, as to her father. Despite the fact that the business had been set up in his name, Sennosuke's personality was poorly suited for a business that required constant interaction with customers. On May 23, a mere ten days after she opened her business, Oume had an argument with her father and went to stay with a friend, Hasegawa Suzu, in Kabukichō. Oume probably conferred with Suzu, who also owned a teahouse, about what to do next, but she also requested that one Kawamura Tsutae act as an intermediary. At the time of her trial, Oume denied that she had ever received money from Kawamura. But it seems clear from the *Confessions* that this wealthy merchant had provided her business with funds. According to the *Confessions*, Kawamura had told Oume, at the time of the original loan, that he was happy to put up one or two thousand yen, but he did not want to give it directly to her, "since he was a prominent man and it would not do to have it rumored that he had become infatuated with a geisha and lent her money." The talks were concluded by deciding that the money would be lent to Sennosuke.[9] It was for this reason that the Suigetsurō's license was made out in Sennosuke's name. The *Confessions* also state that, three days after the argument between Oume and Sennosuke, Kawamura came to Suigetsurō to mediate between the two, declaring that "the real owner of the business is Oume. Although Sennosuke is the formal proprietor, he does not know how to run a business."[10] Kawamura, as the financial backer of the business, recommended that Sennosuke retire from active involvement in it. Although Sennosuke apparently returned home when Kawamura suggested it, he returned the next day with his oldest son, Rokutarō. Together, they put out a sign closing down the teahouse, claiming that it was, after all, Sennosuke's business and Oume had no right to run it as she pleased. The *Confessions* also describes Oume's reaction at the time.

> That day almost 50 customers came to the teahouse after spending the morning at the theater. How astonished they must have been to find the place closed! "Oume, how could you do this to us? We went to so much trouble to arrange this," they complained. I was in a terrible dilemma. I was even more distressed when the actors Hara Gōemon and Senzaki Yagorō arrived. Ah, I cannot remember ever having been so embarrassed![11]

We can glimpse from this just how disturbed and shamed Oume must have been by Sennosuke's capricious behavior and his utter disregard for the conventions of a business devoted to the pleasure of customers. She had, after all, been molded by many years of experience, both in the difficulties of dealing with clients and in the arts of pleasing them. Yet even under these circumstances, Oume appears to have sought to avoid an angry confrontation with her father. She simply left home and went to stay with various acquaintances during the two-week period that preceded the events of June 9. On May 27, she stayed with her samisen instructor, Ogawa Yae. The two went together to the Ikegami Hot Springs Resort and stayed there until May 30. From May 31 until June 4, Oume stayed alone at Kobe Hot Springs. She then returned to Hasegawa Suzu's house on the evening of June 4. On June 6, she went to confer with Ishizaka Asa at the Fukudaya, a floating inn (*funayado*) in Yonezawa.

We should note that all of the people to whom Oume turned at this critical juncture were women who had established economic independence on the basis of their own skill and professional talent. They represented a network she had cultivated during her days as a geisha and they must have been able to provide support and sympathy because their own experiences with business clients were so similar to hers. In her reminiscences of a Meiji childhood, Imaizumi Ume described women who, like Ishizaka, presided over goings-on at the pleasure boats she occasionally visited with her father. "Sitting in the midst of a throng of men," Imaizumi wrote, "it was hard for my eye to pick out the owner of the boat. But I had no trouble picking out the woman in charge. She seemed to be responsible for everything—from the boat itself and the geisha who worked there to the male customers who came to amuse themselves."[12] In an economic context where everything devolved around the abilities of women, we might question just how significant the legal title of "proprietor" was. Moreover, the conflict between Oume and Sennosuke takes on new connotations when viewed against this background. Can we not read it as the conflict between a daughter, desirous of independence and fully capable of realizing her goals, and a stubbornly conservative father, bent on continuing to exercise his patriarchal authority over a daughter he had once sold? Some of Oume's statements suggest she struggled to avoid an outright confrontation with her father. At her trial, she is recorded as saying that she "did not feel it was right to oppose her father." In her *Confessions*, she noted that, "there was something about the very word 'father,' and about the dignity of a parent, that evoked feelings I could never completely overcome, so I refrained from conflict with him."[13] While admitting that "I had no strong affection for him, since we had not lived together in over 15 years," she nevertheless avoided challenging him directly.[14] Could the murder have arisen from a displacement onto Minekichi of the feelings Oume was unable to articulate in the form of a rebellion against her father?

Ishizaka Asa, of the Fukudaya, also went to Suigetsurō on the evening of June 8 to mediate the dispute. Unfortunately, Sennosuke was not there. At the trial, Ishizaka denied that Minekichi had made "slanderous" attacks on Oume at the time that she visited. Moreover, Oume's own references to the "slander" during her trial are sparse. By consulting the *Confessions*, however, we can flesh out the picture. Here, Minekichi is described as having told Ishizaka that "Oume is a drinker. She walks around in an intoxicated state. She has no steady man. She amuses herself with one man after another, aimlessly living for the moment. She spends money like water. She seems to think that since she earned it, she can spend it as she pleases—her finances are in a sorry state. To be blunt, I think Oume is a fool. At this rate, we'll be lucky if she doesn't squander everything the business ever made. She should remember she could never have started it on her own!"[15]

Although there was no doubt some truth to this description of Oume's willful lifestyle, it is also hard to imagine how she could have let such remarks go unchallenged. As Oume recalled after her release from prison, she had given Minekichi work after he had been dismissed, because of some blunder, by his former employer, Gennosuke. It was the Edokko in her, she said, that could not ignore the sufferings of others. At this time, 17 years after the event, Oume still spoke vehemently of Minekichi's betrayal, calling him "lower than a dog, who would remember a person who has cared for it for just three days!" Minekichi, she declared, "even if it were purely out of feelings of obligation," should have been "100 percent loyal to me." In the interview, Oume went so far as to declare that "Minekichi never had what it took to be a man."[16]

This remark suggests something about the nature of the geisha-box boy relationship that needs further contextualization. We can glean insight from a compressed portrait that appeared in this letter published in the *Tokyo eiri shinbun* on June 20, 1877. The letter begins with a verse:

> The eager-to-please
> Dimwit
> Becomes a geisha's box boy

This 17-syllable poem (*senryū*) is extremely astute. Even when his mistress is someone who lacks the qualifications to be a true geisha, he conducts himself like an artist or playboy, accompanying her everywhere but always giving the impression of being an utter moron. To make things worse, when he goes to the parlors where she entertains her guests, he fusses with her *obi*, tunes the strings of her *samisen* and carries it out to her, and even collects the tips, creating a pathetic spectacle of himself. What a shame for someone in the prime of his working life to waste his talents on such an occupation![17]

In Tajima's *Tokyo gijō*, we find this brief description of the box boy:

> He is of average height and has two balls. But despite this perfectly normal body, he belongs to the lowest class of male. There is no existence more demeaning and scurrilous than that of the box boy. He follows behind the geisha, carrying her instrument; he hands her footwear,

folds her clothing, and even takes care of her underwear. He is essentially her slave. Who could ever call him a human being?[18]

Seen in this context, does not the Oume incident afford us a vivid glimpse of structures of discrimination and oppression that existed, not only in the world of the geisha and women who were sold as prostitutes within the patriarchal system, but of those who were the slaves of these women? Yet needless to say, such a tale was never told about the Hanai Oume incident. How, in fact, did readers of the time construct this story?

AN INTERRUPTED TALE

That the Hanai Oume case, as an example of one of the small fraction of Meiji homicides committed by women, received far more publicity than the "Oden incident" of 10 years earlier, largely reflects the enhanced technology for news gathering that had been put in place for journalism, especially newspapers, at that time. After the first accounts of the incident had been published, they were followed by reports that appeared at regular intervals in each of the city's newspapers. These reports described the depositions made by various persons, deemed to have some connection to the event, who were summoned by the court, as well as Oume's personal statements and the appeal that the case be taken to a higher level. Each paper carried accounts provided by reporters who observed the trial proceedings at the higher court and recorded them in shorthand. The astonishing speed of the media's response to developments in the case is perhaps most strikingly revealed by the fact that a book entitled *A First-Hand Account of the Trial of Hanai Oume* (*Hanai Umejo kōhan bōtoku hikki*) was published just one month after her sentence was handed down.[19]

A quick overview of the different types of discourses surrounding Oume's trial suggests that the intense public interest in it was a result of her status as a geisha who had worked at the two well-known districts of Yanagibashi and Shinbashi. This was the era when geisha were "stars" in society. Their glamorous image is reflected in the following *Yomiuri shinbun* depiction of Oume's appearance in court when she was summoned for the preliminary hearings.

The defendant wore a black crêpe jacket decorated with the "three mulberry leaf" crest, over a double-layered undergarment of figured twill on a tortoise-shell ground pattern. Beneath this one could glimpse yet another undergarment of elegant red and white crêpe, and all this was bound by a black Chinese satin sash, fastened with a white crêpe cord. Her freshly washed hair was arranged as specified by prison regulations, and her face looked pale and drawn, because of her days in confinement. She wore straw sandals with white *tabi,* and was led into court by a prison guard. Her quiet, well-mannered behavior and melancholy expression created an air of pathos, more reminiscent of the *ka-buki* character Narukomaya Fukusuke than the "vampire women" played by Onoue Kikugorō.[20]

The *Tokyo eiri shinbun*, which carried four successive days of observer's notes on the trial, carried a drawing of Oume in men's clothing that was purported to be based on a photograph. On each of these days, the newspaper carried pictures of Oume outfitted as a geisha or in man's attire. No doubt, this reflected a craze of the times for purchasing cheap portraits of popular geisha. Those who could not content themselves with these "bromides," as they were popularly called, crowded into the court room to see the real thing. As the *Eiri shinbun* described it:

> Because of the huge public interest in the trial, many would-be observers milled around the court before dawn, hoping to be among the 150 people admitted. There were about a thousand people in all. Some of those who did not receive admission tickets tried to force their way in and several police officers had to stop them. These people were forced outside the gates of the prison. Among those who were denied access to the spectacle were some who protested by throwing rocks and pebbles at the windows.[21]

The presence of the throngs even prompted one of Oume's lawyers to exhort the judge "not to let new criminals be created at the trial of one criminal; please treat all of these people leniently."[22]

As we can see from all this, the horizon of expectations of the audience for Oume's story had a certain fixed orientation even before the tale began to be told. While a case involving a murder committed by a famous geisha was itself both unusual and sensational, the perspectives from which events were interpreted lacked novelty. The readers, indeed, sought to understand Oume's story by fitting it into the framework of existing tales. Let us consider how these perspectives evolved.

In the beginning, immediately after the murder of Minekichi, the majority of newspaper reports appeared sympathetic to Oume. Although there were minor differences in their accounts, they reported Minekichi's murder as a case of justifiable self-defense, assuming that Minekichi was slain because he nurtured a passion for Oume that drove him to commit acts of violence. The June 11 edition of the *Chōya shinbun*, for example, related the story in the following manner, under the headline "Murder by Mistake":

> Perhaps because of the good looks and verve of his mistress, Hanai Oume (24 years old), proprietress of a tea parlor in Hamachō, Nihonbashi, a box boy named Yasugi Minekichi (24 years old) fell in love with her and sought to win her affections day after day. Driven to desperation because his advances were rejected, the day before yesterday

when Oume went out on a rainy night to do some errands, he took a well-sharpened butcher knife, wrapped it in one of the cloths he always used when working, and put it in his breast pocket. When Oume returned, unaware that he was waiting in the shadows along her path, Minekichi apprehended her and threatened her at knife-point to grant his wishes. The terrified Oume struggled to wrest the knife from his hand and somehow, in the scuffle, the knife plunged into Minekichi's side and he was overcome, collapsing in the road. Watching him die, Oume was terrified anew, but since what is done is done, she immediately turned herself in to the authorities. The case has been processed and yesterday she was sent to the prosecutors. A great disaster has befallen her.[23]

It is, of course, possible that it was Oume herself who first narrated the murder of Minekichi as a case of justifiable self-defense (or excessive self-defense) at the preliminary hearings of the Tokyo Court of Lesser Crimes. But even if it was not Oume herself who furnished this interpretation, the materials necessary to incline reporters and readers to such an interpretation, in which Minekichi was cast as the villain, were ready to hand. Just three months earlier, a geisha called Sugaya Ofumi, from Karasumori, had been murdered by her box boy, Shimabara Ginjirō, who was subsequently given a life sentence. The incident appeared to have been related to financial problems. But since the victim was a top-ranking geisha, in high demand, and known for her many affairs with *kabuki* actors, newspapers vied with each other to convey the details to the public. According to one article, the box boy pressed Ofumi for sexual favors, demanding that she return money he had lent her when she refused to accommodate him. If we compare this description with the others cited above, it seems more than likely that the popular image of the box boy as the "lowest species of male" would have helped shape the depiction of Minekichi as a devious young man who harassed Oume.

However, from Oume's testimony and that of others, it is clear that it was Oume herself who purchased the butcher knife that became the murder weapon, and that it was she who called Minekichi to the scene of the crime. It was for this reason that the proceedings were moved, in the following month, to the Tokyo High Court. This development inevitably forced journalists to reconsider their initial tendency to present Minekichi as the villain.

At least two serialized novels, or *tsuzukimono*, based on the Oume incident were featured in newspapers of the time. The novel of greatest interest to our analysis was carried in the *Tokyo eiri shinbun*, and given the title *Tales of Passion on a Rainy Night at Suigetsurō* (*Tsuyugoromo Suigetsu jōwa*).[24] In this tale, Oume was depicted as an outgoing but impetuous woman, self-indulgent and with a weakness for *sake*. In early installments, Minekichi is described "as one surprisingly calculating for a dim-wit box boy." By the sixth installment, however, this characterization had changed to one of Minekichi as a devoted servant, utterly loyal to the haughty Oume. Yet, perhaps reflecting new revelations made when a "Report on the Investigation into the Character of Minekichi" was read in court, after installment 29, Minekichi regains the characteristics of a man "passive and servile by nature." Minekichi's character is not consistently portrayed.

In the second serialized novel, featured in the *Kaishin shinbun*, Minekichi appears but can hardly be called a central character. Before his relationship with Oume could be described, the serialization was suspended. In the case of both newspapers, not only did the incident appear to undergo reinterpretation as the serializations proceeded, but we find that the novels themselves were abruptly terminated.

This second novel was written by Saikaen Ryūka and entitled *Suigetsu manga* (*Scenes from Suigetsu*). Its first scene is set against the backdrop of the opening day of the Ryōgoku River fireworks festival. A large party on the second floor of a restaurant is attended by geisha from both the Shinbashi and Yanagibashi quarters. The proprietress of the restaurant, one Kinoshitaya Tōkichi (representing Oume in her years as the geisha Hideyoshi) is caught up in an argument with an older geisha called Okatsu. One storey below, a party for members of the aristocratic Nakamura family is also in full swing. In the fourth installment, we are given a glimpse of a secret conference, held by servants of the Nakamura family, who make plans to confine the current household head, a man named Kiyodane, to his own home because of his outbursts of violent temper. The title of this particular chapter makes it obvious that the character Kiyodane represents the historical Sōma Masatane. Furthermore, the character Oda Kiyoshi, who makes an appearance early in the novel, is based on the historical figure Nishigori Gōsei. Clearly, then, this second novel attempted to weave together allusions to two contemporary scandals—the Oume affair, and the Sōma family feuds. Since the equivalence between historical and fictional characters in the novel can be ascertained to this degree, we might go even farther and conjecture that the way the novel imputes Kiyodane's "insanity" to his obsession with Tōkichi represented something more than speculation on the author's part, and may have been an attempt to slander someone. But after just 10 days and nine installments, *Suigetsu manga*, also, was discontinued. The author appears to have bungled his attempt to fuse fact and fiction.

The *Eiri shinbun*'s *Tsuyugoromo suigetsu jōwa* (hereafter *Suigetsu jōwa*), however, was also not free from problems arising from the attempt to combine fact and fiction. In this story, unlike *Suigetsu manga*, Oume and Minekichi are introduced with their actual names. While the other characters are given fictional names, the story is nevertheless constructed in such a manner as to enable the reader to guess who they are on the basis of descriptions. The Meiji *tsuzukimono*, we might say, constituted a genre of "novel as reportage," in which factual elements and fictional elements were woven together in such a way as to clarify for the reader the background

and actual facts of an incident. For this reason, the suspension of the serialized novels dealing with the Oume incident may help us glimpse more
clearly something of the context within which such texts were produced.

In a preface preceding the first installment of *Suigetsu jōwa*, the newspaper cited the *rakugo* performer Hakuen as the source of the tale, which
appeared in the pages of the *Eiri shinbun* a mere two weeks after Minekichi's murder. The preface opens with a short eulogy to the contemporary
"era of civilization and progress." Although beauty is not necessarily to be
disapproved of, it declares, "becoming vain over one's appearances is a
characteristic of the vulgar, uneducated woman." The present age "is one in
which our government is determined to reform such attitudes. It is a time
when schools for women are being set up everywhere. Women's reform
societies are also being established. Among our journals, both *Jogaku
zasshi* and *Jogaku sōshi* are devoted to inculcating the kind of education
and behavior we find in Western women. With our country's ancient ideal
of the 'wise woman, faithful wife' as a motto, we are seeking to expand the
rights of women and to elevate them to a position of equality with men."[25]
These sentiments would appear to introduce the narrative that follows as
one intended to enlighten those "vulgar women" to whom the blessings of
progress have not yet been extended. It cloaks itself, we might say, in the
façade of a kind of modernized "promote virtue, chastise vice" ideology
and appears to be narrated from such a perspective. Insofar as it introduces
Oume as an evil woman, somewhat comparable to Takahashi Oden, we
might say that it attempts to insert her story into the framework of a poison
woman tale.

Indeed, the third installment of this narrative was framed by what, by
that time, had become a rather standard epithet for the "poison woman": it
frames Oume as "a Bodhisattva on the outside but a demon within, demure
in appearance but putrid at the core." It conveys to the reader some sense of
the geisha Hideyoshi's history with men and describes the lovers' quarrel
that erupted just prior to Minekichi's stabbing. In Chapter 10, we find a
story, unsubstantiated by any documentation, of how Oume, with her wiles,
brought about the destruction of a young man employed at a haberdashery
establishment. It clearly assigns the guilt in this case to Oume. It was "as
retribution for her cruelty that a shower of blood spattered on the beauty on
that night of spring rains. The fool was not to be blamed. It was as if, in
loving the beautiful woman, he made her sinfulness his own. For the body
of a woman who sells sex also passes on poison."[26] From Chapter 14 (entitled, "Dreams of Little Butterfly, Dance in the Temptress' Teahouse") on,
we find a description of Oume's dreams in prison, and the novel takes on
the tone of a *kabuki* script.

What we can see here is an impulse at work, in *Suigetsu jōwa*, to describe Oume as a woman who drove men mad with lust and then destroyed
them. By 1888, however, the attempt to insert a historical woman into the
dokufu genre that had succeeded so well with Takahashi Oden seemed

doomed to fail. Ten years had already passed since the era of "she-devil Oden," and the conditions of production for such narratives had changed.

FROM *TSUZUKIMONO* TO *SHŌSETSU*

The *Tokyo eiri shinbun* featured the following commentary just three months before the Hanai Oume incident, at a time when the newspapers were flooded with stories about the murder of the Karasumori geisha Ofumi. Entitled, "Not Someone Else's Problem," the editorial ran in the newspaper for a two-day period, on March 15 and 16, 1888.

It has become common for today's tabloid newspapers (*koshinbun*) to make a point of including stories about the lives of "poison women" and villainous men. While one can imagine these stories might convey a moral to discriminating readers, regrettably the members of our society who consume such materials lack that kind of discretion. Rather, they mistake lewd tales of promiscuous women for parables of female virtue and they take thieves and crooks for gallant gentlemen. These stories in the tabloids, then, appear far more dangerous than the stories told in the *kōdan* and *rakugo* halls.

. . . It is the task of the newspaper to be the eyes and ears of a society, and to uplift the level of public discourse. I hear that the recitation of tales about "poison women" and villainous men by *kōdan* and *rakugo* performers has been prohibited by the government. If newspapers take over the job, surely we, too, will meet the same fate. We, who should be providing moral leadership to society, will be in need of discipline ourselves.[27]

This editorial suggests the possibility that *Suigetsu jōwa* was discontinued precisely at a time when serialized newspaper novels were being replaced by journalistic reporting based substantially on actual fact. In the same *Eiri shinbun* just a few days before serialization of the tale began, on June 21, 1888, we can find in the "general news" section the announcement of a performance entitled "Love Between the Rains" (*Tsuyubare jōshi*), dealing with the murder of Minekichi, by the *rakugo* artist Hakuen in the Fukumoto Theater in Hirokōji. On March 25, however, Hakuen is listed as performing a different program entitled, "Strange Tales from Hongō: Araiso no Kenji and the Geisha Kozuna" (*Araiso no Kenji, Geisha Kozuna. Hongō kidan*). The relationship between the two programs is unclear.[28] But interestingly enough, while we can find conversational speech patterns from *kōdan* (such as the endings *gozarimashite* and *arimasen*) in the first installment of *Suigetsu jōwa*, after March 25 the novel completely reverts to the literary style. Occasionally, one will find at the end of an installment, a reporter's note to the effect that his information is based on "street talk" collected by one of the newspaper's scouts, and that therefore, "while what I have related is not groundless rumor, I cannot guarantee its complete accuracy." It is likely that elements of Hakuen's story, as it was delivered in the theater, were picked up by reporters and at some point made their way onto the general news page. Yet because these fragments must have been incorporated without an attempt to reconstruct the actual chronological sequence of events, the contradictions between different sections of this randomly organized material must have become more and more serious, until it became impossible to read them as factual reports.

At this point, the serialization of *Suigetsu jōwa* was discontinued. The reporter offered the following justification at the end of Chapter 30:

> We have now completed thirty installments of the novel *Suigetsu jōwa*, but the narrative itself has not reached a conclusion. This is because no court verdict has been issued dealing with the Oume affair. Since I cannot at this stage reveal the true identities of people involved in the case, nor all the facts connected with it, I find words fail to come when I try to continue my story, and my brush seems to drag. Articles about the matter have appeared steadily in each successive edition of our paper, but inevitably there have been problems and redundancies between them. This is because the factual basis of the incident itself had not been clarified before the newspaper accounts began to appear. The temporal sequence of events was often confused, and because reports were created on a day-to-day basis, truth and untruth were thrown in together. This situation was a source of frustration to the writers, and readers must have been troubled by many ambiguous sentences. For these reasons, I have decided to suspend the novel in its unfinished state. In the future, when the trial verdict has been issued, I will resurrect it.[29]

The author appends the following statement to this apology: "Rather than violating the libel regulations by unwittingly recording untruths that could damage people's reputations, reports should be produced only after the court's verdict has been determined, when the details are clear and all the information is complete."[30] One can surmise from this that the reporter's hasty termination of his narrative must have stemmed from his desire to avoid entanglement with Article 33 of the 1884 newspaper laws, which prohibited newspapers from reporting on a trial before the verdict had been determined. On the one hand, criticisms of the *dokufumono* genre made it difficult for him to continue the Oume tale as a purely fictional "poison-woman" narrative. On the other hand, if he attempted to produce a factual account, based on occasionally gleaned bits of truth, he ran the risk of becoming ensnared in regulations against libel. This was a point in time, we might say, when the attempt to produce a narrative about Oume encountered obstacles on two different fronts.

This was, in fact, a predicament shared by all *tsuzukimono*. A short two weeks after the publication of the commentary "Not Someone Else's Problem," the *Tokyo eiri shinbun* published another article on the same topic. Cautioning, in his title, all illustrated newspapers to take heed, the author Nangō Gakujin offered several points of criticism. As one who believed "newspapers should be the eyes and ears of society," he deplored the way "tabloids pander to the vulgar desires of the readers. . . ." For what reason, he asked, did the *koshinbun* "cater to the trends of the times, stirring up problems in our society? The answer is their practice of publishing works that are something like novels. While there may be a shred of didacticism in these tales, they are for the most part pure fantasies, affording only momentary amusement." Nangō included among the "novelistic writings" at which his criticism was directed the *rakugo* and *shōsetsu* forms, narratives that, because they purported to be based in fact, were "adored by young women, concubines, people of the lower classes, clerks, and apprentices."[31] Clearly, what he had in mind was the emerging form of *tsuzukimono*, which combined fact and fiction.

But Nangō's was not the first attack of this kind to appear. As early as 1883, in fact, the following criticism of the *tsuzukimono* was penned by one Soei Kanjin, published over a three-day period from March 11 to March 13.

Suggestions for Those Who Write for Both Large and Small Newspapers
The mission of the newspaper journalist is to promote public morality. But this has given rise to a paradox in today's journalism. Whenever an event takes place that might lend itself to depiction in a penny dreadful, a *kabuki* script about burglary and sword-fighting, or a lengthy tale of honor avenged, it is featured in the newspaper under a flashy headline, then sold as a multi-volume series, and finally published as a book. We would be well advised to reflect more deeply on this state of affairs. Do not the events of our lives transpire, and our emotions ebb and flow, in a matter quite different from what is described in the genres I have just named? This is because penny dreadfuls, *kabuki* scripts, and the like, are not based on happenings in the present but on those of the past. It goes without saying that their aim was different. While this observation may sound tendentious, let me submit that something has gone a bit awry in a world where newspaper journalists, who bear the weighty responsibility for conveying truth, spend their time writing novels in which fiction is disguised as fact, smugly declaring that there is a kernel of moral instruction in the tale as well.[32]

"Soei Kanjin," under whose name this commentary appeared, was a bureau chief at Ryōbunsha, the company that published *Tokyo eiri shinbun*. (Soei, whose real name was Maeda Kenjirō, also published under the pen name Kōsetsu Sanjin.) As Maeda's remarks reveal, *koshinbun* were launched under the banner of fostering the moral enlightenment of "ignorant women and children." Yet, barely 10 years after their appearance, their role appeared to have become one primarily of furnishing popular fiction written in the late Edo style. This role needed reassessment as the consumption of journalistic writing expanded and the social role of newspapers themselves continued to strengthen. The revised press regulations of 1883 added an additional impetus to this reassessment. These were the regulations that appear to have led to the suspension of *Suigetsu jōwa*. An article on the role of "*furigana* journals," published under the pen-name Gin Nishino, described the impact of the regulations in May 1883. "Since a newspaper is a business, it is perhaps unavoidable that newspapers cater to the public tastes by publishing long fictional-type writings such as erotic or scandalous stories. The press regulations have recently been revised, however. They are stricter than the earlier regulations, and for this reason the responsibility borne by newspapers is weightier. It is imperative from now on that each newspaper exercise even greater discretion, that the content of articles be upgraded, and that even the slightest risk of violating the laws be avoided."[33]

This concern became even more pronounced in the following year and gave rise to a new movement calling for the reform of the *tsuzukimono*. That is to say, newspapers found themselves facing a dilemma. From a business point of view, they relied on the "long, fictional-type writings" that their readers loved, yet now they incurred considerable risk if they took real-life incidents and fictionalized them. The attempt to deal with this contradiction led to a public debate on the reform of serialized fiction. A two-day commentary published in the *Eiri chōya shinbun* on January 10 and 11, 1884, by one Kenkon Koji, asserted that "the serialized fiction in today's *furigana* newspapers is a genre of writing that can be classified as neither fact nor fantasy. It is, rather, a mode of writing that distorts fact in service of fiction, and fiction in the name of fact. Should we not learn from European newspapers, such as the *petit journaux* of France, that fiction can be entertaining and of benefit to society at the same time?"[34] This article provoked an almost immediate response from another writer, who urged that "gradual reform of serialized fiction be undertaken, since the form taken by serialized fiction, not to mention other literary genres, is unsatisfactory."[35] These articles provide evidence that a movement for the reform of prose fiction was ripening in the mid-1880s, with newspapers as its staging ground.

As we can see from Kenkon Koji's invocation of Dickens and Disraeli, of European newspapers and French *petits journaux*, Western literature was often held up as a model for reform. We can see this tendency in another article by Gin Nishino that appeared in November 1884, in the "Commentary" section of the *Yomiuri shinbun*. He noted critically that, "Browsing through several European novels, I discovered that their authors were exclusively members of their nation's scholarly class and possessed of considerable erudition. In addition to being entertaining, therefore, these books possessed scholarly merit, making the actuality of the European novel something quite different from that which is referred to as 'fiction' in Japan. The unevenness of scholarly background among our writers of fiction lies at the root of this disparity." For Gin Nishino, the problem was not one pertaining "only to the established genres of prose fiction," but also to "that writing resembling prose fiction that appears constantly in our newspapers."[36]

There is no need for this article to detail the role of Tsubouchi Shōyō's *Essence of the Novel* (*Shōsetsu shinzui*, 1885) in transforming the state of early Meiji literature, a process that is routinely narrated as the point of departure for Japanese modern literature. The observations of Kōda Rohan reflect what had already become a prevalent assessment of the 1870s and early 1880s. "The tastes of readers were vulgar," Kōda reminisced, "and so were those of the writers of fiction, who were men of limited education, rather than scholars of Chinese and Japanese letters. Literary writing, in this context, was oriented to the crude tastes of the masses."[37] But we should not fail to note that the way had been paved for *Essence of the Novel* to "elevate the tastes of the public by illuminating the nature of Western literature" (as one writer put it) by the contemporaneous movement to reform serialized fiction in the newspapers.[38]

In late 1885, the *Yomiuri shinbun* took a decisive step in announcing the establishment of a new section of the newspaper, which had been created entirely for the purpose of publishing "pure fiction" (*junzentaru shōsetsu*). This innovation had become necessary, the newspaper stated, "to clearly differentiate these texts from the long, fiction-like writings that are carried in the general news section." The newspaper then commenced publication of two installments of "pure fiction" in each edition, modeling itself after the "*petits journaux* of France." This development, of course, did not mean that *tsuzukimono* were banished from the pages of newspapers overnight. In the *Yomiuri*, "pure" fiction by Aeba Kôson appeared together with the *tsuzukimono* of an anonymous author, while in the *Tokyo eiri shinbun* and *Eiri chōya shinbun*—despite the lively critique of the genre appearing in their pages—*tsuzukimono* continued to be featured. We can nevertheless determine that at this historical juncture, a turning point has been reached, with the *tsuzukimono* receding in importance as "pure fiction" came to the fore.

THE EMERGENCE OF NEW NARRATIVES

In addition to the *tsuzukimono* we have considered, the Hanai Oume incident also gave rise to five different "documentary novels" (*jitsuroku shōsetsu*), each with the identical title *Hanai Oume: The Strange Tale of Suigetsu Tea-House* (*Hanai Oume: Suigetsu kibun*). Each of these books appeared within a year of the trial's conclusion in 1888, and although the date and place of publication recorded in the colophon differs in each of them, the tale told in each is the same, consisting more or less of a direct transcription of the contents of *Suigetsu jōwa*.[39] In each case, while the opening and concluding sections of *Suigetsu jōwa* have been maintained, the newspaper installments that constituted the other 30 chapters are arranged according to different chronologies. Notes taken at the trial are also included in each book, with the court's final verdict incorporated at the end. In restructuring the elements of the story, it appears that these authors tried to remedy the effects of the "departure from the original chronology" that was referred to when the serialization of *Suigetsu jōwa* was interrupted. But, in fact, none of the authors succeeded in correcting for the original's problems of "redundancy and contradiction" or for its "admixture of truth and fiction." Like their predecessors, the *tsuzukimono* (the documentary novellas), whether considered as factual or fictional accounts, were unsuccessful. They may, however, be included among the discursive fragments that flesh out our understanding of the Oume incident and the changing narrative frameworks within which it was received.

From the *Suigetsu kibun* and other accounts, we get a picture of lengthy preliminary hearings, held from 10:40 in the morning until 5:00 in the afternoon, with three intermission periods. Once the case had been transferred to the Tokyo High Court, reporter's notes taken at the trial were featured over a several-day period. These reports conveyed the contents of the indictment issued against Oume, as well as of the interrogations that ensued, involving judge, police, defendant, and lawyers. All papers carried the final verdict, which was handed down on November 21, 1888. In the *Tokyo eiri shinbun*, a general report on the trial proceedings was carried for five successive days. After the completion of the trial, however, the newspaper did not fulfill its promise to resume serialization of *Suigetsu jōwa*. We may interpret this as signifying two things: first, that the vast amount of verbiage generated by the trial did not lend itself to clarification of the "facts" in the case, and, second, that it did not lend itself to reconstruction in new forms of narrative.

Oume's stance vis-à-vis her interrogators throughout the trial proceedings is noteworthy in this respect. When Oume described her own state of mind during the trials in *Confessions*, she recalled that, "I said nothing in court. No matter what question was proposed to me, I simply said, 'Yes,' since I believed that, as someone who had committed a murder, I, too, was certain to die."[40] The records show that Oume maintained this attitude consistently throughout the trial. Entered beside her name in the proceedings, we find the statements, "I don't remember" ("*Oboemasen*"), "I don't know" ("*Zonjimasen*"), "I don't understand" ("*Kokoroemasen*"), "I have no clear recollection," or simply four dots (" . . . . ") signifying no response. Perhaps in the case of questions about the nature of her father's business, or Minekichi's place of birth, Oume quite literally was ignorant. Or she may have been too flustered by events to recall details. But she also repeatedly declared that she had "no recollection" of, for example, Minechiki's confiscation of her performance fees, a matter of crucial importance to her lawyers' efforts at plea bargaining. She also refused to corroborate the names of Minekichi's former employer (Sawamura Gennosuke) or of her financial backer (Kawamura Denei), facts that are clearly stated in her *Confessions*. In such cases, it appears that, as she herself stated, she had resigned herself to receiving a death penalty and therefore had decided to refuse to divulge any information that might create problems for people she knew. Whether they were intended as affirmations or denials, Oume's responses amounted to virtual silence and we find no attempt, as in Takahashi Oden's case, to narrate her own story.[41]

I have discussed elsewhere the social conditions that made it possible for Takahashi Oden to tell her story in her own words during her trial, no matter how biased it might have been. Late Edo culture had provided a context for her narrative, a context receptive to both the fantastic narratives of *kabuki* theater and to *jitsuroku*, a genre of documentary. Within this context, Takahashi Oden sought to define her own image as a woman of heroic proportions. Oume's historical context, however, was one in which Takahashi Oden's own narrative had already been negated and transposed within the *dokufumono* genre produced by men, while the *tsuzukimono* was being replaced by the *shōsetsu*. In his consideration of the ways in which images of women in the Meiji novel reflected the narcissistic desires of men, Kamei Hideo has argued that the "poison woman" genre must be understood as a product of the early Meiji official ideology of "promoting virtue and chastising vice." On the one hand, the "poison woman" was a mirror reflecting the masculine desire to seek freedom from sexual conventions through liaisons with women who violated social norms; at the same time, it worked to regulate these self-indulgent fantasies.[42] Kamei abo points out that one aspect of the political novel was to produce an image of woman like that of Yūran, the heroine of *Chance Meetings with Beautiful Women* (*Kajin no Kigū*). The flip side of the poison woman fantasy was the archetype of the geisha as one who "sold her art, and not her body." Kamei argues that, in the political novel, the heroic characteristics of "devotion, gallantry, and self-abandon" were extrapolated from this geisha archetype and projected onto a new type of female heroine.

Complementing the process whereby virtues exclusively compatible with male interests were being extrapolated from the social construct of the geisha to produce a new feminine ideal was a public discourse censuring and criticizing those geisha to whom these virtues could not be attributed. As is suggested by the existence of the term *korobigeisha* or "fallen geisha," prostitution involving geisha had been in existence since the mid-Edo. After the Meiji Restoration, "fallen geisha" began to be referred to as *ōrai geisha* ("all right" geisha, denoting both their response to requests for their services and their easy availability) or "dual licenses" (*nimai kansatsu*, women who had licenses as both prostitutes and geisha, which were supposed to be separate occupations). Such women provided topical subject matter for the general news columns of the *koshinbun*, which adroitly commodified gossip about their doings. At the behest of those who were proprietors of licensed geisha houses, the government took steps to regulate these prostitutes. At the same time, the 1886 promulgation of government guidelines for those who made their living as geisha, became, in turn, the occasion for new efforts at organization among geisha themselves. Many geisha sought to form their own business associations to regulate the three categories licensed by the government at the time—"restaurant-teahouses" (*ryōri-jaya*), "pleasure boats" (*funayado*), and "meeting-and-waiting teahouses" (*machiai-jaya*). This tendency eventually permeated even the worlds of the most elite geisha in Shinbashi and Yanagibashi, stirring up in both areas conflict between the "trade unions" (*kaijō kumiai*), on the one hand, and the "three business unions," on the other. This, in turn, factionalized the individual geisha who belonged to these associations. It was precisely this kind of complication that appears to have motivated Oume's move, as the young geisha Kohide, from Yanagibashi to Shinbashi in 1886.

We can also find an allusion to this situation in a lecture by Nishimura Shigeki, a prominent religious leader of the time. In "Lecture Fourteen" of his series, "In Response to Fifteen Questions," Nishimura inveighed against the geisha and prostitutes of the day. "Surprisingly, even those persons of very high status in our society are lacking in discretion, and seem unaware that the occupations of geisha and prostitute are immoral. Writers, in particular, seem to have a confused sense of propriety and frequently produce stories and playscripts glamorizing these women and stirring up the desires of dissolute young men. Even in such widely read books as the *Famous Sayings of the Notables*, one finds virtuous heroines and geishas and prostitutes lined up side by side, and readers do not even find this strange. What better proof could we have that they are unable to distinguish between the honorable and the base, the pure and the impure?"[43]

On January 15, 1886, the women's journal *Jogaku zasshi*, which had intensified its criticism of the discourse glorifying geisha against the background of the government's promulgation of laws prohibiting prostitution, reprinted Nishimura's lecture. The journal's position on these issues was further clarified in the July issue of the same year, which carried a positive review of Imagawa Shuku's recently published book, *Stories of Virtuous Women: A Manual of Conduct* (*Kenjō shūshin jiseki*). Imagawa's book was praised for "its excellent selection of stories, and for avoiding the common tendency of similar volumes to include stories of geisha among their examples."[44] Somewhat later, the magazine's "Commentary" section ran an article by Nakajima Toshiko on "Today's Fiction," which censured "newspapers, supposedly the upholders of public morality who eschew the corrupt practices of the past," for "not only failing to condemn women who devote their lives to the so-called 'realm of *shamisen* and *shichiku*,' but tacitly express admiration for it."[45]

The publication of arguments like this was not limited to *Jogaku zasshi*, although it is true that it was this journal alone that had single-handedly stirred up interest in the movement to abolish prostitution. In its New Year's Day supplement for Meiji, 1886, the *Yomiuri* published a humorous piece on "Reforming Geisha" written by Minami Shinji, which poked fun at the behavior of geisha. By the following year, critical commentaries on geisha had reached the newspaper's front pages. Gin Nishino's "On the Subject of Reforming Geisha" ("*Geisha kairyōron*") appeared there on January 12, 1887, while a similarly entitled article by an anonymous author was published on September 29. Around the same time, the *Yūbin hōchi shinbun* published an article on *kisaeng*, by one Sankei Sei, which advocated the establishment in Japan of a government-supported *kisaeng* system similar to that of Korea. When a rebuttal to this argument was published soon after, it was clear that the existence of geisha had come to be regarded as a social problem.

A *Yomiuri* article expressing nostalgia for "the golden age of Tamenaga Shunsui's romances, *Plum Calendar* (*Umegoyomi*) and *The Southeast Garden* (*Tatsumi no Sono*)," and lamenting a state of affairs in which the social arts of the geisha were declining, making geisha more like prostitutes, provoked this critical response from a writer with the pen name Jishō Shinshi.

I find it astonishing that your reporter, having concluded that a book like *The Southeast Garden* recorded both actual social relations and nuances of emotion, should have lauded the geisha of that era. In Shunsui's day neither the producers nor the readers of fiction thought of prose narrative as something focused on the depiction of psychology—prose fiction was purely and solely "to promote virtue and chastise evil." But from the viewpoint of a contemporary reader, Shunsui appears to have produced the character Yonehachi, whom he strove to endow with the quality of peerless devotion to her man, simply for the purpose of offering women—be they maidens, wives, or widows—a model for their actions and thoughts. Even in his wildest dreams, he never intended to provide insight into the truth of human emotions or behavior. To me, it seems excessive and a bit absurd that the reporter should have relied on this fictional character, heavily tinged with Confucian moralism, to produce a eulogy of late Edo geisha.[46]

This commentator, who begins with the assumption that geisha who "trade in lust and peddle romance" were not a recent invention, and rejects Shunsui's selflessly devoted heroine as a fictional construct cloaked in Confucian moralism, seems to have astutely surmised that by the late 1880s the "geisha heroine" of political novels was no longer viable, and that the fantasy of her qualities of "devotion, gallantry, and self-abandon" (*sessō, kyōki, jiko hōki*) was a mere delusion. His criticism is firmly based on concepts advocated in Tsubouchi Shōyō's *Essence of the Novel*, which stressed that depiction of psychology, not of society and customs, was the principal aim of the novel, and held that doing away with fiction that sought to promote virtue and chastise evil was the precondition for the emergence of the "true novel." This writer's words suggest, that is, that the transition from *tsuzukimono* to *shōsetsu* occurred in tandem with the evolution of the reformist literary movement that, using the introduction of Western literature as a lever, pursued the "pure novel" and sought to expunge, as a last vestige of the late Edo *gesaku*, the ideology of "promoting virtue, chastising vice."

Needless to say, during the period in which the *tsuzukimono* was the focus of a movement for reform, newspaper reports about the doings of geisha continued apace and yellow journalism was churned out incessantly. Even during the Russo-Japanese War, for example, scandalous reports about Prime Minister Katsura Tarō and his mistress, a Shinbashi geisha, appeared in *Yorozu chōhō* and *Hōchi shinbun*. Nor did the vaunted modern novel, once it had banished the geisha heroine, emancipate women from their role as mirrors of male desire and make them the enunciators of their own narratives. Tales about women continued to be subsumed into tales narrated by men, and female characters, divided into the virtuous and the wanton, continued to be objects of either glorification or punishment.[47]

We might also see in the various defense arguments presented by the lawyers at Oume's trial the emergence of new kinds of narratives told about women by men, who were able to divorce Oume from her own story because of her silence. In *The Confessions*, for example, the "slanderous remarks" of Minekichi that allegedly triggered the murder are recounted in considerable detail. Yet even Ishizaka Asa, who had earlier claimed that she told Oume about Minekichi's remarks, declared that Minekichi "said absolutely nothing." Wasn't this silence a deliberate cover-up on the part of the defense (which included the cooperation of Ishizaka), who hoped to save Oume from a death sentence by asserting that Minekichi's murder was not premeditated or planned, but a spontaneous action? Any indication of a clear intention of murder on Oume's part would have been awkward for the lawyer, Tsunoda Shinpei, who argued that her sentence be reduced on the basis of extenuating circumstances. According to his statement, Oume had only decided to kill Minekichi because of the way he was treating her. Moreover, he held, even if she had decided to do it several hours or the night before, there was no legal basis for considering it premeditated murder, and it was therefore manslaughter.

A "hereditary . . . genetically transmitted mental illness" was also cited as the cause of Oume's tendency to "claim that what never happened happened" by the lawyer Ōka Ikuzō. Ōka declared:

As evidence of this hereditary tendency, let me point out that the defendant's mother becomes mentally deranged under the influence of liquor, and even in ordinary conditions flies into a rage over arguments. I have heard that recently, when she was insulted during a meal, she became furious and threw her rice bowl on the table, and then went on to tear apart some screens. Furthermore, the defendant's grandmother is said to be the type who will rip precious clothing to shreds if something irritates her, and only then regain her composure. Because of this bad blood or insanity . . . particularly after the argument with her father, Oume became afflicted with a uterine disease. Since I have been told by doctors that uterine diseases often cause hysteria, we cannot rule out the possibility that she was insane at the time of the event.[48]

These remarks may be seen as part of a discourse that tries to link Oume's crime to a female "bloodline" traced through her mother, prone to drunken frenzies, and her mother's mother, with her bouts of hysteria. Here, Kanagaki Robun's tale of *Takahashi Oden*, which narrated a causal link between Oden's crime and the "intensely promiscuous, licentious disposition" she inherited from her mother, appears to be recycled with the trappings of new science, that of medical criminology. Such narratives participated in a larger discursive formation of the time, within which woman's body was gradually being exposed to reveal the inner organs that harbored such tendencies. Fukuzawa Yukichi, for example, in his "Treatise on Japanese Women" (1888), expressed the opinion that the "social oppression" that thwarted the open expression of women's "feelings" made them "prone to dejection and melancholy and gave rise to overly sensitive dispositions and frail bodies, transmitted hereditarily from mother to daughter to granddaughter," from generation to generation. "What are commonly called 'female maladies' or 'attacks of nerves'," he stated, "are actually forms of illness such as mental illness, or hysteria arising from uterine disease."[49] Ōka Ikuzō followed up on the statements above by citing, as evidence of the unbalanced mental condition brought on by "Oume's constant nervous attacks," the "exceedingly strange behavior" observed by a third party who saw her "downing platefuls of broad beans" at the Ikegami hot springs resort. The minds and bodies of women, in this discourse, converge in a negative vector of inherited inferiority.[50]

It is not entirely clear how the court responded to these arguments, put forth by the defense on the basis of "medical knowledge." The text of the court's decision merely states that the case was one of premeditated murder, but that "the sentence is reduced to one of life imprisonment because of extenuating circumstances." What these "circumstances" were is never made clear. Yet it appears that the rhetoric of the lawyers who sought to narrate Oume's story as one of "a sick mind" was taken up by newspaper journalists. A report in the *Yomiuri* on May 22, 1895, for example, stated that in the Ichigaya Prison Oume "became psychologically deranged and exhibited abnormal behavior" whenever the season of Minekichi's murder rolled around, and that she had to be treated by a doctor. A report in the *Miyako shinbun* on February 2, 1899, described her as "suffering from fever on the evening of the eighth day of each month" (the day of Minekichi's death).

IN CONCLUSION

In 1909, more than 20 years after the events, the writer Emi Suiin produced yet another book entitled *Hanai Oume*, this one a sequel that narrated, not the cause, but the aftereffects of Oume's crime. It presented her as a "sick mind" who was tormented each night by the ghost of Minekichi. In this tale, the narrator is awakened one night, when he is staying at an inn in Chōshi, by the shrill screams of a woman. When he discovers the name "Hanai Oume" listed in the inn's register, he recalls events that have taken place since the murder of Minekichi years earlier. Many memories come back to him . . . how he learned of the murder through an illustrated edition of the *Chōya shinbun* that had been pasted on the walls outside the newspaper's office, prompting his imagination to run wild, and how he skipped school to stand in the theater gallery and watch Mokuami's drama about Oume performed at the Nakamura Theater on April 20, 1889. Fragments of the other discourses surrounding Hanai Oume, whether bits of news leaked about her "insane behavior in prison," the journalistic uproar occasioned by her release, or stories of her later life as an actress, returned as memories, and the musings they stirred up kept him awake until dawn.[51]

Yet Emi's reminiscences seem ultimately to have little to do with Hanai Oume. For example, we find him commenting, in the following passage where he describes a *tsuzukimono* featured in the *Kaishin shinbun*: "When I look back on it, I can see the Japanese literary world has made great progress. Or rather, in the heyday of *tsuzukimono*, Kanagaki Robun and his followers were still holding on. . . . But they were pushed aside. Now, people are trying to push us aside, but we won't give up so easily. The real struggle is just beginning."[52] As these words suggest, Emi's recollections are, in the final analysis, recollections about the Japanese literary world, about his place in it and his prospects for the future.

When Emi's narrator returns to the inn a few days later, he learns from one of the maids of Oume's present situation: she has become a traveling entertainer, performing a play about the box boy's murder in small theaters attached to inns. But, according to the maid, it is not Minekichi's ghost that torments Oume at night, it is the bill collector! After conveying this information, the narrator concludes:

> This woman, who is visited in her dreams nightly by the man she murdered, and who is so terrified she breaks into a sweat that drenches her bedclothes . . . this woman, terrified as she is, reenacts the murder be-

fore an audience, turning it into a spectacle to win their applause. How could anything be more contradictory? Yet is it only in the case of Oume's art that we see these tragic contradictions? No, I realize they extend to me. The thought gives me gooseflesh and sends a shudder down my spine.[53]

Clearly, when we read this writing, we have left the realm of Oume's tale. This is an authorial confession produced at the height of the Naturalist movement.

Perhaps this clarifies why the Hanai Oume of Kawaguchi Matsutarō's *Meiji ichidai onna* had to be split into the opposing roles of "Kanoya Oume" and the geisha "Hideyoshi." Kawaguchi's is the stereotypical narrative of a woman who dies because of her obsessive love for a man, and was nothing other than the projection onto its heroines of the virtues of constancy and self-abandon fantasized by men. When Takahashi Oden told her tale, she reproduced within it countless narratives about women created by men. By contrast, Oume's silence resulted in a kind of amorphousness that allowed her story to be read differently at different points in time, in ways that reflected the historical conditions of the day. As Emi Suiin observed, the very ambiguityof Hanai Oume's story accomodated many fantasies. Yet needless to say, among these narratives produced by men, not one was the tale of Utagawaya Hideyoshi, an independent geisha who took only the partners who pleased her, nor of Hanai Oume, the young woman caught up in a struggle with her father for her own autonomy.

Translated by Brett de Bary

Notes

1. Kawaguchi Matsutarō, *Meiji ichidai onna* (Tokyo: Shinshōsetsusha, 1936).

2. The tendency to link the names of Takahashi Oden and Hanai Oume may be seen in a number of commentaries on early Meiji literature. For example, in Yata Sōun's *Edo kara Tokyo e*, we find the statement that, "of all the villains and 'poison women' who emerged in the early Meiji period, when the social order of Tokyo was thrown into disarray, Takahashi Oden and Hanai Oume were the most notorious pair" (Yata Sōun, *Edo kara Tokyo e* [Tokyo: Chūō Kōronsha, 1975], 322). In Hasegawa Shigure's *Kindai bijinden*, we also find the women treated together (see Hasegawa, *Kindai bijinden* [Tokyo: Iwanami Shoten, 1985], 37).

After the comment cited above, Yata Sōun added, "In the case of Oume's murder of her box-boy, however, her actions seem to have been without premeditation." By contrast, he describes Takahashi Oden's crimes as "planned, and serial." Thus, "her criminality was more manifold, and the promiscuous nature that motivated these deeds seemed terrifying to the people of the city."

Needless to say, Takahashi was no serial killer, but Yata's way of comparing and passing judgment on the two women was typical of the basic stance of most critics. Like Yata, Shigure was more sympathetic to Hanai.

3. This information is taken from the *Tokyo eiri shinbun* series of articles entitled, "*Hanai Oume no kōhan*," published between November 19 and 25, 1888. References that follow to recordings of the trial proceedings are taken from the same source.

4. Asai Masamitsu, *Hanai Oume zangebanashi* (Tokyo: *Kokueki shinbun-sha*, 1903), 134.

5. Ibid., 137.

6. *Tokyo nichinichi shinbun*, October 12, 1874.

7. *Yomiuri shinbun*, March 7, 1879.

8. Tajima Ninten, *Tokyo gijō*. This book was published by the individual Tōsei Kamejirō, October 12, 1884.

9. Asai, *Hanai Oume zangemonogatari*, 143–144.

10. Ibid., 144–145.

11. Ibid., 145.

12. Imaizumi Mine, *Nagori no yume* (Tokyo: Heibonsha, 1963), 204–205.

13. Asai, *Hanai Oume zangemonogatari*, 140.

14. Ibid., 136.

15. Asai, 141.

16. Ibid.

17. *Tokyo eiri shinbun*, June 20, 1877.

18. See Tajima, *Tokyo gijō*.

19. Satō Eizō, *Hanai Umejo kōhan bōtoku hikki* (Tokyo: Seibundō, December, 1888). A date for the release of the book attached inside the cover records it as the day after the verdict was announced, that is, on November 22.

20. *Yomiuri shinbun*, November 12, 1888.

21. *Tokyo eiri shinbun*, November 19, 1888.

22. Ibid.

23. *Chōya shinbun*, June 11, 1888.

24. This serialized narrative, entitled *Tsuyugoromo Suigetsu jōwa*, commenced with a *hottan* or prefatory statement describing how it came to be written, and was published on June 24, 1888, in the *Tokyo eiri shinbun*. Thereafter an installment was featured almost every day until the "30th Chapter," published on July 29. The second narrative, *Suigetsu manga*, was featured in *Kaishin shinbun* in the same year, but ran only about nine installments. "Part I" began on July 17. The last installment was published on July 27.

25. *Tokyo eiri shinbun*, June 24, 1888.

26. *Tokyo eiri shinbun*, July 4, 1888.

27. "*Tanin no senki ni arazu*," *Tokyo eiri shinbun*, March 16, 1888.

28. On June 24, an article in the general news section of the *Tokyo eiri shinbun*, under the headline "A new tale of Suigetsu," gave the following information: "A story entitled '*Tsuyubare jōshi*' will be performed starting June 24 at the Hirokōji Fukumoto Theater in Ryōgoku. It has been created as a

kōdan, on the basis of investigation into details surrounding the murder of Minechiki by the geisha known as Hanai Oume (formerly called Kohide), the proprietress of the *machiaijaya* called Suigetsurō along the Hamachō shoreline, a woman whose entanglements with men have been the subject of many rumors." A day later, the same newspaper announced the performance by Hakuen of *"Araiso no Kenji, Geisha Kozuna: Hongō kidan,"* a *kōdan* based on events that took place in the early 1800s involving a geisha named Kozuna and an exconvict known as Araiso Kenji.

29. *Tokyo eiri shinbun*, April 1, 1888.

30. Ibid.

31. Nangō Gakujin, *"Kaku eirishinbunshi no chūi o nozomu,"* April 1, 1888.

32. Soei Kanjin, *"Ōkokisha shokun ni teisu,"* *Tokyo eiri shinbun*, March 11, 1883.

33. Gin Nishino, *"Bōkun shinbun no kōyō,"* *Yomiuri shinbun*, May 12, 1883.

34. Kenkon Koji, *"Taisei wa riji ni hairazu,"* *Eiri chōya shinbun*, January 10–11, 1884.

35. Hara Akitomo, *"Bōkun shinbun no tsuzukimono wa nan ni yorite shirusaruruka?,"* *Tokyo eiri shinbun*, January 15, 1884.

36. Gin Nishino, *"Shōsetsu sakusha,"* *Yomiuri shinbun*, November 9, 1884.

37. See *"Aa, Harunoya Shujin"* by Kōda Rohan, in *Rohan zenshū*, Vol. 30 (Tokyo: Iwanami Shoten, 1979), 422.

38. Ichijima Kenkichi, *"Meiji shotō bundan no kaiko"* in *Shunjō hitsugo* (Tokyo: Waseda Daigaku Shuppanbu, 1928), 115.

39. All of these versions have the same title, *Hanai Oume Suigetsu kibun*. Although their publishers, place of publication, and bindings differ, the text has only slight variations, and all have adopted the illustrated installments published in *Tokyo eiri shinbun* without modification.

40. Asai, *Hanai Oume zangemonogatari*, 148.

41. I explore this question in my essay, *"Onna no monogatari, monogatari no onna,"* published in Wakita Haruko and Susan Hanley, ed., *Jendaa no nihonshi* (Tokyo: Tokyo Daigaku Shuppankai, 1995).

42. See Kamei Hideo, *"Dokufu to kyōjo"* in Honda Kinichirō, ed., *Henkakuki no bungaku* (Sapporo: Hokkaido Daigaku Tosho Kankōkai, 1976).

43. Nishimura Shigeki, *Kōdōkai sōwa*, Third edition, Vol. 6, December 1886.

44. *"Hihyō kenjō shūshin jiseki,"* *Jogaku zasshi* 28 (Tokyo: Jogaku zasshisha, 1886), 269.

45. Nakajima Toshiko, *"Tōkon no shōsetsu,"* *Jogaku zasshi* 40 (Tokyo: Jogaku zasshisha, 1886), 191.

46. Jishō Shinshi, *"Geigiron o yomu,"* *Yomiuri shinbun*, October 7 to November 20, 1887.

47. Shōyō's first novel, *Shōsei tosei katagi*, featured a geisha heroine whose name was Tanoji. Following this, Shōyō drew extensively on the dis-

course surrounding geisha in his novel *Imōto to sekagami*. However, even by
this time, the mainstream of the novel had moved beyond the kind of *tsuzukimono* based on stories about geisha that Shōyō acknowledges as one of his
sources in the beginning of the work. Thus, although one of Shōyō's protagonist, called Otsuji, is an uneducated woman, she insists that "she will not be the
plaything of men," while another heroine, called Oyuki, is a talented beauty
who has graduated from a normal school. In the 1890s, there was chorus of
voices criticizing the manners of women students, in which the novel itself became implicated. A certain vulnerability to criticism that had been displaced
from the "poison women" to the "fallen geisha" was now taken on by the *joga-
kusei* or woman student. I hope to write elsewhere about this discourse on
women, which emerged midway between the debate on women's equality that
took place in the first decade of Meiji and the propagation of the ideology of
"good wife, wise mother" in the 1890s.

48. See "*Hanai Oume no kōhan*," in *Tokyo eiri shinbun*, November 19–25,
1888.

49. Fukuzawa Yukichi, "*Nihon fujinron*," *Fukuzawa Yukichi zenshū 5* (Tokyo: Iwanami Shoten, 1959), 460.

It was around the beginning of the second decade of Meiji that advertise-
ments for "uterine pills" began to appear in newspapers. One medication
"Medicine For Improved Circulation of the Blood: An Elixir for Ladies" used a
mermaid for its trademark, yet featured surprisingly realistic diagrams entitled
"External View of Pelvis and Organs" and "Dissected Uterus." The term "uterine disease" (*shikyūbyō*) started to replace "malady of the lower regions" (*shita
no yamai*) in fiction and letters from readers.

50. I am grateful to Tanikawa Keiichi for calling my attention to Eguchi
Jō's *Zōho: Seishinbyōgaku* (The Study of Mental Illness: A Supplement), published in May, 1889, as a supplement to the volume of the same title published
in January of that year, which describes "hysteria" (*hisuterikyō*) as "a hereditary
condition in many people." See Tanikawa's *Kotoba no yukue* (Tokyo: Heibonsha, 1993) for further discussion of ways in which modern medical discourse
objectified the mind and body, and how such objectifications became configured in literary texts of the time.

51. This tale was included in an anthology of Suiin's writings, *Suiin Sōsho*,
published by Hakubunkan in August, 1910. It first appeared in the journal *Taiyō*
in May 1899.

52. See "*Hanai Oume*," in *Suin Sōsho* (Tokyo: Hakubunkan, 1910).

53. Ibid.

Memories of the "Dim-witted War": The Case of Takamura Kōtarō

Nakano Toshio

PRELIMINARIES: POSTWAR JAPAN AND THE MEMORY OF TAKAMURA KŌTARŌ

To begin with, let us acknowledge that today the figure of Takamura Kōtarō, as author of the two works, *The Road Ahead* (*Dōtei*, 1914) and *Chieko's Sky* (*Chieko-shō*, 1941), is one of the best-known poets in Japan.[1] Which is to say, we must consider that the way in which he is known is quite problematic.

Most Japanese first encounter the work of Takamura Kōtarō in middle school or high school Japanese literature classes.[2] These encounters are likely to be with the two poems "The Road Ahead" ("*Dōtei*") and "Lemon Elegy" ("*Remon aika*"), and, in fact, we might say that the image of Takamura, the poet, has been constructed around these two poems. In terms of such an image, Takamura has been considered to be a poet who contributed to the enlightenment of the Japanese by working with such motifs as the development of independent character or ideal love between man and woman. Takamura becomes, that is, a kind of *missionary* of the modern values of idealism and humanism.[3] But something is occluded by this evaluation that we cannot ignore.

As is familiar to many, during the war years (that is, the period of the Asian Pacific War extending from the outbreak of the Sino-Japanese War of 1937 to Japan's defeat in 1945) the poet Takamura wrote many poems lauding Japan's imperialistic war. In this respect, the figure of Takamura was, and remains, problematic within Japan's modern history. Hidden in the shadows of the image of idealism and humanism is this other dimension of Takamura as a poet of war, and in the figure of Takamura, the modern poet, constructed in contemporary Japanese education, a mechanism—conscious

161

or unconscious—is at work, differentiating between what we do and do not want to see about him. To overstate the point somewhat, let me suggest that the very fact that such a phenomenon exists is revelatory of the nature of modernity in Japan.

To be sure, the problems we must take up in relation to the memory of Takamura Kōtarō formed in postwar Japan are somewhat more intricate. If we turn our attention from matters of public education to the arguments of scholars and literary critics, it becomes immediately apparent that the connection between Takamura and the Asian Pacific War has always been a focus of controversy. Far from being ignored, Takamura was one of the central exhibits in the debates over the war responsibility of writers, which aroused such concern at one point after the war. From this perspective, we might conclude that the selective memory of Takamura exercised in public education might indeed be linked somehow to the ways in which he was discussed in the war responsibility debates. Could it be that what is at stake in the problem of Takamura Kōtarō is not so much suppression as the way the debates themselves took a form that allowed for, and even came to promote, the selective remembrance of Takamura? If that is the case, we are facing a problem that penetrates the very core of the mentality of postwar Japan.

How, then, was the figure of Takamura Kōtarō shaped in postwar debates over war responsibility? Whether in discussions of Takamura's social background or biographical analyses, the observations and emphases of those who commented on Takamura are, of course, as varied as the number of participants. Yet looking back from the standpoint of the present, certain common features emerge. If we were to sketch just the outlines of arguments presented by a range of critics, we could point to a shared narrative that explains Takamura's poetic collaboration with the war effort as a "return to Japan," whether along the lines of "the dissolution of a modern self" (as Yoshimoto Takaaki has argued) or along the lines of a "failure of critical consciousness" (as Serizawa Shunsuke asserts).[4] What might account for the fact that so many critics have attempted to interpret Takamura's wartime production according to this shared problematic?

Takamura's early personal history seems, indeed, to lend itself rather well to the notion of a "return to Japan." Takamura Kōtarō was born in Tokyo as the eldest son of Takamura Kōun, an Edo craftsman (a carver of Shinto and Buddhist sculptures) who rose to become a professor at the Tokyo School of Fine Arts. Accordingly, Takamura was designated from birth to be a successor to his father's, and to his household's, occupation of carving, and he grew up grappling with issues posed by this legacy. On the other hand, Takamura admired the modern sculptor François Auguste Rodin, and as a young man went to the United States and Europe to study sculpture. From then on, Takamura appeared to be caught up in a profound internal conflict between the "Japan" symbolized by his father, and the "West" symbolized by Rodin. At first glance, these aspects of Takamura's life seem to conform to a model of psychological development that has been seen as typical of many intellectuals in modern Japan.

And yet, to see the path that led Takamura to produce poetry supporting the war as "a return to Japan," is to interpret it as a story of "collapse and conversion," in which Takamura's newly awakened modern consciousness underwent a breakdown when he confronted the reality of the backwardness of Japan. Yoshimoto Takaaki, for example, describes it this way: "Takamura lost the ability to resist, and when he surrendered to the mentality of the Japanese commoner, Japan's most advanced model of modern identity was destroyed. This was the same kind of inner process that brought communism, as well as humanism, in Japan to the brink of collapse."[5] By way of providing a backdrop for this phenomenon, Yoshimoto says, "There is a point of intersection between Takamura's breakdown and that of many other poets who were his contemporaries: what underlies that point of intersection is a semi-feudal society that had organized itself into a form of modern imperialism."[6] Efforts like Yoshimoto's and others to understand Takamura's war complicity as a story of collapse and conversion share, to a large extent, the historical view of a Japan struggling to come to terms with its defeat in the war (the view of history that became orthodoxy in the postwar "enlightened" era); this is a view that sees prewar and wartime Japan as insufficiently modernized and claims that residual premodernity led Japan into a barbaric war and defeat.

Actually, this interpretation of Takamura's war complicity is in fact Takamura's own interpretation. After the war, Takamura published a series of poems called "*A Brief History of Imbecility*" (*Angu shōden*, 1947), which looked back on his life and which commented particularly on his writings during the war.[7] In these reminiscences, Takamura expresses an attitude of remorse and deep self-reflection. Thus, the point of departure for the postwar Takamura was a self-criticism that determined that buckling under in the face of the backwardness of Japan was "imbecilic." It was this stance, which he called "self-criticism," that allowed Takamura to be reborn into postwar Japan, lauding modern values such as "the pioneering spirit," "a lifestyle of science and beauty," and "the liberation of nuclear energy," while embarking on a new creative project. This new phase of modernism Takamura had entered into corresponded perfectly to the guiding ideology of postwar Japan, then pursuing the goals of scientific technology and industrial development.

When we consider these things together, it becomes apparent that the war responsibility debate (which traced the "imbecilic" or "dim-witted" Takamura's conversion to a stance of cooperation with the war by way of a "return to Japan") and the school curriculum that praises his "idealism and humanism" are conceptually two sides of the same coin. And, precisely because of this, the view that takes wartime Japan as extraordinarily backward and condemns the converted Takamura as misguided comes to be linked with the standpoint that entirely affirms postwar Japan's "moderni-

zation" and positively evaluates the modern poet Takamura. Such a pattern
provides for a kind of convenient "twist," whereby the very process of pursuing war responsibility undermines itself, for what never is subjected to
question is the *continuity* between wartime and postwar through which the
burden of war responsibility persists.

This essay is concerned with modes of remembering history, but is not
an attempt to judge the matter of ethical responsibility. I want to look back
over positive and negative aspects of our ways of recollecting Takamura to
the extent that they are connected with our own historical view of prewar
and postwar Japan. Is it appropriate for the intellectual trajectory of prewar
and wartime Takamura to be taken as a "return to Japan" brought on by a
breakdown of a modern consciousness? Also, what is the significance of
Takamura's transition into the postwar, the transition of one who sought
rebirth by labeling his wartime return to Japan as "misguided"? The purpose of taking up these questions is to reconsider the trajectory of modernity and modern consciousness itself as it occurred in Japan, and to extend
these considerations to our own present.

THE PROTOTYPE OF SALVATION BY NATURE: TAKAMURA'S FIRST CRISIS
AND THE SANCTIFICATION OF "CHIEKO"

The autumn wind comes up and the white clouds fly by,
But this year what hurries south are the ranks of my brethren.
What lies in wait in the south is shellfire.[8]

This is the opening of "Ode to the Autumn Wind" (*"Shūfū no ji"*), published in the newspaper *Miyako Shinbun* just when the Sino-Japanese war
had become full-scale, after the 1937 Marco Polo Bridge incident. Around
this time, Takamura's poetry rapidly took on a pro-war hue. Before long,
Takamura would come to speak of the propriety of the war in the name of
the emperor and Japan. If we were to take what has been called the "postwar value system" as the basis of our thinking, this interpretation of Takamura as someone undergoing "the dissolution of modern identity" or "a
lapse in critical thinking" is not unreasonable. To the extent that one accepts
the presupposition that complicity in a war fought in the name of Japan and
a self-constructed modern consciousness are, by definition, opposed, one
has no choice but to think that Takamura's identity must have suffered a
breakdown or buckled under pressure.

And yet, if we change our perspective a bit and look into Takamura's
personal history, we notice that the period around 1937 was a time of deep
crisis for him personally. At this time, the condition of his wife, Chieko—
who had previously begun to show signs of insanity—had deteriorated quite
a bit, and, in 1938, she would die. Furthermore, just a few years earlier, in
1934, his father, Kōun, whom Takamura had continued to think of as "the
most difficult and most distressing relationship I have to deal with," had

died.[9] This situation by itself was enough to have driven Takamura to the edge.

When we consider these circumstances, Takamura's rapid movement into cooperation with the war effort, when seen as a personal action, can be understood as a self-devised way out of a crisis rather than something that was forced upon him. If we take into consideration that Takamura mass-produced war poetry and even worked as head of the Central Cooperative Council (*Chūō Kyōryoku Kaigi*), we have to assume that the poet Takamura had the ability to take responsibility quite prominently and must have developed the identity to allow that. At the very least, one cannot explain away Takamura's war complicity as simply the result of external pressure and, furthermore, we must see that Takamura's sense of self did not dissolve in that process, but rather was *preserved* through it. If that is so, then perhaps what we need to try to understand is the kind of identity that inclined Takamura to overcome his personal crisis in this manner.

Thus, the problem we should take up is something like the following: to analyze the fundamental structure of the resolution Takamura found to the crisis that visited him, and to try from that perspective to close in on the "self" that employed this solution. When we look back over Takamura's personal history, there are, in fact, three crises in his everyday life that seem to be related to his identity. The crisis around Chieko's insanity and death was actually Takamura's second personal crisis, the first having occurred upon his return from study abroad in the United States and Europe, and the third coming along with Japan's defeat in the war. In what manner did Takamura try to overcome these various crises? But also, what sort of consciousness of identity is displayed in such a process? Let us take these in turn, starting with the first crisis, which is also the original point of crisis for Takamura.

The first crisis, which came upon Takamura directly after his return from abroad, is most clearly revealed in the fact that, at that time, he found that he could not fit into Japanese society and had no alternative but to take up a lifestyle of decadence. However, in order to truly comprehend the meaning of this crisis, we must know the kinds of problems that studying abroad held for Takamura. Takamura returned to Japan in June of 1909, after three years abroad in the United States and Europe. Yoshimoto Takaaki indicates the importance of this study abroad when he says that Takamura "first shouldered the internal motifs of his life during his study abroad in Europe and the United States."[10] This statement seems to be confirmed today by many critics, but exactly why is it that one can say this?

Two aspects of Takamura's experience are salient. First of all, he became aware that he had grown away, and was now estranged, from his father and household, but precisely in this way they continued to preoccupy him as the "most difficult of relationships."[11] In a piece entitled "A Sheaf of Letters Not Sent" ("*Dasazu ni shimatta tegami no hitotaba*"), which was published soon after his return to Japan, Takamura used the epistle form to express his feelings while abroad concerning his father:

> In actuality, parent and child must remain locked in struggle and cannot come to peace. If the parent is strong, he degrades the child and it results in so-called filial piety. If the child is strong, then, like the bell cricket, he consumes the parent. . . . When I think about it now, my going overseas was the mistake of my father's whole life. . . . I myself have become someone who cannot be reigned in. Now I will probably end up doing as the bell cricket does.[12]

Takamura would later say, "I became an adult in Paris,"[13] but the preceding quote shows not simply that he is aware of having outgrown his father; there is also a premonition here that the realization of principles fundamentally different from the father's world gave birth to an irreconcilable opposition to the father. In the background of this premonition, we can see two other oppositions: first, considering that his father's craft was sculpture, Takamura's awakening to the modern fine arts stands in opposition to the craftsman's art of the father; second, he becomes estranged from, and fundamentally critical of, the Japanese commoner's world symbolized by his father. This critical consciousness of Takamura's appeared as a quite shocking criticism of Japan in an essay called "A Country of Grotesque Ornamentals" ("*Netsuke no kuni*"), which ends with the description of "a Japanese like a piece of broken china" (i.e., totally useless and lacking beauty).

In contrast to this, another aspect of the problem Takamura encountered while studying abroad was the intensified and insurmountable isolation that he discovered after taking the necessary step "towards the West" in order to estrange himself from the world of his father. In "A Sheaf of Letters not Sent" this appears in the following form: "Alone. Alone. Why am I in Paris? Paris's awful CRIMSON smiling faces leave me desolate. The voices of pleasure in Paris's streets seem to hurl me down into a bottomless well of gloom."[14] Or in a section entitled "From a Cafe," he recalls the pitiful experience of waking the morning after spending a night together with a Parisian woman, feeling completely Parisian himself yet being startled by his own figure, somehow Asian-looking, reflected in the bathroom mirror: "The keenly painful thought . . . ah, after all I'm a Japanese. JAPONAIS. MONGOL. LE JAUNE."[15] As many of the students who went abroad from the Meiji period on probably did, Takamura, experiencing a sudden scission from that West with which the infatuated self had entirely identified for a moment, became conscious once again of being of "Japan."

Of course, to really know the meaning of Takamura's overseas experience going from New York to London to Paris, it would be necessary to consider a great deal more of that history. However, I have just mentioned the foregoing to convey a sense of the first crisis that visited Takamura. The crucial matter is that—although the binary opposition between "Japan" and "the West" make us tend to think of Takamura's experiences of estrangement from Japan and his isolation from the West as mutually exclusive—in his study abroad, Takamura experienced these two things simultaneously. The feelings of so-called "marginality" and angst attendant upon his discovery meant that he could no longer simply identify himself as either Japanese or Western. Due to these feelings, he could no longer locate a "true place" in which he could live comfortably, either in lands of the West or in the commoner's world of Japan. The urge to criticize Japan that erupted in Takamura after his return from abroad further intensified these feelings of anxiety and loneliness, and threatened his identity once again. There was no place for Takamura to go except to embrace a decadent lifestyle. This was Takamura's first crisis.

Now let us turn our attention to what Takamura did to overcome this crisis. As many critics have pointed out, the adoption of a unique philosophy of "Nature" became Takamura's opportunity for escaping his decadent phase (or "first crisis"). However, the philosophy of "Nature" Takamura embraced was quite different from the pan-humanist view of nature that is usually erroneously read out of the work, "The Road Ahead." The publication in 1914 (by Takamura himself) of the collection *Dōtei* was certainly an announcement to society that Takamura had overcome his crisis, yet in the original version of the poem (which had appeared in a magazine before being revised and included in the 1914 volume) the relationship between "Nature" and Takamura's escape from crisis is presented in some detail. Let us look at some of characteristic passages of the poem, paying close attention to Takamura's use of the expressions "Nature" and "Father."

"Nature"

"Looking back on it / My own path has been frightful / . . . / I look at my own miserable path / And I shed tears at Nature's enormous love / From the midst of that worthless-looking path / Nature showed me ever so clearly the meaning of life."

"They and I both / Are but single parts of that thing called the great human race / Yet the human race freely discards and lets rot useless things / . . . / Nature makes an abundance of humans for the human race / let rot rotting things / Things that defy Nature all rot / At this point I cannot care about them."

"Father"

"'Wake up, wake up,' it was Nature that called / This indeed is the love of a strict father / As the child I keenly felt the thanks due."

"My startled spirit / Suddenly pierced by a voice that said "Walk!" / I rallied my courage / I felt the mission of the child throughout my body / The mission of the child! / It weighed upon my shoulders."

"At that time I once again prayed to my father / My father showed me in that landscape but a few people further on, walking the same way."

"The child is one in whom burns the desire to repay the love of the father."[16]

What Takamura is trying to express here in the notion of "Nature" is clearly not humanism. It is more like the transcendence of nature over humans. And from this transcendental nature, "I" receives commandments to "wake up" and to "walk!" Similarly, the "Father" who appears here is not the actual living, biological father, but is seen as one with "Nature" in the background, which gives ethical commandments to "me." Such a vision in which "Nature" and "Father" are linked, is not, as Yoshimoto Takaaki has suggested, a simplistic "affirmation of personal environment," from which Takamura's earlier "criticism of the Japanese" has been lost.[17] "Nature" and "Father" are elements in a backdrop that we must first of all understand as allowing awareness of one's supposed ethical mission ("the mission of the child") to emerge, but also as producing the conceit of the righteousness of that mission. We can see that, in terms of his own subjective judgment, only *awareness of an ethical mission that transcends the immediate self* was able to generate the power Takamura needed to break out of his crisis.

We should notice that these ideas, in their attempt to entrust the self to the productivity of an enlightened progress ("wake up," "walk"), are a very modernist way of thinking. Of course, this modernism was not of the sort that made a credo out of ideals or modes of life that originated in the modern West. Rather, we could say that Takamura embraced a pure form of modernism insofar as the theme of "let rot the rotting / all that defies nature rots" rejects so-called stagnation and traditionalism, and seems to signify the embrace of an attitude towards life that always wagers on progress. Takamura's "first crisis," then, should be seen as a crisis of identity brought on by the anxiety of finding oneself on the boundary between Japan/biological father and "the West." Rather than identifying with either, Takamura moved forward on his own path, endeavoring to overcome his crisis through a modernist vision.

The problem with such thinking is that, since it lacks a social foundation and goes no further than to indicate an abstract notion of awakening and progress, the path to be pursued can only be a subjective and ambiguous one. This is a condition symptomatic of the solitude and anxiety of the modern person, who would affirm only himself or herself and who tries earnestly to travel his or her own road. Such a condition inevitably gives rise to the search for some kind of rootedness, which can provide the stability and conviction of a direction for that journey. For Takamura, at the time of his first crisis, this "rootedness" and certainty were provided by the encounter with the woman who would become his wife, Chieko. If the relationship with Chieko had simply meant a kind of "psychological support" or "liberation of physical desire" for Takamura, there would have perhaps have been no gap between the historical Chieko's mental and physical state and the reality of his poems. Yet for Takamura, it was necessary to find in Chieko's existence something that could give conviction to his journey toward the destiny assigned by Nature, and also something that purified that endeavor. Only in that way was it possible to overcome his crisis. "Chieko" therefore became for Takamura something beyond the historical Chieko, a sacred being. In a work from the same period as "Dōtei," Takamura extols Chieko in this manner:

When I think of you
I feel closest to eternity . . .
For us everything is the absolute
There is none of what the world calls the struggle between man and woman
Only faith and experience and passion and freedom
And then awesome power and authority
The fusion of one part of humanity with the other
With the same ease that I trust in Nature
I believe in our lives . . .
You are fire . . . [18]

At a glance, this near worship of Chieko may seem to be a beautiful, idealized love, but there is no mistaking the great deceptiveness of this. Takamura's idealization of her was an overly heavy burden for the historical Chieko to bear, and it is clear that eventually this burden plunged her into her own crisis. While Chieko's madness in her last years can be ascribed to various physical, household, and social causes, as far as her relationship with Takamura was concerned, we must also consider it the flipside of Takamura's resolution of his own crisis, achieved by projecting a sense of sacredness onto Chieko. For one who felt he had received the commandments of a transcendent Nature, sustained by the sanctification of Chieko, however, it was inevitable that this "overcoming" should collapse in the face of Chieko's breakdown.

Takamura's scheme to overcome his first crisis, then, was frustrated by these internal difficulties. Because of them, he found himself overwhelmed by a new crisis. How did Takamura respond to this second crisis?

MODERNITY IN SEARCH OF MYTHS: TAKAMURA'S SECOND CRISIS AND THE
SANCTIFICATION OF JAPAN

Takamura's second crisis, which reached its extreme with the death of
Chieko in 1938, came just as Japan was entering its imperialistic war. Many
critics already rely on the idea that Takamura's personal crisis was a crucial
factor in driving him into a position of direct commitment to the unfolding
war. However, we need to skeptically reassess the ways in which this argument has been used as a starting point for critiques of Takamura. For
example, Serizawa Shunsuke makes the following remarks:

> What I want to question is the reason why Takamura was no longer
> able to maintain an internal state in which he could maintain two things
> in tension, and why he needed to abandon his own identity in order to
> move to a position directly implicated in the trends of the times. One
> answer to this question is simply the collapse of "the couple." In other
> words, the crisis of nature symbolized by his deteriorating relationship
> with Chieko had already gone beyond the possibility of repair; the
> foundation that had been supporting Takamura's identity had crum-
> bled.[19]

It is clear here that Serizawa considers the breakdown of the relationship with Chieko to be the definitive cause driving Takamura to produce
war poetry. Let us say that the basic outline of this thinking is correct, as
long as we do not neglect the point that the collapse of this relationship was
itself brought on by difficulties internal to Takamura's own schemes to resolve his first crisis. What we have to problematize is Serizawa's idea that
at this point Takamura "abandoned his own identity." If we are to try to do
a proper historical and intellectual critique of Takamura, shouldn't we start
by disinterestedly tracing what Takamura himself was thinking? When we
introduce determinations such as "the collapse of identity" into our thinking, the line of hypothetical argument is severed, and we lose sight of Takamura's capability for responsibility as a person of his time, as well as of
the intellectual and ideological implications of this matter. The critics who
speak of Takamura's "conversion" and "collapse," are simply re-evaluating
what seems to be Takamura's identity from the perspective of their own
postwar values, and in doing so they evade and suppress what it is about
Takamura, and about themselves, that we actually should concentrate on.
    Let us propose rather that Takamura's conduct at this point be under-
stood as a scheme for overcoming his crisis and guarding his identity, and
on this basis proceed with an analysis of the preparations underlying that
scheme.
    Even before it resulted in actual failure in the form of Chieko's descent
into "madness," it should be clear that, supported as it was by the mystification of Chieko, Takamura's resolution of his first crisis was quite unsta-

ble. Since the cost of resolving his first crisis and maintaining his identity as sculptor was to give up writing poetry, we can deduce from the fact that Takamura resumed writing poetry that he must have become aware of an instability in his first resolution. Already at this point Takamura could not rest comfortably in the mystification of Chieko, and found the craving for a new course difficult to suppress. The metaphor of "the beast" we find in a poem written in 1923 expresses that craving. In the poem "A Stinging Epigram," ("*Togetoge na epiguramu*") the metaphor appears in the following form:

> If you please, don't make up your mind yet
> It is not just cheerful
> It is not just pretty,
> Dark things, filthy things
> Horrible things, brutal things
> Filled with those kinds of beasts
> I am a desert
> That's why I'm impatient for a beautiful world
> To tame this beast
> And send it back to the original Eden
> Dreadful
> My great entreaty.[20]

In light of the instability of the "beauty" that Takamura had set up as a response to his first crisis, one reason for calling forth the beast here is evident. If we then look at the series of poems in "*The Beast Compilation*" ("*Mojūhen*") and pay attention to the way the relationship between "the beast" and Takamura himself is handled, we notice that on either side of the second crisis, there is a gradual, yet significant, change by means of which Takamura comes to identify himself with the beast.[21] First of all, there is this poem, "Polar Bear" ("*Shirokuma*"), one of the early pieces from the series.

> In wind-blown Bronx Park
> Where the snow like granulated sugar remained
> He, with the typical Jap face of a deaf-mute,
> Spent the Sunday standing in front of the polar bear's cage . . .
> The polar bear too was silent and from time to time looked at him.
> For the first time in a week he didn't hear the voices calling, "All right,"
> And bathed in silence he continued standing in front of the enormous white bear.[22]

The beast, which earlier in "A Stinging Epigram" appeared just as an object that had to be kept and tamed, here becomes an interlocutor that meets the gaze of the narrator. Then, in the 1937 "Elephant" ("Zō"), the beast comes to appear as "me."

> The elephant walks on slowly.
> Enough of the stockade trap that once confined me . . .
> They think they've already caught and tamed me
> I can't stand their complacent smugness
> I break the chains and come out.[23]

Finally, in the 1938 "Fish of the Northern Darkness" ("*Hokumei no sakana*"), this beast that is "me" is transformed into a "U-boat of the northern sea," which represents the southward advance of the Japanese military itself.

> The great fish Kon of the northern darkness has now become a U-boat
>   of the northern sea.
> Such a terribly small thing it has become,
> But the will to drive south has not shrunk . . .
> Deftly swimming amidst the mines,
> With bated breath it draws near its selected prey
> And fires a torpedo hitting the target with a single shot . . .
> For what purpose does the underwater boat drive southward?
> Stop asking for what purpose!
> This is not something a human can know.
> Behind the answer is another answer
> The terrible physical law of limitless reality.[24]

In the process of writing the series of poems later compiled as *Mōjūhen*, Takamura, through gradually identifying himself with the beast, became more and more involved in the events of the period. Let us note that, at the same time that the poem dismisses questions about that involvement ("Stop asking to what purpose!") there is a positive answer: "The terrible physical law of limitless reality." Here, too, Takamura seems to use the idea of "Nature" to justify his gradual commitment to the state of affairs. In the two collections of Takamura's wartime poetry, *Towards That Great Day* (*Ōinaru hi ni*, 1944) and *A Record* (*Kiroku*, 1944), we can quite clearly discern a revival of the thought of "Nature" as a foundation upon which Takamura's self-justification rests. The following images of nature are taken from Takamura's poems written between 1927 and 1939:

> "At last, Autumn has come," and "Salut, Autumn!," "Northeastern Wind, Rain" ("*Hokutō no kaze, ame*," 1927)[25]

> "That rustic combustible, the sun, just burns," "Un-European" ("*Hi-Ōbeiteki naru*," 1932)[26]

"This year the autumn that visits Japan / is a vast autumn, such as our ancestors never knew." "Ode to the Autumn Wind" ("*Shūfū no ji*," 1937)[27]

"An unprecedented time approaches in the silence / covering everything, it is a time when to die is to live / Such a time is already at hand." "An Unprecedented Time" ("*Mizou no toki*," 1937)[28]

"A storm now rages over the Eastern corner of the world." "Then Morning Will Come" ("*Sono toki asa wa kuru*," 1938)[29]

"For two years, and no matter how many more, / The nation's people steel their will and drive away doubt. / Inevitably, the laws of this universe flow swiftly on." "The Second Anniversary of the Manchurian Incident" ("*Jihen nishūnen*," 1939)[30]

Of course, this "autumn," which is accepted as an "inevitable law of the universe," was nothing other than the unfolding events of the time: the progression of events occurring between the so-called Manchurian Incident and the Marco Polo Bridge Incident, which led to all-out war with China. It follows that Takamura found the power to overcome his immediate crisis in a fatalistic thinking that let him accept as "Nature" the great transformations in the situation that seem to transcend his individual self, and that allowed him to think that "Nature" required as his mission a commitment to that state of affairs. This is a solution that takes the same form as the response to his first crisis.

And yet, when we trace the process by which Takamura justified, once again by means of "Nature," his commitment to the wartime state of affairs, we notice that it led to the appearance in Takamura's poetry of references to "Japan" and to "the Emperor." Takamura's poetry, which in the 1930 poem "Friend" ("*Tomo yo*") had claimed "for me there is no privileged country," began speaking of the "homeland" called Japan in the 1937 "Ode to the Autumn Wind," and eventually this led to the following verses in "Japanese Autumn" ("*Nihon no aki*," 1938):

If it is something that must come,
It doesn't matter what kind of squall or storm it is . . .
Long ago the residents of these islands knew
That after the storm, heaven brings
The beautiful, jewel-like weather of autumn . . .
That Japanese autumn has come again,
It's better to think how nice autumn is.[31]

In the 1939 poem "On the Two Thousand Six Hundredth Year of Imperial Reign" ("*Kigen nisen roppyakunen ni atarite*," 1939), Takamura wrote:

What sort of age is it now?
The Emperor is our parent,
Wherever he deigns to guide us
Naturally follows the opportunity of heaven
No different from the past, the children of Kume[32] cross the ocean
And now fight in the vast expanses of Asia.[33]

As is quite clear here, "Japan" and "the Emperor" are thought to be part of the flow of natural time, just as "autumn" and "the opportunity of heaven" are. But also, "Japan" and "the Emperor" are the foundations that enable Takamura to ascertain that he himself is being made to participate in that "natural" time. In this sense, Takamura's turn to "Japan" and "the Emperor" in this second crisis fulfill the same role as his creation of "Chieko" did at the time of his first crisis. Takamura, having lost "Chieko" to that foreign land of insanity and death, now attempts to secure a new basis of conviction by sanctifying "Japan" and "the Emperor." "The Emperor" is called a "parent" in these verses, but let us note that this emperor/parent differs from both Takamura's biological father, Kōun, and from the actual, flesh-and-blood emperor. "The Emperor" here takes on a mythical form. As with the use of Chieko, in this second crisis, Japan and the emperor transcend actual entities and become quasi-mystical ideals.

Beginning with Yoshimoto Takaaki, past critics have deemed Takamura's sanctification of "Japan" and "the emperor" either as the manifestation of "a pseudo-Asian philosophy, rooted in the semi-feudal attitudes held by the common people, which flowered out of season" (Yoshimoto), or "a complete repatriation from the West to an Asian communality" (Serizawa). However, it is a great mistake to conflate Takamura's sanctification of "Japan" and "the emperor" with a simple reactionary sentiment (a return to Asia, and to Japan). Takamura's sanctification of "Japan" and "the Emperor" is rather the acceptance of an actual on-going state of affairs as a "natural" phenomenon, a state of affairs that requires that one "waken" and "walk forward." As such, it is nothing other than ideology *structured by the deliberate citation of myth*. In this sense, exactly as was the case with the myth of "Chieko," the myth of Japan and the emperor are being invented and/or created out of a necessity to respond to the state of affairs. We have to think that, far from being "Asian," Takamura's views were those that the progress of Japan's modernity demanded, and that it was Takamura's modern consciousness that gave birth to this scheme in response to that demand.

Clearly this mythically justified Japanese modernity, with its pseudo-ethical driving force, brought about a very brutal violence, whether against Asia or against the commoners of Japan. Two years after the Marco Polo Bridge Incident, Takamura, while fully conscious of the cruelties of this war in which so much blood had been spilled, nonetheless justified it by addressing a hypothetical Chinese readership in the following terms:

From the greed of those who wish to colonize China,
You shall be saved, and the real "you" found
Isn't this why blows must rain down on your head?
Trying to restore our "Way" over their profit,
Today, again, the nation's people dedicate their lives.[34]

That the self-justification of one's own course should attain this grotesque and dangerous form can, of course, not be attributed to a collapse of identity. It can only be because inextricable from Takamura's expression here is a modern sense of mission, according to which belief in the self alone is the basis for moving into the future. The sanctification of "Japan" that accompanied this scheme for overcoming the second crisis would at length come to the same end as the collapse of the mystified Chieko. Yet, it would come to ruin in what was socially an extremely catastrophic situation: Japan's defeat in the war. This led to yet a third crisis for Takamura, which we will now examine.

REMORSE FOR "IMBECILITY" AND SALVATION THROUGH MODERNISM: THE THIRD CRISIS AND THE SANCTIFICATION OF LIFE

After Japan's defeat in the war, Takamura withdrew to a mountain village in Iwate and started a lifestyle of self-subsistence farming. He referred to this as a form of "self-imposed exile." It was from this location that, in 1947, he published a collection of poetry looking back upon his own life, entitled *A Brief History of Imbecility*. In taking up the question of how Takamura's prewar and wartime thought might be related to his postwar intellectual stance, we must first turn our attention to this collection. Let us start by analyzing the structures of two poems, "Pearl Harbor Day"("*Shinjūwan no hi*"), collected in *Angu Shōden*, and the wartime poem "The Eighth of December" ("*Jūnigatsu Yōka*," 1941). The outbreak of war between Japan and the U.S. is the common theme of both poems.

First, from the wartime poem, "The Eighth of December":

Record it, the eighth of December.
On this day world history has been renewed,
Anglo-Saxon domination
On this day was rejected in East Asian lands and seas.
What was rejected was their "Japan"
A tiny country of the eastern seas
But also our "*Nippon*," land of the gods.
A god in human form bestows his rule upon it.
The ones who monopolize the world's wealth,
The Anglo-American family of bullies,
Have been rejected by our homeland.
This denial is just.

We only ask that Asia be returned to Asia.
Neighboring countries all languish under their exploitation.
Truly, we are striving to break their grip.
We will garner our own power and rise once again,
Old and young, men and women, all are soldiers.
We will fight until the great enemies admit their wrongs.
This is the great divide of history
The eighth of August,
Record the date.[35]

In *A Brief History of Imbecility*, we find this poem written in 1947:

"Pearl Harbor Day"

Before the declaration of war, I heard that
There was a battle in the vicinity of Hawaii.
At last there was fighting in the Pacific.
When I heard the imperial proclamation my body trembled.
During this uneasy moment
My mind was suspended in an alembic,
Yesterday became the distant past,
The distant past had become now.
The emperor was in danger.
This single phrase
Determined everything for me.
The grandfather of my childhood,
My father and mother were there.
The clouds and fog of the house of my younger days,
Rose and filled the room.
My ears filled with the voices of the ancestors.
His majesty, His majesty
My struggling consciousness swooned.
There is nothing to do now but to throw one's self away.
Protect His Majesty.
Let us write poems abandoning poetry.
Let us write the record.
Let us prevent, if we can, the ruin of our brethren.
That night at Komagomedai, when Jupiter sparkled brilliantly,
So did I simply, seriously, decide.[36]

When we juxtapose these two poems, we can see that the wartime composition is structured in a certain order. It begins with a hailing of the renewal of history (history is here seen as the naturalness of the flow of time), proceeds to lines exalting "Japan" and "the Emperor" through reference to myths, and ends with the acceptance of the imposed mission. The outlines of Takamura's response to his second crisis, which we analyzed in the preceding section, are distinctly visible here. In Takamura's postwar poem, however, that structure has completely disappeared. Instead, we encounter the following progression of images and themes: first, the theme of the delusion of historical understanding that conflates "the past" and "now"; second, the image of a beloved Japan in which emperor, grandfather, father, and mother appear together; and finally, the articulation of an earnest wish to try to protect this Japan. How might we understand this shift in structure from the wartime to the postwar work?

First, in order to get a more complete picture of Takamura's self-criticism that occurs in the postwar "Pearl Harbor Day," let us expand our field of vision to include other poems from *A Brief History of Imbecility*. When we examine some of the motifs from these poems, we can see that the chronology of the self's fall into the delusion ("dim-wittedness," mis-guidedness) of historical understanding is made into a sort of confessional narrative in this collection. The following phrases are taken from poems in the anthology:

"The Russo-Japanese War—a candy proffered at the start of Japan's tragic path of expansion—was of no interest to me." "Dedication to Sculpture" ("*Chōkoku ichizu*")[37]

I became an adult in Paris.
The modern arose in Paris,
Beauty incubated and germinated in Paris,
The brain's new cells were born in Paris . . .
With a sense of sadness, yet unavoidably,
I felt the incomparable gap.
Japanese ways and things, all of them,
I longed for, yet rejected.
"Paris" (*Pari*)[38]

My becoming unfilial was something
That had to be done in the name of humanity.
I want to live as an individual human.
In this country where nothing tolerates humans,
That was nothing short of rebellion.
"Unfilial" ("*Oya fukō*")[39]

When we read these phrases in this order and include the postwar "Pearl Harbor Day," they seem to constitute a summary by Takamura of his own life. It is as if he were explaining, "I, who was disinterested in history, became struck by progressive aspects of modernity in the West (Paris). While for a time I sought to oppose a backward Japan, when war with America broke out, I made the error of confusing the past with the present."

Takamura indicates that the cause of this delusion about history was his stumbling upon a "beloved Japan in which the emperor, grandfather, father, and mother appear together." Accordingly, the historical interpretation that Takamura presents here assumes a dichotomy between "the modernized West" and "a backward Japan, carried along by affection." The "dim-wittedness" of being swayed by one's love for Japan, despite the absolute gap in the level of modernity between Japan and the West, is the culprit responsible for entry onto the path of war collaboration and defeat.

At a glance, Takamura's reflection on his life does indeed seem to be sincere and consistent. The great trickiness of his schema, however, becomes apparent when we consider it in relation to the excerpts quoted above, and to the wartime poem "The Eighth of December."

To start with, note that the "us" of the wartime poem, which sees history clearly, changes in the postwar piece into the misguided "I" who is deluded about history. Furthermore, the revered "god in human form," who in wartime transcends mundane reality, in the postwar becomes the human "emperor" who is set alongside Takamura's grandfather. These transpositions make it difficult to raise questions of agency in relation to either the emperor or the grandfather. There is nothing to do but to forgive stupidity. The poet's surrender to the demands of a beloved collectivity must be accepted as human weakness.

A more crucial point, however, is that what is taken in wartime to be a "renewal of history" is declared, after the war, to be a return to the Japan of the "past." In other words, Takamura asserts that the problem lay in having been made dizzy and allowing oneself to regress, but not in the call to awaken and advance that dominated his wartime writing. This kind of emphasis deflects our attention towards a "backward Japan," and away from the modern imperialistic war and the Japan that pursued that course. Hence a reflection on "backwardness" flips to its opposite face of praise for "the modernized West." Such a critique, in fact, is just a step away from the position that expresses remorse—not about having fought an imperialistic war—but about having been defeated in that war. It is just such an attitude that produced the postwar policy that, while conceding defeat in the war, exhorted the nation to fight even harder to modernize.

Thus the message that initiates Takamura's postwar work is once again a call to accept "Nature" as the flow of time into the future, and to continue advancing forward. The final piece in *A Brief History of Imbecility*, "Mountain Forest" ("*Sanrin*"), puts the message in the following way:

I am now in the mountain forest . . .
Since I saw so distastefully my own foolishness
I accept gladly any evaluation of my work
I listen humbly as I am lashed by a thousand attacks
If that is society's convention
I gladly submit to the harshest punishment

Poems are born naturally,
My passion for sculpture burns ever more fiercely
I communicate every day with masters of ancient times.
I neither struggle excessively
Nor rest, but move forward step by step
When I can walk no longer, the day is done.
The skeletal structure of a Japan that is no other country
Stands, severely, in the mountain forest
The reason our nation exists in this world
Must be rooted there ... [40]

Takamura, in essence, has not changed at all. Confronting the new crisis of being a well known war poet in defeated Japan, he still attempts to
find a solution with the methods used in earlier periods. Because of this, we
must acknowledge that Takamura salvages his modernist vision in this way
as well. This is the modernism that rejects so-called stagnation and traditionalism, and which gambles on endlessly advancing as time moves naturally forward.

Of course, ascribing this kind of modernism to the Takamura who has
retreated to a mountain village at first may seem somewhat strange. However, in Takamura's poetry after *A Brief History of Imbecility*, we find
many images and phrase that suggest such a modernist outlook. For example, we find terms such as "natural principle" (in the poem "Touchstone" or
"*Shinkinseki*") or "physical necessity" (in "Jottings" or "*Gūsaku*") appearing with unexpected frequency. On the basis of these principles, Takamura
praises "pioneering spirit" in the poem "To The Reclamation Effort" ("*Kaitaku ni yosu*") and "a lifestyle of science and beauty" in "Let Us Look
Clearly" ("*Meiryō ni miyo*"). Finally, the motif of "advancing, no matter
what" occurs repeatedly, for example, in the poem "Ten Years After Reclamation" ("*Kaitaku jūshūnen*"), and others. In the light of such examples,
it does not seem so unreasonable to define Takamura's poetry as modernist.
Furthermore, when we look at Takamura's last poem, "The Great River of
Life" ("*Seimei no taiga*"), which appeared in the *Yomiuri shinbun* at the
beginning of 1956 as a message to the people of the nation of Japan, we can
see how that modernism was attuned to the mood of postwar Japan as it
proceeded down the path of modernization, emphasizing scientific technology and industrial development. "The Great River of Life" loudly extols
those sentiments:

The great river of Life flows on endlessly
Permitting all contradictions and contrariness and evil
Hurrying noisily towards that place where the far off time is realized ...
Science allows no stagnation.
Science plunges into danger.

Science overcomes danger.
In the face of radioactivity, science does not look back
To conquer radioactivity
For benign uses
It risks everything.
The liberation of atomic energy
At last has transformed everything for humanity
An era of human life beyond our capacity to imagine draws near . . .
Scholarship, art, ethics, and the like
Are momentarily sucked into the vortex of Life's great river
Emerging again as elements of a new age
This is the Great Way of Freedom and Nirvana.[41]

"Nature," then, is a consistent presence in Takamura's poems, from the first to the very last. Even in this last poem, the concept opens up a new sense of mission. Moreover, the object of veneration in this poem is no longer Chieko, Japan, or the Emperor, but "Life" and "Nature" themselves. There is no doubt that postwar Japan, in its mad rush from reconstruction to high-speed growth, shared deeply the same belief in science that Takamura exhibits here. Only at great cost have we become aware of the danger of maintaining such a reverent attitude toward science—the injury done to Minamata victims and countless others. This notwithstanding, Takamura, at least on an intellectual level, was able to ride the currents of postwar history by means of the same modernism that had helped him to resolve his earlier crises.

CONCLUSION

According to Maruyama Masao, immediately after the defeat in the war, Japanese intellectuals composed a "community of remorse" that was defined by the common desire to find a new starting point in critical reflection on the wartime past.[42] Indeed, when Takamura expresses his regret about the "imbecility" of cooperating with the war, we can consider him to be one member of this community of remorse. But, as we have come to see in the course of this argument, if we are to do so, we must question anew the nature of this state of mind called "remorse" and also rethink the meaning of the "transformation" to the postwar that was made possible by mobilizing it.

Of course, Takamura's personal characteristics and daily surroundings strongly affected his experiences and intellectual career. We should be careful not to exaggerate the importance of this one example, or to too broadly generalize on the basis of it. Yet, we must acknowledge that the anxiety and sense of marginality that Takamura experienced in his study abroad are above all things more or less shared by many people who experience the modern in the form of cultural contact, and, furthermore, that modernity itself has evolved through the repetition of such encounters on a global scale. From this perspective, we can see Takamura's responses to his crises as somewhat prototypical of the attitudes of modern people confronting their own age. To the extent that this is true, what I have described as Takamura's "modernism"—his cooperation with the war effort and his remorse after the defeat—is not something to be dismissed as particular to Takamura. While Takamura's trajectory may have taken a more extreme form than most, it should be submitted to rigorous examination for what it reveals of characteristics displayed by many modern people.

Also, although Takamura went through the motions of carrying out a severe self-criticism, we should note that the mode of reflection he calls "remorse" takes the form of his reasoning that the nature of the war was "something that I should have understood from the beginning, but somehow was not able to." Thus, his was a mode of reflection that could serve to ward off doubt concerning the real reasons for being remorseful. What we have come to see in Takamura, in fact, is the way in which "remorse" became a kind of impasse, leaving many problems unresolved and forming a continuity between wartime and postwar Japan.

If this has been the case, then we must try to reconsider what kind of "reflection" the whole "community of remorse" (which included Japan's postwar intellectuals) engaged in. Could that "remorse" itself have provided a bridge through which certain elements that led to Japan's imperialist war were reintroduced in the postwar era? We need to undertake a new kind of analysis based on such considerations. This analysis must avoid the pitfalls of previous theories that spoke of "the dissolution of the modern self"—criticism that, in the end, makes the agency of the Japanese subject more ambiguous—or that deplored "premodern" aspects of Japanese society from the lofty perspective of enlightenment thinking. Rather, we should carefully reflect on how modern subjects dealt with the pressures of their age, keeping ourselves aware both of factors internal to Japanese society and of the simultaneity of many modern phenomena in a global context. An analysis based on such considerations might, indeed, be able to illuminate the problematic of the continuities between prewar and postwar Japan, and might even offer something of universal significance by way of reflection on modernity itself. This is the least that a study of Takamura Kōtarō can offer us.

Translated by Joshua Young

Notes

1. Where applicable, I have consulted the translations of Soichi Furuta, *Chieko's Sky* (Kodansha International, 1978), and Hiroaki Sato, *Chieko and Other Poems of Takamura Kōtarō* (Honolulu: University of Hawaii Press, 1980). Sato's translation includes most of the poems in *Chieko-shō*, all of Ta-

kamura's later *Angu Shōden*, and a scattering of poems from other volumes. (Translator's Note)

2. The first-year high-school literature textbook in use for 1995, "Kokugo I," included 21 poems, of which nine were Takamura's. Since there are so many of his poems in the textbook for just one grade, it is safe to say that during the six years of middle school and high school, just about every Japanese student is exposed at least once to Takamura's poetry.

3. For Takamura's poetry and personal data, I have used Kitagawa Taichi, ed., *Teihon Takamura Kōtarō zenshishū* (Tokyo: Chikuma Shobō, 1982).

4. Yoshimoto Takaaki, "*Sakkaron II*" in *Yoshimoto Takaaki zenchosakushū* 8, (Tokyo: Keiso Shobō, 1973) and Serizawa Shunsuke, *Takamura Kōtarō* (Tokyo: Chikuma Shobō, 1982).

5. Yoshimoto, "*Sakkaron II*," 217.

6. Ibid., 35.

7. Takamura Kōtarō, "*Angu shōden*," in *Takamura Kōtarō zenshū* 3 (Tokyo: Chikuma Shobō, 1976), 267–308 (hereafter, this text will be referred to as *TZK*). Hiroaki Sato, *A Brief History of Imbecility: Poetry and Prose of Takamura Kōtarō* (Honolulu: University of Hawaii Press, 1992). I have kept Hiroaki Sato's title translation for this essay, but I must add a brief explanation of the term *angu* and its use in this essay. While "imbecility" is a common translation of this word, the characters of the word literally mean "to be foolish by reason of being in the dark." This nuance of being "dim-witted" or "misguided" is crucial to the author's argument in this essay, and was, according to Nakano, relevant to Takamura's choice of the word for use in this autobiographical work. Thus, I have at times translated this word as "dim-witted" or "misguided" in order to emphasize Nakano's interpretation and use. (Translator's Note)

8. Takamura, "*Shūfū no ji*," *TKZ* 2 (Tokyo: Chikuma shobō, 1976), 196.

9. Takamura, "*Chichi to no kankei*" in *TKZ* 10, 225.

10. Yoshimoto, "*Sakkaron II*," 8.

11. Concerning the kinds of problems that Takamura had in his relationship with his father and household from childhood on, see the detailed analysis of Serizawa in *Takamura Kōtarō*.

12. Takamura, *TKZ* 9, 52–53.

13. Takamura Kōtarō, "Paris," in *A Brief History of Imbecility*, 137.

14. Takamura, "*Dasazu ni shimatta tegami no hitotaba*," *TKZ* 9, 57.

15. Takamura, "*Kōhiten yori*," *TKZ* 9, 44.

16. These passages are taken from the original 102-line poem of the same title, published in the magazine *Bi no haikyō*, 1914.

17. Yoshimoto, "*Sakkaron II*," 70.

18. Takamura, "*Bokura*," *TKZ* 1, 249–250.

19. Serizawa, *Takamura Kōtarō*, 197–198.

20. Takamura, "*Togetoge na epiguramu*," *TKZ* 1, 378.

21. Takamura gave the title *Mōjūhen* to a series of poems about imaginary animals he began in 1925. The series was unfinished.

22. Takamura, "*Shirokuma*," *TKZ* 2, 8–9.

23. Takamura, "Zō," *TKZ* 2, 192.
24. Takamura, "*Hokumei no sakana*," *TKZ* 2, 272–273.
25. Takamura, "*Hokutō no kaze, ame*," *TKZ* 22, 77.
26. Takamura, "*Hi ōbeiteki naru*," *TKZ* 2, 171.
27. Takamura, "*Shūfū no ji*," *TKZ* 2, 197.
28. Takamura, "*Mizou no toki*," *TKZ* 2, 205.
29. Takamura, "*Sono toki asa wa kuru*," *TKZ* 2, 231.
30. Takamura, "*Jihen nishūnen*," *TKZ* 2, 258.
31. Takamura, "*Nihon no aki*," *TKZ* 2, 226.
32. "Children of Kume" is a reference to the Kume clan that, according to the *Nihon Shoki*, acted as allies to the mythical emperor when he subdued of the lands of Yamato.
33. Takamura, "*Kigen nisen roppyakunen ni atarite*," *TKZ* 2, 277–278.
34. Ibid.
35. Takamura, "*Jūnigatsu yōka*," *TKZ* 3, 4
36. Takamura, "*Shinjūwan no hi*," *TKZ* 3, 297.
37. Takamura, "*Chōkoku ichizu*," *TKZ* 3, 285.
38. Takamura, "*Pari*," *TKZ* 3, 287.
39. Takamura, "*Oya fukō*," *TKZ* 3, 289.
40. Takamura, "*Sanrin*," *TKZ* 3, 305.
41. Takamura, "*Seimei no taiga*," *TKZ* 3, 426.
42. Maruyama Masao, *Kōei no ichi kara* (Tokyo: Miraisha, 1982), 114.

Maruyama Masao's "Japan"

Hirotaka Kasai

Maruyama Masao, the first son of the well-known journalist Maruyama Kanji, was born in Osaka in 1914. He majored in political science in the Law Department of Tokyo University and, in 1937, became a faculty member of the same department. Until his retirement in 1971, Maruyama lectured on political science in general and the history of Japanese thought in particular. His work spans the periods of drastic social change from World War II to its end, and from the economic revival under the postwar system to the period of rapid economic growth, after which Japan became known as an advanced nation.

Maruyama's achievements in intellectual history, broadly speaking, can be divided into two periods or genealogies. The first period extends from the publication of the essays collected in *Studies in Japanese Political Thought* (*Nihon seiji shisōshi kenkyū*, 1952) to that of *Modern Political Thought and Behavior* (*Gendai seiji no shisō to kōdō*, 1956–1957).[1] Maruyama's writings during this early postwar period were primarily concerned with the formation of the modern subject in Japan (and its implications for intellectual history), with the critique of Japan's wartime ultra-nationalism, and with democratic thought. During this period, Maruyama garnered the reputation of being the intellectual who was most representative of postwar Japanese democratic and social scientific thought. It was in this context that Maruyama was often praised highly for presenting deep and insightful views about Japan's future. He was also, however, criticized by conservative intellectuals for being symbolic of the pitfalls of progressivism. A second period in Maruyama's thought might include works dating from the publication of his book *Japanese Thought* (*Nihon no shisō*, 1961) through publication of his 1972 essay, "On the 'Substratum' of Historical Consciousness" (*Rekishi ishiki no "kosō"*).[2] In these later writings, Maruyama could be said to attempt to construct a culturalist argument, based on the schematization of Japanese culture as a whole.

Of course, there are common themes underlying these two periods and we cannot separate them too neatly. Yet, it is possible to say that the earlier period includes numerous works, starting with the critique of fascism in the essay "Theory and Psychology of Ultra-nationalism" (*Chōkokkashugi no ronri to shinri*), collected in *Modern Political Thought and Behavior*, that made Maruyama into an icon of the postwar enlightenment and brought him both adulation and censure for his modernist, democratic stance. Yet a different tendency becomes discernable in Maruyama's work after the late 1950s. As Maruyama's attention turned toward issues of methodology in Japanese intellectual history, and toward a structural understanding of Japanese culture, he seemed to retreat from the intellectual ground he had staked out in the early postwar. There was a corresponding decline in the critical energy he directed toward contemporary society. Perhaps it is possible to salvage the outlines of Maruyama's early vision as a modernist by arguing that his turn toward the notion of "substratum" in the late 1950s can simply be attributed to lapses or setbacks in his setting forth of the idea at that time. And perhaps it is still possible, from the vantage point of our own time, to revive the elements of a critique of Japan, and a critique of modernity, in Maruyama's history, if we simply disregard his discussions of a "substratum." Regrettably, this essay must argue otherwise. This is because a critical perspective on the relation between Maruyama and nationalism and, furthermore, between postwar thought and nationalism, has been decisively missing from existing evaluations of Maruyama.

Keeping in mind the above-mentioned political contexts within which Maruyama has been read, I would like to discuss Maruyama's texts from the standpoint of their reproduction of nationalist ideology. While it is true Maruyama discusses nationalism as a theme in many essays, I will not pursue a detailed evaluation of the historical descriptions in such essays. My subject is, rather, the relation between nationalism and Maruyama's intellectual historical methodology. In other words, what will be considered here is not the question of whether Maruyama Masao identified himself as a nationalist, but how his arguments function as a discourse of nationalism and what enables his epistemological framework to function as a discourse of nationalism. I hope to make clear the ways in which Maruyama's intellectual history works as a mechanism that reproduces the ideological narrative of Japan's cultural identity. In order to examine this question, I would like to posit two axes. First, I would like to posit a necessary relation between the logic of nationalism and the spirit of democracy in the construction of the modern subject. Second, I would like to trace, in the epistemological register, processes of the mutual transference between universalism and particularism. From the perspective of these axes, the development of Maruyama's analyses can be formulated using terms he himself devised, as a shift from the emphasis on "nationalism as invention (*sakui*)" to one on "nationalism as nature (*shizen*)"—or what I would describe as a shift from universalism to particularism. Those familiar with Maruyama's work might protest that his intellectual and ideological trajectory was just the opposite. But as I hope to make clear in the course of this essay, just as surely as Maruyama's writings narrated a story of "invention," they spun out a vision of "nature." While Maruyama attempted to narrate the shifting logic in the Japanese mental structure (*seishin kōzō*) from "nature" to "invention," that is, he reproduced "nature" on the methodological level through his emphasis on "invention." Through this paradoxical structure, his argument came to function as the narration of the cultural identity of Japan.

NATIONALISM AS "INVENTION"

Modernity as an Ideal Type
By taking on his "investigation of the process of the maturation of modern thinking in Japan" in his 1946 essay "Modern Thought" (*Kindaiteki shii*), Maruyama Masao emerged as a severe critic of the mental structure (*seishin kōzō*) of not only wartime Japan, but of modern Japan itself.[3] At this point in time, a certain kind of schema was necessary in order to objectify and critique Japan as a particularity. In the case of Maruyama, this schema of objectification could be called "modernity as an *Idealtypus* (ideal type)." What were the characteristics of modernity as an ideal type for Maruyama? It was a pure form of the modern state ("the neutral state"), abstracted from an image of the nineteenth-century European state, which was characterized by political rule based on the formal validity of laws and by the establishment of the principle of inner, private freedom of thought, scholarship, religion, and so on. It is only through the establishment of the "neutral state" as a universal ideal type, and by means of comparison with it, that "Japan" as a particularity could emerge for Maruyama. Undoubtedly, this epistemic schema itself, in which the so-called "West" and "Japan" are juxtaposed and comparatively examined on the basis of a binary opposition, is not specific to Maruyama. For it probably can be said that this conceptual apparatus based on the oppositions of "the West" and "the East" or "the West" and "Japan" has defined the basis of the social scientific cognition of the majority of modern intellectuals. In Maruyama's case, however, since the ideal type is posited as an abstraction from nineteenth-century Western Europe, it is not effective merely to criticize his argument as another "theory of lack," which reifies "the West" and blames Japan for being different.

Rather, the problem lies somewhere else. What I would like to draw special attention to in Maruyama's methodology of intellectual history are the epistemological conditions that enable him to constitute his conceptual apparatus, and their political effects. In his reminiscences, Maruyama recalled that during the war "when we were inundated by cases of ideological conversion (*tenkō*), I rethought—or perhaps I should say came to a new recognition of—things like bourgeois democracy and liberalism."[4] "Amidst all the calls for 'overcoming' or 'rejecting' modernity," he explains, "my focus on the modern aspects of the Meiji Restoration and on the maturing of modern elements in Tokugawa society was a kind of desperate stance I took in an era of fascist historiography. . . . My motivation for struggling with issues of Tokugawa intellectual history was, so to speak, extra-academic."[5]

The political goals of Maruyama's early research, alluded to in the word "extra-academic," are here expressed in terms of his sense of opposition to the idea of "overcoming modernity."[6] Maruyama's political concern, consistent throughout the wartime essays he published in *Studies in the Intellectual History of Tokugawa Japan*, was the defense of modernity and the resistance to the contemporary regime through discussion of the possibility of a modernity particular to Japan. Therefore, when Maruyama wrote in "Modern Thought" just after Japan's defeat in the war, "it has finally become clear to a number of people that, far from modern thinking having been 'overcome' in our country today, it has not even been acquired," it was a kind of call for re-embarking on the "project of modernity," defined as the acquisition of "modern thought."[7] It was out of this kind of vision that Maruyama's notion of modernity as an ideal type was constructed and came to function as an index according to which Japan's modernity could be analyzed and criticized.

Maruyama's argument for the particularity of modern Japan in relation to the idealized universality of Western European modernity, therefore, should be seen as based on a very personal, political choice made by Maruyama, rather than on his sense of the inherent, logical superiority of the ideal type of modernity that undergirds his arguments in these essays. In this sense, it might be said that Maruyama reached, of his own accord, the position of modernist during the war. In this sense, it was out of opposition to the ideology of "overcoming modernity" that Maruyama simultaneously constructed "Western European modernity" as a universal standard and particular "Japan" as an object of analysis.[8]

"Nature" and "Invention"

How did Maruyama thematize the historical process of the modernization of Japan in this epistemological framework? How did he discuss the possibility of a Japan that could be deduced through comparison with an ideal type?

According to Maruyama, who saw the theme of intellectual history as "the transformation in ways of thinking," the birth and development of the modern spirit can be seen as the relative shift in mental structure from the logic of nature to the logic of invention.[9] This motif of "nature" and "invention" occupies a crucial position in Maruyama's methodology as an intellectual historian. It is easy to find this motif, for example, in his war-time reading of Tokugawa intellectual history in *Studies in the Intellectual History of Tokugawa Japan*, or in the several essays on Fukuzawa written during the period when Maruyama acknowledges having been "smitten with Fukuzawa."[10]

Maruyama first formally established his use of these two concepts in *Studies in the Intellectual History of Tokugawa Japan.* Here, he sought to "view, from the perspective of the transformation in ways of thinking, the growth of modern consciousness through processes of self-analysis developed in Confucian thought" that had been "the orthodox worldview of feudal society."[11] Maruyama designated the mode of thinking (*shii yōshiki*) of the Zhu Xi school (the official school of the Tokugawa regime) as a logic of "nature" in which natural law and moral standards were characterized as continuous in the form of transcendence *qua* immanence and substance *qua* principle. Maruyama described Ogyū Sorai's thought as a logic of "invention," in which the natural order of the Zhu Xi School was overcome and the invented character of social standards was posited. In place of the absolute transcendence of ideas (*rinen*), Sorai made the human Sages, who were producers of the Way, the starting point of philosophy.

In a manner that could be compared to Ferdinand Tönnies pointing out the shift from *Gemeinschaft* to *Gesellschaft*, Maruyama read in Tokugawa intellectual history the historical development of a logic of invention out of a logic of nature. While this is admittedly a summary reading of Maruyama's account (I have omitted a detailed examination of the development of its logic or its description of Motoori Norinaga), such a characterization enables us to propose that Maruyama sought to point out, in the emergence of the logic of invention (an "invention" that we might more precisely define as creation through the act of reading), a possibility of modernity in the premodern. Moreover, Maruyama's extremely positive evaluation of Fukuzawa Yukichi can be attributed to Fukuzawa's attempt to achieve a thorough-going shift from the logic of nature to the logic of invention as Japan's modernization process began (a shift that included calling on the individual to internalize the state). As Maruyama emphasized in his writings on Fukuzawa, it was what Fukuzawa called "the spirit of physics" (*butsuri seishin*), an independence from nature, that made possible the modern citizen's spirit of "independence and self-respect." The "spirit of physics" was a product of the emancipation of both nature and the individual from society, and the modern citizen was one who, because of his or her autonomy as a subject, became a human being who "actively participated in the social order" rather than "simply accepting it as an external given."[12] The modern civil spirit Maruyama discovered in Fukuzawa was, indeed, a spirit of "invention" that could affirm the relativity and plurality of value judgments (this was Maruyama's concept of *fukuganshugi* or "multiperspectivalism") and that was constantly transcending itself, having escaped from the form of reification of the spirit Maruyama called *wakudeki* ("irrational attachment"). Such a spirit could sustain what Maruyama conceived of as democracy. At the same time, we must note that establishment of individual autonomy based on the "spirit of physics" could only take place in relation to the state, and for Maruyama this had the greatest significance. As he wrote in the same text:

> If each person in a nation does not feel the state to be his or her own possession and is not conscious of the state of the nation as his or her own destiny, how can the state maintain its firm independence in the severe international arena? If Japan should develop normally as a modern state, it is necessary to make the national masses (*kokumin taishū*), who up to this point have not known anything beyond mere passive obedience to the political order, wake up to their subjective and active positions as members of the nation. In such a case, a certain number of intellectuals must carry out the enormous duty of moving the national and the political dimensions from an external milieu to the inner depths of individual consciousness. Fukuzawa was the pioneer who faced this unprecedented problem with a surprisingly vigorous fighting spirit.[13]

It is in this context that Maruyama highly evaluates Fukuzawa for "being a true nationalist by being an individualist." In the conclusion to a prize-winning essay written while he was still a student in 1936, Maruyama stated that "while the individual can be concretely positioned in society only through the state, the individual's relation to the state must be one of a ceaselessly negative independence vis a vis the state."[14] We can clearly see in these examples that, for Maruyama, the establishment of the modern individual's autonomy based on the spirit of "invention" was the equivalent of the establishment of a national subject. Furthermore, Maruyama always discussed democracy in relation to nationalism. In the conjuncture following the Pacific War, for example, Maruyama upheld the notion of a synthesis of the spirit of nationalism and the spirit of democracy by discussing early Meiji thought in terms of a narrative running from Fukuzawa to Kuga Katsunan.

> Katsunan's Japanism (*Nihonshugi*) aims at the synthesis of nationalism (*nashionarizumu*) and democracy (*demokurashii*). While his analysis may not have been absolutely thorough, it was an essentially correct view of the direction of Japan's modernization. . . . Unfortunately, in the past, Japan failed to synthesize nationalism and democracy. Instead, there is a form of "nation-ism" ("*kokumin*shugi") that links the thought of Fukuzawa Yukichi to that of Kuga Katsunan, a "nation-ism" that manifested its weaknesses from the start, and in the end was drawn into the strong rule of statism (*kokkashugi*) from above. Today, more than ever, when nationalism has escaped from the long-lasting regime of ultra-nationalism, we must combine the democratic revolution with nationalism in its proper sense and with true nationalist movements. Even as we pick up the unfinished legacy of Katsunan and others, we have to reject that project's lack of thoroughness and its constant tendency to compromise.[15]

This passage demonstrates the way in which democracy, for Maruyama, could never be separated from nationalism (*"kokuminshugi,"* as opposed to what he called *"kokumin*-shugi"). Indeed, Maruyama's concept of democracy included not only aspects of external legal institutions such as parliamentary democracy, but also a notion of the solidarity of autonomous individuals, whose inner freedom would be sufficient to enable them to support these institutions. Maruyama calls this democracy "a social system based on an accumulation of daily practices."[16] Seen from the point of view of the mental structure of the citizen/subject, the establishment of both nationalism and democracy were always made possible by the logic of "invention." It is none other than this synthesis that provided the telos for Maruyama's narrative about the creation of a modernity, which, while gauged in relation to modernity as an ideal type, was particular to Japan. When read from this perspective, the political dimension of Maruyama's famous early postwar arguments on ultra-nationalism and nationalism stands out in relief. Surprisingly enough, this conceptual trajectory became the discursive mechanism that, as it protected and conserved nationalism, produced as its "nature" the homogenous ethnos of "Japan."

The Critique of (Ultra) Nationalism/Defense of Nationalism

What does Maruyama consider "proper nationalism" (*tadashii kokuminshugi*)—a term he actually uses in his essay on Kuga Katsunan—to be? How does he differentiate between "proper" nationalism and "improper" nationalism? In the following pages, I will try to shed some light on Maruyama's nationalism and its different facets by discussing the use of a number of related concepts in his work: "nationalism" (*kokuminshugi*), "statism" (*kokkashugi*), and "ultra-nationalism" (*chōkokkashugi*).

In his writings, Maruyama frequently uses the loan word *"nashionarizumu"* with a meaning that we may see as equivalent to *"kokuminshugi."*[17] This is because nationalism, for Maruyama, had to do with the ideological formation of a national people, or ethnos, based on modern thought. Such a conception of nationalism can be seen in the following passage from *Studies in the Intellectual History of Tokugawa Japan*. Here we can see how Maruyama defines what might be a "proper" nationalism by extrapolating from his ideal type of modernity.

It has been said that a nation (*kokumin*) is something that wants to be a nation. . . . In other words, we can say that a "nation" exists only if the members of a given group are aware of the common characteristics they share with each other, and that distinguish them from other nations, and possess some desire to preserve and foster this unity.[18]

Maruyama's concern with modern thinking received its major stimulus from his interest in the question of how a nation is formed. Thus, in Maruyama's analytic framework, arguments about the mental structure involved in modernization and modern subjectivity become reduced to arguments about people living as a "nation." The "nation," however, is not born from nothing. Maruyama defines "nationalism" as "ideologies or movements that push toward the unity, independence, and development of a nation" and he defines "national consciousness" (*minzoku ishiki*)[19] as "the subjective moment of the nation (*nēshon*) that gives vitality to nationalism (*nashionarizumu*)."[20] In Maruyama's terminology, then, it is the transformation of premodern "*minzoku ishiki*" into "*kokumin ishiki*" that indicates the emergence of nationalism or *kokuminshugi*. Maruyama argues that "it is this *kokuminshugi* that serves as an indispensable spiritual driving force for the existence of the modern state as a modern state." Thus, the identity of the "natural" ethnos (*minzoku*) discovered in premodernity is assumed to shift to the identity of the "invented" nation (*kokumin*). It is in this manner that a certain "nature"—that of the ethnos—is actually presuppposed as the basis of Maruyama's "invention."

The task of Japan's nationalism after Japan's defeat in war, according to Maruyama, was to democratize the social formation, or to break premodern modes of social bonding and "establish a new national homogeneity."[21] Maruyama argued that "democratic forms function smoothly only on the basis of this national and social homogeneity" and that "the expansion of the former is made possible by the expansion of the latter."[22] He further pointed out that "nationalism must be rationalized to the same degree that democracy is irrationalized."[23] Threading through these statements seems to be the proposition that the political future of postwar Japan should be envisioned in terms of a balance between democracy and nationalism, built on the stable base of a homogeneous ethnos. In this sense, nationalism and national homogeneity become, for Maruyama, indispensable elements in democratic politics.

By contrast, Maruyama's "improper" nationalism was "statism" (*kokkashugi*), a deviant form produced when nationalism fails to combine with democracy. What Maruyama most sought to criticize in fascism was its "*Gleichschaltung*" ("compulsory homogenization"), or the replacement of the modern principle of "rule by consent" by a "rule of uniformity," based on "homogenization from within" and a dictatorship of fear.[24]

On the basis of his analyses of fascism, Maruyama presented Germany, Italy, and Spain as models of "classical fascism." These were examples of the classical form of fascism from below in which state power is grasped monolithically and a single-party dictatorship was established. Moreover, Maruyama regarded Japan's "emperor-system fascism" (*tennō-sei fashizumu*) not simply as statism but as ultra-nationalism (*chōkokkashugi*). This was because, for him, "there was a qualitative difference between the internal motive force that spurred Japan's policies of expansion abroad and oppression at home" and "classical fascism from below".[25] The qualitative difference was that Japan's imperial state (*tennōsei kokka*) was not a neutral state in which state sovereignty occupied a middle ground, a neutral position. In the absence of such a neutral principle, both spiritual authority and political power in Japan were monopolized by a sovereign state. Thus:

> The standard according to which the nation's (*kokka*) actions are judged as right or wrong lies within itself (that is, in the "national polity"), and what the nation does, whether within its own borders or beyond them, is not subject to any moral code that transcends the nation.[26]

According to Maruyama, it is in this kind of ultra-nationalism, in which "autonomy of inner value" for the individual is not established, that the Emperor, as the "ultimate substance," becomes the spiritual motive force that embodies absolute value. The Emperor, however, is not a dictator who alone possesses subjective freedom. Rather, "saddled with a burden—in his case the authority of a tradition that derived from the infinitely remote past," the Emperor is "an axis of ordinates (the time dimension) running perpendicular to the plane of the circle."[27] This is what Maruyama calls the "ultra-character" of the imperial state.

Through this type of argument, Maruyama asserted that a responsible subjective consciousness did not exist in Japan's imperial state and that, in place of dictatorship, "there emerged the phenomenon in which spiritual equilibrium is maintained by the transfer of oppression." This "transfer of oppression" (*yokuatsu ijō*) was defined by Maruyama as a system where "by exercising arbitrary power on those who are below, people manage to transfer in a downward direction the sense of oppression that comes from above, thus preserving the balance of the whole." Furthermore, he stated that "this phenomenon is one of the most important heritages that modern Japan received from feudal society."[28] Thus, the cause of ultra-nationalism was sought not in modern nationalism, but by Maruyama in the premodern character of Japanese society. This was also the case when Maruyama pointed out that, in contrast to the model of fascism from below, Japanese ultra-nationalism was characterized by fascism "from above." According to Maruyama, it is its degree of maturation as a democracy that determines whether a society exhibits fascism from above or from below. "In the process of fascization," he wrote, "the strength of influences 'from below' is determined by the strength of democracy in that country. In other words, in countries where a democratic movement has not taken place, one cannot find the growth of typical fascist movements from below."[29]

To illustrate this point, Maruyama analyzed Germany's experience of Weimar democracy. In comparing Japan's "Serve the State through Industry" movement (*Sampō Undō*) to Germany's "*Kraft Durch Freude*," Maruyama emphasized the relative strength of democratic character in the Nazi system. For Maruyama, it was the lack of a bourgeois democratic revolution in Japan and the pathology of the mental structure of Japanese society that led to the ultra-nationalist character of Emperor-system fascism in Japan.

Maruyama, through reference to an ideal type, tried to analyze the pathology of Japanese society by comparing it with Germany. It is not difficult to detect, however, that in the process of his analysis, he implied that German Nazism was a relatively "superior" fascism, due to its more democratic character. It is possible, however, to point to a series of methodological assumptions in his writings that make this logic inherent to Maruyama's analysis.

First, Maruyama assumed the German form of fascism as a model and used it as a standard of comparison in his analysis of Japan's imperial state. In this framework, Japan, analyzed as an object, was defined as irrational and imperfect in relation to an ideal type, while the reasons for its aberrations were always sought in external factors that were not essential to the ideal type. Hence, what was made visible in Maruyama's analyses was the feudal, premodern, and particular nature of Japanese society. Since Maruyama analyzed modernity in terms of modern thinking, the cause of problems was always located in a mental structure particular to Japan. Ironically, while analyzing fascism as a modern political phenomenon, Maruyama ended up seeking for the causes of fascism outside of modernity. Maruyama thus reductively made a modern phenomenon the product of Japan's premodernity, which then became the cause for whatever was incomplete in Japan's modernity. According to Maruyama's definition, statism (*kokkashugi*) was nationalism that had abandoned any union with democracy; statism's political function was that of *Gleichschaltung*. In contrast, nationalism was defined as that which creates "national homogeneity" when it is synthesized with democracy. Both phenomena create a homogenous "nation." Their difference lies in the degree of their maturity as a democracy, or in the degree to which they have realized the principle of the sovereignty of the people based on a notion of the plurality of values. By differentiating nationalism and statism on the basis of the difference in the degree of democracy a society had attained, then, Maruyama's argument ironically served to cover up the fact that fascism is a form of modernity, and that, through the implementation of fascism, certain forms of democratization can occur. But it is the modern, not the premodern, nature of fascism that we need to problematize—and not only in the case of Japan.[30] In Maruyama's argument, the possibility of this type of questioning has already been foreclosed.

By now the difficulties inherent in Maruyama's use of the two concepts of nationalism and statism should be clear. He proposes the alternative concept of "statism" in order to rescue a "nationalism" based on modernity as an ideal type.[31] Because of this, however, the source of anything problematic is always sought outside of the ideal type: not in nationalism but in statism; not in modernity but in premodernity; not in a universal ideal type but in an objectified particular "Japan." In the logic Maruyama uses in his analyses of Japanese society, he invariably begins with a general model, and then in relation to that model, argues that Japan has a particular mental structure.[32] This is why Maruyama's critique of Japan always becomes an analysis of Japan's pathology. And this is why, while attempting to problematize fascism (or, we might say, in the very process of problematizing fascism), Maruyama constructs a theoretical framework that not only fails to analyze fascism, but makes it logically impossible for Maruyama to disclose the problematic nature of nationalism itself. Today, however, what Maruyama called "national homogeneity," or the problem of the homogeneity of the ethnos, should be seen as one of the most pressing problems to be raised in relation to modernity.

Maruyama's tale of modernization (the creation of the nation state) as "invention" posited a smooth transition from the cultural identity of the ethnos to the "homogeneity" of the nation as a political subject, and, insofar as it is built on a distinction between "nationalism" and "statism," envisioned a linking of democracy and nationalism. Undoubtedly, in the intellectual milieu that prevailed just after Japan's defeat, Maruyama's emphasis on the combination of nationalism and democracy could take on a certain critical force in relation to more naive forms of naturalistic ethnic nationalism. At the same time, however, if the powerful logic of "national homogeneity" inherent in his logic of democracy is overlooked, we ignore the ways in which Maruyama's logic contains within itself the same logic as does his object of critique. What we find in Maruyama's arguments is a process of smuggling the logic of "nature," in the name of "national homogeneity," into the spirit of "invention" he promotes. Precisely because the basis of Maruyama's "spirit of invention" was the ethnos, posited without qualification as a social homogeneity, Maruyama's thought lacked the capacity to consider the violence that takes place in the very process of producing that homogeneity in the name of the nation state. This is a violence that is characteristic of modernity itself, and is not limited to either Japan or fascist societies.

If it is possible to describe the epistemological framework in which Maruyama objectified and criticized Japanese society, with reference to modernity as an ideal type, as a universalist one, it took the form I have just described. But, in the late 1950s, the timbre of this universalist epistemological framework changed, and a particularist character came to the fore in Maruyama's reasoning. We can understand this as a shift where nationalism defined as "invention," with a strongly universalist cast, became nationalism defined as "nature," which, in Maruyama's methodology, entailed producing a substantialist notion of Japanese culture as tradition. As the foregoing has made clear, however, we should not see this as a radical shift. It was rather the logical outcome of Maruyama's universalist perspective, for what was consistent throughout was Maruyama's discourse on nationalism.

NATIONALISM AS "NATURE"

The Tradition of Asystematicity (Mukōzō no dentō)
When, in 1957, he first wrote the essay "Japanese Thought" (later incorporated into his 1961 book, *Japanese Thought* [*Nihon no shisō*]), Maru-

yama began to thematize the issue of "tradition" in Japanese intellectual history, giving particular attention to the problem of the methodology of intellectual history. We might say that at this stage Maruyama moved away from his early postwar emphasis on the moment of "invention" and embarked on a process of revision, even recantation, of his former views. He now strove to produce a notion of "national homogeneity" as a concrete instance of "the natural."

In his essay, "Japanese Thought," Maruyama explained the particularity of Japanese intellectual history in terms of its nature as a "tradition of asystematicity." This was because "Japan never formed an intellectual tradition in which the self could occupy the position of a core or coordinate axis of history."[33] By contrast to Maruyama's early postwar writings, this essay, which described the Japanese "tradition of asystematicity" as one in which modes of thought succeeded one another without conflict and in which there was a "limitless embrace" of ideas, did not find Japan lacking or pathological in relation to the ideal type. Rather, Maruyama located the prototype of this "tradition of asystematicity" in "Shintō," Japan's singular "indigenous" religious belief. Maruyama's emphasis was now on defining "the unique character of Japanese modernity, in which the pre-modern and the ultra-modern are combined."[34] The aspects Maruyama had objectified and criticized by contrast to the universal ideal type of modernity in the early postwar period were now positively recognized as the difference of Japanese modernity (and moreover of Japan) itself. Now Maruyama assigned "Japan" and "the West" static characteristics, based on what Homi Bhabha calls the viewpoint of "cultural diversity," one determined according to structural elements rather than moments of historical praxis.[35] Indeed, it is in this period that Maruyama declared, "Japan does not follow either a Western model or an Asian model. It is its own model."[36] The elements of a static, formulaic, culturalist argument have become very pronounced in this view, according to which Japan's epistemological structure is identified by contrast to an idealized West.

In keeping with the ideas expressed in the essay, in Maruyama's book, *Japanese Thought*, Maruyama's recognition of the deficiencies of Japan's intellectual tradition compelled him to replace his earlier emphasis on the spirit of invention with a clear vision of the "natural" values out of which a tradition is constituted. The values of "being" and "doing" were reversed again. Maruyama, who had called attention to the way "invention" superseded "nature" in Japanese modernity, now called for a reassessment of the "living meaning" of such cultural values as "caesura" and "inaction." In so doing, Maruyama subtly shifted the emphasis of his argument: it became a matter of insisting on the indispensability of a "natural" basis for cultural production in order to guarantee the existence of that spirit of invention that builds a "tradition" out of accumulating traditions. Moreover, by the time of the 1972 publication of the essay, "On the 'Substratum' of Hostorical Consciousness," as we shall see, Maruyama had reached the point where he began to produce his own formulation of what constituted the tradition of Japanese thought: the idea of a "substratum" (kosō) of historical consciousness. This way of thinking, however, should not be seen as emerging after an abrupt shift that occurred when Maruyama wrote *Japanese Thought*. We have seen that Maruyama's early postwar work had already posited a premodern "national consciousness" (*minzoku ishiki*) as the natural ground that generated the invented logic of nationalism. When he wrote *Japanese Thought*, Maruyama simply brought the task of how to render this Japanese historical consciousness a positivity to the center of his argument.

The Evolution of the Concept of "Kosō" (Substratum)
    In the gradual shift of emphasis in Maruyama's argument from *Japanese Thought* onward, there is a matter with implications for the methodology of intellectual history that cannot be overlooked. This is the question of what Maruyama calls "cultural contact" (*bunka sesshoku*), a concept that shapes his theoretical development from this point on. Since, in fact, it is in his analysis of what "cultural contact" is that Maruyama talks about the process that led him to develop the idea of "substratum," we can learn more about the latter from his discussions of "cultural contact" than from reading the essay on "substratum" itself, and we will turn to this question first.
    Maruyama first came upon the notion of "substratum" long before he published "On the 'Substratum' of Historical Consciousness," when he was trying to introduce a horizontal vector (what we could think of as a spatial dimension) into the historicist, and heavily Marxist influenced, sense of linear history that characterized his early postwar work. At this point, he turned to a notion of "cultural contact" to explain the existence of Japan's "tradition of asystematicity," whose development could not be accounted for in terms of purely internal factors. It is clear that, as of 1960, Maruyama began to distance himself greatly from the Marxist idea, which he formerly held, that "there should be stages of historical development applicable to the entire world." In a discussion of his work at Nagoya University in 1978, published as the essay, "Groping for a Methodology for Intellectual History" ("*Shisōshi no hōhō o mosakushite*"), Maruyama recalled how, departing from the notion of stages of development, he had hoped to "introduce to the study of Japanese intellectual history the question of the transformation of thought through cultural contact." This led him, he said, to "rethink Japanese intellectual history, not from the late Tokugawa period" (which had been his point of departure up until that point) "but from ancient times."[37]
    Maruyama described how, in the course of this attempt, he came to expand the ideas about the "difference" of Japanese modernity and "the tradition of asystematicity" that he had broached in "Japanese thought" to the whole of Japanese intellectual history. His thinking, at this point, appears to

have undergone a kind of mutation in which what he had seen as the particularity of modern Japan became the particularity of Japanese culture itself. In "Groping for a Methodology for Intellectual History," Maruyama
described how, in order to explain this particularity, he began to resort to
the concept of a "prototype" (*genkei*) of the Japanese world image
(*sekaizō*). He defined this prototype as "a pattern of thought that comes into
play repeatedly at moments when 'foreign' thought is revised and 'made
Japanese.'"[38] In turning his attention to this "moment of revision," Maruyama consciously tried to avoid what he saw as two errors that had inevitably led to failure in modern Japanese intellectual history. The first error was
to be found in the methodology that took "Japanese intellectual history to
be the history of the distortion of foreign thought." The second error was to
look for "an 'internally developed' Japanese way of thinking that is independent from 'foreign' thought." Maruyama saw these two erroneous tendencies in modern Japanese intellectual history as a product of the "repeti-
tious pattern of revision" itself.

> If we were to speak of what constitutes the dominant "melody" in
> Japanese intellectual history, we would have to say it is "foreign"
> thought. Some might ask, then, if there is anything we can call "Japa-
> nese." But once a system of thought with a well-defined doctrine enters
> Japan, it does not maintain its original form but invariably undergoes
> revision. Isn't what is "Japanese" that very process of transformation?
> If we examine various processes of making something Japanese, we
> find a common pattern, and surprising similarities. This is what I am
> talking about when I refer to a historical 'substratum.' And that sub-
> stratum is not the "dominant melody" itself, but the moment in which
> the "dominant melody" is transformed.[39]

It is against this background that Maruyama came, in the essay "Prototype, Substratum, and *Basso Ostinato*" (*Genkei, kosō, shitsuyō, teion*), to
define "substratum" as "the moment that modifies the foreign universalist
world views that Japan has received since ancient times."[40] Here Maruyama
has modified the concept of "prototype" into that of a "substratum," in an
endeavor to emphasize the existence of a "substrate layer transcending particular historical epochs, which continue to have an effect."[41] According to
Maruyama, the "substratum" cannot be an independent ideology. This is
because "the pattern that is the substratum is in every case fused with im-
ported thought, creating a symphonic sound."[42] We can see in this conception Maruyama's attempt to historicize the Japanese mind (*Nihon seishin*)
in a manner very different from "histories of the Japanese mind" (*Nihon
seishinshi*) produced during the "overcoming modernity" debate during the
war. He wanted to produce an account that would, as he put it, "intersect
with the most ordinary of scholarly concerns." Certainly, it is undeniable
that Maruyama attempted to counter the logic of "overcoming modernity"

by taking a universal ideal type of modernity as his reference point in the early postwar years. But when we consider the evolution of Maruyama's later notion of the "substratum," we have to wonder how much he had really freed himself from the influence of those discourses on "the Japanese mind" that he once denounced.

In order to examine the above question, it is necessary for us to consider how Maruyama's methodology produced a narrative of "Japan's" cultural identity through its deployment of the concept of "substratum." By considering the epistemological assumptions that ground this theory of the "substratum," we should be able to see how this conception of intellectual history functions as a political narrative, and how it is related to Maruyama's concerns from the early postwar period.

The most significant characteristic of Maruyama's notion of "substratum" is that it is not introduced as a doctrine about the "origins" of what is Japanese. Rather, Maruyama attempts to grasp the "substratum" as a *"pattern of transformation"*—something akin, perhaps, to the concept of "formless form" developed by the philosopher Miki Kiyoshi.[43] If most studies of the "Japanese mind" have presented a certain doctrine about the origins of that which is Japanese, then Maruyama's theory of "substratum" does not attempt to delineate this type of direct, substantial origin. Rather, it almost seems that Maruyama's argument is founded on the impossibility of this kind of positivism.

This, however, presents us with several problems. As is evident from Maruyama's statement that "something remains after one eliminates from Japan's myths all that is clearly based on the categories and ways of thinking of ancient China," Maruyama's notion of "cultural contact" always takes the form of a calculation based on subtraction.[44] Because this method is based on elimination, his explanation implies that he assumes as logical premises both the existence of "that which is Japanese" and the unchanging nature of "Japan" as a space and object of analysis. In other words, the existence of "that which is Japanese" is already included in his problematic—guaranteed as a "pattern of transformation" (if not a doctrine)—and from the beginning there is no possibility that the result of subtraction could equal "zero." Thus, in Maruyama's hypothesis of "substratum," "that which is Japanese" is first set up as that which should already exist and then is discovered through subtraction. In this regard, although Maruyama recognizes that the method of his theory of "substratum" is "a certain type of tautology," he still emphasizes that there are historical facts to support his theory.[45]

Compared to the other "civilized nations" of the world, our country is characterized by a degree of homogeneity that is absolutely *exceptional* in terms of geography, ethnic groups (*minzoku*), language, the mode of rice production, and the related forms of villages and festivals. Our country has maintained these characteristics for over one thousand and several hundred years, dating back to at least the late Tumulus Period. It is this vast historical reality that lies before us.[46]

According to Maruyama's understanding, *regardless* of the repeated "cultural contacts," Japan has been homogeneous in geographical, ethnic, linguistic, and cultural form, and continues to be historically identical. Thus, there exists a "substratum" as a "continuous substrate layer" and the theory of "substratum" is possible. This argument, however, should be understood as a logical inversion. For it is *through* his act of narrating the theory of "substratum" that Maruyama discursively produces the homogeneity of Japan. Even before he enters into a concrete demonstration, Maruyama's theory of "substratum" has also already guaranteed the existence of "Japanese identity" and the "Japanese spirit." Therefore, Maruyama's two theories of the "substratum" that have been published to date can be read as having produced the positivity of a Japanese identity through their narration of history.

The Repetition of History
In the 1972 essay "On the 'Substratum' of Historical Consciousness," Maruyama turned for a model to Motoori Norinaga, who wrote in his commentaries on the *Kojiki* that "the meaning of all things goes back to the age of the gods." Like Motoori, Maruyama found in the *Kojiki* and *Nihon shoki*, especially in the opening sections describing the creation of the world, a framework of thought that he described as "a mash of conceptualization that can be extrapolated from the opening narration." He stated that this constituted a "prototype" (or "substratum") of "the Japanese mentality" that has "continued to flow beneath the various evolving modes of historical consciousness, persistently, into the modern age."[47]

Having established this prototype, Maruyama went on to set forth three basic categories and proceeded, quite tautologically, to use historical materials to demonstrate their existence. Ultimately, referring to the "substratum" with the phrase "energy that randomly becomes one thing after another," Maruyama asserted that the substratum is, "not exactly Hegel's 'Bad Infinity,'" but something that takes the form of a straight line that can be extended infinitely, a "limitless genealogical continuity" or a Japanese form of the "eternal present."[48] This "continuity" inherits the "tradition of asystematicity" Maruyama described in "Japanese Thought," constantly moving toward the new without accumulating a past. It is such a tradition, in which there is continuity but not accumulation, and in which the accumulation of traditions never takes on a structure, that this "limitlessness" itself becomes the immutable element of history.

Even when he discusses the "*basso ostinato*" of political consciousness, the premises and methodology Maruyama uses are the same as those used in the case of historical consciousness. Again he extracts, from the *Kojiki*, *Nihon shoki*, *Manyōshū*, and so on, all the ancient transitive verbs that take politics (*matsurigoto*) as a grammatical object and, using these as keywords, produces a schematic structure to explain decision making and processes of legitimization in politics. According to Maruyama, the characteristics of Japanese politics that can be found in these ancient texts are "to separate the level of legitimacy from the level of decision making" and "the concept of joint rule." He then concludes that there has been no change, in that "these patterns of institutional modification that occurred in the seventh and eighth centuries were repeated again and again in the course of Japanese history." [49] Also, Maruyama states that "ultimate legitimacy always lies in the Imperial Family." [50]

What takes place is that Maruyama, in setting forth a pattern of repetition in "Japanese" history, reinforces the notion of the "historical identity" of the "Japanese state," which is necessary as a methodological premise. In fact, in this way, he dehistoricizes Japan. The trajectory of this argument, then, is very similar to the way in which, since the early postwar period, "national homogeneity" had been posited in Maruyama's writing as authentic and unchanging, and thought to be indispensable to the synthesis of democracy and nationalism.

Although Maruyama considers modernization of the mental structure to be a relative shift from "nature" to "invention," the "national homogeneity" that appears here is actually a kind of "nature" created through the "invention" of his discourse on Japanese intellectual history. The narration of nation as an apparatus may be seen in classical form in Maruyama's constitution of this logical series. In other words, Maruyama's discourse of nationalism creates its own "tradition." The identity of "Japan" is presented as a "natural" bond, or what Benedict Anderson calls the "beauty of *gemeinschaft*."

[I]n everything "natural" there is always something unchosen. In this way, nation-ness is assimilated to skin-colour, gender, parentage and birth-era—all things one cannot help. And in these "natural ties" one senses what one might call "the beauty of *gemeinschaft*." To put it another way, precisely because such ties are not chosen, they have about them a halo of disinterestedness. [51]

Thus, we could say that Maruyama has produced a Japanese version of "imagined communities" through his theoretical practice ("invention") that he describes as "nature" in the form of "substratum." Interestingly, Maruyama's choice of the geological metaphor of the "substratum" could also be seen as symbolic of the way in which the "inventiveness" of the researcher's practical activity is concealed in his discourse. In Maruyama's writings from the period of "Japanese Thought" through the introduction of the concept of "substratum" (1961–1972), the concept of "nature" that had been smuggled in behind the spirit of "invention" in his earlier postwar writings is rendered into a positivity. The modernization of mental structure that had earlier been defined as a shift from "nature" to "invention" becomes its obverse, a shift from "invention" to "nature." The concepts of "invention" and "nature" are, it turns out, accomplices of one another.

Although at first glance, the two sides of Maruyama's intellectual history—the universalist argument about "invention" and the particularist argument about "nature"—appear to be different, in fact, they constitute a consistent discourse of nationalism that produces a narrative of national identity. The practical moment of research, i.e., the "inventiveness" of the act of research, must always be concealed behind the image of the cultural identity of "Japan," which is narrated as the moment of "nature." Moreover, since Maruyama's concept of "nation" (*kokumin*) is based on an uncritical sense of its equivalence to "ethnos" (*minzoku*), posited as a given and natural identity, Maruyama produces the notion of a dehistoricized "national homogeneity" in the face of his own emphasis on the inventedness of the logic of nationalism. Contingent and hybrid elements, which exist from the start in all democratic movements, are excluded from this view. As a result, Maruyama's posited synthesis between nationalism and democracy must inevitably become reduced to an identical "national homogeneity" that serves as the premise of both nationalism and democracy. Although it may be possible to speak of Maruyama's work in terms of "postwar democracy," it is democratic only to the extent that it is nationalist first.

However, if we return to Maruyama's argument, through consideration of his concept of "substratum," we can see that a certain revision has been effected with regard to Japanese particularity, as well. In "Groping for a Methodology of Intellectual History," Maruyama had claimed that "the introduction into intellectual history of the perspectives of cultural contact and revision, which include problems of *language* (that is, translation) must entail a rejection of the theory of universal stages of historical development."[52] Because of this need to reject a theory of universal stages, in the essay "Prototype, Substratum, and *Basso Ostinato*," Maruyama proposed a new category of "individuality" (*kotaisei* or *kosei*), which he differentiated from "particularity" and which he held could not be subsumed in his early universalist postwar schema of Japanese particularity versus modernity as an ideal type. Maruyama stated:

> It is necessary also to try to grasp Japanese thought as an "individuality" (*kosei*). The term "particularity" calls attention to discrete elements but then dissolves them within something that exists somewhere in the world. The concept of particularity itself is merely a sub-category of "universality." . . . It is not such "particularity" that I am talking about but rather the "individuality" of Japanese intellectual history (*seishinshi*) as a totality.[53]

From the writing of *Japanese Thought* onward, Maruyama investigated what he called the "epistemological structure of the Japanese state," and concluded that "Japanese national culture, as a structural totality, is unique in all the world."[54] As Maruyama put it, "almost all of the most important intellectual products of the past thousand years of world history are still 'in stock' in Japanese intellectual history."[55]

Is Maruyama's explanation, however, really free from the binary opposition of the universal and the particular? His own position would seem to be a kind of particularism. While Maruyama tries to find in Japanese culture a symmetrical relation with "modernity as an ideal type," which he posits as a reference point, he still depends on the apparatus of the binary opposition between the two imagined identities of "the West" and "Japan." Maruyama has simply shifted his position from a universalism based on an imaginary West to a particularism that narrates, as a kind of universal, the authenticity of a closed and dehistoricized "Japan." If so, this discourse that emphasizes the "individuality" of Japanese culture, could be said to have the same political effects as the arguments about "Japaneseness" that have been tirelessly spun out in the name of "*Nihonjinron*" or "Japanese culturalism" in academic and journalistic discourse since the 1970s. Like them, it is a discourse of Japanese uniqueness.

The transition in Maruyama's methodology shows us that even as he advocates universalism, features of particularism gradually come to the fore in his writing. It also shows us that modernist universalism is not only insufficient as a critique of particularist discourses on Japanese uniqueness, but that that this universalism ends up being complicit in the construction of national identity.[56] It follows then, that when we read Maruyama today, we can neither accept the particularist hypothesis of his discourse on "substratum," nor defend his early postwar universalism simply by making a distinction between that and his later discourse on "substratum." This analysis should also provide a clue to understanding recent developments in Japan, because we can see that the social scientific discourses that have developed in connection with postwar democracy do not possess discursive strategies that can effectively challenge the neo-conservative discourse that has declared an end to the "postwar." Emphasizing the spirit of nationalist democracy, as Maruyama did, can no longer be either a necessary or effective method of criticizing the new forms of nationalist discourse that have prevailed since the 1980s. The real problem lies with the processes of homogenization that accompany the creation of a national identity, a homogenization that nationalist democracy tacitly assumes. What we need today, then, is a conception of democracy capable of resisting the discourse of national identity—in other words, a denationalization of democratic thought. Of course, this does not mean the construction of another "authentic" identity to replace that of the "nation." Our task, rather, is to move toward an understanding of the indeterminacy of identity itself.[57] Such a project, which would entail rereading the intellectual history of the twentieth century, can be understood as the attempt to deconstruct the nationality, which has been, more or less, the premise of postwar social science and history.

Translated by Lewis Harrington

Notes

1. There are English translations of both of these works. *Nihon seiji shisōshi kenkyū* has been translated as *Studies in the Intellectual History of Tokugawa Japan*, trans. Mikiso Hane (Tokyo: University of Tokyo Press, 1974). There is a partial translation of *Gendai seiji no shisō to kōdō* entitled *Thought and Behavior in Modern Japanese Politics*, edited by Ivan Morris (London: Oxford University Press, 1963). Unless specifically noted, references in this essay are to page numbers in the original Japanese texts.

2. *Nihon no shisō* was published by Iwanami Shoten in 1961. The article "*Rekishi ishiki no kosō*" may be found in Maruyama Masao, *Chūsei to hangyaku* (Tokyo: Chikuma Shobō, 1992). In formulating a theory of *kosō* or "substratum," Maruyama envisioned three aspects: "historical consciousness," "political consciousness," and "ethical consciousness." In what he has published to date, Maruyama has theorized the first two aspects of this substratum using the terms "*rekishi ishiki no 'kosō'*" ("'substratum' of historical consciousness") and "*seiji ishiki no 'shitsuyō teion'*" ("the '*basso ostinato*' of political consciousness"). Maruyama's "theory of substratum," in this essay, can be taken as shorthand for these two discussions.

3. Maruyama Masao, "*Kindaiteki shii*," in *Senchū to sengo no aida* (Tokyo: Misuzu Shobō, 1976), 188–189. This essay was first published in the journal *Seinen bunka kaigi*, no. 1 (Tokyo: Seinen Bunka Kaigi, 1946).

4. Maruyama Masao, "*Fuhenteki genri no tachiba—kataritsugi sengoshi*," *Shisō no kagaku*, (May 1967), 111. All emphases in quotations are from the original unless otherwise noted.

5. Maruyama Masao, "*Atogaki*," *Nihon seiji shisō kenkyū*, (Tokyo: Tokyo Daigaku Shuppan-kai, 1952), 372. This epilogue is not included in the English translation of this work, entitled *Studies in the Intellectual History of Tokugawa Japan*.

6. For recent work on this point, see Koyasu Nobukuni, "*Nihon no kindai to kindaika-ron: sensō to kindai nihon no chishikijin*," in *Datsu seiō no shisō: Iwanami kōza gendai shisō*, 15 (Tokyo: Iwanami Shoten, 1994), 84.

7. Maruyama, *Senchū to sengo no aida*, 188–189.

8. It is in this context that Naoki Sakai points out that Japan's desire for identity is channeled through its desire for the West. "It is through the imitative relation to 'the West' that the student of the history of Japanese thought acquires the possibility of representing 'Japan,' and 'Japan' as an object of personal identification, at the same the time." Sakai Naoki, "*Nihon shakai kagaku no hōhō josetsu*" in Yamanouchi Yasushi et al., eds., *Nihon shakai kagaku no shisō* [*Shakai kagaku no hōhō* III] (Tokyo: Iwanami Shoten, 1993), 31.

9. In his book *Nihon no shisō*, "nature" and "invention" become respectively "to be" and "to do." Maruyama explains that the dynamics of the modern

spirit "is born from the shift in relative importance from the logic and value of 'to be' to the logic and value of 'to do.'" Maruyama Masao, *Nihon no shisō* (Tokyo: Iwanami Shoten, 1961), 157.

10. Maruyama Masao, *"Fukuzawa ni okeru chitsujo to ningen,"* *Senchū to sengo no aida*, 144.

11. Maruyama, *Nihon no shisō*, 369.

12. Maruyama Masao, *"Fukuzawa ni okeru chitsujo to ningen,"* op. cit., 144.

13. Ibid. For more on Maruyama's relation to Fukuzawa Yukichi and Kuga Katsunan, see J. Victor Koschmann, *"Minshushugi kakumei to kokka"* in *Gendai shisō* (January 1994).

14. Ibid., 32.

15. Maruyama Masao, *"Kuga Katsunan: hito to shisō,"* in *Senchū to sengo no aida*, 29.

16. Maruyama Masao, *"Keiken, kojin, shakai,"* in *Tenbō* (January 1967).

17. In translating this essay, I have used the English word "nationalism" as a translation for both *kokuminshugi* and *nashionarizumu*. The author of this essay, in analyzing Maruyama's thought, consistently uses the term *kokuminshugi* to refer to Maruyama's "nationalism." This is because he wishes to link it to Maruyama's concept of ethnos, or *kokumin*. In the Japanese text of this essay, the author generally "translates" Maruyama's term *nashionarizumu* as *kokuminshugi*. (Translator's Note.)

18. Maruyama Masao, "The Premodern Formation of Nationalism" in Mikiso Hane trans., *Studies in the Intellectual History of Tokugawa Japan* (University of Tokyo Press, 1974), 323. (Translation slightly modified.)

19. In the original, Maruyama uses the English phrase "national consciousness" to gloss the Japanese term *"minzoku ishiki."*

20. Maruyama Masao, *"Nashionarizumu, gunkokushugi, fashizumu,"* in *Gendai seiji no shisō to kōdō* (Tokyo: Miraisha, 1964), 274. (This essay is not included in the partial English translation of this work.) In Maruyama's concept of *"minzoku,"* cultural identity is established without foundation and hence its modernity becomes concealed. For more on this point, see Sakai (1993, 28) and Sakai Naoki, *"Maruyama to chūsei"* in *Gendai shisō* (January 1994): 185.

21. Maruyama Masao, "A Critique of De-Stalinization," in the English edition of *Thought and Behaviour in Modern Japanese Politics*, 215.

22. Maruyama Masao, *"Stalin hihan ni okeru seiji no ronri,"* in *"Atogaki,"* of the original Japanese *Gendai seiji no shisō to kōdō*, 545.

23. Maruyama Masao, "Nationalism in Japan: Its Theoretical Background and Prospects," in the English edition of *Thought and Behaviour in Modern Japanese Politics*, 152.

24. Maruyama, *"Nashionarizumu, gunkokushugi, fashizumu,"* 299. Maruyama also calls *"Gleichschaltung"* a form of *"kyōseiteki sementoka"* ("coercive cementing").

25. Maruyama Masao, "Theory and Psychology of Ultra-nationalism," in the English edition of *Thought and Behaviour in Modern Japanese Politics*, 3.

26. "Theory and Psychology of Ultra-nationalism," 8.

27. "Theory and Psychology of Ultra-nationalism," 20. This argument is related to the discussion in *Nihon no shisō* of the "infinite embrace" (*mugen hōyōsei*) of Shintō.

28. "Theory and Psychology of Ultra-nationalism," 18. (Translation modified.)

29. "Theory and Psychology of Ultra-nationalism," 76. (Translation modified.)

30. To see (ultra)-nationalism as a deviant form of nationalism and to reduce it to a problem limited to wartime leads one to lose sight of the relationship between postwar democracy and "the system of wartime mobilization." This form of discourse, in emphasizing the abnormality of war, tends to endorse the relative legitimacy of the "postwar" era. Recent studies on the system of wartime mobilization problematize this view by stressing the continuity, as opposed to the discontinuity, between the wartime and the postwar. Until now, the relationship between the wartime and the postwar has been discussed in terms of a rupture or break. For recent discussions about wartime mobilization, see Yamanouchi Yasushi, J. V. Koschmann, and Narita Ryūichi ed., *Total War and Modernization* (Ithaca, New York: Cornell University East Asia Series, 1998).

31. See Satō Takumi's translator's commentary in George L. Mosse, *Taishō no kokuminka: nachizumu ni itaru seiji shinboru to taishū bunka*, trans. Satō Takumi (Tokyo: Kashiwa Shobō, 1994). This a Japanese translation of G. L. Mosse, *The Nationalization of the Masses: Political Symbolism and Mass Movements in Germany from the Napoleonic Wars through the Third Reich* (New York: H. Fertig, 1975). By contrast to Maruyama's analysis of Nazism as being based on nondemocratic elements, Mosse demonstrates that Nazism first existed on the basis of such core notions of democracy as a form of "national sovereignty" and "parliamentary democracy." Satō criticizes Maruyama for dividing the term nationalism into *kokuminshugi* (nationalism) and *kokkashugi* (statism)—a division that even today, for the most part, has not been problematized in studies of Maruyama's work. He also criticizes Maruyama for "a neglect of intellectual effort in his examination of the demonic (*masei*) nature of nationalism" (p. 235–237). I agree fully with this criticism of Maruyama.

32. This can easily be detected if one reads Maruyama's essays from the early postwar period. I will cite two representative examples here. "Nationalism in Japan has evolved along unique lines; consequently any study of Japanese nationalism involves difficulties of a special nature. To explain the particularity of its evolution, we are obliged in the last analysis to focus on the unique pattern of Japan's evolution as a modern state." (Maruyama, "Nationalism in Japan" in the English edition of *Thought and Behaviour in Modern Japanese Politics*, p. 135). "It's an enormous subject. If I were to give you an explanation [of the problem that spirit is not independent from nature], I'd have to start with a general description of the development of modern society. And then I'd have to mention the Emperor system and the family system, which form a unique

historic foundation for Japanese society. It would turn out to be quite an undertaking." (Maruyama, "From Carnal Literature to Carnal Politics," also in *Thought and Behaviour in Modern Japanese Politics*, p. 253).

33. Maruyama, *"Nihon no shisō,"* in *Nihon no shisō*, 5.

34. Ibid.

35. Bhabha contrasts the notion of "cultural diversity" with that of "cultural difference." He sees the former as having to do with culture as an epistemological object, with knowledge of a culture and customs whose content is *assumed*. The viewpoint of "cultural difference," on the other hand, problematizes the notion of a culture's identity, and is attentive to the fact that all signifying processes entail practical acts of enunciation. Homi Bhabha, *The Location of Culture* (London and New York: Routledge, 1994), 34.

36. Maruyama Masao, *"Gendai wa ikanaru jidai ka—haisen jūgōnen ni tatte,"* in *Asahi jānaru* (August 9, 1959): 13.

37. Maruyama Masao, *"Shisōshi no hōhō o mosaku shite,"* in *Nagoya Daigaku hōsei ronshū 77* (Nagoya: Nagoya University, 1978): 26. See also Kawahara Akira, ed., *"Nihon shisōshi ni okeru 'kosō' no mondai—Maruyama Sensei o o maneki shite,"* in *Keiō Gijuku Daigaku Uchiyama Hideo Kenkyūkai* (Tokyo: Keio Gijuku Daigaku Uchiyama Hideo Kenkyūkai, 1979): 61.

38. Maruyama, *"Shisōshi no hōhō o mosaku shite,"* 27.

39. Maruyama Masao, *"Nihon shisōshi ni okeru 'kosō' no mondai":* 61–62. Maruyama seems anxious lest the term "prototype" (*genkei*) be misunderstood as referring to the "oldest" in *developmental stages*, so he uses the term "substratum" (*kosō*) instead. However, these two terms indicate the same phenomenon. Later, Maruyama will use the musical metaphor "*basso ostinato*," to suggest a comparison with persistently repeated bass notes.

40. Maruyama Masao, *"Genkei, kosō, shitsuyō teion"* in Takeda Haruko, ed., *Nihon bunka no kakureta katachi* (Tokyo: Iwanami Shoten Dōjidai Library v 84, 1991), 142.

41. Ibid., 150.

42. Maruyama, *"Nihon shisōshi ni okeru kosō no mondai,"* op. cit., 69.

43. For an elaboration of *"mukeishiki no keishiki* (the forms of the formless)," see Miki Kiyoshi, "The Japanese Character and Fascism" (*"Nihonteki seikaku to fashizumu"*), in *Miki Kiyoshi zenshū*, vol. 13, (Tokyo: Iwanami Shoten, 1967), 251–255.

44. Maruyama Masao, *"Genkei, kosō, shitsuyō teion,"* op. cit., 148.

45. Ibid., 149.

46. Maruyama Masao, *"Rekishi ishiki no 'kosō',"* op. cit., 298. Maruyama argues the same thing in his discussion of the "*basso ostinato*" of political consciousness. "Japan is characterized by a degree of homogeneity—homogeneity in terms of race, language, mode of agricultural production, etc.—unusual among the highly industrialized nations of the world." (Maruyama, *"The Structure of Matsurigoto: the Basso Ostinato of Japanese Political Life,"* Henry and Lehmann, eds., *Themes and Theories in Modern Japanese History: Essays in Memory of Richard Storry* [The Athlone Press, 1988], 27). There are two

essays concerning the "*basso ostinato*" of political consciousness. One is Maruyama's 1984 presentation "*Nihon shisōshi o meguru shomondai,*" which is included in *Gendai shisō*, January 1994, under the title of "*Matsurigoto no kōzō: seiji ishiki no shitsuyō teion.*" The English article contains a more detailed argument. For a critique of Maruyama's discourse on the "substratum" of historical consciousness, see Koyasu Nobukuni, "'*Kosō' ron e no kaigi,*" in the journal *Gendai no riron*, July 1986, and Yonetani Masafumi, "*Maruyama Masao no Nihon hihan,*" in *Gendai shisō*, January, 1994.

47. Maruyama, "*Rekishi ishiki no 'kosō',*" op. cit., 295.
48. Maruyama, "*Nihon shisōshi ni okeru 'kosō' no mondai,*" op. cit., 77. Also, "*Rekishi ishiki no 'kosō',*" 350.
49. Maruyama, "The structure of *matsurigoto,*" 40.
50. Maruyama, "*Matsurigoto no kōzō: seiji ishiki no shitsuyō teion*" in *Gendai shisō*, op. cit., 74.
51. Benedict Anderson, *Imagined Communities: Reflections on the Origin and Spread of Nationalism* (London and New York: Verso, 1983, 2nd ed. in 1992), 143.
52. Maruyama, "*Shisōshi no hōhō o mosakushite,*" 27.
53. Maruyama, "*Genkei, kosō, shitsuon teiyō,*" 135.
54. Ibid., 134.
55. Maruyama, *Nihon no shisō*, 187.
56. For the complicity between particularism and universalism, see Naoki Sakai, "Modernity and its Critique: the Problem of Universalism and Particularism" in Masao Miyoshi and H. D. Harootunian, eds., *Postmodernism and Japan* (Duke University Press, 1989), 93–122. See also, in particular, the conclusion of Naoki Sakai's *Voices of the Past: the Status of Language in Eighteenth-Century Japanese Discourse* (Cornell University Press, 1992).
57. For radicalization of the concept of democracy, see Ernesto Laclau and Chantal Mouffe, *Hegemony and Socialist Strategy: Towards a Radical Democratic Politics* (Verso, 1985).

III. Contemporary Nationality

The Modern World System and the Nations of the Periphery

Iyotani Toshio

THE EMERGENCE OF EAST ASIA AND THE MODERN WORLD SYSTEM

The end of the Cold War system has once again brought the North-South problem to the surface. However, the disposition of the countries of the South has changed considerably from 30 to 40 years ago, when they were advocating "trade, not aid" under the banner of economic independence. Surface approximations of modern society, such as the permeation of mass consumer culture, a political posture advocating democracy, and policies based in economic liberalism, have reached these countries and the trend appears only to be gaining strength. Looked at from the perspective of their modernity, the majority of the countries of the world demonstrate common characteristics. Highly industrialized countries, however, have come to regard modernization like a worn jacket to be shaken off and discarded, while the countries of the so-called Third World continue to regard modernity with an envious gaze. The difference between these two groups of nations makes it difficult to adopt a thoroughly relativized perspective on the contemporary world.

The modern nation-state, whether in the case of Western or non-Western countries, was brought into being through the fixing of a boundary between "we national citizens" and an "other," and the fabrication of a time and space held in common by "us." It must be emphasized, however, that the formation of this homogeneous time and space entailed both contact with, and absorption of, heterogeneous realms. The modern nation-state has never been able to exist as a world closed off from others, but has rather been born out of its engagement with other societies and the impact they have had upon it. While, on the one hand, it ceaselessly produces its difference from others, and excludes them, on the other it is inclined toward expansion towards its exterior, and the absorption into itself of others.

This mutual relationality between states is perhaps most plainly illustrated in economic negotiation. The modern nation-state has been incorporated from the start in an integrated global division of labor, and has been cultivated within the ties established through foreign trade and other forms of economic exchange. Nationalism habitually emerges as a mode of resistance to internationalism, and its legitimacy is guaranteed through state-to-state relations. While capitalism is nourished within the body of the nation-state, insofar as the capitalist division of labor can only come to completion as a global division of labor, it must eventually reveal itself as world system. One of the keys to understanding the dynamism of the modern world system lies in this gap between the constitution of a delimited time and space in the form of nation-states, and the expansion of economic activity on a global scale.[1]

The extension of a net of commodity exchange throughout the world has incorporated a variety of regions into a single unified division of labor, and a flow of commodities from these various regions makes its way into daily life. From the standpoint of economic activity, national boundaries are nothing more than convenient demarcations for solidifying political and cultural difference, what we might call buffers on the same order as those constituted by spatial distance. The circulation of commodities and flow of information causes dramatic change in people's lifestyles and standards of value, and has brought about homogenization on a global scale. The capitalist world has in a very real way created a variety of "experiential modes" that humanity holds in common.[2] It is precisely this commonality of experience, then, that has separated large numbers of people from the land of their birth, driving them onto new lands. Within such a modernity, political, economic, and cultural changes have emerged in a particularly dramatic fashion in regions labeled peripheral or semi-peripheral.

In context of our present era, in which nationality is said to be being deconstructed, I would like to take up the problem of the peripheral countries, which have heretofore been seen as "distorted" in their formation as nation-states. In the process of the globalization of economic activity, the nation-state that once accomplished the role of midwife to industrial society is being shaken to its foundations. How has the above-mentioned disparity between the nation-state's development and the globalization of economies projected itself onto the precipitously industrializing nations of the "Third World"? To pose this kind of question signifies perhaps nothing so much as the rethinking of modernization in the countries of the periphery.

The constitution of the modern nation-state in the regions of the periphery starts with the so-called "impact of the West." Through coercive creation of the institutions of the modern nation-state in peripheral regions, a blueprint was laid to secure designated territories as colonies, introduce central military or administrative authority, and/or to rearrange existing power structures. Though national authority was secured through a suzerain state, and economic bases were fragile, these regions were incorporated as "candidates" for sovereign status within the interstate system of the modern world. The distribution of power among nation-states—that is, the very framework of center/periphery—received its form in the process of colonization. Regardless of the arbitrariness with which boundaries were drawn, in the nation-states of the periphery, histories were written, and new traditions invented.[3] Colonial domination created the modern nation-state, and gave birth to nationalism. While it is true that domination by the center engendered the constitution of nation-states in the periphery, nation building in that periphery was destined eventually to clash with the domination of the countries of the center. For this reason, peripheral nationalism has frequently been dispersed through the intervention of the countries of the center. In many countries, the dismantling or rearrangement of traditional power structures proceeded apace, but the formation of an "imagined community" to take its place was not successfully completed.[4]

With the dissolution of imperial rule brought about by the two world wars, these nations of the periphery separated from the yoke of colonial suzerainty. In tandem with the shift to wartime economic systems in the countries of the center, the countries of the periphery had pushed ahead precipitously in the direction of unification. Within the shift from the nineteenth-century imperialist system to a new interstate system, countries of the periphery drove forward the movement to constitute nations based on a system of bureaucratic authoritarianism, and to promote industrialization as the material base of such nations. The regional power structures and agrarian societies that had formed the base for traditional ruling establishments in the peripheral countries were rapidly dismantled and new arrangements took their place. The breakdown of existing forms of power was more radical here than in the countries of the West. Bureaucratic authoritarianism in the peripheral nations has been heretofore said to be a sign of backwardness. Typical in this respect was the evaluation of Chang Kai Shek's *Kuomintang* government in the former Chinese republic. This, however, is mistaken. The formation of states in the periphery under the dissolution or weakening of the colonial system proceeds apace even while no new order has been constructed to take its place, and it would perhaps be better to regard this gap as giving rise to systems of bureaucratic authoritarianism.

The end of imperialist domination in its nineteenth-century form signaled the collapse of the principle of global economic formation that had taken the United Kingdom as its center. In the context of the confrontation between East and West and the direct infiltration of Western economic influence into the countries of the "Third World" following the Second World War, bureaucratic authoritarianism had to take on a new form within the new interstate system. In response to incursions by big business in the form of multinational corporations, and the massive transfer of state capital in the form of aid, the majority of the nations of the periphery came to develop new structures of power and authority. Because it was unavoidably wrapped up in internationalization, the industrialization of the periphery meant that the formation of nation-states there would be subject to the direct cultural and economic influence of the advanced industrial nations.

Somewhere around the late 1960s and early 1970s, the large-scale infiltration of foreign capital reached a turning point and rapidly expanded its influence from enclave economies set up in peripheral countries, such as the plantation, to the establishment of comprehensive industrial production processes, including reproduction there.[5] For our purposes, we may call the period that follows this turning point the era of globalization. As I will discuss later, the concept of "globalization" implies an era where economic conflict on a global scale does not necessarily take the form of opposition between nation-states. Under the process of globalization, the states of the peripheries promote national unity on the basis of a fierce nationalism, while at the same time becoming enmeshed in international capital through outward-looking industrialization. For this reason, the countries of the periphery typically find themselves situated in a kind of gap between nationalism and internationalism.

The peripheral states experienced precipitous change in an extremely short period of time as they underwent the transition from being states comprehended under the colonial system to their restructuring as nation-states under globalization. The region where the greatest transformation has been evident during this shift to globalization is East Asia.

Over the course of thirty years of massive global economic transformation from 1960 to the 1990s, nations of East Asia enjoyed continued economic growth, achieving an effective average growth rate of 5.5% per year. At the same time that the countries of the West were slipping from high growth into low growth, this region posted such an astonishing economic development that a report from the World Bank did not exaggerate when it described it as "The East Asian Miracle."[6] Over the course of this period, the share of world trade occupied by the countries of East Asia, including Japan, rose from 7.9% in 1965 to 18.2% in 1990, while the figures for trade in manufactured goods rose from less than one-tenth of the world's share (9.4%) to greater than one-fifth (21.3%), a dizzying ascent in an extremely short time period. East Asia during this period became a major manufacturing base, was taken as a model for development economics, and was made much of as the new center of economic growth in the world.

From the standpoint of globalization and economic development, therefore, we may speak of the "East Asian region" in terms of a number of characteristics I set forth below.

First, the industrialization of East Asia occurred over the same time period as the structural transformation of the global economy that locates its turning point in the late 1960s or early 1970s. The end of high economic growth in the advanced nations, the collapse of the Bretton Woods order, the oil shock, and the dollar crises were major turning points for postwar world economics. That these structural changes in the advanced nations were not simply the result of a cyclic economic movement but a structural transformation in capitalism is a point on which the majority of commentators agree. Theories have been developed on the movement from a mass-production system to flexible production system, from a classic to a new international division of labor, from the age of industrialization to the "deindustrialized society," or to a service economy in an era that is seen as an age of internationalization, borderless economics, and the end of organizational capitalism.[7] The industrialization of the East Asian region proceeded in connection with these structural shifts in global economics.

Second, the industrialization of East Asia occurred in countries that were formerly subject to colonial domination. Since the establishment of the nineteenth-century-style global economic order centered on the United Kingdom, industrialization of colonial or formerly colonial territories has been thought to be extremely difficult to attain. The very proliferation of development economics studies attests to how difficult the industrialization of these countries has been. Originally the notion of "center/periphery" had been used to assign positions in functional hierarchical relations of economic domination, but subsequently the concept came to be understood under the specific, geographically fixed connotation of "countries of the center/countries of the periphery." As a result, the problem of industrialization in non-advanced nations has been discussed in a framework that makes it appear that once the global economy became differentiated into center and periphery, these relations remained fixed and unchanging over several centuries. To grasp the world in terms of this kind of dichotomy was to understand the dynamism of the world economy as residing exclusively in the countries of the center, and carried the unspoken premise that center/periphery relations were irreversible. The fixed, hardened character of this kind of center/periphery analysis is blatantly visible in the notion of a postwar North-South problem. This spatial framework for analyzing the global economic division of labor, which would geographically fix the relations of center/periphery and regard them as unchanging over a period of several hundred years, however, has difficulty accounting for the industrialization of the countries of East Asia. Their industrialization thereby brings into question the very framing of the question in terms of a "North-South problem."

Third, I would like to suggest that the emergence of industrialized East Asia constituted the formation of a new sphere of the regional division of labor in the non-European world. What we refer to here as the industrialization of the region of East Asia began with the high economic growth of Japan, but this was succeeded in the 1970s by the Asian NICS (newly industrializing countries), as South Korea, Taiwan, Hong Kong, and Singapore came to be called. And when we enter the 1980s, the ASEAN countries of Thailand, Malaysia, and Indonesia underwent a similar industrialization. In 1990, the seven countries of the NIES (newly industrializing economies) plus ASEAN made up 56.3% of the trade of the so-called Third World. The region's manufacturing exports actually reached 73.5%. In the early 1990s, the coastal regions of China, Vietnam, and the Philippines also sustained high levels of growth.

Of course, there is no denying that economic growth in the East Asian region gave rise to "distortions" in the internal economies of the various countries. The disparity in income levels between the highly developed countries and the countries of East Asia also remains high as before. The economies of East Asia have embraced, along with modern industry, vast slum economies, and the irregular employment strata is disproportionately high. The infiltration of consumer culture into low-income levels has given rise to new forms of poverty. The assessment of industrializing East Asia as little more than a group of subcontractors to Western capital or Japanese industry seemed, at one point, not so far off the mark. However, when compared to other regions, these countries showed striking progress in areas like education, level of infrastructure, and in the reduction of domestic disparities in income. The standard of living of the people rose, and a material prosperity was realized to a considerable degree. Further, this kind of visible transformation in lifestyles was extended to agricultural village society.

My purpose in recording the accomplishments of these East Asian nations in their "development" is not to praise them. When we take into consideration the character of their development, or the pros and cons of their export-oriented developmental strategies, each country harbored serious ongoing problems. But what I would like to call attention to is rather that there was a geographically concentrated and sustained development in this specific area. It came to constitute a sphere within which its own division of labor was operative, formed in a non-Western region independent of the existing economic center in the West. In other words, the diverse collection of countries that makes up East Asia entered the world stage as an economic sphere possessing its own set of mutual relations.

The countries of East Asia all brought about their industrialization through a bureaucratic authoritarianism with an intense nationalism at its base. However, this kind of bureaucratic authoritarianism geared for development was a common posture of Third World countries. East Asia cannot be said to differ greatly from other regions in this respect. Heretofore a number of hypotheses have sought the source of East Asian development in some essential particularity of the region of East Asia. The view has been advanced that it was non-European structural principles rooted in Confucian culture that enabled economic development. In the past, Confucianism was held to be the cause of Asia's stagnation but, in the 1990s, the judgement was reversed and Confucianism was positively praised by various regimes and interest groups. There have also been a number of arguments on industrialization that have stressed the particularity of the East Asian cultural sphere. One would perhaps not be mistaken to say that, before Western impact, a broad cultural sphere had been formed in Asia with China or India as its center, and that the existence of that cultural sphere gave form to the particular history of the region. However, it is certain that the Asian cultural sphere thus indicated did not have the kind of global dimension that could have stood in opposition to the Western European world, and it is impossible to link the existence of an East Asian cultural sphere directly to the contemporary fact of industrialization. There are also those who stress the effect on economic development of the flow of American capital into the East Asian region during the Cold War, or the extraordinary economic demands produced by the Vietnam War. Certainly, one cannot ignore America's postwar global strategy, but one would expect the same conditions to be applicable to Latin America and other regions of the "Third World."[8]

If each of the factors I have just listed shows, to some extent, characteristic peculiarities of East Asia, nevertheless these factors in and of themselves cannot be said to have brought about East Asia's contemporary industrialization. It would appear to be impossible to maintain, as the Report of the World Bank does, that this region's economic development has been brought about through some kind of factors particular to the region. It seems rather more plausible to think that the economic development of the countries of East Asia has been brought about by the successful unification of each country's people through intense nationalism, and the forced creation of a modern society compatible with the world system. In the next section, I would like to take up the question of how the policies of forced modernization in these countries of the periphery relate to the transformation of center/periphery relations in the world system.

MODERNIZATION OF THE PERIPHERIES AND THE RETURN OF IMPERIALISM

The assertion that modernization in Asia is different in kind from that of the West has been often repeated. Moreover, in recent years, the thesis of Asian particularity has come to be asserted not just from the Western side but also from within the countries of Asia. Even with a concept like democracy, prefixes are added to yield terms such as "Thai-style democracy" and the like. The discrepancy between the understanding of the concept of "human rights" in the West and in Asia has time and time again given rise to friction in international politics. Terms such as "human rights," which have a fundamental relationship to modernity itself, are now being advocated and affirmed in Asia itself, in contexts utterly different from the so-called "Western" one. In conceptions of the economic integration of East Asia one can see a disparity in thinking between America and East Asia, as for instance in ways of thinking about an "EAEC" itself. In opposition to an APEC modeled on a Pacific Rim economic sphere, the notion of an "East Asian Economic Community" that excludes the United States—the EAEC—has been advocated by some countries in East Asia. That Japan, the first Asian nation to industrialize, constitutes an ambiguous point of slippage between these different conceptions, is significant.

But to what extent is the notion of Asian "particularity" that has been put forth (often in the context of anti-Euro-American discourse) in Asia truly a rejection of modernity? It is true that individual countries or regions have their own specific histories. After all, the notion of a "Western" modernity itself is no more than an "invented tradition." But the thesis of "East Asian particularity" also refers simply to specific characteristics of different regions discerned against the background of a simultaneous of modernity. All too often, the "theory of East Asian particularity" has presented itself as an affirmation of an anti-modernity or amodernity, implying that it is an ideology of reaction against the Euro-American order. Although I will not develop this point in detail here, it should be possible to at least point out that arguments for Asian "particularity," while on the surface presented as anti-modern or non-Western discourses, in fact take economic development for granted and are argued within frameworks of "human rights" or "democracy" that have long been the discourses of modernization. That is to say, these arguments do indeed differ from assertions of "Asian difference" made in the West, but—while taking on the guise of critiques of modernity—they are, in fact, expressions of nationalism and function simply as extensions of modernization theory. What I would like to clarify here is the central economic role played by the nation-state in the evolution of capitalism. The process of industrialization in East Asia should not be spoken of in terms of East Asian particularities, but rather in terms of its strong orientation toward the modern nation-state. If, as Octavio Paz has written, all societies have modernity as their "fate," then East Asian nations must be understood to be ineluctably imbricated in the universality of the modern.

In economic terms, the modern nation-state guarantees the reproduction of human life processes, the maintenance of the infrastructure needed by capital, or else by society, and the formation of a consciousness of order with respect to social institutions including the nation-state itself. In this way, it functions to support and maintain the reproduction of capitalism. The modern nation-state guarantees a minimum level of subsistence for people from whom the means of production has been taken away, provides water, energy, transportation, and other public capital, and further constructs a social order based on racism or sexism and the like. Capital commodifies things to the greatest extent possible, and produces them as commodities. However things like human beings, an environment held in common, and the order and regularity of society will not be produced and reproduced through the independent movement of capital. The rational activity of capitalism itself, in the absence of systematic mediation, cannot function to guarantee the reproduction of capitalism.[9]

In this sense, then, capitalism as a system can be said to have been produced by a nation-state whose sovereignty is restricted to a fixed sphere. The material base of the modern nation-state is industrialization and the degree of its development determines the strength or weakness of the state. The nation-state has promoted political and cultural unification through the exclusion of the heterogeneous. It is precisely this kind of national unity that brings to fruition a homogenized labor force, the city as a site for the activity of capital, and a social order rooted in fixed norms and value consciousness. It is this national unity that has driven industrialization.

At the same time, however, economic activity has already developed to the point where it exceeds a national framework. Thus, modernity is a system in which there is a divergence between political and cultural domains, and the domain of economic activity. The modern nation-state, while on the one hand ceaselessly excluding heterogeneity, must encompass heterogeneity within it to fill in the gap between the sphere of political control and the spread of economic activity. One of the ironies of the modern state is that, even while its material base is provided by capitalist production, the global nature of capitalist production provides for the introduction of heterogeneity to the nation-state.

The material base that supports the modern state situates itself within a global division of labor. Relations of center/periphery within global economics are clearly defined by economic power, and economic domination is the mode by which countries of the center most effectively exploit peripheral countries. Wage gaps are fixed in the relation between nation-states, and relations of exploitation are embedded in market relations of international trade. Unequal relations between nation-states take the form of market relations, and no coercion at all is required to transfer wealth from the peripheries to the center. It goes without saying that exhortations of "anti-expansionism" and "free trade" repeated to the present day are nothing more than the ideology of the nations of the center.

Regardless of the type of country one is dealing with, though, to sever economic relations with other countries is to endanger the state's material basis. The modern nation-state is supported through vast practices of consumption, and severing the commodity chain would shake modern society to its foundations. Hence, the countries of the center, to the greatest extent possible, overshoot the domain governed by the nation-state, and strive to exercise influence and power in the domain defined by economic activity. The countries of the center do not simply exercise economic domination over the periphery, but also political and cultural hegemony. In this way imperialist domination finds its way into an organization of global economics based on relative economic strength.

The countries that have successfully industrialized are the countries that have succeeded in unifying as a nation-state. However, these countries that comprise the center, because they have succeeded in industrialization, have reverted to imperialist domination. Imperialist domination here may be conceived as an expansion of the political and cultural domination that corresponds to economic expansion. In correspondence with expanding economic activity, these countries have subsumed a polyvalent politics and culture that exceeds a nation-state framework, and have come to include heterogeneity.

Though modernity is a capitalist economic system, it nevertheless harbors within it the ceaseless potential to turn to imperialist domination. Wallerstein understands the modern world to be a transition from global empire to global economics.[10] The gap, however, between economic globalism and political nationalism has brought about a return to imperialist forms of domination within modernity. The modern age has not constituted the nation-state as pure homogeneous space, but rather always contains within itself the potential to turn to imperialist domination. One can take mercantilism, or nineteenth-century-style imperialism, as prototypical examples of the propensity to imperialist hegemony in practice. The propensity to imperialist domination that characterizes modernity, however, is not to be construed as a particular historical stage, but as the universal mode of existence of the nation-state in the countries of the center within the global capitalist economy.

The center has always harbored this recurring tendency to imperialist domination. It reveals itself most directly in struggles over spheres of influence, or hegemony. This type of imperialist domination is based on the cultural superiority of the center, and has the structure of enlightened domination, aiming for integration on a symbolic level. Setting aside the question of whether or not the British Empire had a systematic logic of domination, it manifested itself as a single integrated body. Europe, America, and Japan, as well, defined their colonial administration as part of a single imperialist project.

However, this return to imperialist domination does not simply entail the absorption of heterogeneous culture into the domestic sphere; it also requires huge financial expenditures. Insofar as political domination is not directly exercised, this means the weakening of the material base of the nation-state. The opening of domestic markets and transfer of the industrial base overseas brings about a rapid deterioration of trade income and revenue structures, and with increasing transfer of funds as foreign aid, it becomes difficult to maintain an international balance of payments. Insofar as these processes take place in parallel with growth in the industrial structure, problems do not surface. However, imperialist domination frequently brings about a reversal in international competitiveness and a parasitism of the economies of the center on the outside.

One of the distinguishing characteristics of the world system is struggle or competition between the countries of the center. However, it is precisely this competition that has imperiled the economic bases of these countries and prepared for the dynamism of the world system. The drama of the rotation of hegemony among the countries of the center does not mean simply that successive nations occupy the position of a center around which the globe pivots. It also entails shifts in the principles by which the world system is constituted. These shifts, in principle, carry over into changes in the relations between center and periphery in ways that open up the possibility of transforming the global hierarchy or transforming the structure of the system itself. An example of the kind of movement that can destabilize relations of center and periphery emerged most sharply in the arms race that accompanied the Second World War and the Cold War. The Second World War, in particular, resulted in a decline in power of the countries of the center. Organized around systems of total mobilization, it enveloped various countries around the globe, required vast wartime procurements and manpower mobilization, and, in its aftermath, led to vastly increased human and material costs of maintaining modern weaponry. Yet, perhaps the most dramatic shift in center/periphery relations was manifested in the collapse of the colonial system. While the countries of the center declined, however, this did not mean that these countries were peripheralized. The slackening of center/periphery relations simply opened new fissures in the world system. Only those countries and regions that were able to interpret these shifts in the world system and choose a compatible direction were able to slip through these cracks and successfully industrialize.

The so-called modernization strategy taken by the countries of East Asia after World War II was one of extreme fidelity to nation-statist aims. Though we cannot describe each country in detail here, a rough enumeration of the basic policies of bureaucratic authoritarianism in East Asia might look like this: (1) the forced implementation of a policy of equality; (2) high-handed unification of the population as national citizens, despite the existence of a variety of ethnic groups; (3) the promotion of the homogenization of the population in areas like universal primary schooling; and (4) the creation of systematized modern spaces such as cities and industrial zones. (Of course the countries of East Asia are diverse, and the policies suggested here have been implemented in a variety of forms.)

One may perhaps sum these policies up as the promotion of national unity based on an intense nationalism. Nation or religion, or in some cases anti-communism, have been advocated as a matter of national policy, and made symbols of national unity. The patriarchal family system, once the symbol of Asian backwardness, became stressed as a basis of national unity—it became both the fundamental basis for industrial organization in these societies and the wellspring of a stable labor supply. Some in East Asia even assert that it is precisely because of the stable survival of the patriarchal family system that capitalist development has been possible. In overcoming complicated ethnic problems, these countries have reinvented traditions based on religion and ethnicity and offered as an enticement the tangible evidence of a higher standard of living. Anticommunist dictatorships have time and again, for example, carried out agendas for social renewal, aggressively pursuing policies on the environment, hygiene, and education, or building organizational infrastructures for local areas. In East Asia, the rate of government investment in education has been extremely high, and vast improvements are said to be visible in rates of attendance at primary schooling and literacy rates. It has been bureaucratic institutions that have implemented these policies, and the majority of technocrats have studied abroad in Europe and America. Economic policy under such bureaucracies pursues a scientific rationality, and is extremely faithful to western economic theory and development theory. This is why, for instance, the rate of inflation in such countries remained low.

Prototypical examples of the bureaucratic authoritarian system would include the Park regime in South Korea, the government of Suharto in Indonesia, the Marcos regime in the Philippines, and the Saliht regime in Thailand. That, in the process of implementing their policies, these regimes oppressed labor and social movements and engaged in the unseemly amassing of wealth is a well-known fact. It is also a fact that systems of bureaucratic control have created structures of corruption. These governments have accordingly been attacked as dictatorial, anti-democratic, and authoritarian. Yet, however autocratic and corrupt they may have been, under these regimes the banners of "development" and "democracy" were hoisted, and a new middle class of bureaucrats and industrialists emerged. These regimes, in other words, gave rise to the very middle class that would eventually form the core of democratization movements seeking to topple them. Most books discussing the successful industrialization of East Asia have positively assessed the policies of these regimes as having provided the basis for economic development.

Systems of bureaucratic authoritarianism are often approached in terms of the dilemma of democratization versus development.[11] According to such a view, giving priority to development policies is incompatible with democratic political forms, and gives rise to authoritarian political power. Economic development itself, however, is what creates the material base on which democracy can be raised, and dictatorships that have led modernization efforts have toppled. Can it not be said that from the first (and not only in peripheral nations but also in most countries), modernization carries within it the contradiction between economic development and democracy, that is to say, the contradiction between the unfettered expansion of production and its regulation? And if that is the case, should we understand bureaucratic authoritarianism in these nations not as a deviation from modernization, but as the form of the modern nation-state itself? It seems undeniable that bureaucratic authoritarianism constitutes precisely the kind of power structure necessary to carry out enforced modernization.

What makes the assessment of industrialization in the countries of East Asia so difficult is that it took place in the midst of a major structural transformation of the modern world. Before undertaking any assessment, then, we must consider the implications of the fact that development dictatorships emerged in tandem with a major transformation in the world system itself, the shift to the age of globalization.

IMPERIALISM TO GLOBALIZATION

While the criteria invoked may differ, it is a shared assumption of many different academic fields that the late twentieth century witnessed a major transformation of the modern world. The notion is widely held that the modern world order with the West as its pinnacle eroded, and that the modern nation-state, which had been the fundamental modern unit of politics and culture, went into decline. The outlines of the nation-state tended to recede in debates concerning the nature of this transformation: they now revolved around notions of universalism and globalism.

In his book, *Cultural Imperialism*, John Tomlinson argued that the late twentieth century must be understood as one of globalization.[12] In his conclusion, Tomlinson used the phrase "from imperialism to globalization" to characterize the shift in the way countries of the center had come to imprint the stamp of modernization on the regions of the periphery. Imperialism here means the configuration of power according to which global domination is seen as rooted in Western cultural dominance and enlightenment ideology. In the West, the history of the human race has been seen as a history of progress, and the goal of human society as the advancement of science and the pursuit of rationality. Progress and economic development came to possess an absolute value. Imperialism, in this sense, was not simply a system of global domination based on economic superiority. It entailed the formation of a Eurocentric global order suffused with a sense of moral mission based on cultural superiority.

The age of globalization, however, seemed to signal the collapse of the cultural domination of the West over other regions, the loss of legitimacy of its the quest for world domination, and the decline of enlightenment ideology. Western economic development and the progress of scientific technology are seen by some as bearers of environmental destruction and the pathologies of industrialization. The development of scientific technologies has outstripped the capacity of humans to control them. For Tomlinson, the age of globalization has been characterized by "uncertainty, lack of moral legitimacy, and cultural indirection."[13] In the age of globalization, although problems of environment and technology emerge on a scale that surpasses existing national frameworks, there is no sign of any unified political body capable of controlling them. Imperialism was a world order based on the ascendancy of specific nations. We now need to try to understand what new configuration of power will replace imperialism in the age of globalization.

There is no need to point out anew that Eurocentric social science and historical consciousness have already been subject to critique from a variety of perspectives.[14] However, multiculturalism, pluralism, and other proposals for new value systems have wavered on the question of how best to overcome, or succeed to, the legacy of modernity. Even if a situation where diverse values are recognized could be brought about, what would serve as a common basis for mutual recognition and respect? At the present juncture, as a legacy of modernity, we have only the belief in universality. "The problem for the critique of modernity is how to criticize its discontents whilst recognizing its comforts, thus to avoid the self-indulgence involved in romanticizing 'tradition'," as Tomlinson says.[15] This observation hints at how difficult the relativization of modernity may be.

I am not trying to pose this question about globalization as one of "cultural domination." Rather, I am concerned with how economic processes relate to cultural processes. What is the nature of the material base that will be generated as a new configuration of power replaces imperialism, and how will the center/periphery configuration that held sway in the modern world system be transformed? Our evaluation of East Asian industrialization must also be carried out from this point of view.

The activity of capital has been global from the first, and the modern nation-state has been formed within a global division of labor. What calls for our attention now, however, is capital's "loss of nationality" and a corresponding attenuation of the national identities of peoples. A great deal of research has already been done on the global movement of capital in the age of globalization. Some of the emphases of this research have been on (1) an expansion in the size of firms corresponding to the emergence of systems capable of very high volume production, and the development of intra-firm division of labor on a global scale; (2) the formation of a network of global cities as nodal concentrations of capital, people, and information; (3) the dissolution of rural societies on a global scale with the incursion of consumer cultures; and (4) a kind of aestheticization of value that has accompanied the shift from the production of things to the production of services. The nature of the age of globalization is revealed most boldly, moreover, in the way a certain fantasy—that of the "global dream"—has become incorporated into commodities themselves, taking precedence over function or quality.[16]

Huge corporate organizations now exceed the frame of the nation-state, and have developed a functional global division of labor from a global perspective. The standardization of production processes has refashioned the world into a single market, and production is organized in accordance with a distribution of production sites dictated by efficiency. The core functions of an industry's economic management are concentrated in the head office, while a stratified network of production and sales has subsumed the far reaches of the globe. Rural societies of the Third World, which up until now had not been greatly affected by market economics, have become subsumed into networks of production and sales. With the evolution of mass media technologies, consumer culture has penetrated to the furthest flung regions of the earth, bringing about vast changes in life-ways. With the penetration of rural societies by market economies, great numbers of people have been deprived of their livelihoods, leading to urbanization on a scale not yet witnessed in history, and creating a vast pool of wage laborers in the Third World. We now have the emergence on a global scale of a usable stratum of low-wage labor. For corporations, failure to take advantage of this inexhaustible supply of low-wage labor means a loss of competitiveness. One of the conditions that has enabled the expansion of corporate organization on a global scale has been the revolution in transportation and communication. The real-time transmission of decisions and the development of large-scale sea and air shipping methods enable an industrial organization with a global reach to be centrally managed from the head office. The needs of these head offices have given rise to the demand for corporate services, including finance, in the global cities that have arisen wherever these vast corporations and their corporate services are concentrated. In the new global city, we find concentrations of population and information from various countries, along with concentrations of capital. These global cities place a higher priority on their ties with world cities in other countries than on their ties with regions inside their own countries—on the basis of the economic activity and information they share in common, they create a shared culture. Thus, the globalization of the city is demolishing the foundation on which the nation-state rests. It is the de-nationalization of the (global) city that most decisively demonstrates the globalized space and time of the contemporary world.[17]

The industrialization of East Asia has taken place within the context of precisely this kind of globalization of capital. Various ways of explaining the relationship between East Asian industrialization and this context have emerged. For example, on the one hand, the success of the East Asian NIES has been understood in terms of their movement from the periphery to the center, or else in terms of historical stages that mark the diffusion of the industrialization that began in the West. On the other hand, the process has also been described as a form of international subcontracting by the center. All these appraisals have in common the notion that the industrialization of East Asia must be situated within a world constituted through mutual relations between nation-states. However, the possibility that the East Asian NIES will emerge as a kind of new imperialist bloc of industrialized nations, on a par with Japan and with the U.S. and Europe, is quite slim. Their emergence should rather be grasped as representing a structural transformation of the modern world system that had earlier taken the form of a geographical division of labor between center and periphery.

The control of the periphery by the center—in a word, imperialism—has until now been taken to be the plundering of the wealth of the periphery and the obstruction of its development by the center. However, the industrialization of these countries of the periphery has now clearly advanced, and the peripheries are overflowing with the commodities of the center, creating a new situation. Some would blame this penetration of the peripheries by the capital of the center for fanning the flames of consumer society in the peripheries. In other words, according to this view, the industrialization of the periphery is not to be criticized from the standpoint of its failure to reach all strata of society, but rather because the penetration of the center's capital and consumer culture is to be deplored. Tomlinson characterizes the view this way: "on the one hand, capitalism is seen as guilty of denying its material benefits to some but on the other it is guilty of spreading a shallow 'material culture' . . . of 'delivering the goods.'"[18] But bringing about the penetration of consumer culture into the peripheries has not been a matter of some kind of political coercion. To adopt a familiar metaphor, it has been born of rational choices about consumption made by the modern individual. It is easy to criticize the penetration of consumer culture that was brought about through massive advertising on the part of multinational corporations in the media. This type of criticism, however, is the equivalent of maintaining that the ordinary people in the peripheral regions are so ignorant as to be easily taken in by advertising. This problem of consumer culture purveyed through the mass media, moreover, is in no way restricted to the peripheries. Hence, the critique of consumerism in the Third World cannot be separated from the critique of consumerism in capitalist Europe and America. And what can be said in this regard about the diffusion of consumer culture is applicable *in toto* to the dispersion of production sites and the utilization of low-wage labor by big business. The difficulty of assigning a value to industrialization of peripheral nations in the age of globalization lies partly here.

This is as much as to say that, in the age of globalization, center and periphery relations can no longer be grasped in the framework of political domination and subordination as they once were. The various economic relations between the advanced industrial nations and the contemporary Third World need to be understood, not in terms of the global division of labor between the countries of the center and the countries of the periphery, but rather as the global activity of capital that exceeds the framework of the nation-state. The image of a modern world economy from the ages of imperialism and colonialism cannot simply be projected onto the present age. If modernization of the peripheries more accurately poses the question of "how a cultural practice can be imposed in a context that is no longer actually coercive," or must be studied as "a process not of cultural imposition but of cultural loss," as Tomlinson suggests, then the shift from imperial domination to globalization may be said to pose the question of what kind of world will be created by the de-nationalization of capital and by the migration of peoples.[19] In the face of the functional activities of capital that fall outside regulation by the nation-state, what kinds of frameworks of control will be instituted by which subjects?

We find ourselves today placed in a global configuration of power that differs both from nineteenth-century colonialist domination under European enlightenment ideology, and also from the American hegemony of the 1950s, under the aegis of a modernization theory dressed up as an ideology of prosperity. The age of imperialist domination has already announced its own demise. In the past, imperialism was even able to reap a species of profit economically. The countries with key currencies had no restrictions on balance of payments, and were able to carry out their activities overseas. In this way, it was possible to push the risk of fluctuating exchange rates off onto other countries. These days, however, the advantages of being a country with a key currency are rapidly diminishing.

Our present age has been called the age of interdependency, but one might just as well phrase it as the end of the age of hegemony. That is to say that the age of world orders based on a specific country is over. However, the new configuration of power that will take the place of imperialism in the modern world has yet to make its appearance. Local problems experienced in everyday life—environmental issues, or matters having to do with immigration, refugees, and the like—have also emerged as problems that exceed the scope of individual countries, and it is already clear that such problems cannot be managed by individual countries in isolation. The advent of borderless economies means the advent of a variety of borderless problems. This is to admit that, despite the fact that our daily lives have become overwhelmed by problems that are beyond the reach of the nation-state, we have been unable to produce a political mechanism capable of responding to them.

The East Asian region has indeed accomplished economic development, but this is not to say that it will become a new center for imperialist domination in the world, nor is it to say that it will replace Japan as a new power in Asia. As it has turned out, the modern world has not ultimately evolved according to a pattern in which a single culture establishes hegemony over the entire globe through the osmotic power of its culture. In the present age, with the global unfolding of capital replacing imperialist hegemony, the indifference of capitalism with respect to culture has straightforwardly revealed itself. The age of globalization is rendering the notion of the political, economic or cultural expansion of a particular nation-state meaningless.

The East Asian NIES at one and the same time promoted national unity under high economic growth through a fierce nationalism, and carried out "open-door" policies rooted in internationalization, policies that nimbly adapted to structural shifts in a world economy undergoing globalization. Industrialization in these countries was forged out of world economics in the age of globalization. While the success of their industrialization depended on its taking a nationalist form, then, the globalized nature of world economics also ensured that they would be kept on the run by forces of both nationalism and internationalism. The countries of the former center now seem to be rapidly losing the cultural characteristics typified by nationalism. However, the countries of East Asia, even as they assert an intense nationalism and carry out industrialization within a national framework, seem no better equipped to give birth to new cultural features that would take the place of those associated with modernization.

Translated by Joseph Murphy

Notes

1. Immanuel Wallerstein, *The Modern World-System* (New York: Academic Press, 1989).

2. John Tomlinson, *Cultural Imperialism: A Critical Introduction* (London: Pinter Publishers, 1991).

3. Eric Hobsbawn and Terence Ranger, eds. *The Invention of Tradition* (Cambridge: Cambridge University Press, 1983).

4. Benedict Anderson, *Imagined Communities: Reflections on the Origin and Spread of Nationalism* (London: Verso, 1983). (Revised, 1992.)

5. T. G. McGee and Warwick Armstrong, *Theatres of Accumulation: Studies in Asian and Latin American Urbanization* (London: Methuen, 1985).

6. See the World Bank, *The East Asian Miracle: Economic Growth and Public Policy* (Oxford and New York: Oxford University Press, 1993).

7. This view has been argued in Richard Peet, ed., *International Capitalism and Industrial Restructuring: A Critical Analysis* (London and New York: Routledge 1987), and in Michael Piore and C. F. Sabel, eds., *The Second Industrial Divide: Possibilities for Prosperity* (New York: Basic Books, 1984). See also S. Lasch and J. Urry, *The End of Organized Capitalism* (London: Polity Press, 1987), S. Lasch and J. Urry, *Economies of Signs and Space* (Sage, 1994), and Malcolm Waters, *Globalization* (London and New York: Routledge, 1995).

8. Hirakawa Nao, *NIES—Sekai Shisutemu to kaihatsu* (Tokyo: Dōbunkan, 1993).

9. Toshio Iyotani, *Henbō suru sekai toshi*, (Tokyo: Yuhikaku, 1993).

10. Wallerstein, op. cit.

11. Suehiro Akira, *Tai: Kaihatsu to minshushugi* (Tokyo: Iwanami Shoten, 1993).

12. See Tomlinson, op. cit.

13. Tomlinson, op. cit., 175.

14. Immanuel Wallerstein, *Unthinking Social Science: The Limits of Nineteenth Century Paradigms* (London: Polity Press, 1991).

15. Tomlinson, 175.

16. Richard Barnes and John Cavanagh, *Global Dreams: Imperial Corporations and the New World Order* (New York: Simon and Schuster, 1994).

17. Saskia Sassen, *The Global City: New York, London, Tokyo* (Princeton: Princeton University Press, 1991). See also Manual Castells, *The Informational City: Technology, Economic Restructuring, and the Urban-Regional Process* (New York: Basil Blackwell, 1989).

18. Tomlinson, 107–108.

19. Tomlinson, 173.

Morisaki Kazue's
"Two Languages, Two Souls": Language, Communicability, and the National Subject

Brett de Bary

READING INTERRUPTED: THE AREA STUDIES TEXT

If two people, one Japanese and the other not, could not talk to each other about Japan, would Japanese Studies (as constituted outside of Japan) exist? It is in relation to this unabashedly rudimentary question that I undertake the reading of a short essay by the contemporary author Morisaki Kazue (b. 1927). In formulating such a question, let me make it clear from the outset that I do not wish to speak from the idealist and solipsistic position that some would call "linguistic relativism," nor would I deny the reality (however one chooses to define that term) of that knowledge that is now constituted and legitimated by the institutionalized discourse known as Japanese Studies. But I wish to call attention to how pervasively, indeed unnoticeably, such a model of transparent communication between subjects, one Japanese and one not, informs writing in our field. Put even more simply, one might say that the model of communication between Japanese subject and foreign scholar is premised on yet another model, that of communication among Japanese subjects themselves, a communication that constitutes the authentic knowledge of Japan transmitted to the non-Japanese world by the foreign Japan scholar. While the implications of this model of communication for scholarship in the social sciences, often based on fieldwork and interviewing, would seem to be immediate, they are no less far-reaching in the case of humanistic disciplines. Insofar, for example, as the interpretation of literary texts takes as its key an author's life and intentions, or an historical period itself, the interpretation assumes that the text, like speech, is an adequate and faithful communication of the extra-literary.

I have chosen to work with certain texts by Morisaki Kazue because, throughout her life, Morisaki persistently problematized the speech act, and its relation to writing and research, as well as to relations of knowledge, power, and exclusion. Morisaki's work may thus be used to raise a number of provocative questions about the constitution of Japanese Literature as a discipline. Let me first acknowledge that, in undertaking such a reading, I am performing a task well sanctioned by my academic discipline. At the same time, and as is far less frequently acknowledged, I do not see this reading as providing me with immediate access to some kind of knowledge (typically "expert," or authoritative) of either Morisaki Kazue or that Japan that has been so conspicuously absent from my own work of reading in America. My reading, like any reading, has been and will continue to be an intersection in terms of which any hypothetical "actual" encounter between Morisaki Kazue and myself is displaced in countless ways.

Not the least of these have been my consultations with other speakers of Japanese (and among these I will include my reading and citation, in this essay, of Fujimoto Kazuko's translations of Morisaki's writings into English), conversations that have interrupted and assisted my reading, making it hardly a solitary enterprise, and to whose "expertise" I, the "Japan expert," am always indebted. When, in negotiating my way through a Japanese text—experiencing, indeed, a poetry and terror similar to that Morisaki Kazue has frequently attributed to linguistic encounters—I invariably reach a point where I must, as the professional argot has it, "consult a native speaker," I am keenly reminded of this dependence. In so doing, moreover, I must vividly confront a "Japanese" that is no longer the supposedly stable, neutral medium through which I seek to decipher a meaning, but rather a form of commodified information whose international circulation involves me in diverse and subtly articulated hierarchies of relationships.

Against a background of modern global relations, for example, the phrase "consult a native speaker" may itself be seen as setting forth at least two (as it happens, contradictory) sets of hierarchized relationships, a verbal surface where language and history intersect. For insofar as the role of "native speaker," within the institutionalized practices of area studies, often overlaps with that of "native informant," the term evokes the hierarchized schema of modern disciplinary knowledge according to which, as Gayatri Spivak has noted, "the dominant subject position" (presumably the "Western" scholar) "constructs the subordinate as other" while attempting to efface its dominance by endowing this other with the "curious, objectified subject position" of native informer, or native speaker.[1] I will take up later the historical ambiguity of Japan's own role as a colonizing power dealing with "native speakers" in Asia. At this point, let me simply note that, in American academic parlance, the subjectivity with which the native speaker or informant is endowed is undone and contradicted by the overpoweringly objectivizing force of the designation "native" (for a native speaker is generally seen to be so from the positionality of the non-native, outsider), as noted by Spivak. What I would like also to call attention to is another level of ambivalence in this construction, which posits, and appears to recall the dependence of the foreign scholar on, the authority of the native speaker. While what is evoked by this phrase will certainly be construed variously in different historical contexts, for American area specialists it is most likely to be periods of time spent abroad for research, periods when one's claim to authority as a specialist has to coexist with, and be daily discomfited by, one's position as member of a linguistic minority. When the language being negotiated is Japanese, the non-native speaker must always implicitly acknowledge the superiority of the "native speaker" and feel, to varying degrees, disadvantaged. At its most difficult, research abroad entails prolonged exposure to such vulnerability, in which the sense of risk and uncertainty in social relationships is high. Johannes Fabian's admittedly caricatured description of the anthropologist's fieldwork experience may also ring true for those who recall the low points of doing field work in Japan or any other site abroad. How often has the "aura of empirical research" served, Fabian asks, "to legitimize as field work varying periods spent on getting over culture shock, fighting loneliness," coping with "the claims of local expatriates," as well as with the local bureaucracies?[2]

Once returned to the home context, however, such memories of inadequacy, and the autobiographical narrative they might constitute, are generally suppressed or deemed irrelevant to the presentation of the "objective" scholarly project, the expert's dispensation of knowledge of/about the researched culture. Furthermore, the expert may now, in the institutionalized context of area studies, continue to consult with native speakers, with a much reduced (although, I emphasize, not always and entirely eradicated) sense of risk, since, as it happens, most are language instructors of lower rank within the institution, who well know their places as assistants to the experts (or know, in the humanities, that language teaching is routinely assumed to be ancillary to the higher pursuits of literary interpretation, and so forth). Yet ironically, highly conventionalized allusions to concrete encounters between the foreign scholar and members of the other society continue to circulate in area studies discourse, as that which (together with written texts) ultimately authorizes the knowledge of the scholar. In literary studies, moreover, there tends to be an even more blatant suppression of the sociality of so-called "texts in the original," whose reading is assumed to have been purely the product of the solitary scholar's/subject's encounter with printed artifacts. Nevertheless, the scholar's fluency in the language and sensitivity to cultural nuance, presumably nurtured during periods abroad, is an important credential.

What I hope to have called attention to in the preceding is a need to reexamine the institutionalized notion of "reading the Japanese text," a need to redefine that reading in its multiplicity as well as in its dialogic dimensions. What has been institutionalized as the product of the scholar's individual (and privileged) subjectivity must be seen rather as an intricate concatenation of processes, one in which the hierarchical positioning of subject and object of knowledge has been historically mediated but may also be locally modulated, and is thus always capable of being reversed, disrupted, or contested. To call attention to the ways in which multiply configured social relations are systematically effaced in the disciplinary conventions of "reading the text," may be one step toward what Spivak has called "occupying or cathecting" the "representative space or blank presupposed by the dominant text" of area studies. For those who, from a number of different theoretical perspectives, would see their involvement in such studies as a process of—and indeed a commitment to—the representation cultural difference, reflection on how we are implicated in the institutional processes that produce that representation will be a necessary part of the task of transforming them.[3]

AREA STUDIES, FEMINISM, POSTMODERNISM

The foregoing remarks, very much a response provoked by Morisaki Kazue's work, have been an attempt to open up the reading of the area studies text to dissonances and heterogeneity. By contrast to the fetishization of the written text within, particularly, humanistic disciplines, I have emphasized the materiality of the verbal artifact, a signification produced through absence. At the same time, however, I have opposed to the equally powerful reification of the written text within the academy, a concept of language as sociality. From this perspective, the individual scholar subject appears to dissolve into a plurality of language games, in which gender, national, and racial subject positions ("identities") may be variously constituted. Depending on the locality, the rules of the game may be changed. Thus the attention given by post-modern philosophers such as Jean-Francois Lyotard to the existence of a heterogeneity of language games with locally determined rules seems useful in destabilizing the notion of the area studies text. Institutions such as the university, according to Lyotard, may exert a powerful constraint on language games. They function to "filter discursive potentials, interrupting possible connections in communications networks" by privileging certain classes of statements and censoring others.[4] But Lyotard would also emphasize that it is in language games that constraints are always at stake and contested. Reading the area studies text, similarly, does not entail the same hierarchized relations in every situation. The institutionalized notion of the text works to interrupt some connections in the reading process but also to impose continuities where none exist. Local contexts of reading in America and Japan, for example, will be multiple and dissonant.

In deconstructing the fetishized notion of the area studies text, then, the concept of language games can provide a helpful means of mediating the (usually firmly differentiated) categories of the material (text) and the social (text), making it possible to posit reading as a heterogeneity of processes entailing multiply constructed subject positions. Such an approach, in turn, may help us avoid unwittingly perpetuating the rigid West (subject)/East (object, other) dichotomy characteristic of Eurocentric discourses. Only a constant awareness of the tension between the destabilizing potential of language games and the force of such historically constructed identities will enable us to question the assumed objectivity of the area studies text.

In the following pages, I would like to consider ways in which writings by Morisaki Kazue may be productive of such a tension. Rather than deconstructing Morisaki's texts, I will read them as deconstructive texts; texts that, by "putting the subject on trial" (as Julia Kristeva once described it), raise provocative questions about the constitutive categories of area studies. For Morisaki's texts convey a palpable awareness of the risks of claiming to represent cultural others. They thus share a reluctance, articulated at a critical juncture in North American feminism by Elspeth Probyn, "to assume that anyone could speak for One woman and all women."[5] By enacting, through their critique of communicational transparency, the impossibility of representing the Other, Morisaki's texts aggressively project back to the area specialist who would read "the other woman" in them a defamiliarized image of that process in which the area studies text is engaged. It is in the dialectical tension between the acknowledgement of the universalization entailed in any use of language (universalization as "an irreducable moment in any discourse," as Spivak puts it) and a critique of the violence of representation as commensurability—of representing the other as the same—that Morisaki's texts situate themselves.[6]

Furthermore, Morisaki's texts demonstrate an engagement with the local, as writing's site of production, which can counter the tendency of a critique of communicational transparency to drift toward "some unspecified local that becomes the site for an unnamed politics." Probyn, for example, distinguishes between a sense of the "local" (in which women are interpolated as subjects in specific, geographical locations) and what she calls "location," referring to the *ordering* of knowledge within dominant discourses that delimit what qualifies as knowable, rendering certain representational practices scientific while others are excluded. "This epistemology most often works to keep the subaltern outside the sanctified boundaries of knowledge."[7]

In what follows, I would like to propose ways in which Morisaki's writing can be read against the grain of the "area studies text," particularly with regard to the local and location as Probyn has defined them. I will discuss the essay, "Two Languages, Two Souls" (*"Futatsu no kotoba, futatsu no kokoro"*), first published in the journal *Space of Language* (*Kotoba no uchū*) in May 1968, and subsequently included in the anthology *My Imagi-*

nary Marriage to my Motherland (Haha no kuni to no gensōkon), published in 1971.[8] The anthology includes essays of Morisaki's written against the background of over a decade of involvement in "local" cultural production and political struggle in the Chikuhō mining areas of northern Kyushu. It was a period during which she challenged the hierarchical "location" of knowledge by producing oral histories (*kikigaki*), essays, and bulletin/newsletters with groups (women miners, Yoronese laborers conscripted in the prewar period) whose access to literacy was limited and for whom standard Japanese was a second language.

Born the daughter of a school administrator for the Japanese colonial government in Korea, Morisaki had come to Japan as a "returnee" (*hikiagesha*, the term used for settlers in former Japanese territories in Korea, Manchuria, and elsewhere) at the end of the war. In 1958, as a mother of two young children with an interest in poetry writing, she joined the *Sākuru Mura* (Circle Village) collective of artists and political activists in the mining city of Nakama, in Fukuoka Prefecture, whose founder, the writer Tanigawa Gan, was her lover. Labor leader Ueno Eishin, and Ishimure Michiko, whose celebrated books about Minamata disease were written during this period, were also members of the collective. While at *Sākuru Mura*, Morisaki participated in two major strikes against the rationalization of the Japanese coal mining industry, at the Taisho and Miike mines, carried out in tandem with protests against the 1960 renewal of the U.S.-Japan Security Treaty. These involvements took place at a time when many Japanese intellectuals were seeking to turn away from the early postwar emphasis on internationalism and the autonomy/agency of the subject as "individual" (*kojin*) and to reaffirm concepts of autonomy through community (*kyōdōtai*), the study of folkways, and submergence in the local. Although Tanigawa left Kyushu in 1965, Morisaki remained in Fukuoka, where she continues to live and write.

In the afterword to her volume of essays *My Imaginary Marriage to my Motherland*, Morisaki described the table at which she wrote them during the time of the Taisho and Miike strikes, setting forth a notion of interrupted textuality that might be counterposed to that of the fetishized area studies text.

> As someone who could never settle down in anything resembling a study, I have written most of the essays in this volume at the large kitchen table at which we prepared, as well as ate, our meals. Since we often shared meals or had meetings with the miners around that table, I had to time and again clear away my manuscripts and take them to another part of the house. To have my writing repeatedly interrupted while under the pressure of publishing deadlines was physically exhausting. Nevertheless, as we sat around working out the details of our actions for the following day, often until three or four in the morning, I would feel energy bubble up, as if from some white source beyond the

limits of my physical stamina. I thought of this as a process whereby the exhaustion produced by manual labor converts itself into will, and it seemed to me I could glimpse the traces of this process in the eyes of the miners, too. When our meetings ended near dawn, they would go off without sleep to wherever they worked. With similar physical and psychological sensations, I would go and retrieve the manuscript that had been cleared away.[9]

"TWO LANGUAGES, TWO SOULS": THE "KOREA WITHIN" AND THE MYTH OF POSTWAR HOMOGENEITY

Morisaki Kazue's twenty-page essay published in 1968 uses the trope of "Two Languages, Two Souls"—representing the subjectivity of the returnee, or *hikiagesha*, from the dismantled Japanese empire—to disrupt the postwar myth of a homogeneous Japanese nation. Like much cultural production associated with the political activism of the 1960s and 1970s, Morisaki's many essays from this period were originally written for journals published by small presses. Composed in an idiosyncratic language that was autobiographical, impassioned, and often explicitly sexual, yet which just as frequently digressed into highly abstract philosophical argumentation, Morisaki's essays garnered avid readers among some student radicals and young women involved in the "second wave" feminism that emerged in the early 1970s.[10] Today she is better known for more narrative works like *The Third Sex (Daisan no sei)* and *Karayuki-san*, while her more obscure essays have, for the most part, fallen out of circulation.[11]

There is much to be learned, however, from the intense and erratic prose arguments penned by Morisaki before the breakup of the *Sākuru Mura* collective. Although there is a risk in imposing thematic coherence on her fragmented and elliptical prose, it is also possible to find in it a sophisticated challenge to certain highly naturalized modern notions, especially the notion of a shared language as the basis for national community, and the notion of language as a neutral medium of representation. In the discussion that follows, I will analyze Morisaki's prose—both in its figurative moments and in its fragmentary philosophical speculations—in order to highlight salient aspects of this critique. Although Morisaki's essays are not academic, and are thus unconcerned with providing an intellectual genealogy for her assertions, I will also call attention to striking parallels between the ideas (often suggested in condensed form) in her prose and modern theoretical arguments that have evinced a similar concern for understanding the relationships among language, the social, and issues of colonialism and discrimination. I incorporate a number of translated passages of the essay into my analysis, so that the reader may have a better sense of Morisaki's language and the questions her style itself engages.

The Colonizer's "Crime of Birth," Two Languages, Dementia

In "Two Languages, Two Souls," Morisaki's narrator poses her subjectivity as a returnee as that which shatters the supposed *heimlichkeit*, or familiarity, of Japanese culture after the war. For Morisaki, it appears, the *hikiagesha* could only be represented as a site of dissonance, capable of disrupting both the myth of similitude and the amnesia (of the former colonizers) that sustained it. As we may observe in the passage below, the narrator from the start of her essay rejects the pretense of writing objectively about the former Korean subjects of Japanese colonialism. She freely admits that her writing can only pursue a circuitous logic, and she presents the reader from the first with apparent paradoxes. Insisting that her birth was a "crime" (despite the fact that she, of course, did not will it), she claims that she cannot write about Korea as a knowing subject but only as a subject of "dementia." Far from presenting Korea as an object of knowledge to be described by an efficacious and instrumental language, the narrator presents Korea as that which cannot be detached from her existence itself. To write is a painful labor she compares to a process of birth.

> To talk about Korea is a burden, it makes me feel so heavy-hearted I hardly know where to begin. I was born in Mikasa-chō, Taegu, Kyong-sangpukto, Korea.
>
> Sensing that your birth—not the way you lived your life but the fact of having been born—was in itself a crime is not something you speak about easily. Ordinarily, I try to maintain my mental composure by telling myself that the fact of my birth is linked to the nucleus of history. Since the end of the war, I've managed to survive by blending in with masses of other Japanese. Yet unlike them I am not allowed the comfort of believing that the crimes of colonialism occurred at a national level, and had nothing to do with the ordinary people. . . . It does me just as little good to think that I was only a child, that I wasn't born in Korea because I wanted to be. It is the very fact that I was born in that land without having chosen to do so, that I absorbed its culture, which in turn gave shape to my being, that gives rise to my dilemma. I find it impossible to remain objective about Koreans or the activities of Koreans; I lose my composure. The hair of my Korean mother (*omoni*) and the nurse (*neya*) who carried me on their back still sticks to my lips. It fills my mouth with memories I never would have had if we had parted in a different way . . .
>
> Perhaps my sensibility is truly split, perhaps there is one part of me that is irrevocably Korean. I need to have Koreans around me. I want to open their graves and give them voice (which is the same thing as acknowledging that my split personality itself is my very reason for being, and that I am seeking to free myself intellectually from that reality by violently severing my ties with it). My reasoning is circuitous. Yes, that is me. Although what I want to say is straightforward and not cir-

cuitous in the least, I am the kind of person who becomes circuitous as soon as I attempt to recruit the medium of language. Just as powerfully as I wish the Japanese language would become real for me, I wish I could give words to the reality that is Korea for me: I want to give birth to Korea.[12]

As these opening passages suggest, Morisaki's essay from the outset aggressively problematizes language, while also refusing the notion of a stable boundary between the writing subject and "Korea." As an attempt to represent the narrator's relationship to the victims of Japanese colonialism and its aftermath, these paradoxical assertions seem to represent a strategy for dealing with historical trauma described by Dominick LaCapra in his study of European writings about the Holocaust. The conscientious witness of a nation's past crimes, he suggests, may choose to forego the stance of detached narrator and "pleasures of narration" it affords, in favor of "acknowledging implication" in the processes represented, even at the risk of exposure to their "destabilizing or radically fragmenting effects."[13] Moreover, perhaps precisely because it risks exposing itself to fragmenting effects, it is possible to see Morisaki's essay as raising far-reaching questions about the relationships among language, subjectivity, and subject-as-nation. Her title represents language and subjectivity as doubled, an image through which she will later characterize as a "dissonance" (*bure*) her attempt through writing to give birth to the Korea of her childhood in the colonies.

This is a "Korea" that the narrator depicts as saturating her language itself. The narrator's apparent obsession with what one critic has called the "inadequacy of language as a means of communication," reflects not so much a poetic sensibility ill at ease with the harsh exigencies of political struggle, as a desire to make language precisely the arena in which such a dichotomy between private and public selves breaks down.[14] Language, as a historically specific practice, is foregrounded by Morisaki as the site of subjectivity's discursive constitution and, as such, seen as inseparable from the function and signification of power. By foregoing truth claims and questioning its own ability to communicate a message, "Two Languages, Two Souls" elaborates, not so much existential despair as a rigorous critique of the role played by notions of consensus and communicability in the ideological construction of transparency between subject and nation in modern Japan.

Thus, throughout her essay, Morisaki's narrator associates her most intense statements of affect with the unsayable or almost sayable, frequently associated, in turn, with Korea, the land of her birth as a member of the colonizing Japanese. Through the tears, clenched teeth, and eccentric behavior enacted by its narrator, her essay repeatedly poses language over and against what cannot be put into language but remains powerfully felt. It thus refuses the conception of language in which words, or signs, are seen as already existing "referents to which are attached significations validatable under the cognitive regimen," as Lyotard has written.[15] Rather, the narrator takes pains to suggest that the feeling of frustration vis-à-vis language may have a positive valence: the process of pointing to what exists in excess of signification serves precisely as an incitement to desire and to speech. For Morisaki, as for Lyotard, for whom not only the *differend* but the sign itself may "indicate that something that should be able to be put into phrases cannot be phrased in the accepted idioms," there is a dynamic relation between signification and "the feeling of pain that accompanies silence."[16]

In "Two Languages, Two Souls," this feeling of pain is counterposed to the pervasive sentimentality of postwar Japanese life. For "sentimentality," Morisaki uses the word *naniwabushi*, referring to traditional popular ballads (with their origins in the late Edo) associated by some intellectuals of the time with an attitude of political apathy. In the light of the close link Morisaki posits between language and subjectivity, however, it becomes clear that, for her, sentimentality refers to an ideological effect far more pervasive than what might be described through a simple opposition between passivity and political activism. For Morisaki, the sentimental is whatever reinforces the antinomy between the private and the social, perpetuating the fiction of an autonomous, purely spiritual or psychological interiority or freedom. This is a freedom the narrator rejects from the outset of her essay, opening up a thematic she sustains until the end. Indeed, it appears that, for the author of "Two Languages, Two Souls," the fiction of individual will is predicated, precisely, on a *misrecognition* of the discursively constituted nature of subjectivity. It is *because* each subject must use a language that bears in itself the material traces of history that there is an ethical obligation to take responsibility for wrongs of earlier generations. Morisaki's narrator, whose language and psyche retain the traces of a childhood in colonial Korea, is merely a more vivid example of what is true for postwar Japanese in general.

Written within the context of debates about the direction and nature of citizens' movements in the wake of the anti-Security Treaty demonstrations in 1959, then, "Two Languages, Two Souls" advances an argument about language and subjectivity that attempts to call into question two related (although apparently separate) tendencies in postwar thought: the belief in the freedom of the individual, and the concept of national consensus or communicational transparency. On the one hand, Morisaki's essay suggests that the modernist emphasis on the autonomous individual in early postwar thought promoted a kind of national absolution from war responsibility. It was an absolution that took the form of the "victim complex" through which, as Oda Makoto once observed, "everyone had been betrayed; no-one had been the betrayer, and thus all blame was placed at the door of the state."[17] The modernist notion of the autonomous individual, Morisaki maintains, was surprisingly easily accommodated to this discourse of national irresponsibility.

The insistence that it is, rather, the un-freedom of the individual that is the locus for social responsibility is the source of the paradoxical rhetoric that characterizes many passages in "Two Languages, Two Souls." Indeed, Morisaki had alluded to her obsession with this idea elsewhere, citing the verse of a Fukuoka mining song—"Down in the mine since I was seven or eight, Carrying a lantern for my parent's sins"—as one of her favorite songs. ("This is not the sort of thing one calls a favorite poem, not, that is, unless a favorite poem is one that has made its home in your mind, one that has permeated your very depths and refuses to be moved.")[18] As it happened, in Morisaki's own life, her maternal grandmother had regarded her birth as a "sin," since Morisaki's mother had gone against the family's will in marrying a Japanese colonial in Korea.[19] Yet, the ethical inquiry pursued in "Two Languages, Two Souls" is more complex than one that can be reduced to matters of authorial experience. It is neither a narcissistic preoccupation with individual past nor a form of determinism that the narrator expresses in her notion of the crime of her birth. Rather, this notion of crime is opposed precisely to the postwar mentality that would absolve the individual subject from responsibility for history by invoking the notion of a private, inner realm untouched by public events. For Morisaki, it is the precisely the belief in the inviolability of the private self that sustains the conviction of Japanese citizens that, because they were "ordinary people," or "children," and did not individually "will" the war and colonialism, it is no longer their concern. It is precisely an un-freedom that impels her narrator to write. "It is not as a matter of choice that I set down facts about Korea—that which became my flesh and blood."[20]

Yet, as we shall see, while she argues that collective history is a responsibility from which the individual subject cannot be "free," Morisaki's essay takes pains to avoid collapsing individual subjectivity into subject-as-nation, or advocating the notion of the social or communal (kyōdōtai) as the realm of the Same. While the notion of "two languages, two souls" alludes to the divided and dissonant subjectivity of the narrator, it also proposes Japan itself as a multilingual site and therefore as a site of coexisting, incommensurable regimes of signification. The Japanese and Korean languages referred to in the title exist in a hierarchized relationship in Japanese everyday life is made abundantly clear by the narrator, who describes, among her many eccentricities, her habit of provoking fellow passengers on Japanese trains by riding with a Korean language textbook open in her lap. (Like most Japanese in the colonies, Morisaki herself attended separate schools for Japanese and did not learn to speak fluent Korean). The scene invariably provokes curiosity. ("'Korean?' the man says as he undresses me with eyes. 'I didn't know they had writing in Korea.'"[21]) The narrator's actions make clear that the ideological construction of modern Japan as a linguistic unity has been predicated on the exclusion and marginalization of heterogeneous language communities within its territorial boundaries.

Morisaki, Watsuji, and Commonality

Having foregrounded Japan as a site of linguistic heterogeneity, Mori-saki's essay proceeds to make the "fact" of this heterogeneity the basis for a critique of transparent communication and an instrumental view of language. While passages of her essay in which she proposes this view are among its most abstract and condensed, her descriptions of language—far from being merely haphazard or eccentric—articulate an astute rebuttal of reified notions of national community. Though she does not refer explicitly to the ideas of such celebrated interpreters of Japanese culture and daily life as Watsuji Tetsurō or Yanagita Kunio, for example, Morisaki's conceit of "two languages, two souls" may nevertheless be fruitfully read as a stance that refutes their influential constructions of commonality in modern Japanese life. Particularly interesting is a passage in which Morisaki, pursuing a logic similar to that of the linguist Emile Benveniste and post-structuralist theorists who built on his observations about language, compares different uses of the words "I" and "we" in Japanese and Korean. Morisaki's passage, in which we can see how abstract inquiry and affect-filled statement commingle, is as follows:

The time-space that is my "I" is marked in overlapping ethnic hues (*minzokuiro*). This is not an explanation I offer in self-defense. The essential function of the pronoun "I" is to indicate a singular history in terms of a totality. For this reason, the pronoun "I" contains two different, conflicting tendencies. On the one hand there is a movement of reduction through which the self tries to differentiate its singular history from that of others. On the other hand, there is an extensive movement whereby the word "I" would have no meaning in language unless it included an indefinite number of others, unless there were a part of the word in which the singular histories of self and other overlap. In ordinary speech in Japan, the latter function is closer to the surface. It somewhat amorphously indicates an area of responsibility within everyday life that that singular history entails.

When I came to Japan after the war, I learned that in the life of the Japanese masses, the word "I" revolves around the axis of this latter function. But I myself had been accustomed to thinking of "I" in terms of the former. Confronting masses of Japanese, I marveled at discovering a human species that could not grasp the full range of functions of the word "I."

In any event, it seems to me the word "I" has this latter bias in daily life in Japan. Perhaps this is not an appropriate example, for I am not sure I understand it completely, but in Korea when one wants to convey the same meaning that Japanese convey when they say, for example, "Come over to my house," ("*watashi no ie ni asobi ni irasshai*") or "I'd like you to meet my mother" ("*haha ni atte kudasai*"), one would not use a singular possessive like "my" house ("*nae jip*") or "my" mother ("*nae ŏmŏni*") but state quite explicitly "our" house ("*uri jip*") and "our" mother ("*uri ŏmŏni*"). I would like to suggest that in ordinary Japanese speech this nuance (that of reference to possessions in common, trans.) is carried by the simple word "I" ("*watakushi*"). In Japanese, moreover, this way of speaking does not function simply to distinguish between singular and joint ownership or between singular and plural, but seems to point to a commonality of experience, a realm of overlapping experience. Of course this sense of commonality is also suggested by the Korean term for "our" ("*uri*"). But for some reason—although I experience no perplexity when a resident Korean friend addresses me as "friend," or "comrade," I am quite intensely shaken when someone speaking Korean includes me in the Korean plural pronoun for "we." A painful doubt about the constitutive grounds for my inclusion in that plural makes it difficult for me to maintain my composure. With all the strength of my experience and my being, I am no match for the history entailed in that word. It is all that can do at such moments to stand in place, pretending I do not notice that my face has gone pale.

Yet it is also true that when I am sitting alone and lost in thoughts of Korea (or Japan), at some point without my knowledge the shadows of those indefinite numbers of others that make up my "I" steal across my entire existence. Of course, these are the shadows of formless, nameless Koreans. Or, they are the undulations of the land and mind of Korea. Were my consciousness to deny this, my existence itself would cease.[22]

To begin, we might briefly juxtapose Morisaki's reflections here to the arguments about the relationship of language and commonality proposed in Watsuji Tetsurō's influential text, *Fūdō* (*Iwanami Shoten*, 1935, translated as *Climate and Culture*, Geoffrey Bownas, 1962). In this book, originally written by Watsuji after his return from a year's study of German philosophy, familiarity with Heideggerian thought is evident in an argument that attempts to overcome a rigid subject-object dichotomy by describing how the human subject discovers itself as *already* a social being whose very existence is in "exteriority," as suggested by the Latin term "*exsistere*." To demonstrate how the human subject discovers, only retrospectively, that it is a social being, Watsuji turns, like Morisaki, to examples taken from everyday speech. Thus he describes the subject's phenomenological apprehension of cold: "That we feel the cold is an intentional experience, in which we discover ourselves in the state of '*ex-sistere*,' or ourselves *already* outside in the cold," Watsuji writes.[23] While such an argument is compatible with the notion of a dialectical relationship between the subject and an exteriority that may be construed as social (Watsuji indeed makes it clear that he so construes it), Watsuji, nevertheless, quickly moves to *collapse* subjectivity with this sociality by alluding to the reassuring mutuality found in everyday speech about the experience of cold:

> We have considered the problem in terms of individual consciousness in the experience of cold. But, as we have been able to use the expression "we feel cold," *without any contradiction, it is "we," not "I" alone that experience the cold.* We feel the same cold in common. It is precisely because of this that we can use terms describing the cold in our exchange of daily greetings." (Italics added.)[24]

It is precisely the kind of slippage "without any contradiction" between "I" and "we" that is asserted in Watsuji's thought that Morisaki's text contests. Its misfit narrator (who is told by her friends to "try to be more rational" when she speaks of her difficulties in adjusting to life as a returnee) finds herself suspended in the difference between "I" in Japanese and "I" in Korean. Through the figure of multilingualism, or subjectivity constituted in a heterogeneity of languages (a scandalous admixture of Japanese and Korean, at that) "Two Languages, Two Souls" challenges the continuum between subject and commonality that Watsuji sought to find in everyday speech.

While Watsuji implies that the existence of a transparent national language guarantees the existence of "we," Morisaki does the reverse, proposing that it is the fact of existence in more than one language that exposes division of "I." Moreover, it is precisely her consciousness of multilingualism that makes Morisaki's narrator aware of the inadequacy of language, of the gap between language and the real. The oscillation of the writing subject of "Two Languages, Two Souls" suggests the possibility of occupying multiple positions, including the incommensurable (because historically specific) Japanese and Korean "I"s. This notion of existence in overlapping linguistic regimes enables Morisaki to develop a notion of subjectivity as both discursively produced and unstable. Neither a "Japanese" nor a "Korean" identity is a reality for her. Her oscillation also provides the basis for deconstructing ideological appropriations of the national "we." For her narrator can use the perspective of the *hikiagesha* to skillfully challenge the belief in a reified communal body inhering in the national "we."

In fact, when we carefully consider Morisaki's reflections on the nature of "I" in Japanese and Korean cited above, we may note that Morisaki articulates a far more sophisticated notion of the "commonality of language" than Watsuji. Because she does not shy away from contradiction, Morisaki can insist that language has "two conflicting tendencies," the capacity to both divide and to universalize. As she says above of the pronoun "I," it functions as both a "movement of reduction through which the self tries to differentiate its singular history from that of others" and an "extensive movement whereby the 'I' would have no meaning in language unless it includes an indefinite number of others." By emphasizing these apparently conflicting tendencies, Morisaki can account for the way in which language is a medium of sociality, without falling into the trap equating of linguistic terms with substantialized social entities. Her nuanced description of the function of "I," indeed, is very close to that of the post-structuralist theory that, drawing on the certain insights of Benveniste and others, posits language as that which enables social life, but at the price of alienating the singular subject from itself. The word "I" in this view is seen to be "empty" of any individual personality because anyone can use it. Yet precisely because it is a linguistic convention that anyone can use, "I" can signify meaning to others. Morisaki's attempt to account for the "I" that reduces and excludes at the same time that it includes "indefinite numbers of others" resembles the linguistic conception of "I" as a "shifter," an empty structure that must be repeatedly grounded through deictic signs to specific instances of discourse. The post-structuralist sense of "I" as "a *division that joins all the same*" is quite close to the notion of the two "conflicting tendencies of 'I'" that Morisaki specifies.[25]

We should also note that is only *after* setting forth such a definition of "I" as a shifter that Morisaki proceeds to her comparisons of the different functions and morphology of the words "I" and "we" in Japanese and Korean. This is important to remember, for while her discussion might seem to essentialize differences between the two languages, her strategy is rather to compare Japanese and Korean as a way of suggesting that the word "we" can never have a transparent meaning, nor signify a true "union" or identity of subject positions. In describing her bemused reactions, as a returnee, to the uses of the word "I" in everyday Japanese, for example, Morisaki uses the subtle morphological difference between Japanese and Korean singular and plural pronouns as a springboard from which to defamiliarize the sense of a collective "we" that is taken for granted in everyday Japanese speech. In Japanese, the singular and plural pronominals "I" and "we" closely coincide because they share the same stem. "*Watakushi*" is pluralized in the form "*watakushi-tachi*," while the plural of "*ware*" is "*ware-ware*," and so forth. In Korean, on the other hand, "I" (*na*) and "we" (*uri*) are morphologically distinct words. Furthermore, she suggests that in Japanese conversational usage "I" or "my" can easily be used to signify "we" or "our"—one can speak of "my school" (*watakushi no gakkō*) despite the fact that it is not an individual possession, while in Korean instances of singular possession (*na ŭi*) and plural possession (*uri ŭi*) are clearly differentiated.[26] By showing that the conflicting dynamics of the "I" receive different emphases in Japanese and Korean daily conversation, however, Morisaki reaches a conclusion quite like Benveniste's assertion that the pronoun "we" can never represent a "multiplication of identical objects," but only a kind of "*junction* between the 'I' and the 'non-I.'"[27] Watsuji's assertion that "I" and "we" are interchangeable in everyday speech, for example, is suggestive of the Japanese pattern described by Morisaki, in which "I" frequently stands in for "we." Unlike Watsuji, however, Morisaki's narrator emphasizes the inherent ambiguity of the "I" as a linguistic shifter. It is purely the work of ideology to obscure the ambiguity of this distinction and to assert, as we have seen Watsuji do, that, "without any contradiction, it is 'we,' not 'I' alone who experience the cold," thus reinforcing the notion of a substantive national linguistic community. It is a defamilarization of this ideological reading of "we" as a sign of national community—rather than the notion of an essentialized difference between the two languages—that Morisaki wishes to bring out in the comparison. The passage we have analyzed, in this sense, seems closer to the following insight of Benveniste than to that of Watsuji. Beveniste writes:

> It is clear, in effect, that the oneness and subjectivity inherent in "I" contradict the possibility of a pluralization. If there cannot be several "I"s who are speaking, it is because "we" is not a multiplication of identical objects, but a junction between "I" and "non-I," no matter what the content of this "non-I" may be. This junction forms a new totality of a very special type whose components are not equivalent . . . "[28]

Finally, we should remark that Morisaki's narrator links the ambiguous "I"/"we" distinction in Japanese linguistic practice to a system of inclusions and exclusions that produces sameness in everyday life. This sameness is the product of the assimilationist ideology that Morisaki sees as a consistent element in colonial and postwar nationalism:

> The responsibility of the Japanese population for the colonial experience lies in the following fact. Both before and since the war, they have continuously maintained the social and psychological structures that enable them to live in a nation whose administrative structures represent a thorough-going politics of discrimination without feeling that they discriminate in their everyday lives in any way. Guilt is the refusal to grapple with this structure. . . . Its distinguishing feature is that through a certain process whereby I am just like you, and you are just like me, and so we are just like each other, there is no responsibility to be found any place . . . furthermore, anyone can participate in this structure at the level of everyday life.[29]

The effect of the ethos of sameness is to create an atmosphere in which "to introduce the principle of legitimate opposition into a community is improper . . . it offends the sensibilities of everyday life."[30] By contrast to this, Morisaki's *hikiagesha* proposes the notion of living precisely as an oscillation (*bure*) borne out of her own cultural and lingustic instability. She commits herself to that "swerve" of the "I" through which both its "emptiness" and its sociality are held in tension. For if linguistic forms are "empty" in an existential sense, they are also "full" of history in their sociality. Already alienated in language, the *hikiagesha* subject cannot find an abiding home in any national linguistic regime. It is "haunted" by an otherness that it can neither control nor create. Through language as a material trace, the past, which this narrator names "Korea," comes back to her.

Rather than going in the direction that arises when one mobilizes the exclusionary force of "I" that differentiates oneself from another, I swerve in the tension-producing direction of that indefinite number of others. Of course, this does not mean that I speak as one of the colonial masses. But the source of my language is somehow there. . . . And there are moments in the life I lead, insulated among Japanese as I engage in social affairs or political struggle, when I feel almost haunted by that source. Many condemn my attitude. They say that I am uncooperative. I pray for the courage to go on confronting my oscillating "I."[31]

Traces of History in Language, Gendered Representations of Korea
  While Benveniste's discussion of "I" in the discrete discursive instance is based on a synchronic analysis of language as a network of elements that signify in relation to each other, for Morisaki the diachronic is also crucial. Thus, in the rhetoric of her essay, the relational structure of subjectivity is never merely apprehended in its purely abstract and formal aspect. Subjectivity can only be encountered insofar as it is figured, in symbolic systems and in history. Nor is meaning entirely "contained" in the "frozenness" of the formal signifier. As Morisaki writes, "Words are shrunken, unable to contain the fullness."[32]
  If Benveniste's synchronic analysis of the speech act has enabled us to understand Morisaki's deconstruction of "I" and "we," then, we may apprehend the images she deploys to suggest the *diachronic* aspect of language through reference to Julia Kristeva's early writings on semiotics. For it is clear that Morisaki's dense considerations of language also insist that meaning unfolds in time. As Kristeva has asserted, meaning is produced "only through the . . . diachronic unfolding of a signifying chain." Kristeva emphasizes that signifying systems must always pre-exist the writing subject in history. Thus, we can understand better why Morsaki's musings on language drift into daydreams about a very specific past ("the undulations of the land and mind of Korea" that "haunt" the narrator). Moreover, if the signifying system itself precedes the subject, the signifying system can be seen as "the addressee, the other, the exteriority," through which every speaking or writing subject must pass. Invoking a Bakhtinian concept of the dialogical, Kristeva writes that, since "literary structure does not simply exist but is generated in relation to another structure," the literary word is an intersection, a "dialogue among several writings: that of the writer, the addressee (or the character), and the contemporary or earlier cultural context." In the act of writing, which is in fact a rewriting, the author must in-

sert herself or himself into the text of history. Kristeva's language invokes the same imagery of birth and death so prominent in Morisaki. "This is why problems of birth, death, and sex appear," Kristeva writes, "when literature touches upon this strategic point that writing becomes when it exteriorizes linguistic systems."[33]

Through its reference to the diachronic structure of signification, we might say that "Two Languages, Two Souls" returns us by yet a different route to its opening motif of "birth as crime." The narrator's preoccupation with the past and with "the Korea that nurtured me" now appear in another light, as we come to understand how Morisaki's writing brings the synchronic dimension of the relationship between subjectivity and language into contact with the diachronic one of the relationship between *history* and language. Why is it that the narrator's "I" is haunted by the "an indefinite number of others"—why does she insist that "what has made me what I am" are the "shadows of formless, nameless Koreans, and the undulations of the land and mind of Korea"?[34] Through her invocation of Korea as that which gave rise to her being, Morisaki calls attention to the historical specificity of any discourse in which the subject is produced. Through the mediation of language the subject has access to specific, culturally inflected subject positions. In this sense, Morisaki's language of "birth as crime" resembles Lacan's description of the subject as enveloped in a network of symbols so total that "they join together, before his birth, those who are going to engender him by flesh and blood; so total that they bring to his birth . . . the share of his destiny."[35]

Moreover, as we now turn to Morisaki's reflections on history, it is easier to grasp why she insists on the paradoxical rhetoric of responsibility based on "un-freedom." For Morisaki's notion of the "crime of birth" is similar to the idea of the "givenness" elaborated in Rey Chow's discussion of Chinese diasporic identity (a discussion that draws, in turn, on work by Wlad Godzich). Describing, in *Woman and Chinese Modernity*, the hybrid "subjectivity of which and in which I write," as neither Chinese nor Western but an "unstable dialectic between the two," Chow introduces a concept of subjectivity as "givenness." According to her notion of "givenness," subjectivity is not purely "individual but an effect of historical forces that are beyond any individuated 'consciousness.'"[36] Moreover, Chow proposes, turning to the writing of Godzich, that this notion of subjectivity necessarily entails contradiction and paradox because, insofar as subjectivity emerges in a specific, materialized, symbolic system, the subject can never simply know itself "directly." For Godzich, "givenness" describes that which eludes direct cognition by the subject while (here again, the language resonates with Morisaki), it is the very "ground" or "field" upon which the subject is constituted. Because the subject's relationship to givenness can never be a direct or conscious one, it is "knowable only through its figurations."[37]

This idea furthers our understanding of the positive political valence that seems to be attached to Morisaki's insistence on the unsayable, the unknowable. The *hikiagesha* subject is inexorably linked to the colonial past. Yet this "Korea" is never a subject of direct knowledge that can be mastered. To redress colonial crimes requires a constant work of negotiation and interpretation of the relationship between the past and the present, a relationship in which the victims, especially those who have died, can never be recompensed in equivalent terms. As we have seen above, Morisaki is inclined to locate the ethical task of postwar Japanese in their confrontation with a continuing history of discrimination *at the structural level*, rather than in the pretense that the sins of the past can be adequately known, mastered, and left behind.

Gendered Korean Figures: Omoni and Kim Hui Ro
Finally, it is in terms of the "givenness" of Morisaki's narrator's subjectivity that we turn to the use of gendered figures in her essay. Two prominent, gendered Korean figures are linked, in "Two Languages, Two Souls," to the narrator's linguistic and subjective "oscillation," to her "dementia." The first, as we have already seen, is that of her Korean surrogate mothers, the second that of the historical Kim Hui Ro, a Korean resident of Japan who held thirteen people hostage during a four-day struggle with police in February, 1968, about two months before the publication of "Two Languages, Two Souls." Both figures, although in quite different ways, are linked by the narrator to moments of the inadequacy of speech—and thus may help us to conclude our consideration of Morisaki's deconstruction of national language and the national "we."

It is at the opening of the essay that the figure of a lost mother is associated by the narrator with the impossibility of talking about Korea. This is not an image of the narrator's natural mother, but of Korean nursemaids who cared for her when she was a child. Morisaki's narrator's speech itself is represented as permeated with traces of loss, which she imagines as hairs of these Korean women who carried her on their backs, which continue to stick to her mouth whenever she tries to talk about Korea. Within the context of Morisaki's participation in the movement to "return to the local" in the early 1960s, a movement accompanied by a revival of interest in the work of Yanagita Kunio, this thematization of origin in terms of a lost Korean mother's body is provocative. As Harry Harootunian has argued, Yanagita sought in Japanese folklore a narrative that aimed to "forget the eventfulness that transported Japan into industrialization." In theorizing the *jōmin* ("ordinary and abiding folk") as the homogeneous subject of this discourse, Yanagita sought the condition for "eliminating the Other, radical difference, and history" and restoring the Japanese Same.[38] For Morisaki, rather, "origin" is the lost and inaccessible Korean mother. This represents yet another refusal to essentialize national culture in terms of an origin. But, in the light of the synchronic and diachronic dimensions of language we have already seen analyzed in Morisaki's essay, we may relate the lost Korean mother to "givenness" itself. As a surrogate mother, the Korean mother functions as a screen memory, as a stand-in for the unfigurable, like an inaccessible memory of the "originary," traumatic moment of separation from the maternal body. The image of the Korean mother also suggests the necessary temporality within which Morisaki insists the relation to the past is constructed, thus again making origins inevitably irretrievable. The Korean mother may, indeed, be seen as a kind of "screen memory" described by Laplanche and Pontalis as that fantasy that tries to "cover the moment of *separation* between *before* and after," just as a linguistic sign connotes both an object and its absence.[39] This interpretation, too, lends strength to the idea that Morisaki's thematization of the insufficiency of language is not nihilistic, but productive or "generative," in the same sense that the "shot of a shadow, 'photographed' on stone, of someone killed at Hiroshima" represents how a graphic trace can generate a new text in Alain Resnais' film *Hiroshima Mon Amour*.[40]

Following Chow and Godzich, I would suggest that Morisaki implies that it is *because* the real (Korea) remains unrepresentable, knowable only in its figurations, that the desire of her narrator to bridge this gap is elicited. Again, we find in Morisaki the language of un-freedom.

> It is not as a matter of choice that I put down facts about Korea—that which became my flesh and blood. I have expended great effort to suppress those facts. By suppressing them I have suppressed my nanny, pushing her farther and farther away. Somewhere here, in my flesh, is her grave. Until today, with the strength that has enabled me to avoid dealing in the currency of facts, I have lived, trying to build something. I have just wanted, indiscriminately, to be.[41]

The constant eruption and return of the screen memory, the narrator's inability to forget Korea ("I have suppressed my nanny, pushing her farther and farther away . . . ") is the source of her "dementia," her inability to represent Korea, that which became her "flesh and blood," objectively. Yet, as the essay demonstrates, the narrator is compelled by this return of the repressed not to stop but to continue writing.

A second significant gendered figure is that of the historical Korean Japanese Kim Hui Ro. In February, 1968, Kim, accused of shooting two members of the Imagawa-gumi gang with whom he had had a long and complex relationship, fled to the central Japan Alps, and held thirteen people hostage in a small hot springs resort before being arrested by police. Postwar historian Ide Magoroku notes that the incident took place just at the point when television had permeated the majority of Japanese households, and constituted a gripping media spectacle. While on television, Kim Hui Ro, who had dropped out of primary school after attending 47 days of fifth grade, and learned to read while serving a prison term, read his own poetry and condemned Japanese prejudice against Korean Japanese.[42] The figure of Kim is just as consistently linked to language in Morisaki's argument as the Korean nanny is. "By embracing crime," the narrator of "Two Languages, Two Souls" asserts, "Kim Hui Ro achieved the ability to express himself publicly in words." Moreover, and this must be emphasized, Morisaki theorizes the "meaning" of the Kim event primarily in relation to Japan as a linguistic community predicated on notions of sameness and consensus. What the narrator finds rare about the Japanese reaction to Kim is an unease over speech that the event has stimulated among the general population, a mutual fear among Japanese of being misunderstood.

> At the time, Japan was in something of an uproar. Or rather, a current of linguistic repression flowed through Japan, indicating people's determination not to make statements they might later regret. . . . I knew, however, that Japan was not a country to maintain this mood of self-repression long.[43]

That "spokesmen" will emerge who diffuse this tension and return the population to their comforting assumption of mutual understanding is what Morisaki calls the "peculiarly Japanese tragi-comedy" the narrator fears will too soon evolve. At the same time, she expresses doubts about an essentialized, "artificial Koreanness" to which some Korean Japanese aspire. Thus the narrator's reactions to the event are conflicted. Television reportage of the four-day siege dominates her home. She describes her children, immobilized before the television set and sneaking "guilty glances at me clenching a towel between my teeth as I raised havoc with the grease spattering in the frying pan." On the one hand, the narrator feels isolated, unable to understand the sympathy for Kim of liberal Japanese friends who write to her praising the daring of his "suicide tactics, taking on the whole of Japan single-handedly." On the other, she finds "nothing in the least peculiar" about the fact that "Japanese are at times and at random unsuspectingly, without the least personal reason, taken hostage by Koreans."[44]

The threatening figure of Kim Hui Ro is one that any reading of "Two Languages, Two Souls" must attempt confront, for it is particularly in terms of this figure that Morisaki seems to suggest that subjectivity must be seen as linked to the exercise of power in any given social formation, and that, as such, it is a relational (rather than fixed or univocal) position. In Morisaki's essay, we may infer this interpretation from the presentation of a fantasy the narrator experiences as she views the televised image of Kim. She envisions herself as having fallen into a "well" separating her from those friends who sympathize with Kim, and she figuratively defines this well as the "position" of hostage.

From the well I had fallen into I was unable to understand my friend's support for Kim Hui Ro. But where exactly was I? I was in the position of one who had been taken hostage. Then what was I doing? I was standing tense, glaring at Kim, holding back my words. This is what I had always done as a child. At those times, did I have something lucid to convey? Yes. Was I able to say it? No. And now? No. I cannot say it. I am about to say it and then I cannot. Kim's bare backside is visible between his shirt and his pants. I can see what Kim is saying and at the same time what he is not saying."[45]

It is from this position—one in which speech is deferred in the face of a threat, a scene superimposed on the memory of a childhood scene—that the narrator unleashes the scathing words she directs at Kim's Japanese sympathizers. For them it is "the easiest thing in the world to discharge words towards that Korean . . . without staking the least bit of themselves." The furor over Kim is a "tragi-comedy" because Japanese sympathizers do not put themselves at risk, cannot conceive of themselves as held hostage by a Korean. "Without sacrifice or fear," and "without being cut off from their fellows, they can arrogate to themselves the role of apologists," the narrator observes. But in their manner of response, they perpetuate the notion of Kim and of any Korean Japanese as thoroughly "other." In so doing, they merely reinforce the ideology of national community, which, with its politics of structural difference (as well the dichotomy between "private" and "social" the essay challenges from the start) enables them to believe in the essentialized and discrete nature of identities produced by this very structure of difference. They therefore do not perceive that their "Japanese" identities are, in fact, put at risk by Kim Hui Ro. By misrecognizing the relational nature of their own subject positions, these sympathizers ironically forfeit the possibility of inventing new, non-stereotypical responses to Korean Japanese, as well as of discovering a new dimension of themselves. Their response is easily accommodated to a power relationship that functions through differentiation of ethnic identities. They help perpetuate, that is, what Michel Foucault has seen as an indispensable element of any power relationship: "that 'the other' (the one over whom power is exercised) be thoroughly recognized and maintained to the very end as a person who acts."[46]

The reference to the Kim Hui Ro event enables Morisaki to problematize relationships among language, subjectivity, and national identity in a manner far more complex than would have been possible only through her comparison of Korean and Japanese language practices. Gendered subject positions are among the range of discursive positions available at any given time in language, and thus the threatening Kim functions as a counterpart to the nurturing Korean mother, producing a structure of sexual difference projected across linguistic and geopolitical "Koreanness" in the essay. It is vital to note that, while the existence in Japanese society of a hicrarchical structure privileging the apanese language over Korean is stressed in the discussion of "two languages, two souls," Kim's action temporarily and partially (because the narrator is also aware of what he is *not* saying in Japanese) reverses that hierarchy, causing the narrator as a figurative hostage to shift into an overdetermined position of subordination vis-á-vis the male Korean Japanese Kim, both as Japanese and as female. Having introduced the language of the Korean Japanese minority to demonstrate that the "Japanese" subject position is neither "pure" nor univocal, the essay introduces the image of the "hostage" Japanese woman to demonstrate the similarly shifting and relational nature of the "Korean" subject position. Thus, as the essay runs its course, we are able to see how relations of power are "multiple in any given society," and "how they are superimposed, they cross . . . sometimes cancel one another out, sometimes reinforce one another.[47] As Chow notes, by foregrounding women who occupy the lower rung in the male-female opposition, a text can call attention to the way "purely structural, systemic differences" signify and relay power, and can clarify subtle relations between different forms of discrimination."[48]

The superimposition of the narrator's fantasy of herself, as a speechless hostage of Kim, over her memory of speechlessness as a child marks the concluding stage of essay's probing of national subjectivity. Imagining her silence as a hostage, a situation that makes her aware of something "lucid" or distinct within her that nevertheless cannot be uttered in Korean or Japanese, calls up for the narrator the powerful image of "doubly or triply layered perceptions" she experienced as a Japanese colonial child in Korea. Everyday life as a child entailed constantly traversing two linguistic and ethnic communities: the narrator describes walking, often nervously, from the Japanese settlement on the hilltop, along a "road traveled by both Koreans and Japanese to meet with the grass and touch the water." Although, as a child, the narrator experienced Koreans "individually" as "soft and warm," when she encountered them as an "anonymous" majority they imposed upon the narrator a "regimen of tension," a "corset of speechlessness," which she describes as forcing her to "find within myself the fountainhead of words." In the following scene, the narrator's fantasy of Kim Hui Ro's eyes opens into the memory of a childhood encounter with Korean boys, one described in the almost mythical terms of the assumption of a gendered subject position in the face of a threat (and in this sense, something like the entry into the Lacanian symbolic order of language). The narrator sees in the glare of Kim Hui Ro's eyes the eyes of a "throng of Kim Hui Ro's surrounding me as its hostage," eyes before which the narrator is constituted as a *"Korean nisei girl child"* (emphasis in the original).

The Kim Hui Ro herd surrounds me as its hostage. They stand a little boy about four years old in front of me. The little boy is facing me while everyone else turns away. That is the world of a little girl born a Korean nisei. No one laughs; everyone is as silent as ice.[49]

Elsewhere, Morisaki has spoken in similar terms of her sexual maturation as a Japanese child in colonial Korea.

> You have to remember that when I think of the "woman" inside me, it always has a connection with Korean boys. I can always see their eyes. It was their eyes that made me mature sexually. There was something contemptuous in those eyes. It was these eyes which made me become aware of myself as a woman.[50]

Moving back and forth constantly as a child between the position of linguistic majority and linguistic minority, the narrator was unusually aware of the painful nature of the subject's initiation into the symbolic, and of the relational nature of subjectivity itself. Although, for every subject, entry into the symbolic order of language is traumatic, it may be doubly so for such subjects. Thus, Morisaki here seems to be drawing a parallel between the state of "being held hostage to a Korean" and her discovery, within that "regimen of tension" and "corset of speechlessness," not only of the "fountainhead of words" but of a glimmering of what Godzich call's "givenness"—the very ground of her constitution as a subject. In the image of the narrator as hostage, Morisaki presents that subject as driven to seek beyond the relational structure in which desire is always invested, for the elusive prediscursive "ground" on which such relationships are constituted. It is for this reason that the narrator can paradoxically maintain that the situation of being taken hostage by a minority is not in the least "unnatural" and may even be salutary for Japanese. To be taken hostage is to symbolically experience being a minority, to suddenly become aware of all within one's being that exists in *tension* with the purely arbitrary and impersonal designation of oneself as Japanese: it is to ask, "why am I being taken hostage just because I happen to be Japanese?" As the narrator says quite explicitly, to be taken hostage "is to be in a situation of constraint vis-á-vis the Korean's subjectivity." She deplores the fact that most Japanese, finding such a situation intolerable, would miss the chance "to use that sense of vital danger to discover the Korea within."[51]

CONCLUSION

In contrasting Morisaki's writing with that of the area studies text, I have emphasized its thematization of, and acknowledgement of its own implication in, the sociality of writing. As such, Morisaki's text may be seen as exposing its language to the "fragmenting effects" described above by Dominick LaCapra, and as admitting its inseparability from historical processes that, nevertheless, are beyond its ability to master. Through this process, Morisaki's text challenges the notion of transparent communication between national subjects, and even the notion of discrete, knowable, national identities.

In pressing its exploration of subjectivity toward the final exhortation that the national "majority" subject must discover the grounds of its constitution by becoming figuratively hostage to the minority subjectivity, in fact, Morisaki's essay calls to mind the work of certain anti-apartheid African writers considered by Godzich in his discussion of "givenness." In his books *The African Image* and *Voices in the Whirlwind*, for example, the South African writer Es'kia Mphahlele similarly problematized biologically grounded notions of ethnic consciousness.

As Godzich interprets it, Mphahlele, studying in England, discovered that he was "white inside" by virtue of his colonial education, a discovery that may be paralleled with Morisaki's discovery of ways in which she was "formed" by Korea because she was raised there. This prompted him to reject the notion of skin color as the basis for black consciousness. For a time, Mphahlele attempted to define "black consciousness" paradoxically, as a knowledge, attained through effort, of a "whiteness within." Because of the effort required, this was utterly different from the casual way in which whites knew themselves to be whites. Eventually, however, Mphahlele rejected even this position. By placing the African point of view within the sphere of what could be known, and therefore mastered, he realized it would make it possible for the South African know to understand his or her subjectivity "casually, the way whites know they are whites."[52] According to Godzich's interpretation, for Mphahlele, "the casualness of white knowledge is the result of its univocity and reliance upon a stable and fixed positionality."[53] For Mphahlele, both blacks and whites should seek the "non-casual" knowledge according to which the notion of a univocal subject position may be painfully, perhaps, thrust to the "ground of its production." The position of being held hostage in Morisaki's text would seem to evoke the notion of a search for "noncasual" knowledge advocated by Mphahlele. Morisaki's writing appears to generate, and be generated by, such an impulse.

Notes

1. Gayatri Chakravorty Spivak, "Imperialism and Sexual Difference," in *Oxford Literary Review*, Vol. 8 (1986), 229.

2. Johannes Fabian, *Time and the Other: How Anthropology Makes its Object* (New York: Columbia University Press, 1983), 94.

3. Spivak, op. cit., 229, 225.

4. Jean-Francois Lyotard, *The Post-modern Condition*, translated by Geoff Bennington and Brian Massumi (Minneapolis: University of Minnesota, 1984), 17.

5. Elspeth Probyn, "Post-modernity and the Local," in Linda J. Nicholson, ed., *Feminism/Postmodernism* (New York and London: Routledge, 1990), 177.

6. Gayatri Spivak, *The Post-Colonial Critic* (New York and London: Routledge, 1991), 11.

7. Elspeth Probyn, op. cit., 177.

8. Morisaki Kazue, *Haha no kuni to no gensōkon*, (Tokyo: *Gendai shisōsha*, 1976). This essay was translated as "Two Languages, Two Souls" by Kazuko Fujimoto, in *Concerned Theater Japan*, 2, No. 3/4 (Spring, 1973), 153–154 (hereafter referred to as *CTJ*). In most cases, citations from this essay are from Fujimoto's English translation, with appropriate page numbers. When I have used my own translations, I cite the Japanese text with reference to page numbers in *Haha no kuni to no gensōkon*.

9. Morisaki, *Haha no kuni to no gensōkon*, 340.

10. In an interview with Morisaki featured in the inaugural issue of *New Feminism Review*, Ueno Chizuko recalls her keen interest in Morisaki's writing when she was a university student. This article helped, in the 1990s, stimulate renewed interest in Morisaki as a kind of forerunner of second-wave feminism. Morisaki's apparent discomfort with the discussion of same sex relationships and unproblematic notion of the "natural," however, suggest that a recuperation of her writings *in toto* by contemporary feminists will be difficult.

11. Other representative collections of Morisaki's early essays include *Hishoyū no shoyū* (Tokyo: *Gendai Shisōsha*, 1965), and *Izoku no genki*, (Tokyo: *Yamato Shobō*, 1971).

12. I have slightly modified Fujimoto's translation. See "Two Languages, Two Souls," *CTJ* and *Haha no kuni to no gensōkon*, 178.

13. Dominick LaCapra, *Representing the Holocaust: History, Theory, Trauma* (Ithaca: Cornell University Press, 1994.)

14. Livia Monnet, "The Metaphysics of Defeat: The Work of Morisaki Kazue," in *Bulletin of the European Association for Japanese Studies*, No. 23, June, 1985: 17–24.

15. Jean Francois Lyotard, "The Differend, The Referent, and the Proper Name," trans. by Georges van den Abbelee, *Diacritics*, 14, no. 3, 1984, 14. The article contains extracts from Jean Francois Lyotard, *Le differend* (Paris: Minuit, 1984).

16. Ibid., 7.

17. Oda Makoto, "The Ethics of Peace," in Koschmann, 157.

18. See Morisaki Kazue, "*Tsuchi no soko no utagoe—watakushi no suki na hitotsu no shi*," in *Haha no kuni to no gensōkon*, 135–138. These lines are translated by Kazuko Fujimoto, "Singing Voices from the Bottom of the World: One of My Favorite Poems," in *CTJ*, 165.

19. Morisaki Kazue, "*Watakushi o mukaete kureta Kyushu*" in *Haha no kuni to no gensōkon*, 200–212.

20. Ibid.

21. Ibid, 159.

22. I have largely modified Fujimoto's translation of this passage. See *Haha no kuni to no gensōkon*, 181–182.

23. Watsuji Tetsurō, *Climate and Culture*, trans. Geoffrey Bownas (Tokyo: Hokuseido Press, 1961), 4.

24. Ibid.

25. Stephen Heath, *Questions of Cinema* (Bloomington: Indiana University Press, 1981), 86. Heath's discussion of the "I", which also draws on Lacanian psychoanalytic notions, is cited in Sharon Willis' helpful analysis of the function of "shifters" in Alain Resnais' *Hiroshima mon Amour*. Sharon Willis, *Marguerite Duras: Writing on the Body* (Urbana: University of Illinois Press, 1988), 40–50.

26. "Two Languages, Two Souls, *CTJ*, 155.

27. Emile Benveniste, *Problems in General Linguistics*, trans. Mary E. Meek (Coral Gables: University of Miami Press, 1971), 202.

28. Benveniste, ibid.

29. I have followed Fujimoto's translation, with some modifications. See "Two Languages, Two Souls," *CTJ*, 163, and *Haha no kuni to no gensōkon*, 194.

30. "Two Languages, Two Souls," 161.

31. "*Futatsu no kotoba, futatsu no kokoro*," 182. Like Benveniste, Morisaki's language seems to posit of every speech act an addressee who is an "other," as well as the speaker. As Benveniste writes, in a synchronic sense, every speech act has an addressee. ("We will never find an originary 'I,'" "exercising his wits to conceive of another.") Morisaki's complex insistence on the "opposing dynamics" that produce "I," a word that would have no meaning without reference to others, resembles Benveniste's analysis of the way in which language produces "empty" forms that the speaking subject, in the discursive situation, "appropriates to himself and which he relates to his "person," at the same time defining himself as *I* and a partner as *you*. Benveniste concludes from this that "thus the old antinomies of 'I' and 'the other,' of individual and society, fall. It is in a dialectical reality that will incorporate the two terms and define them by a mutual relationship that the linguistic basis of subjectivity is discovered." Benveniste, ibid., 227.

32. "*Futatsu no kotoba, futatsu no kokoro*," 178.

33. Julia Kristeva, "Word, Dialogue, and Novel," reprinted in Toril Moi, *The Kristeva Reader* (New York: Columbia University Press, 1986), 35–61.

34. "Two Languages, Two Souls," 155.

35. Jacques Lacan, *Écrits: A Selection*, trans. Alan Sheridan (New York: Norton, 1977), 68.

36. Rey Chow, *Woman and Chinese Modernity* (Minneapolis: University of Minnesota Press, 1991), xii.

37. Wlad Godzich, "Emergent Literature and the Field of Comparative Literature," in *The Comparative Perspective on Literature*, ed., Clayton Koelb and Susan Noakes (Ithaca: Cornell University Press, 1988), 26.

38. Harry Harootunian, "Disciplining Native Knowledge and Producing Place: Yanagita Kunio, Origuchi Shinobu, Takata Yasuma," in Thomas Rimer, ed., *Culture and Identity: Japanese Intellectuals in the Interwar Years* (Princeton: Princeton University Press, 1990), 106.

39. Jean Laplanche and Jean-Bernard Pontalis, "Fantasy and the Origins of Sexuality," in Victor Burgin, James Donald, and Cora Kaplan, eds. *The Formation of Fantasy* (New York: Methuen, 1986), 24.

40. Sharon Willis, op. cit., 50.

41. "Two Languages, Two Souls," 154. I have modified the first sentence of the translation.

42. Ide writes: "The 'Kim Hui Ro event' was the first time, in my own memory, that an ongoing event was brought right into the *cha-no-ma*. With shock we encountered the live footage of Kim—he was dressed in hunting clothes and standing in a run-down hot springs resort called Sumata-kyo in the Central Japan Alps (a place I had never heard of or visited), armed with a rifle and 72 sticks of dynamite—in our living room." Ide Magoroku, *Sengōshi*, Vol. II, (Tokyo: *Iwanami Shoten*, 1991), 39.

43. "Two Languages, Two Souls," 157.

44. "Two Languages, Two Souls,"159.

45. "*Futatsu no kotoba, futatsu no kokoro*," 184.

46. Michel Foucault, "The Subject and Power," translated by Leslie Sawyer in *Michel Foucault: Beyond Structuralism and Hermeneutics* (Chicago: University of Chicago Press, 1982), cited in Paul Bove, "Discourse," in *Critical Terms for Literary Study*, Frank Lentricchia and Thomas McLaughlin, eds. (Chicago and London: The University of Chicago Press, 1990), 59.

47. Foucault, op. cit.

48. Chow, op. cit., 52.

49. "Two Languages, Two Souls," 157.

50. Morisaki Kazue, Ueno Chizuko, "*Mihatenu yume*," in *New Feminism Review*, I, no. 1 (Tokyo: *Gakuyōsha*, December, 1990):14.

51. "*Futatsu no kotoba, Futatsu no kokoro*," 185.

52. Es'kia Mphalele, *Voices in the Whirlwind* (New York: Hill and Wang, 1964), 76–77.

53. Godzich, op. cit., 30–31.

CORNELL EAST ASIA SERIES

Order online: www.einaudi.cornell.edu/eastasia/CEASbooks, or contact Cornell East Asia Series Distribution Center, 95 Brown Road, Box 1004, Ithaca, NY 14850, USA; toll-free: 1-877-865-2432, fax 607-255-7534, ceas@cornell.edu

IBT/11-05/0.5M pb/.2M hc